Library Management Problems Today

Library Management Problems Today

Case Studies

Edited by Wayne Disher

ROWMAN & LITTLEFIELD
Lanham • Boulder • New York • London

Published by Rowman & Littlefield
An imprint of The Rowman & Littlefield Publishing Group, Inc.
4501 Forbes Boulevard, Suite 200, Lanham, Maryland 20706
www.rowman.com

6 Tinworth Street, London SE11 5AL, United Kingdom

Copyright © 2021 by The Rowman & Littlefield Publishing Group, Inc.

All rights reserved. No part of this book may be reproduced in any form or by any electronic or mechanical means, including information storage and retrieval systems, without written permission from the publisher, except by a reviewer who may quote passages in a review.

British Library Cataloguing in Publication Information Available

Library of Congress Cataloging-in-Publication Data

Name: Disher, Wayne, editor.
Title: Library management problems today : case studies / edited by Wayne Disher.
Description: Lanham : Rowman & Littlefield, [2021] | Includes index. | Summary: "This book uses case studies gleaned from today's library world to help students take analytical approaches to library problems. Case studies are often used in business, law, and medical schools; this text will enable library management instructors to help their students apply what they've learned to real world situations"—Provided by publisher.
Identifiers: LCCN 2020037173 (print) | LCCN 2020037174 (ebook) | ISBN 9781538135921 (cloth) | ISBN 9781538135938 (paperback) | ISBN 9781538135945 (ebook)
Subjects: LCSH: Library administration—United States—Case studies.
Classification: LCC Z678 .L4857 2021 (print) | LCC Z678 (ebook) | DDC 025.10973—dc23
LC record available at https://lccn.loc.gov/2020037173
LC ebook record available at https://lccn.loc.gov/2020037174

Contents

Preface	vii
Acknowledgments	xiii
Notes for Instructors	xv

Part One: Planning

1	Alice in SWOTerland: A Planning Scenario Using Problem Solving	3
2	Hide the Plan: A Planning Scenario Using Supposition	13
3	I Hear Music: A Planning Scenario Using Supposition	23

Part Two: Organizing

4	Book Selections Can Be Challenged: An Organizing Scenario Using Skills	37
5	My Time Is Valuable Too: An Organizing Scenario Using Problem Solving	51
6	The 38 Percent Reduction: An Organizing Scenario Using Supposition	61

Part Three: Leading

7	The Mean Girl: A Leading Scenario Using Problem Solving	77
8	Challenging the Challenged: A Leading Scenario Using Difficult Professional Topics	87
9	Budget Woes: A Leading Scenario Using Problem Solving	99
10	The New Guy: A Leading Scenario Using Supposition	109

Part Four: Controlling

11	The Cops: A Controlling Scenario Using Skills	125
12	Story Times Can Be a Drag: A Controlling Scenario Using Difficult Professional Topics	135
13	A Sticky Situation: A Controlling Scenario Using Problem Solving	151
14	Transitioning to a New Job: A Controlling Scenario Using Difficult Professional Topics	163

Part Five: Staffing

15 Experience or Skills: A Staffing Scenario Using Problem Solving 177
16 Jack of All Trades: A Staffing Scenario Using Problem Solving 185
17 Weeding Out Bad News: A Staffing Scenario Using Skills 195

Part Six: Communicating

18 A Failure to Communicate: A Communicating Scenario Using Difficult Professional Topics 209
19 Professor Privileges: A Communicating Scenario Using Difficult Professional Topics 221
20 She Seems Creepy: A Communicating Scenario Using Difficult Professional Topics 233

Index 245
About the Editor 247

Preface

I vividly remember sitting at the kitchen table as a young child, trying to explain to my mother why I had done something I shouldn't have been doing. "But, Mom, everyone else was doing it!" I said. Like everyone else's mother has likely done, mine replied, "Wayne, if everyone else jumped off the cliff, would you follow them?" I remember creating a picture in my mind of all my friends running to the edge of a cliff and motioning to me—"Come on, Wayne. Let's jump!" That visual representation made a lasting impression on me. Visualizing a scene has the very potent power to influence the way we think.

Decades later, while sitting in one of my library school graduate courses, I had a similar epiphany. My instructor handed students copies of a column from one of our library professional journals. That column was titled "How Do You Manage?" and presented a fictionalized library management situation typically faced by library staff. The column then provided two differing perspectives from library leaders on how the situation should be resolved. For nearly two hours, my class colleagues and instructor engaged in a spirited discussion on which perspective was right. I couldn't believe how engaged I was in a library situational conflict I'd never even considered, let alone conceptualized. It was such an invigorating debate. I was envisioning characters in my mind, thinking about what they'd say, wondering how they'd react. At the same time, I was able to create library environments I never knew existed. I soon realized this technique of creating fictional library situations could be a unique way for those entering the library profession to learn practical and analytical skills.

When I became a library and information school instructor myself, I began teaching library management and administration. It wasn't long before I realized a misconception in my teaching philosophy. I was struck by the number of students who told me that they'd never worked in a library or had little knowledge about the library profession beyond volunteering in their local information center. I had been expecting students to hand in essays and assignments that conveyed experience and competency they had yet to accumulate. I needed a way to put these students at the center of actual library problems and see how they reacted. I recollected the value I had received from the situations and scenarios I had used when I was a student, and the "what would you do?" lessons I learned from my mother, and thus the seed of an idea for this book was planted.

The purpose of this book, then, is to engage students with real-world library problems and situations that put them in charge of challenging library issues. The overarching goal is to provide a more interactive method for students to think about the root causes of library problems. By using library-related scenarios and situations, students—especially those with little actual library experience—can quickly learn how library policy decisions and organizational structures hinder, or enhance, problem-solving abilities. As an instructor, I appreciate the fact that scenarios allow students to learn from different perspectives and approach problems from various points of view they may never have considered before. Such is the power of the process of visualization and role playing. Thus, this book was created.

INTENDED AUDIENCE

The primary audience for this book is students—especially those in a library and information school or library technical college—who will soon be entering the professional field. In creating these scenarios, focus was placed on the art of problem solving. For this reason, students wishing to pursue a management track in the information profession will derive the most benefit. Those who wish to improve judgment, intuition, and perception, and, in turn, make themselves more marketable in the workforce, will certainly find this book to be of value as well.

Much research points to the fact that students are more inductive than deductive reasoners. But there is little available in the current instructional body of work that builds students' logic and inductive skills. Therefore, books like this, which provide actual examples to explore and think about, are far more useful than many of the existing texts that start with theory and basic principles. Case studies and scenarios are often used in business, law, and medical school instruction, but they can be useful in any discipline, and with most any audience, in which instructors want students to explore how the lessons they have learned apply to real-world situations, making them more adept at acclimating to the library environment they aspire to enter.

This book is also intended for instructors of library and information studies programs as well as library technical colleges and school library media centers. Instructors will find more information about using scenario-based learning as part of their curriculum in the "Notes for Instructors" section that follows. Generally, however, instructors will note that these library scenarios immerse students in the subject you are teaching. By using the strategies and concepts you will be teaching them, your students will experience library problems while dealing with the real-life consequences of their choices—all without real-life risks.

There is yet another audience this book will benefit—current library managers and employees. The text uses scenarios that are gleaned from *today's* library world and industry-specific characters that will be immediately relatable to many current library employees. Furthermore, the scenarios herein will encourage current library employees to access previously acquired professional knowledge. These advantages—and the potential for scenarios to foster lively discussion, interactivity, and engagement—mean current library managers may find value in presenting and using these scenarios as part of staff development and training programs.

SCOPE

With scenarios depicting sexual harassment, censorship, budget cuts, and governing board dysfunction, the library situations represented in this book reflect a broad range of topics familiar to many of those in the profession. These are topics that many instructors already include in their lesson plans and will add depth to the overall instruction. Other scenarios explore unfamiliar, perhaps even uncomfortable, topics that many students may—up to this point—be unaware of and could therefore lack the understanding and knowledge necessary to process them without directives and discipline from the instructor. These scenarios explore issues of diversity, transgender employees, controversial children's programs, and patron privacy. These types of scenarios expand students' knowledge of operational situations they could likely encounter.

Certainly, working through a scenario and thinking about the who, what, why, and so on is a valuable practice for students wishing to gain practical and situational knowledge of library issues and functions. What makes this textbook even more desirable to would-be library professionals is the fact that over fifty library leaders—virtual mentors, if you will—were asked to read these same scenarios and provide their own perspectives on how to resolve the problems presented. This sort of content gives students the invaluable opportunity to evaluate multiple actual leadership styles to truly acquire successful library managerial skills and knowledge.

FORMAT

This book includes twenty library-themed scenarios organized into sections that highlight the six basic managerial functions: planning, leading, organizing, controlling, staffing, and communicating. Within each of these sections, at least three library-themed scenarios are presented that depict a real-world library problem with that managerial function as a core feature. Following each scenario are three responses solicited from library leaders from the United States and Canada. These library leaders have read that scenario and provided their own perspective on how best to resolve the issue.

Students will need to use one of four levels of triggers, or tools, to help them successfully explore that scenario. These triggers address the complexity and difficulty of the scenario and clue students in to the logic necessary to resolve it. These triggers include skills, problem solving, difficult professional topics, and supposition. Each trigger is further explained in the "Notes to the Instructor" section that follows. To make it easier for instructors and students to choose an appropriate scenario to enhance a lesson, each scenario is labeled with the basic managerial function at its core as well as the trigger most useful in its resolution.

EXPLORING AND ANALYZING A SCENARIO

Not unlike the analysis and evaluation of a case study, the analysis of a scenario will require the reader to explore the background and environment and identify the key elements of the problem and potential resolutions to the challenges presented. However, whereas the study of a case history normally requires structured and extremely detailed analysis of research already provided, some of the relevant information in a scenario may not be explicit, leaving readers to fill in certain gaps by quickly inferring from the information provided what is *likely* happening. For this reason, there may be no better approach to using a scenario in a classroom setting than simply having a "read and discuss" session. After reading the scenario, leaders often begin group discussion with the prompt "What is your first move?"

Rather than try to find the "perfect" answer, it is useful to generate many different approaches worth considering while exploring the pros and cons inherent in various possible resolutions. This informal approach is easy to set up and will foster a good deal of participation from the entire group.

However, there are certainly drawbacks to such an informal and unstructured approach. Some individuals may find that certain elements are ignored or addressed out of sequence, so it might take more time to get through the whole scenario effectively. Informal and unstructured discussions risk being "hijacked" by more vocal group members who want attention to focus on them or who want to appear more knowledgeable than others. Additionally, some group members may find certain scenario topics too complex or even too uncomfortable to discuss in a group setting—even with encouragement and prompting by a leader. Finally, logistics and geography may make it impossible to create groups. For whatever reason, then, a more structured and formal scenario analysis and evaluation method may be more productive.

A STRUCTURED APPROACH TO WORKING WITH THESE SCENARIOS

Guiding discussions in any form or situation can be quite challenging for a leader or facilitator, and when working with scenarios and case studies it can be even more so. Group leaders must be skilled in leading discussions on the wide range of complex issues inherent in these short scenes, and, since most of these scenarios do not have clear-cut paths to resolution, participants may experience some discomfort and frustration when working through them, which can ultimately cause resistance to the learning process. Additionally, some discussions and scenario evaluations may occur online or across geographic and cultural boundaries, which can present its own set of communication challenges.

What follows are questions, or prompts, created with the intent of helping a discussion leader (or an individual working alone) produce more formal discussions (or thought) without a facilitator providing content. These prompts should encourage readers to take a proactive role in self-directed learning by analyzing and evaluating the scenario. When applied to the analytic process, these questions will create a far more engaging, interactive, and immersive experience for readers—regardless of whether they are working in a group, working with others online, or evaluating the scenario individually.

What Do You See as the Key Issue/Challenge Presented in the Scenario?

These scenarios often represent multiple management issues that may all seem pertinent. In many cases, problem solvers will rush to a decision based on the last thing they remember. Or they may base solutions on irrelevant or surface information. This can often lead to what are called "quick fixes." Asking this question necessitates that the reader back away from a quick fix and look at the totality of the situation. Starting off a scenario discussion or analysis with this question is comparable to a photographer adjusting and fine-tuning a camera's lens before snapping a picture of a subject. The question also facilitates a better understanding of the various pieces of the scenario, gaining insight into specifics and helping to define the complexity and importance of issues needing discussion as the analysis goes forward.

Because these scenarios present a good deal of peripheral information within a relatively small story, it is natural to overlook information that may—on its surface—seem irrelevant. Likewise, some detail may be missed on the first reading. For this reason, it is beneficial to read the scenario several times and from several perspectives. This will help readers to question characters' statements and decisions and begin to understand the judgment and actions of the many individuals portrayed.

What Do You See as the "Context" of the Problem? (What Causes or Influences the Problem?)

In writing the scenarios, context and background information has been added to assist readers in understanding vital situations or experiences—especially since the experience or situation can't often be adequately explained by a single word or phrase. Therefore, it may be necessary to define the circumstances and environment contributing to the key issue or issues identified by asking about context. This question will help to identify specific goals, constraints, and environmental conditions that have likely influenced the situation portrayed in the scenario. Since a good deal of the context of the scenario may be hidden, or remain unstated by the characters in the scenario, looking for context within the background information will improve overall meaning and specificity. Obviously, by understanding context in this way, readers can avoid making inappropriate interpretations and attaching incorrect significance to certain elements in the scenario. As a benefit to answering this question, students may find value in using it as a comparative tool, searching for similarities (or dissimilarities) with what they are familiar with at their own library or place of employment.

What Information or Facts Do You Feel Must Be Taken into Consideration Before Making Any Decision Regarding the Issue/Challenge?

Like a detective at a crime scene, readers must have an unwavering quest for "just the facts" as they evaluate and analyze the case. A discussion question that asks which relevant facts and figures shouldn't be ignored when considering the scenario should help focus attention on finding the core problem or issue. It will also help eliminate trivial information that doesn't need to be a part of the ultimate decision-making process.

What Information or Facts Are Missing from the Context of the Scenario That Would Influence How You Might Respond to the Issue?

Continuing on the fact-finding mission started above, it is just as important to identify what information is missing from the scenario. As any future manager in the "real world" will quickly find out, not all key facts and information will be readily available to the decision maker. Therefore, it is critical to understand what missing information would be necessary to know—and what missing information would be nice to know—before progressing too far down the problem-solving path. As individuals analyze and work through these case scenarios, they may need to make assumptions about missing information that are based on knowledge and reasoning learned in classroom instruction. For this reason, this particular question provides opportunities to evaluate—and ultimately improve—professional skill, objectivity, and judgment.

Who Will Most Likely Be the Key Decision Maker in This Scenario?

There are often several key characters in a scenario. However, it is unlikely that each of them would play a significant role in making decisions to resolve a specific issue. As readers work through a scenario, they will begin to see different professional perspectives, different roles and responsibilities, and different tactics displayed in the use of management power, authority, and politics. Appraising all the "actors" in a scene, and comprehending how or why they do the things they do, will not only provide information on who makes the key decisions in that situation but also offer opportunities to analyze how employees leverage power, negotiate agreements, and maneuver within the confines of organizational bureaucracy.

What Alternatives Does the Key Decision Maker Have Available?

The true goal of analyzing the case studies is to be able to confidently state what one believes is the "best way" to resolve the challenges presented. However, before this can happen, it is beneficial to generate as many potential alternatives as possible. These alternatives must be logical and rational. Some alternatives may even require a level of innovation and creativity that is grounded in personal experience and observation rather than classroom instruction. Because of this, some scenario users will find themselves outside their comfort zone and have difficulty considering this question. Processes that help generate ideas (such as brainstorming, mixing/matching possible solutions, and reexamining internal and external constraints within the situation) are to be encouraged and explored.

Given the Information You Have Right Now, Which Alternative Do You Feel Is the Best Course of Action to Resolve This Case?

Once as many alternatives as possible for resolving the problem described in the case have been generated, the process of ranking and prioritizing them should be undertaken. Readers should evaluate and rank these alternatives from their own perspective, since they can see the whole picture and have knowledge that the actors in the scene may or may not have. Before deciding on the best alternative to recommend, readers should also ensure the chosen alternative covers the entire range of the issue under analysis. For example, the best alternative within a scenario may be to terminate an employee for bullying and constant harassment. However, to ensure that a similar situation does not arise again in the future, the chosen alternative might also need to include a full-staff training program centered around the organization's harassment policy (if one exists) and the proper procedures employees should follow when confronted with the issue.

How Can You Apply What You've Learned to Your Current (or Future) Library Environment?

After arriving at a satisfactory conclusion to a scenario, it is extremely helpful to reflect on the entire process in order to enhance what was learned, determine which skills need improving, and access how those skills may be improved in the future. Additionally, a full debriefing of the process should lead those analyzing the scenario to begin understanding how to apply information they have learned once they are on the job.

READY TO BEGIN!

For many, immersing yourself in the middle of a challenging, often dysfunctional, management crisis may seem like a counterintuitive way to gain insight into the library information science profession. For professionals who value finding answers to serious questions, and who strive to organize and categorize, embracing the ambiguity and uncertainty inherent in scenario cases seems foreign to our service standards. And yet there are few better ways to apply principles learned through class instruction—to practice what we've been taught—without fear of making mistakes and being judged harshly. As you work through this book, and as you immerse yourself in the challenge of reality-based library management situations, continue to ask questions, evaluate your skills, and envision how *you* would respond. Have fun in this nonthreatening environment of scenario-based case studies. You'll soon be experiencing your own scenarios in real time. Rest assured, you'll now be far more prepared.

Acknowledgments

The professional world would certainly be a better place if there were more leaders who willingly gave of their time to share their expertise. I am grateful to have found so many of those leaders while creating this book. Its completion would not have been successful without their participation and assistance. I am honored that these library leaders offered to share their experience, even while many are still working in our nation's libraries, struggling with daily operational problems and crises far worse than the fictional ones herein. Many of these library leaders and managers also participated as our world has been in the midst of a global pandemic—a time in which many of their own library and information facilities were closed. And yet they gladly accepted the opportunity to contribute their time and expertise so tomorrow's library employees could better understand the professional environment in which we are employed. For this, I sincerely appreciate their unconditional support during the most difficult of times. While these library leaders are cited—along with their affiliation—in this book, I know there are others who cannot be cited but whose contributions were nonetheless significant. I particularly want to acknowledge Christopher John Garcia for his creative mind and help in creating dialogues and environments for some of the fictionalized scenarios in this book and allowing me to act out the scenes with him. This was incredibly beneficial in ensuring these vignettes accurately reflect the realities of today's work environment. My heartfelt thanks.

Notes for Instructors

Armed with book loads of knowledge, heightened academic skills, familiarity with theories on information-seeking behavior, and a great deal of optimism, students in today's library and information studies (LIS) programs often enter the workforce with underdeveloped managerial abilities and judgment necessary to cope with problems and issues that can—and will—arise in the field. When faced with complex operational issues, or when pressed with seemingly insurmountable management problems while on the job, a common refrain heard in just about every information environment is, "We never learned *that* in library school!" How do students acquire and apply knowledge that engages a whole new set of skills currently absent from most of their coursework? Certainly, there is a need to prepare students with practical, hands-on knowledge in order to bridge the gap that currently exists between much of the theory taught in LIS programs and the practice needed to become successful library professionals. Scenarios that model true-to-life experiences and challenges commonly faced in the work setting are extremely useful tools to help students navigate real-world work environment challenges. Sadly, the availability of such material in our profession is minimal. To make matters worse, the body of case and scenario-based material that *is* available lacks currency and relevance to today's library world. To rectify that situation, this book provides twenty library workplace scenarios that put students in the middle of the action. These scenarios—each designed to simulate actual language, tasks, and processes found in today's library world—present authentic challenges that ultimately encourage students to role play, to explore, to discuss, and to consider what they would do if placed in similar professional situations.

The scenes presented in this book should not be confused with actual case histories or studies. Technically, a case history involves *actual* events, organizations, or people that have been studied over a period of time—using a far greater depth of scrutiny and formal research methods—and then recorded for the purpose of specific data review and analysis. Unlike traditional case history studies, the scenarios herein have been designed to be engaging *stories* that provide relevant information in fictional format. They are intended to be used as teaching lessons that contain many traditional dramatic elements, such as plot, dialogue, character, tension, conflict, and mood. While *based* on synthesized professional knowledge of actual events, circumstances, professional settings, and incidents, these scenarios are not real and do not represent any actual library or library personnel. Instead, the scenarios have been artificially created with the purpose of allowing students to use learned experience, accumulated research, knowledge of theories, and personal judgment in order to interact and exist within each situation.

When presenting or using these case scenarios in instruction, it should be stressed that there are no perfect answers. Yes, some methods are better than others when resolving complicated issues. Without actually implementing a suggested resolution and observing what occurs in real time, we can't be sure that one particular resolution would be better than any other. Therefore, in order to generate robust dialogue, it is always helpful to remind students or readers that there are many ways—as opposed to right or wrong ways—to approach the incidents presented in these scenes. To illustrate that concept, and to help facilitate even more discussion and thought, each of the scenarios in this book has been reviewed by accomplished library managers, educators, and information professionals who are working, or have worked, in the library and information field. These individuals have provided their own insights on the incidents portrayed and have contributed their own thoughts on how they would react in the situations if *they* were placed within that scenario. While their responses are not intended to be the sole correct answer in each scene, they do represent actual approaches to resolve the prevalent issue and give insight as to how the problems may have occurred and how they might have been prevented. These responses will provide an excellent benchmark that students can consider, evaluate, and measure against their own responses. By so doing, students should be able to hone their professional skills and see significant improvement in the quality of their judgment and professionalism.

WHY USE SCENARIOS IN THE LEARNING PROCESS?

In his many contributions to the study of education, American philosopher and psychologist John Dewey argued his belief that schools would be most successful in their educational mission if they provided lessons that represent real life. Students need to learn by example by considering situations that are just as real as what they'd find in the home, in the neighborhood, or on the playground. Dewey further believed that schools should provide lessons that reproduce activities in ways that students can gradually learn from them and become capable of playing their own part in relation to them. In designing a theory of education that focused more on the learner as a *participant* in instruction (as opposed to a passive *recipient* of it), Dewey broke ground at the time by arguing that the most effective lessons and instruction for students enabled them to link what they had learned in classroom instruction with actual experiences and practice—thereby developing a personal connection between theory and practice. From this school of thought, it can easily be argued that students are more apt to succeed if they can *learn by doing*. Giving students the tools that allow them to complete a process is only one piece of the puzzle. Actually allowing them to *use* those tools within simulated practical situations provides them with opportunities to gain experience without actually being on the job. Unfortunately, some educators—particularly those involved in the instruction of would-be library and information professionals—may have lost touch with this "theory-to-practice" concept. Students cannot learn to be effective library professionals solely by reading journal articles and listening to instructor lectures. Instead, they need to play a more active role in the learning process. The use of scenarios in instruction can afford students the opportunity to identify interrelationships between the theories they are learning and the realities of the profession they will enter and the environments in which they intend to work.

BENEFITS OF USING SCENARIOS IN GRADUATE-LEVEL LIBRARY INSTRUCTION

As already discussed, scenario-based instruction bridges the perceived gap between theory and practice while at the same time helping students link instruction to eventual experience. However, if this were the sole benefit of using scenarios, there are other effective methods that might produce the same results (computer-based simulations, media-based instruction, digital content, competency-based instruction, job shadowing, etc.). A deeper investigation of scenario-based learning, however, reveals additional benefits not easily found in other teaching methodologies.

Increasing Comfort in Handling Badly Structured, Complex Problems

Students of management often learn that problems are divided into two categories. There are those problems that are well structured and have a clear path leading from the current state (where you are right now) to the goal state (where you want to be). Resolving these problems simply requires using known operators that provide a correct answer. For example, in resolving the problem "What is two plus two?" the problem solver simply uses addition and comes to the conclusion that two plus two equals four. What a perfect world it would be for managers if all the problems they faced were as well structured as this. Unfortunately, most of the problems a manager will confront will be ill-structured—that is, there is no clear path or answer for how to resolve the issue. These issues are fraught with ambiguity and uncertainty. "How can we achieve world peace?" is an example of an ill-structured problem. Ambiguity and uncertainty create a great deal of angst for potential problem solvers and managers who find it difficult to react effectively when there are no rules for handling a particular set of problems. The scenarios presented in this book are open-ended with no clear direction on how best to move from the current state to the goal state. In exploring and discussing each scenario, students will begin to develop their own systems for identifying and interpreting elements within complex and ill-structured problems. Students who discover commonalities between the problems presented in these scenarios, who create processes for cataloging data derived from these complex problems, and who learn how to distinguish between what is relevant and what is trivial in each scene will begin to gain a higher level of tolerance and competency in handling the many ill-structured problems they are bound to face in the workforce.

Scenarios Provide Safe Environments in Which to Engage in and Discuss Difficult Themes

There is nothing more unsettling to new managers than being confronted with their first emotionally charged incident. Whether it's a complaint of sexual harassment, an active shooter in the building, or the threat of having to dismiss an employee who has stolen something from the library, every library manager will be broadsided by a challenge that will literally change their lives. Scenarios offer instructors an opportunity to place students into such emotionally charged situations within a "make-believe" context. Several scenarios in this book will challenge students to make critical decisions involving a highly charged library-related incident. Because these scenarios involve fictional settings and people, students will feel more comfortable using their judgment and discussing the personal, political, cultural, or structural challenges that caused them to make the decisions they did in each case. Fiction provides the safety necessary for students to freely explore disruptive incidents—and fine-tune their critical thinking skills—without the burden of shouldering the responsibilities of making a wrong decision in the real world.

Discovering the Usefulness of Small Group Decision Making

LIS instructors are often surprised to be met with resistance and disdain from students when asking them to work in small groups. Scenario-based learning is an engaging way for students to acquire a deeper appreciation for working in groups. As stated earlier, these scenarios present complex and thought-provoking problems that don't often lead to clear resolutions. When reading a scenario in this book, students may develop what they believe is the best course of action. However, the diversity of opinions that can be generated in group discussion will likely result in many different alternatives coming forward that the individual may not have considered or even known existed. For this reason, scenarios are excellent tools to help students understand the benefits of sharing knowledge, generating more ideas, identifying differing styles of problem solving, and learning to listen and communicate effectively.

Learning from Industry Role Models

One of the unique attributes of this text is the presentation of insight from various library and information industry leaders on each of the scenarios. Each of these individuals bring respected leadership skills, excellent communication, strategic organizational knowledge, and valuable professional experiences to the exploration of the scenarios. In many cases, these exceptional professionals may have already experienced or handled similar situations in their libraries. By reading these insights from industry professionals, students can take advantage of the important knowledge already acquired by others in their profession. Importantly, this knowledge may include not only what *to* do but also what *not* to do in certain situations. Ultimately, the scenario responses provided by these library industry leaders may help identify more realistic and creative alternatives or resolutions. This can also help learners develop judgment and intuition that is based on a foundation of known library expertise. This is particularly important when using scenarios in online coursework where small group formation may not be possible.

Learning to Participate within Uncertain and Unfamiliar Professional Cultures

Whether they are researching an essay topic or checking out a textbook, certainly every LIS student has used a library in some way. But how many students have actually been employed—or currently work—in a library? Even those students who *are* employed in a library are likely only working at a novice or intermediate level. As such, they likely have not yet gained the necessary knowledge of key duties and responsibilities attributed to various library personnel, the relationships between power and authority at different levels, and the current organizational etiquette of today's library and information environments. Scenarios place students within today's library culture. They will explore library organizational relationships, learn responsibilities associated with various library activities, be introduced to professional jargon, and dissect library operations from the standpoint of either an active or passive observer within each scene. Scenarios allow students, then, to encounter real-world situations in which they will soon be involved and instantly become a "virtual" part of the professional community they wish to enter.

Understanding Various Perspectives

Understanding different perspectives is a key leadership skill, and scenarios will allow students to see many different library roles from the point of view of those characters operating within each situation. This forces students to question motives and look at what may be influencing the actions of those within the scenario. One of the most complex concepts students need to understand is that various library roles come with differing biases and agendas. When asked about library budgets, a children's librarian will likely have a completely different perspective about how much money to allocate for programming than would, say, the adult services librarian. Although we each have the capability of taking a different perspective on issues, we seldom like to abandon our own points of view or consider differing realities. Scenarios help change that. Not only can students identify what motivates certain characters in each scene; they can also begin to evaluate the appropriateness of the motives of the characters involved and decide if certain actions and reactions are caused by shifts in perspective.

CLASSIFYING SCENARIOS

To make it easier for instructors and other users of these scenarios to synthesize them into specific lesson plans or areas of coursework, each scene has been broadly classified in two ways. First, each scenario will be roughly grouped into one of the six management functions being applied (planning, organizing, leading, controlling, staffing, or communicating). Second, each scenario has been labeled according to which of four teaching "triggers" (skills, topics, problem solving, or supposition) it employs. These functions and triggers are further described below. Obviously, some scenarios employ combinations of several functions and triggers and can therefore be useful in several ways. However, the dominant function and trigger has been identified and labeled for each scene (e.g., Scenario Name: A Planning Scenario Using Skills, or Scenario Name: A Staffing Scenario Using Supposition). The following chapter will help both instructors and students understand how to define and approach each scenario and will illustrate how each scene has been constructed to target broad management classifications and enhance specific professional capabilities.

BASIC MANAGEMENT FUNCTIONS

The name Henri Fayol is instantly recognizable to any student of management. However, few if any LIS students are likely to be familiar with the name. They would, however, be more familiar with Fayol's accomplishments in defining theories of management—specifically his role as the first to define five basic management functions: planning, organizing, commanding, coordinating, and controlling. It is Fayol's five functions that are most commonly used around the world in the study of management, and those functions have been named—with some modification to reflect today's language—as the basis for scenario classification herein. Additionally, every professional (whether in a library or other organization) recognizes the importance of effective communication in being a successful manager. Therefore, *communication* has been added as a sixth management function in classifying these scenarios. It is not the intent of this book to contribute any extensive examination of each of these management functions or principles. However, since each of these scenarios has been classified to show where it fits within these broad categories, what follows is a brief explanation of each of the six managerial functions in order to help students to understand the concepts used and illustrate how the scenario fits into the learning process.

Planning

Often thought of as the first—and arguably most important—management function, planning involves setting appropriate goals or objectives and developing strategies that will get the organization there. Characters within these scenarios must make decisions regarding the best actions and policies for their organization's future success. Incidents portrayed in these scenes show strategic, tactical, and/or operational activities that shape the organization's current and future position. Working with these scenarios will help students identify organizational strengths and weaknesses and enhance their ability to make effective decisions based on known and unknown environmental conditions.

Organizing

Once a plan has been created, managers must marshal the resources necessary to enact the plan. Identifying the appropriate roles of authority, chain of command, and interdepartmental coordination makes organizing an important consideration in these scenarios. Working with these scenarios, students will learn to evaluate organization charts, divisions of labor, and positions of authority as part of ensuring organizational success.

Leading

Perhaps the most interesting of the management functions because of its reliance on observing human behavior and motivation, leading considers the factors that influence employees to perform essential tasks. Since the most effective managers are those who can motivate subordinates to continually improve and attain the organization's objectives, students will find it necessary to identify those qualities within many of these scenarios. Scenarios that focus on this management function will be useful for students in helping them understand different types of formal and informal power as well as in helping to identify effective—and even the most ineffective—ways to inspire and motivate others.

Controlling

In order to measure organizational success or failure, it is necessary to have controls and standards in place against which to measure performance. An organization's policies and operational processes help determine when—and if—employees have deviated from established controls. Working with these scenarios will require students to identify and evaluate organizational controls to determine how they reflect actual performance. Students will learn to relate components such as budgets and performance to organizational goals. These scenarios will also be helpful in addressing how organizations deal with the lack of controls or controls that have unintended consequences.

Staffing

Staffing is the management function concerned with the process of recruiting, selecting, evaluating, rewarding, and retaining the human resources of an organization. Since staffing deals with job functions and labor management, it is often thought of as a subtask of the management function of organizing discussed above. However, because it is just as important for students to learn more specifically about the types of individuals performing certain jobs as it is to learn about the jobs themselves, the management function of staffing needs more attention. These scenarios present situations that allow students to determine if the right people are in the right positions and if they are performing the right jobs. It helps build connections between job function and job performance. In the simplest terms, working with these scenarios will assist students in understanding employees as they relate to organizational productivity and morale.

Communicating

Clear and appropriate communication is the basis for success in every management function. For example, a strategic plan that is not communicated properly cannot be implemented successfully. Likewise, a manager who cannot communicate effectively with the staffing resources employed at the organization is doomed to fail. Because communication plays such a vital role in management functions and organizational success, students cannot ignore it as a factor in becoming proficient library employees. Working with these scenarios allows students to discover many types of communication challenges and analyze how and why they occur. Additionally, students can observe the emotion and volatility inherent in situations where poor communication skills are present. This will help students cultivate steps to avoid barriers in the successful communication process and develop methods that can improve—if not eliminate—poor communication skills in organizations.

DEFINE THE TRIGGERS

The goal of most any student in a library and information science program is to gain the technical experience and knowledge necessary to secure employment after they have completed their academic program. The scenarios herein use one of four triggers to help target professional elements that many prospective employers in the field desire, if not require. The scenarios use a particular approach that helps initiate or precipitate a chain of events or process. Not unlike a gun's trigger, the particular scenario trigger actuates the mechanism that helps resolve the issue being explored. Since these scenarios present situations that are open-ended and unresolved, students are left to use one of these triggers to reveal how they would react to, or resolve, the scenario. The trigger they will need to use in each scene will be one of the following: their acquired academic skills (skills), their problem-solving abilities (problem solving), their knowledge of difficult professional topics (difficult professional topics), or their logic in supposition (supposition). What follows is a brief explanation of each of the triggers the scenarios intend to address. By classifying the scenarios this way, instructors and students can more easily select those scenarios that fit best into a particular learning module or that enhance specific abilities.

Skills Scenarios

These scenarios allow students to demonstrate the factual knowledge, theory, and principles of library science they have already acquired. These scenarios can best be described as having the most basic path toward resolution. To resolve these scenarios, students will likely use established practices or procedures. Students' thoughts are normally based on their acquired knowledge of the common roles or responsibilities they have already associated with librarianship. A scenario that presents a situation in which a librarian is sitting at a reference desk and is approached by a patron who needs some specific piece of information would be a skills-focused scenario example. Students would be required to demonstrate their acquired knowledge of conducting a reference interview and display explicit knowledge of known reference sources. Scenarios that focus on skills are certainly most useful for instructors who wish to provide "practice" to students. They can compare the practice against established benchmarks of acceptable procedures and provide immediate feedback for students. This is particularly beneficial in identifying omissions in professional performance and providing concrete pathways to improve. Skills-focused scenarios can also be quite useful in demonstrating that even set practices and set procedures do not resolve every situation. Think, for example, how different the situation described above (in which a patron needs some specific piece of information) would be if the person who has approached the librarian is a non-English-speaking patron.

Problem-Solving Scenarios

Once more complex elements have been added to a skills-focused situation, the scenario becomes more challenging. Students can no longer rely on acquired knowledge of set procedures and processes and must face open-ended questions that are not as easily answered. The non-English-speaking patron who has approached the reference librarian described above would be an example of a problem-solving scenario. Using their acquired professional knowledge, students will need to identify the known quantities within the situation and make decisions regarding unknown variables presented therein. For example, the student knows the non-English-speaking patron in the situation above has approached the reference desk for help of some sort, but it is unknown what *kind* of help is needed. The student must assess how to obtain the missing information in the situation and then must make subsequent decisions regarding that information in order to provide solutions. Problem-solving-focused scenarios are excellent tools to familiarize students with decision-making techniques and how to use them effectively. Additionally, these scenarios are useful in introducing the role of ambiguity and uncertainty to the problem-solving process and in illustrating how students can reach a higher level of tolerance and comfort when confronted by it.

Difficult Professional Topics Scenarios

In continuing with the example of the non-English-speaking patron at the reference desk, consider how the scenario might change when (during the problem-solving process) it is learned that the patron is homeless. Libraries are certainly not immune to facing difficult societal, legal, technological, environmental, or economic topics. There isn't a librarian working in the field today who would not be familiar with issues of, say, homeless people in the library, latchkey children, "fee for service," or censorship. Several scenarios in this book focus on difficult professional topics that will require students to debate and begin to develop a personal perspective on such issues. Learning to research these topics, provide evidentiary support for a position, and express a professional understanding of difficult topics will benefit students as they prepare to enter the workforce. Using scenarios that require students to explore these difficult professional topics from several perspectives will help them foster an awareness and an appreciation of the important role library personnel play in society.

Supposition Scenarios

Scenarios that start from a "suppose you . . ." or "what do you think would happen if . . ." perspective can best be described as using a technique that relies on students using broad supposition. These scenarios can often be the most challenging because they require students to use all the triggers previously discussed in some respect. Several of the scenarios in this book are useful in targeting students' use of logic in supposing future events or situations.

Using what they have already learned, students will develop a hypothesis about something that is expected to change in the future. Furthermore, they will need to provide support and evidence for their hypothesis in order to frame their ideas into a logical context. These scenarios may also require students to look for past and present actions and trends to predict future behavior. To use the example of the non-English-speaking patron at the reference desk one final time, a supposition scenario might ask, "What would happen if demographic trends predict that within twenty years, 50 percent of the potential library users in this community will speak a language other than English?" Unlike the triggers of the other scenarios already discussed, those that use supposition often call for a far more creative approach. Students can be encouraged to think outside their professional comfort zones in order to provide logical resolutions to events or situations that may, or may not, occur. In doing this, students can contemplate the future of their professional environment while developing their own identity and sense of place within that environment.

A FINAL WORD FOR INSTRUCTORS

Scenario-based instruction is meant to be just one engaging part of the overall academic learning process for the prospective library and information professional. Whether you are using the scenarios in this book as a source of knowledge transfer in order to introduce students to the myriad of management-related challenges they will soon be facing in their chosen field or whether you are taking a more proactive approach to skill training, the scenarios in this book are not meant to *replace* instruction in any way. For this reason, before using a scenario, instructors should design lesson plans that will allow students to first acquire the basic core knowledge necessary to respond to concepts at the root of each scenario's topic. Once equipped with the appropriate tools, students should be expected to analyze and evaluate the scenario and, ultimately, create satisfactory solutions.

Part One

Planning

Chapter One

Alice in SWOTerland

A Planning Scenario Using Problem Solving

SCENARIO

She was not a morning person. In fact, Alice Cumberland had considered phoning in sick today. Her boss, the university librarian, had set today as a mandatory training and staff development day at Chasten University Library, and Alice was sure she wouldn't be missed. It's not like the library's administration recognized all the work she was doing anyway. She couldn't remember the last time she had received a performance review. Yet Alice knew her absence would not look good to the university librarian, and she might even require some sort of proof that she was unable to go to the mandatory meeting. So instead she struggled out of bed and readied herself for work.

Upon arriving at the staff entrance to the library that morning, Alice was beginning to feel a bit better. Being out in the cold, crisp morning air seemed to clear her mind. As soon as she set her purse on her desk, that feeling instantly evaporated. Sitting at the place on her desk she had identified as the place for "things that are important" were five folders representing five major projects that had been set in her lap for completion. The top folder, marked "Microfilm Project," was the one project Alice was finding the most difficult to complete, and here it was staring her in the face. Alice had been tasked with devising a plan for preserving, storing, and making searchable the library's entire Hirshfeld microfilm collection of historical documents. The project included not only the library's microfilm rolls but also the thousands and thousands of microfiches, microfilm jackets, and aperture cards. The Hirshfeld collection contained land documents, medical documents, personal diaries, historic newspapers, and precious local history images—all of which was currently in analog format. Since this format required specialized microfilm readers or scanners to be viewed, the library needed a plan to transfer the current collection to digital images so that the specialized microfilm hardware would no longer be required.

When this project had been passed off to Alice, she had been told that she was the fourth person to work on it. This raised some red flags in her mind. Why were so many previous staff members unsuccessful? She learned that, because of a university restructuring plan years ago, the project never seemed to settle on one person long enough to carry it through to completion. So, Alice was the fourth person, and maybe there wasn't anything to infer from that. What she really couldn't understand was why she had been chosen for the task at all. She didn't even know what analog meant.

It was a long, hard learning curve, but Alice had gotten herself to the point where she felt she at least had a grasp on what was needed. Still, she only knew *what* was needed. She didn't know *how* to accomplish it. From what Alice had learned, she knew that special equipment (which was quite pricey) was needed. There was also the option of contracting the services of some sort of digitization provider (which was also quite pricey) to perform the process for the library. Then there were complicated questions such as technical specifications, the time necessary for conversion, and deciding about value-added services such as image enhancement, data extraction, and cloud storage. How was she going to get all of this done? The project was obviously a high priority for the university. It had been in the pipeline for so long, faculty members were continually bringing it up at staff meetings, and students were more and more perplexed about using the old—and often broken—microfilm reading equipment in the library. As a result, the Hirshfeld collection was becoming obsolete in their eyes. Just as Alice reached for the "Microfilm Project" folder, the library's public address system boomed over her desk.

"Attention, all staff. Today's training session is about to start. We look forward to hearing everyone's thoughts today as we work on a key part of our ongoing library strategic plan—our SWOT analysis. Identifying our library's strengths, weaknesses, opportunities, and threats will help us plan for Chasten University's next decade. Please make your way to the staff auditorium as quickly as possible."

Alice heaved a heavy sigh and pushed the project folder she was reaching for a little farther to the back of her desk. She got up from her chair and headed to the training session on planning.

On her way to the elevator, Alice walked alongside her colleague June Burnett. "Hi, Alice! Well, this is exciting, huh? I'm really looking forward to seeing what strategic direction we all come up with today, aren't you?" June asked.

I don't even know what I want for dinner tonight, let alone what I want to see in our library in five to ten years! Alice nearly blurted out loud. Instead she gave a casual "uh huh" as they rounded the corner and entered the meeting room. Nearly all the chairs were full, but there were several seats up front. It looked as if staff members were reluctant to be front and center in the planning session, but Alice's options were few. Short of returning to her desk, she had nowhere else to go. Alice took a seat in the front row.

Standing at the podium in front of Alice was a highly paid consultant from Delaney Analytics, a firm the university had contracted with to develop an important piece of its strategic plan called a SWOT analysis. The university had closed the library so all employees could participate. Alice immediately thought of the money the university had spent on hiring a consulting firm as well respected as Delaney Analytics to perform this morning's session. *It could easily have paid for at least a portion of the cost to get my digitization project off the ground*, she thought. As she looked around the meeting room, waiting for the training session to start, Alice could only see dollar signs. The amount of money being spent in just paying the staff to sit there and listen was in the thousands of dollars. If they couldn't use that money for some of Alice's projects, couldn't they just close the library for a day to allow the staff to catch up on the backlog of work they were all experiencing? Instead, here she was being required to attend yet another university library planning session that would most assuredly follow the same "path to nowhere" that the previous strategic plan had taken.

A few weeks prior, Alice had walked through the university's reference section looking for records of the previous training sessions conducted over the years. She remembered finding two large black binders on the shelves marked "Chasten University Strategic Directions—A Visioning Voyage." They were dated a decade earlier. As she quickly thumbed through the table of contents in the binder, she had to laugh. There it was. A SWOT analysis—conducted over ten years ago. She turned to the SWOT pages. The strengths listed were the same as those she noted today. The same was true for the weaknesses that had been identified. As she browsed the threats reported back then, she was surprised that those threats had indeed materialized and caused the university some major problems. The opportunities listed were some that had never been acted on. In fact, there was even a short mention in the opportunities section of taking advantage of digital technology! Why hadn't anyone used this plan to develop strategies to address those issues? Seeing these binders of previous strategic plans that had gone nowhere simply reinforced Alice's belief that the meeting she was going to attend was a colossal waste of time.

A squawk of microphone feedback from the podium suddenly brought Alice's attention back to the Delaney Analytics consultant.

"Welcome, everyone!" the university librarian, Rosario Cortez, said. "Let's get started. We have a lot to get through today." She gave a brief introduction of the university's strategic planning push and explained some logistics. She then introduced the morning's trainer.

"Good morning. My name is John Beachum, and I work for Delaney Analytics. Over the course of twenty years, our company has been helping organizations such as yours successfully chart a course to the future. My job today is to help your library uncover opportunities that you are well placed to exploit. I hope to also help your organization understand the threats surrounding your library so you can manage or prepare for them and not be caught by surprise. In order to be successful in these two things, organizations need to build objectives and strategic priorities around their strengths and find ways to downplay their weaknesses, so we'll need to identify what those are as well. By doing all of this, Chasten University can start to craft a strategy that ensures your library will remain relevant and successful for years to come. That's the general plan for today. Everyone on board?"

"Oh brother! Here we go," Alice said—a little louder than she had intended.

The consultant glanced her way. "I'm sorry? Did you say something?" he asked.

Caught like a deer in the headlights, Alice squirmed. She decided to just lay it all out there. She was tired of all these trendy staff workshops. There were important things on her desk waiting to get done. She was tired of what she saw as useless training. She thought of the failure of their big customer service training last year. The university restructuring plan they had completed earlier in the year had done little—except move staff around from department to department without changing any duties. And, of course, there was the previous strategic planning—the "Visioning Voyage"—that she had seen in the binders on the reference shelves. That activity certainly produced a strategic plan that looked good on paper, but, after it was published, what had happened to it? It was never heard from again. So here Alice was, caught in the spotlight. She just let it out.

"Let's be honest with ourselves, everyone," she said. "These strategy sessions are practically worthless. Instead of a tool that helps our organization focus and act to position ourselves in the future, it produces something that sits in a big thick binder on our reference shelves, or in our university librarian's office, gathering dust on a shelf next to other thick binders that nobody reads. Our operating environment is changing so much. There isn't enough certainty in our profession to be able to strategize effectively. Strategy emerges naturally . . . why force it?" There was a smattering of applause from the crowd, though she wasn't sure where it came from or who had started it. She felt such a rush of relief. But she wasn't done yet.

Alice had found her wings, and she was gonna fly . . . even if it meant she'd eventually have no nest to return to when she came back from wherever it was she was going. She stood up and faced the entire staff. "If I ask every one of you to make a list of all the projects you're working on right now, and then I told you to cross off all the ones that aren't important, I'll bet that not one thing will get crossed off your list. And why? Well, because every single project we are working on is important to someone somewhere somehow. If our projects aren't adding value to our library, why in the heck would we be working on them?" Alice sensed that she had hit a nerve with her audience. She went on, perhaps a little more forcefully than she meant to. Turning to John Beachum, the consultant, she finished, "That's why debating about what is and what isn't important seems futile to me." She stepped off her figurative soap box and sat down.

The entire staff of the Chasten Library sat silent and turned to look at John. Rather than anger, there was a wide smile on his face. "I'm glad you asked that. It indicates that what we are doing here is even more important than I thought. I understand the frustration employees feel when they are doing more with less. Remember, what we are doing here today is just a piece of the overall planning process. Think of it as data gathering. We can't identify how to be more successful if we don't have the data necessary to understand what successful means to Chasten University Library. A SWOT can help you do that."

There was some murmuring among the participants at that point, and John waited for the crowd to quiet. He walked over to Alice and calmly said, "We certainly can't change the past. I've taken the time to review the university's previous strategic planning processes. I saw that there were some definite problems with them, and we will all ensure that those problems are not repeated. We will be transparent here, and we'll discuss how and why previous sessions failed so we don't repeat past mistakes. As we all become strategic thinkers, we'll decide where to focus the library's attention first—rather than trying to focus on what's most important." Alice somehow didn't see the difference. Was there a difference?

"At Delaney Analytics, we always stress to our clients that eighty-five to ninety-five percent of an organization's time is consumed handling its day-to-day operations," John went on. "Strategic planning," he assured everyone, "is about managing the remaining small amount of time—the five to fifteen percent—that staff can squeeze out of the day to invest in making the future what the organization wants it to be instead of relying on chance or luck to take you somewhere you never intended to go." This was all beginning to sound like doublespeak to Alice.

The consultant turned to Alice and said, "I'm sure you've heard of the children's book *Alice in Wonderland*?"

Alice blinked, not letting on that her name was Alice and that she'd always loved that book. She loved that book for many reasons, the least of which was because it had her name in the title. But she couldn't figure out what that whole story meant, so she'd learned to just enjoy the book for what it was—entertainment.

John continued. "I think there are a lot of lessons in that book that we could apply to our strategic planning process. For example, in that book, when Alice meets the Cat, they have a conversation. Do you know which one I'm talking about?" Alice was impressed when John went on and quoted the following *Alice in Wonderland* passage from memory:

"Would you tell me, please, which way I ought to go from here?"

"That depends a good deal on where you want to get to," said the Cat.

"I don't much care where," said Alice.

"Then it doesn't matter which way you go," said the Cat.

"So long as I get somewhere," Alice added as an explanation.

"Oh, you're sure to do that," said the Cat, "if only you walk long enough."

The consultant smiled at Alice as if she would certainly understand what his point was. She didn't. Alice decided she'd hear him out. She knew these were just things that organizations had to do and that she'd at least have job security with all the important stuff still remaining to be done on her desk. But just what the heck do strengths, weaknesses, opportunities, and threats have to do with all this?

John posed a simple question to Alice: "What one project are you working on that you're finding most difficult?"

Alice took the bait. "A digitization project of an important library collection."

"If, by the end of the day, I can show you how a SWOT analysis can be extremely valuable in shaping your strategy in getting that project completed, will you agree to hear me out? It will give you a chance to see things from a new perspective. It will likely help you discover some previously untapped talent or market niche that will allow you to pinpoint obstacles that are preventing you from moving forward. Agreed?" John stared at her. Alice's head started to pound.

Just then, Rosario Cortez, the university librarian, walked over to her and whispered in her ear, "Alice, come on up to my office at the next break. We need to talk." She smiled and patted Alice's arm.

Alice looked at John as Rosario walked away. "Agreed," she said.

Had Alice said too much? Maybe the university librarian wanted to terminate her? Alice had spoken the truth, and she knew it. Sometimes, though, you had to just jump through the hoops. What would she say to defend herself? She kept repeating those lines from *Alice in Wonderland* as if they were supposed to mean something to her. Her headache was getting worse now. At the break, Alice took four ibuprofen tablets and headed to the university librarian's office.

Rosario instructed her to sit down. As Alice sat, Rosario pulled a folder off her desk. In fact, the folder looked a lot like the folders sitting in Alice's own pile of important folders.

"Alice, I've been meaning to talk to you about this for a few days. This seems like an appropriate time." Written on the top of the folder were the words "Alice Cumberland Performance Evaluation."

It was all or nothing now. Rosario was going to put a quick end to her employment right here and now. Or Alice was going to listen to her supervisor and figure out how to turn over a new leaf. Either way, Alice's adventures at Chasten were coming to a most dramatic turn.

ALICE IN SWOTERLAND RESPONSES

Response 1
By Kayla Kuni, library educator, Pasco-Hernando State College, New Port Richey, Florida

The situation that Chasten University librarian Alice Cumberland is in depicts what happens when staff members feel overwhelmed and underappreciated. Alice seems to have a lack of excitement for her work, as evidenced by the desire to call in sick. Perhaps she has too many projects and not enough help on said projects. Perhaps Alice's feeling of frustration is even felt by other staff members, evidenced by the applause that Alice receives from colleagues after her speech at the training session. Everyone on the university library team probably wants their job, and the work they provide, to have some meaningful impact on their organization. It is difficult for anyone to feel valued when an organization lacks consistency, does not provide adequate feedback, does not assign projects based on skill sets, and uses funds in problematic ways.

Information and consistency are important in any organization. In libraries, having a project like the one Alice is working on go through four different staff members is, indeed, a red flag. Based on this case study scenario, it does not appear that Alice was provided with notes or feedback from past staff members that would have enabled her to understand the project's background. The university also seems to be pushing the responsibility of this very important project off on someone who already has a full plate and who does not have the skills to complete the project. Pushing a project off on the next person down the line does not show value in the project, though; it depicts the project as a problem no one wants to deal with. In this situation, the project actually does have significant value in that faculty and students want it to be completed. The best person to address this problem, however, is one with the skills to handle the needs of the project—and librarian Alice Cumberland is clearly not that person.

The project that Alice was assigned requires a certain set of skills that she does not seem to possess. She understands the "what" of the project but not the "how." In this circumstance, it is essential to know how a project should be completed. Based on the needs of the project (technical issues, time issues, additional services), Alice should not have been assigned this project. If leadership really wants Alice to lead this project, then Alice should have been given access to the experts in various departments that this project would impact to ask for their feedback. If everything is in silos at an institution, and there is no communication between departments, that leaves people—like Alice—left guessing on projects. When people are guessing on projects that they know will have major implications, a few things can happen. Employees can overwork themselves and produce something that *might* work for the time being. They could create something that does *not* work at all and then lose confidence in their skills. Or they could just put the project off and wait for the fifth person in line to take a turn at it. In any of these situations, the employee leading the project is not provided the necessary resources, be it access to other people, more time for project completion, or money.

Money and expenses are a big deal to library staff, particularly during times when budgets are being cut. Alice was likely not the only participant who was thinking about the fees associated with the consultant and how far that money could have gone in other work. In situations like this, it is more than money that bothers people; it is the lack of respect paid to the team. If Alice asks for money for project completion and is denied, she will immediately think back to the consultant's fee and feel further frustration with the organization. It is important for organizations to keep in mind that their teams have a good idea as to what consultant fees are and how far that money could have gone toward other projects.

Looking more specifically at the incident at the heart of this scenario—the all-staff SWOT training session—it is clear that Alice did not have the most positive attitude going into the meeting. She was aware of the several previous SWOT analyses, and she knew how unproductive those reports had been. Understandably, this seems to heighten Alice's annoyance in participating in one more attempt when the others had failed. Knowing that an employer had not acted on previous suggestions, and knowing that much of the SWOT report is the same as it was ten years ago, would make anyone question leadership. However, Alice did not actually *do* anything with this information. In many instances, Alice is not acting but is instead reacting. Perhaps the university had ignored Alice's feedback in the past, or perhaps it was simply not sought out. Either way, there are ways to communicate concerns as opposed to letting them ruin the outlook on an entire day. What will end up happening with frustrated team members is exactly what happened in this case. Alice spoke up about issues experienced on the project. While colleagues may agree, and even support Alice's words, the leadership of the library may feel differently.

Alice's comments during the meeting come from a place of frustration. When Alice blurts out "Oh brother!" two things happened. First, Alice got the attention of the consultant. The reaction from Alice, and the information she provides in her speech, may actually be very helpful for consultant John Beachum to hear. Second, Alice got the attention of the university librarian, Rosario Cortez. Alice's information may have been just as helpful for Rosario to hear as it was for John. Rosario, however, has the power to immediately impact Alice's future with the library. Hopefully, Rosario took note of, and carefully reviewed, Alice's employee records. She may then have realized that Alice had not received an evaluation in some time and decided now is the opportune time to do that. An evaluation following the behavior that Alice displayed could potentially be negative. However, there is also the chance that Rosario could use this opportunity to apologize for library leadership not communicating better with Alice and other members of the team. Rosario could lay out a positive plan—with goals and objectives—that outlines for Alice just how she can complete her project and how management will assist her in doing so.

Leadership in this scenario could have done many things differently, but it really all starts with evaluating and communicating with staff in order to make the university library team members feel valued. Alice displays frustration at the number of unproductive meetings and workshops staff are required to attend—like the SWOT training at the center of this scene—and it is likely that she is not the only staff member feeling this frustration. No one is communicating with them or evaluating their performance. Furthermore, no one is consistently communicating a strategic message. Staff members at Chasten University Library are basically left on their own to ensure organization success. This is certainly a failure of library management to communicate why change is needed and how specific change will result in better outcomes for the staff.

Speaking of outcomes, performance measures are just as important in evaluating staff as they are in evaluating strategy and operations. Performance evaluations should be done regularly without employees having to ask for them. Evaluations are an excellent communication opportunity for an employee and employer to work together to create professional development goals and make future plans. These evaluations can help make clear to staff why and how organizational changes are made and may prevent future outbursts like the one Alice felt needed to be made at the training.

Finally, this scenario clearly illustrates how important it is to recognize that managers and leaders are not the same thing. Managers handle the day-to-day operations, while a leader strategically guides the organization. This case shows what happens when one person (Rosario) tries—unsuccessfully—to assume both roles.

Response 2
By Dina Schuldner, academic library manager, Virginia Beach, Virginia

Successful management of employees requires communication, including coaching, encouragement, and feedback. The reader of this scenario may be tempted to focus only on the current SWOT training taking place at this library and how inflexible and unreceptive Alice is being toward that training. However, Alice's attitudes seem to be a symptom of a much larger problem. There seems to be an issue in effective communication in this library, with the primary error being in university librarian Rosario Cortez's management style. The university librarian has chosen not to communicate with Alice in a timely manner. In fact, other than the meeting Alice is summoned to at the conclusion of the scenario, it seems Rosario hasn't met frequently with Alice at all. Because of this, Alice seems to be just as lost in her work responsibilities as the fictional Alice in Wonderland portrayed in the passage that the consultant quotes; she doesn't seem to know where she is going but is just hoping to get somewhere.

People in management need to be aware of the efforts of each of their employees. They need to have face-to-face communication time with their employees to identify what projects they are working on, understand what—if any—difficulties they are facing, and determine what could be improved on. This can be achieved by meeting with employees on a regular basis—perhaps weekly.

If employees are having difficulties with a project or service they are performing, they need to feel free to communicate that to their manager. The manager can act as a coach and a way-maker. In Alice's case, she was having difficulty with her digitization project. If she knew that she would be having a weekly meeting with her supervisor about her work, she could feel free to express her concerns at that time. Rosario could have informed Alice about the available budget and resources she had access to in order to complete the project. In working with Alice, Rosario may have recommended reaching out to other university libraries in order to research what their methods of digitization were and put that information into a report that the two could discuss in more detail after the research was done. The two could have discussed what options were available, and—if necessary—Rosario could have opened up a couple of doors for Alice so she could plan her project, implement the plan, and assess the effectiveness of the plan as it unfolded. They even could have done a specific SWOT analysis together that focused directly on the project. This could have given Alice a clearer understanding of the strengths, weaknesses, opportunities, and threats that would prevent the project from being completed within a defined time frame.

Alice also has no idea why the project has gone through so many hands before landing on her desk. The manager should have been open enough to explain why she was assigning this project to Alice. I suspect that this digitization project was mismanaged from its very inception. Assuming there were no other more pressing projects that supplanted the need to get the digitization project completed, the first person assigned to it should have been coached into success. Rosario dropped the ball with the first person who had the project, and now that it is in Alice's hands, she needs to correct her previous negligence and work more closely with Alice to analyze the needs of the project.

Alice may not be a morning person as stated in the scenario, but she is clearly a motivated employee. The fact that she took it upon herself to read the SWOT report filed in the past and reflect on the university's effectiveness in acting on threats and opportunities shows that she cares about the state of the university library and has a vested interest in improving it. In fact, had Alice been involved in the previous strategic planning session, she may not have been in the predicament she now finds herself with regard to her digitization project. Alice seems better equipped and motivated to have done a better analysis on her project at that time and gotten it off the ground far more effectively than those before her. As a result of being left out of the process, Alice now expects the SWOT training to be useless instead of a valuable step toward making the library and the university as a whole stronger and more relevant. Alice would likely learn a great deal by listening to the new consultant at the all-staff training session she doesn't want to attend. However, without the necessary changes in communication and management style needed to support the training, it is likely to produce the same results as the previous SWOT failures with which the university has apparently been involved.

Alice has never been given any amount of encouragement. She cannot remember the last time she had a performance review. This is yet another indication of a lack of communication on her manager's part. Although many managers recognize that employee performance reviews are stressful (to both the employee *and* the manager), and can take a good deal of time to prepare and deliver, they are nonetheless a critical component of the manager's oversight responsibility and should not be ignored—as has been done in Alice's case. Instead, performance appraisals should be conducted more frequently and should provide employees with motivation, goals, and encouragement. Alice should never have been placed in a position where a discussion with her manager about a performance review could cause such stress that she considers ending her employment with the university. If Rosario and Alice were used to communicating on a regular basis, Alice would not feel as much stress and uncertainty about her performance. She would have felt comfortable enough to discuss the discoveries she made in the former SWOT analysis and her concern about the direction of her project, and she would not feel like her efforts were being overlooked by management.

The reader is not sure what will happen at the meeting Rosario calls Alice to at the end of this scenario. In an ideal world, we can only hope that university librarian Rosario Cortez has come to the realization that she has an opportunity here to completely overhaul the way she manages her employees. She needs to open herself up to feedback from Alice and other direct reports on the library's team. Hopefully Rosario will take time in her meeting to find out what is going well with Alice's project and to identify ways she can help improve on them. Once Rosario acknowledges the shortcomings of her current management to Alice, she can begin the more productive task of becoming a more integrated part of her team's work lives.

Response 3
By Julia McKenna, circulation services manager, Jacksonville University, Jacksonville, Florida

Overall, the key issues in this scenario are Alice's attitude, a lack of communication in the department, and a lack of support for individual employees and their initiatives. Alice is understandably frustrated with the library and the lack of support it provides her to undertake her projects. Without performance reviews, employees cannot know where they stand and how to address any issues. In addition, there seems to be a large amount of planning with little follow-through on many library projects and goals. This can be frustrating as well, especially when a new project, such as Alice's microfilm one, falls on your plate.

However, Alice's remark in front of the entire staff was not an appropriate way to address her frustrations and concerns. Her concerns are valid, but they need to be brought to her direct supervisor, not aired in front of the entire university staff. Doing this creates—or contributes to—negative morale and is not conducive to departmental progress. As Alice's supervisor, Rosario Cortez should note if this is a pattern or a new behavior that Alice has been exhibiting. Depending on how recently these sorts of behaviors have emerged, there are different tactics she can take to correct the behavior.

The supervisor has three primary options when it comes to addressing the issues with Alice. The first is an informal conversation to address the issues. This would include reviewing what the supervisor has noticed, asking Alice for her perspective, and creating an action plan for how to improve issues on both sides. This may include Alice agreeing to present a more positive attitude as well as the supervisor agreeing to support her through more feedback and providing her with the resources necessary to undertake her projects. The supervisor can also use Alice's feedback to examine managerial practices and may implement various strategies to improve communication and formalize feedback in the department. The supervisor should document this conversation in an email and send it to Alice after the meeting in order to create a paper trail if future performance issues emerge.

The second approach is to place Alice on a formal performance improvement plan (PIP). This would involve the supervisor writing up the current behaviors, what benchmarks Alice needs to meet to improve, and the dates she must reach these goals by. The supervisor would then monitor Alice's progress and either note the improvement or terminate her if she does not make the necessary changes in the time period allotted. The benefits of a PIP are that it very clearly demonstrates the severity of the issue to the employee and gives clear goals so that Alice knows exactly what is expected of her. Finally, it allows for the supervisor to document the discussions about Alice's performance in a concrete and standardized way.

The third option is to fire Alice. The supervisor may take this action if she has observed and documented a long history of this behavior or feels that improvement is not possible. However, this is the least effective option, as Alice has not received any formal feedback previously and thus has not had the opportunity to improve or correct the behavior. In addition, hiring a new employee can be a long and expensive process that should not be undertaken lightly. Considering the current lack of communication and protocol at the university library, if these issues are not rectified, a new employee might end up behaving in precisely the same way as Alice. While employee termination is certainly an important option to keep on the table, it should be a last resort to be used when the employee either violates a no-tolerance policy or shows an inability to meet the necessary performance level.

If I were managing Alice, I would begin by having an honest conversation with her and acknowledging that the library has some issues that need to be addressed. Communication and follow-through clearly have not been executed well in the past. However, the new strategic plan is a genuine effort to correct this, and the library is committed to improving over the next year. Alice needs to understand that progress is not going to happen overnight and requires the buy-in of the whole staff, including herself. I'd also make it clear that Alice's behavior in the meeting was unacceptable and that while I understand her concerns, she needs to voice them to me rather than air them in public. I cannot assist her if I do not know what issues exist, and she needs to do her part as well to keep the line of communication open. I'd follow up with an email documenting this conversation, then closely monitor her performance over the next month. If no improvement is seen, especially relating to her attitude, I'd place her on a formal PIP, then either note an improvement or fire her at the end of the plan.

Chapter Two

Hide the Plan

A Planning Scenario Using Supposition

SCENARIO

Williamson Park Public Library director Samara Haines had come to dread the first Wednesday of the month. She called it Chaos Day—the day the library's board of directors met each month. The library board meetings wouldn't be so bad if they actually managed to accomplish anything other than members sniping at one another. The level of personal animosity between the eleven of them seemed to have grown stronger as the years passed, the edges of their civility having worn away due to the consistent grind of dysfunction these monthly meetings brought.

As was normal practice, board meeting agendas were prepared and sent out by the department's executive secretary, Ben Fields. Samara would forward agenda items to Ben and attach documents and reports she wanted distributed with the agenda one week before the board meetings were to take place. Ben would prepare the agenda and send a final draft back to Samara for approval. Once approved, Ben would distribute the agenda and accompanying documents to all the pertinent people. Samara had been sent the agenda last week and quickly approved it for distribution without even opening it. Ben had distributed the entire agenda packet to everyone just a few days ago. In preparation for this afternoon's board meeting, Samara had printed her agenda without even looking at the contents. After all, she knew what was on there and knew that every item would come complete with those library board member "asides" that drove her crazy and those broadsides from one member or another that seemed to deflate any productivity in the boardroom. This was a group that couldn't even come together long enough to approve the previous meetings' minutes without lengthy discussion. It was no wonder the library board had never managed to accomplish anything significant—either in their meetings or otherwise. Sure, they'd managed a few annual library fundraising events, but the big issues that faced the library were never dealt with or even debated. Samara wasn't ready, now, to deal with the kind of debate the library's strategic plan would bring, and knowing it was on this agenda only made her sense of dread even worse.

Knock knock.

The assistant library director, Leslie Geno, opened the door and stuck her head in.

"Boss?"

"Yeah," Samara replied.

Leslie pushed the door open with her foot, carrying a cup of coffee and a vegan oatmeal cookie. She set them on the desk in front of Samara, then walked over to the seat on the other side of the desk.

"Coffee and cookie," Samara said. "You must know this is library board meeting day."

"It's in the air," Leslie said. "Feels like the air's been sucked out of the entire place."

Samara took a sip of her coffee, though her stomach was far too knotted to get down an entire cookie.

"It'll be fine," Samara said. "I'll hand them the visioning document, they'll calmly debate the merits, add significant insight to the issues, and then make the necessary movements to enact it without delay."

Leslie chuckled. "I didn't know you liked science fiction." She picked up the agenda where it lay on the desk.

"It's a marvelous dream, isn't it?"

The smell of the cookie finally untied a few of the knots in her stomach, and Samara took a bite, then dipped the cookie in the cup and chased the first bite down with another.

"So, when's the great debate on the visioning document and strategic plan?" Leslie asked.

Samara rolled her eyes. "Take a look. You're the one holding the agenda. I haven't looked at mine yet."

"That's what I mean . . . " Leslie handed her the paper across the desk. Samara somewhat begrudgingly put down the cookie to take it from her.

"Look. It's not on there," Leslie said.

"What do you mean?"

"It's not listed. See for yourself," Leslie said, reaching over and breaking off a small piece of the cookie for herself.

Scanning the page, Samara noted that the agenda item for the strategic plan wasn't listed. Instead, there was a single item labeled "Director's Report—Samara Haines—10 minutes."

Samara was dumbfounded. "I sent Ben everything, along with the plan and visioning document to accompany the agenda. Why didn't he include that? Did he at least include the supplemental attachments?"

"Nope. Just some of the other reports. But no strategic plan or visioning document. Ben must have missed it," Leslie said, chewing the cookie. "Doesn't surprise me with the quality of his work, honestly."

Samara scanned the agenda again and again, making sure there was no other item that could have been meant for discussion of the strategic plan or visioning document. Perhaps Ben had couched it in another item by mistake. She couldn't find anything among the dozens of committee reports and simple library board business. Had she forgotten to hit Send when she emailed that stuff to Ben? Maybe she was dreaming and hadn't actually sent it. She slid her laptop over and looked through her emails for the original email with the agenda approval she had sent Ben. Yes, it was there, but she had to admit that the strategic plan stuff for the agenda was at the bottom of that message to Ben, and it was listed after a good deal of other less significant business. She had sent along a lot of attachments for Ben to include in the packet—over a dozen—but she had, in fact, neglected to include the actual strategic plan. The visioning document was attached but not the strategic plan. So perhaps Ben had missed her request to add the agenda item completely and—if he'd seen the visioning document among the other attachments—had accidentally left it off. Out of confusion, had Ben left both documents off, meaning to get clarification, which he later forgot to do?

"Well, you're right. It's not there," Samara said.

"Samara, that could be a very good thing, right?"

"How so? I've got ten minutes to go over the entire strategic plan and visioning document, and no one on the board will even have had an opportunity to read it yet. That's not remotely possible with this dysfunctional board!"

"No," Leslie said. "You're off the hook now. You've got ten minutes to do a report, and since the board doesn't know anything about the strategic plan, you don't need to bring it up."

Samara saw where this was headed.

"So," she said as she picked up her cup of coffee, "I just give my report and then bring the strategic plan business up next month? Hold back my trip to the gallows?"

"Not quite," Leslie said, "but what if you didn't present it? Not today or even next month? What if instead we just, you know, sort of started circulating and implementing it?"

"You mean completely bypass the library board?" Samara exclaimed.

"Think about it," Leslie said. "We did this whole strategic plan business ten years ago—not because the library board asked us to but because the city manager required it. And what did that accomplish? Nothing! It was a complete waste of time. Sure, the process could be different this go-around, but we're the ones who are going to be making any strategic plan happen anyway, so if you don't bring it to the board, what does it matter?"

"They're the library board, Leslie! They're supposed to be involved."

"They're a poorly framed, ineffective board," Leslie said. "Half of them don't even attend meetings regularly and don't participate in any significant way—other than argue with each other—and you pretty much said yourself that they'll only get in the way."

Samara had indeed said that. In fact, she remembered screaming it into her pillow in bed a few times. Typically, she described the library board as maddening, but that really downplayed the level of impact they had on her well-being. They would fiddle and twiddle, and in the end, nothing would happen with anything she put in front of them. Just last meeting they had spent hours on whether the library would participate in the Art in Public Spaces program the city was sponsoring. After nearly two hours of sniping and debate, the issue was put aside to discuss more later . . . and "later" meant at tonight's meeting. Would they need another two hours to resolve that issue? How could she now include the library's strategic plan on this same agenda? The board would need days to argue this over. In the end, the library's board would set the strategic plan aside and not make any decision, and she'd not be able to implement the plan as the city required. If the strategic plan was hidden from the board, she could implement it without their knowledge. In other words, as always, Leslie was making sense. Samara grabbed all her materials—including the strategic plan and visioning document—and headed toward the meeting room. *It's showtime, folks!* she thought.

Williamson Park Public Library's board president, Marco Lapeota, brought the gavel down. He was impressed. Somehow, he had actually managed to get the board to approve all the minutes from previous meetings, which, until then, they had continually punted down the road. There were a few objections, and a couple of small nits were thoroughly picked, but they had managed to get through the backlog.

The library board members were seated in their usual cliques. Samara always placed herself between Marco and board treasurer Louise Hidalgo. The two were friendly with her and seldom found themselves embroiled in the worst of the board attacks.

"All right," Marco said. "Moving on to old business."

The meeting moved along slightly more briskly than usual. The usual suspects seemed to be quieter than normal. As they moved into the assorted committee reports, it was almost a quiet, peaceful afternoon.

"Now, to an item deferred from last month's agenda. Let's hear from Helen and the library programming committee regarding the city's Art in Public Spaces program," the board president said.

Here we go, Samara thought as she rubbed her temples. *Better settle in for the fight.*

Two more hours went by as the board engulfed itself in a vocal bruhaha. Half the board argued for participating in the program to show support for the city, while the other board members objected to moving prominent local history portraits already hanging in the library to accommodate the new pieces.

Marco banged the gavel. "Please, people," he said, "let's finish this. We've spent too much time trying to decide. I call for a vote." In the end, to Samara's surprise, the board voted in favor of participating. *Apparently, some of the board members* can *be swayed*, Samara thought. *If only it didn't take so darn long.*

Samara got up, grabbed a bottle of water from the side table, and returned to her seat. She looked down and saw the strategic plan in the folder she had brought with the printed copies of the visioning document summary. She hadn't noticed at the time, but the longer the art show debate had gone on, the more material she had piled on top of that folder. Now the folder was barely visible. She uncovered the strategic plan packet and moved it to the top of her materials . . . although she did find herself leaning her elbows on it, as if trying to keep it from floating out into the room.

Samara looked down at the agenda again, one more item before she was set to give her director's report, and she knew this item would be contentious too. Samara was sure of it. In fact, she was so sure of a pending fight that she had piled her now-closed laptop, her notebook, and two empty water bottles on top of the strategic plan packet.

It was time for a break. The mingling took the form of the folks who always sat next to each other standing in tight little groups, sipping coffee and cracking jokes at the expense of the tight little circles peopled by those they saw as small-minded. The group giggled, they snickered, and Samara always suspected this was where they plotted. She sipped at her third water bottle of the afternoon, and as Marco called everyone to return to their seats, she was less sure than ever how she should spend the time she had been allotted on the agenda. Was Samara's audience the thoughtful, intelligent debate club that had been present the last quarter-hour of their board meeting or the pack of snarling wolves that had been the norm the rest of the meeting? One would certainly benefit the proposal, while the other might sink it forever.

Marco moved to his seat again and gently banged the gavel twice.

"Come on, everyone," he called out. The group unraveled themselves as they moved toward their unassigned, but consistently occupied, seats. "Samara, it's time for your report."

Should she or shouldn't she? Should she "hide the plan" or put it out there? She kept hearing Leslie's "waste of time" comment repeating in her mind. Samara stood up, looked down at her strategic plan packet, looked out at the board members around the table, and began to speak. She wasn't exactly sure where this report was headed, but she opened her mouth and began.

HIDE THE PLAN RESPONSES

Response 1
By Helen Palascak, director, Upper St. Clair Township Library, Upper St. Clair, Pennsylvania

Williamson Park Public Library director Samara Haines is in a very difficult situation. Unfortunately, it is one at least partly of her own making. Library director and library board relationships need careful cultivation to create a partnership whose goal is supporting excellent library services. The library director manages, and the library board governs. Neither should micromanage the other.

Samara's problems with the board seem long-standing. From the scenario as presented, she has not taken any positive action steps to improve board functionality. Have the board members received training in their roles and responsibilities? Has she spoken privately to the board chair about doing more to control the meeting and counseling members individually on inappropriate behaviors? Cliques and personal attacks should not be tolerated. Have she and the board chair reviewed the board bylaws concerning term limits? The very fact that Samara dreads "Chaos Day," that years of animosity have worn away civility, demonstrates she has been ineffective in promoting positive board interactions.

The limits on the areas of library board responsibilities seem nonexistent. The agenda prepared completely by library staff is not best practice. The agenda should be a cooperative effort, with the library board chair having final approval. This isn't Samara's meeting to dictate. It is the library governing board's meeting, and the library board president presides over it and decides what goes on the board's agenda. Certainly, library staff should assist in preparing documents and reports for the consent agenda for the board's information. No discussion needed. Discussion items on the agenda should be limited to broad, forward-thinking initiatives, fundraising ideas, or governance and policy issues. Action items, on which the library board votes, would include major decisions, the yearly budget, starting a new program or branch, or changing the fee structure. Depending on where in the process it is, the strategic plan Samara is hesitating on presenting would be either for discussion or a vote to accept. It is completely inappropriate to suggest hiding the new strategic plan from the library board.

This library board is definitely micromanaging, and Samara seems to encourage it with all the reports and information she presents for approval. It should not take two meetings and over four hours to discuss participating in a city-sponsored program. One would expect the board to promote a positive relationship with their primary funder. Art in Public Spaces should have been first presented as an information item. No discussion, no vote; the library is participating. Where the art hangs within the city's building is the director's responsibility. The presentation of the strategic plan, required by the city manager, should provide a summary of the main objectives and the library's implementation plan, which the staff have already prepared. Unless there are significant impacts on the library budget, or major changes to policies, the library board need only support the plan and support their library.

Given the information of so many submanagement positions—such as a department executive secretary, Ben Fields, and an assistant library director, Leslie Geno—we can assume that the Williamson Park Public Library is a fairly large organization. It is hard to totally understand, therefore, how the issues presented in this scenario have come to pass. In many library systems, especially large organizations like Williamson Park, one would expect library board term limits, library board training sessions and strategic planning retreats, and library board orientations that review responsibilities and standards of conduct for members. Library board chairs receive training in how to conduct meetings and stop inappropriate behavior immediately. Why isn't this done in this large public library? It may be a process that the library director is expected to facilitate. Which brings us back to the library director, Samara Haines.

Clues in Samara's behavior—the dread of the meeting, expecting chaos, not reviewing the agenda, the snipe against the quality of Ben's work, knowing the board is dysfunctional yet doing nothing about it—lead one to believe she has been ineffective in working with her library board and perhaps with her staff as well. She needs help. Could the city manager be asked to suggest a consultant to work with the board on understanding their legal and fiduciary responsibilities? Is there a state library association or neighboring library system whose director could help mentor Samara and perhaps speak with the library board members and help resolve this dysfunction? A last resort could be terminating board members who continue to bring personal issues into the meeting or who attempt to micromanage library operations. Indeed, Samara needs help. She just has to be more proactive in seeking it.

Response 2
By Donald Barclay, deputy university librarian, University of California, Merced, California

Before considering whether Williamson Park Public Library director Samara Haines should or should not hide the plan, let's consider what she needs to do in terms of advisory board management. For most library directors, having an advisory board comes with the job. In the best case, a good advisory board provides a director with valuable advice gained from experiences and perspectives outside of the narrow world of libraries and librarians. It can be a real plus to hear how, say, a teacher, a physician, a building contractor, a stay-at-home parent, or a stockbroker views the issues confronting your library. A good board also serves as a true advocate for the library. Obviously, Samara's board is far from the best case. But what can she do about that?

First off, library board members are not Supreme Court justices with lifetime appointments. Could Samara reach out to the (presumably elected) city officials who appoint citizens to the library board about freshening up the board membership? Given how unpleasant the board meetings are, some members might be delighted to be asked to step down, "with the grateful thanks of the city for your service." Could Samara reach out to citizens who care about the library and encourage them to apply for seats on the board? Changing the membership of a board is a long-term solution, but that makes starting the process today—instead of a week from today—all the more important.

Another approach in board management would be trying something that would shake the current board membership out of its poisonous routine. Even little things like meeting at a branch library instead of the main library or meeting in a different room in the main library might help. The scenario stated how Samara sat between the same two board members every time—that sends a message to others regardless of whether you think it does or not. Others may think you are sitting by favored individuals or individuals with more power than others. Switching up seats now and again would prevent the wrong message getting out. How about organizing a purely social event that brings the board members together to eat, drink, and socialize without any library business before them? How about a board retreat (of one day, or a half day, or even just the length of one regular board meeting) during which the subject is not agenda-driven library business but rather how to function more effectively as a board? Samara could bring in an outside facilitator who doesn't carry any baggage with board members to lead the proceedings, and the retreat could be couched in terms of "building a stronger team to guide the library" rather than a more blunt "teaching you monsters how to get along with each other." A retreat could include both soft team-building activities as well as more practical skills, such as agenda management or proven techniques for advocating for the library.

One of the glaring problems presented in this scenario deals with bad board meeting agenda management. Why was the discussion of the Art in Public Places program allowed to go on for two hours? Agendas should be clear and delineate time frames for discussion. Either the time allocated on the agenda for discussion of that item was ignored (in which case the blame lies with the chair of the board for not sticking to the agenda) or the person who created the agenda didn't allocate a set amount of time for discussion of that item (in which case the blame lies there). If Samara wants a better board, she needs to pay careful attention to the agenda of every meeting, including the time allowed for each item, the sequencing of agenda items, and which board member is given primary responsibility for leading the board through each item. Don't leave it to the chair to lead the discussion of every agenda item; spread the wealth among board members. Also, always get the agenda out in plenty of time for board members to become familiar with it and prepare themselves for the meeting.

Turning to the issue at the heart of this scenario, what should Samara do in the ten minutes left for the board meeting? Obviously, there is not enough time to go over an entire strategic plan with the board, so that is out of the question. Since trying to sidestep the board is a mistake for reasons both practical and ethical, Samara's only option is to fess up that the strategic plan was unintentionally left off the agenda and that the board will be asked to address it at a future meeting—perhaps even a special emergency meeting. But what to do before that meeting comes around?

"Being a waste of time" is a property of far too many strategic plans, but it is not an inherent property of strategic plans. Unlike bad strategic plans and vegan cookies, good strategic plans are not at all a waste of time. A good strategic plan is, in the end, a contract among employees, management, and customers (as represented, in this case, by the board). A good strategic plan spells out

- what we are going to do,
- when we are going to do it, and
- what resources are required so that we can do it.

If, in the formulation of a strategic plan, the resources to carry out goal X are not available, then goal X is either eliminated or pushed back until those resources are available. A good strategic plan ensures that nobody—willingly or by coercion—underbids a goal by promising to achieve a goal for which sufficient resources are not available. A misconception about strategic plans is that they are all about new and/or highly aspirational goals. A strategic plan could well consist of nothing other than sustainability goals focused on allowing an organization to continue doing what it is already doing. Example: For a library that is open until 10:00 p.m. Sunday through Thursday, a reasonable sustainability goal would be to continue offering those opening hours to the public.

A good strategic plan is built from the ground up with input from the full spectrum of stakeholders—shelvers, circulation clerks, librarians, department heads, the library director, the public, and the board. Assessment via tools such as surveys and focus groups are essential for public input. (NB: Input does not mean that everyone gets everything they ask for. It means that everything that is asked for gets fair consideration.) Even if board members are much less involved in writing the plan than library staff, they should be aware of the process, periodically made privy to progress and drafts, and given the opportunity to provide feedback. And once the strategic plan is finalized and approved by the board, everyone must be held to it. If, for example, one year into a three-year strategic plan the board comes up with a bold new initiative to keep the library open around the clock, seven days a week, that initiative must be incorporated into the plan, possibly at the cost of removing one or more existing goals in order to create the capacity to take on the new initiative.

In the end, there is no sliding a strategic plan past the board if the board has been—as it should be—involved in the development of the plan from the beginning. And, in a best-case scenario, the work of being involved in strategic planning might be just annoying enough to inspire some of the less committed, less useful board members to step down in favor of new members who can breathe new life into a group that is badly in need of some fresh air.

Response 3
By Beth Wren Estes, faculty member, San Jose State University School of Information, San Jose, California

In order to be an effective team, the library director and members of the library board must work together for the common good of the organization. Several members of the library board in this scenario create a toxic environment to work in, and they appear to be incapable of working together without an intervention taking place.

Samara Haines, the library director, appears to just accept that the library board operates ineffectively and does not recognize that there are things that she can do to try and change the library board's behavior. She is directing the day-to-day operations of the library and in turn needs to present herself to the library board as a leader. From what we see in this scenario, the library board doesn't seem to see their library director in any sort of leadership role.

Samara's relationship with the library board is of serious concern. What has she done to try and change the atmosphere other than to accept that the library board members are dysfunctional; to commiserate with Leslie, the assistant director, on how bad things are; and to continue to be generally frustrated with the library board's attitude and behavior? Samara should be looking for ways she can help facilitate positive change. She should have done this at the first sign of dysfunction. But the boat has not left on her ability to turn it around now. So why has she resigned herself?

In a close examination of this scenario, the following specific issues need Samara's immediate attention and action.

The Personnel Issue

Samara appears to be in charge of creating the library board meeting agenda, but she has relinquished responsibility and accountability to her assistant, Ben. To ensure that the agenda is accurate in the future, Samara should implement a more formal agenda creation and distribution process. For example, she may want to set aside time to have a short meeting with Ben prior to distributing any library board meeting materials to ensure that he has included all the agenda items and attachments she has sent him. She could also use this meeting to add any last-minute additional materials for distribution with the agenda. If she had done such a face-to-face meeting with Ben before the library board meeting presented in this scenario, she would have seen that the attachment for the strategic plan was missing and could have included it in time for the library board members to review. Samara, as the library director, bears the ultimate responsibility for the accuracy of the library board packet that was distributed in this scenario, but Ben seems to have been the cause of the missing documents in the case. Samara needs to determine why he neglected distributing the items, and he must also be held accountable through established performance evaluation procedures to ensure mistakes like this do not occur in the future.

Review Governance Documents

The library board meetings are obviously dysfunctional and, in certain situations, toxic. There doesn't seem to be a common goal or a level of respect for each other. As the library director, Samara should have clarified the following questions about the library board the moment she saw how dysfunctional it had become: Does the library board's bylaws or policies determine how meetings are conducted—for example, adopting parliamentary procedures outlined in Robert's Rules of Order or a similar manual? Is there a definition in the bylaws that describes the powers and responsibilities of the library board and job responsibilities for each of its members? Is there an adopted library board of directors' code of conduct? These governance documents could easily have helped Samara gain better control of the meetings. For example, having a code of conduct that has been adopted by the library board might help stem the number of interruptions and speaking out of turn.

Additional questions that are not described in the scenario, but for which Samara will need immediate clarification, are as follows: Is the Sunshine Act applicable? Under the Sunshine Act, depending on the type of organization, the agenda may need to be posted in advance of the meeting and open to public comment for a period of time. This may dictate a different timeline for distribution of the agenda for official action. Who elects or appoints members to the library board? What are the library board members' term limits? It seems that several of these people have been on the library board for a very long time. If that is the case, it may be possible to replace the negative members with members who are willing to assume a more positive attitude toward their role as a library board member.

Time for Library Board Training

Samara must consider bringing in a consultant who specializes in library board training and—in the case of this library board's behavior—one that is trained in conflict management. A training for a half or full day would benefit this group of individuals. Organizations like the American Society of Association Executives and the Public Library Association are good organizations to contact to get input on consultants. Samara should be discussing this with the leadership of the library board to suggest that this is something drastically needed.

The Strategic Plan

While it is not clear from what we read in the scenario, the strategic plan formulation has not been given the attention it deserves. It is an important document that should dictate much of the library's future. It is unlikely that Samara was not aware of the city's strategic planning process, and she should have been well aware of the timeline. A strategic plan is not a last-minute discussion and should take several monthly meetings to develop. So why is it only now appearing on Samara's agenda? Since the scenario mentions that the entire city is undergoing strategic planning, it is likely that Samara has been involved in the citywide efforts in this regard. She should have involved the city manager and library board president in early discussions. Armed with information from the city manager and library board president, Samara could decide the library's strategy more effectively.

Samara needs to objectively assess her approach to the library board. The scenario describes a victim rather than a library leader. From the opening paragraphs, she has already given up and believes she cannot improve the dysfunctional and toxic operation of the library board. Her assistant has the same attitude. So, "misery loves company" is how the two library leaders have chosen to approach working with the library board. Where is the discussion about how they could change library board behavior? Samara needs to take a good long look at how effective her communication skills are and who she looks to as an ally on the library board. Just expecting that the library board is dysfunctional, and believing she is helpless to improve it, is not going to make her an effective library director. Samara seems to act from a position of weakness, deflecting blame onto staff and the library board instead of dealing head on with what she can do to show more leadership in the situation. This would include arming herself with the library board's governing documents, verifying how the library board members are appointed and for how long they serve, and finally seeking immediate help by bringing in a trained consultant to work with the library board.

Chapter Three

I Hear Music

A Planning Scenario Using Supposition

SCENARIO

Terry had almost fallen asleep in Mika Lorenzo's office as she waited for her to come back from checking to see if the assistant regional manager, Cresta, was available for the meeting. It was the music playing through the small speakers attached to the laptop on Mika's desk. The music was gentle, quiet, calming, and ultimately nap-inducing . . . at least to Terry. Terry understood Mika's need for calming and relaxing music. As the regional manager for six branch libraries, Mika was obviously stressed. *And now that she's acting city librarian, until the position is permanently filled, Mika must be out of her mind with problems*, Terry thought.

Terry wasn't opposed to the sound of the music, but it did remind her of being in a dentist's office, and it sure did make it hard to keep her eyes open. The gentle tones were lulling her into a sleep state. It might have been the best rest she'd had in ages. But a couple of minutes into the soothing sounds, Mika reentered her office on high heels that seemed to click-clack abnormally along with the music's beat as she walked in.

"Cresta's in another meeting," Mika said. "So it'll just be you and me."

Terry sat herself upright in the chair, reversing the mighty slump induced by the music.

"Sorry," Terry said. "I was being soothed into a very deep dream; that music is awfully hypnotic."

"You like the music?" Mika asked.

"It's very nice," Terry answered.

"Soothing, no?"

"Without a doubt."

"That's what I was hoping you'd say," Mika answered, finally settling into her own chair and tapping the space bar on the laptop to stop the music.

"Is this a part of what you'll be presenting at next week's staff meeting?" Terry asked, starting to feel her attention return but also in serious need of a cup of good strong black coffee.

"It certainly is. I want to make a case for piping in some music to make our library environment a more pleasant space and experience for our users," Mika said with a smile. "But more on that later. Let's talk now about the really important thing."

"What's that?"

"Well, there's your promotion," Mika started, having only informed Terry of the fact that she was the library's new special projects manager the afternoon prior. "And there's the reading room and study space upgrades that are coming. Oh, and I'm getting donuts for the meeting!" Mika chuckled.

"Well, that's the best news I've heard!"

"I know, right?" Mika said, obviously excited.

Putting the issue of piping in music to the back of her mind, Terry said, "And what are the building upgrades you mentioned?"

"Mostly accessibility ramping and alert systems . . . and a couple of add-ons," Mika said with a sly smile.

Terry was a bit concerned about what the add-ons entailed, but she let it slide for the moment.

"So, you'll be running the meeting?" Terry asked.

"One last time," Mika said, smiling, "then it's your party. As the library's new special projects manager, you'll be the best person to run those meetings. There'll be a lot of change coming, and change management seems to be an interest of yours."

That made Terry happy. Getting a little extra management experience would help with her résumé credentials when she was ready for promotion to library director herself, so she was thankful for the new responsibility. Of course, she understood that Mika was in charge of the entire library system as the acting city librarian, but now Terry—as the library's special projects manager—would be coordinating everything from special programs to technology and innovation at this facility.

Mika continued. "You know we have so many special projects in the pipeline! I'm glad to be getting some help from you in coordinating and managing them. First and foremost, Terry, you'll be opening our first new library branch in twenty-five years! It's so exciting. It's going to be a very different library, though I know with you at the helm, it'll only be a *better* library."

Different? How? Terry wondered. But the thought was pushed out of her mind by the sheer confidence Mika had expressed in Terry's abilities. As Mika transitioned her own role to allow for more time long-range strategic planning and interfacing more with the city government, she was more than happy to have Terry's expertise to guide the implementation of projects Mika could only conceptualize. It was the best possible thing for Terry's career, and her career was important to her. The library was her spiritual home, and she would protect her career in order to be able to work in her heart's profession. And yet, her mind wouldn't let go of the question she had just pondered: *Different? How?*

"All right, back to it," Mika said as she reached for another compact disc case. "I've got a lot to prep for the transition, and you've got a branch to open! Oh, by the way . . . " Mika rifled through a stack of magazines on her desk. "I wanted you to read this article in the new issue of *Library Innovation Today*. The mayor read it a few months ago and thinks it's brilliant. I showed it to the library board president too, and she shared it with the other board members because she loved it so much." Mika looked in the issue's table of contents and turned to the page. "Here it is." She handed the issue over to Terry. It was opened to an article titled "Should Your Library Be More Like a Retail Store?" Mika quickly shepherded Terry out of her office. "Let me know what you think."

Terry walked away from Mika's office wondering where this was all going. As she turned the office corner, she could hear the drone of ambient new age music flowing out of Mika's laptop, ready to bring cold sleep to any who might enter her cave.

That evening, Terry sat in her favorite comfy chair in her home and dug out the issue of *Library Innovation Today* so she could read the article Mika had given her. It obviously was the key to a lot of the questions that had been running through her mind. As the system's new special projects manager, Terry felt she had been left a little behind by Mika in her vision of the new branch library. If Terry was going to be left to manage this new *different type of library*, well, she reckoned she better get an idea of how different it was going to be. She opened the magazine to the article "Should Your Library Be More Like a Retail Store?" and began to read. Thirty minutes later, Terry closed the magazine and slowly let out a heavy sigh, thinking to herself that trouble lurked on the horizon for her as the special projects manager. Was she up to this?

The article, while heavy with statistical evidence on the shopping behaviors of customers, had little to do with library users, Terry thought. While the article was full of interesting information about traffic flow, merchandise displays, store lighting, and strategies to keep shoppers in the store longer, Terry noted that the author hadn't really linked the retail and library environments well. Terry was finding it hard to understand similarities between the two and why librarians would find any relevance at all in retail store experiences. In her mind, information-seeking behavior and shopping behavior were completely separate and couldn't be compared. The article did present some interesting facts on the need for change in libraries, and it had raised red flags on the declining role libraries played in the lives of today's communities, but Terry certainly wasn't willing to embrace the call to make libraries more like retail stores as the article had suggested. She looked forward to talking more about the article with Mika. She closed the magazine and readied herself for bed.

"I want to thank everyone for coming," Mika said, opening the meeting several days later. "It's been an incredibly busy time, and I'm so excited to make a very special announcement. It's an announcement representing the next movement in the Axfall Public Library System. First, I am proud to announce I have been officially named the permanent city librarian." The room erupted in applause and congratulations. "Thank you, everyone. It's very scary to be moving this fast, but I appreciate the Axfall library board and the mayor for putting trust in my abilities. Now, there's more good news to share! Since I will be moving out of my office here and officially moving into City Hall as city librarian, I have selected Terry Laffler to take over here in a new position I have created called special projects manager."

The applause was enthusiastic, even if the news was a shock to literally no one in the room; the rumor mill had long since made this announcement for Mika. Terry stood up, waved, and smiled. Mika continued. "I'll be handing over the coordination of our library's many project management duties to Terry. Her first order of business is concentrating on . . . " Mika paused to create a dramatic effect, then continued, "opening a new library branch!" The room erupted again, and it took several minutes for the murmurs to die down and the questions to stop.

"But I've got some other very exciting news! And I know nobody has heard this news because I've not shared this information with anyone—not even Terry." The room turned to stare at Mika.

"The new branch is going to be a very different kind of place," Mika said.

There's that word again, Terry thought. *Different? How?* she wondered. She thought back to the article that Mika had given her. She had an idea of where this whole business was going, and she wasn't sure it was the right move. Terry's questions were soon answered in the announcement Mika made next.

"The mayor and I want to take our library to a new level. I think it's a good idea. The mayor wants this new branch to be a place of innovation and discovery, collaboration and change," Mika said. "Our new branch library won't even be called a library. We're naming it

The Discovery Station, and the mayor has convinced me that the community is going to love how different it is!"

Terry had to jump in here. "Define 'different' for us all, Mika, so we get a better picture of where we are going with this library." She knew it had to do with that article, but she just couldn't wait until later to talk to Mika about it.

Mika looked at Terry and smiled. "Well, we will be adding on some exciting features that will genuinely change the way the library is seen."

Mika clicked a button on the small remote she carried with her, and a projector threw up an image of an artist's conception of the new library's large reading room. The room was brighter, with a new skylight, and included soft beanbag-type chairs, meeting rooms, and digital scanners. There were no books in sight.

"As you can see, we added the overhead cupula, have made the room accessible by all, and have brought scanners and self-checkout stations to the library! All this while bringing new, comfier seating, new tables and desks, and perhaps most importantly, independent air conditioning and environment controls with zone-specific sensors that will save the library tens of thousands of dollars a year."

She clicked the remote again, and more detail for the new library appeared. She pointed out laptop checkout kiosks, something labeled a "creation station," a music and film production area, and hundreds of computers and printers. Mika clicked the remote again and continued, "The new library will have energy-efficient windows with full UV coating and new carpeting and sound-proofing, and it will be our most environmentally self-sufficient building in the entire city! But my favorite addition is along the upper portions of the room."

Mika clicked the remote again, and there was a close-up of the top of one of two large, mysterious pillars. At the top of the pillars, a set of speakers had been attached.

"We've installed a seventy-two-speaker setup," Mika said, "which will allow us to broadcast messages to patrons and, more importantly, set an atmosphere of calm during periods of heightened stress."

Mika clicked the remote again, and the same soothing music from her office began to play.

"Starting with finals this week," Mika said, obviously incredibly excited, "we will be testing a program of providing a soothing environment for studiers here at *this* library by playing gentle, ambient music throughout the building."

Mika pressed the remote again, and the slide returned to the original bright-light form of the study room, which then animated and became more subdued.

"Testing this program now will allow us to get a better sense of what will constitute a better study environment and what will provide the perfect study experience in our new Discovery Station." Mika continued on, describing statistics and points Terry recognized from the article she had read the previous evening. It was all beginning to make sense now. The mayor had read the same article Terry had read. He'd been impressed and challenged Mika to change the mission of the library without involving the staff. She wondered if Mika had agreed to all this only because she didn't want to lose out on being named the new city librarian. If she'd have shown any reluctance to the mayor's idea, Mika could have been passed over for the job and Terry wouldn't be the new special projects manager. Terry shook her head. She was being ridiculous. Wasn't she?

Mika turned the projector off, quieted the music, and looked around the room. There were general looks of enthusiasm mixed with dropped jaws, confused looks, and concern from the staff. "Now, I'm heading over to my new office at City Hall, and I'm sure Terry will continue talking with you all about the new library and looks forward to your input. Back to work, everyone. We're about to open the library." She left the room.

Back in her office, Terry was looking at the artist's conception of the new library. She focused particularly on the two giant pillars and the speakers that had been attached to the top of them. She was stunned that such a huge change in service models had been created in a vacuum. Could the mayor and Mika seriously have planned such a change without any word whatsoever being shared with library staff? As far as strategic plans went, Terry was shocked at how her two superiors had evaded the normal planning process. There was no buy-in from key staff. Instead, the powers above had seemingly been so caught up in the excitement of the "new" that they forgot to allow enough time to manage existing business activities. Terry could only wonder why all of this was being dropped in her lap. She returned to looking at the artist's conception.

Terrible, Terry thought. She could already envision homeless people and young people curled up asleep on the comfy furniture. How would anyone be able to focus, let alone stay awake, with that music playing? Add to that the planned soft mood lighting or natural light, and she could easily see the Discovery Station becoming a napping place.

Cresta, the library's assistant director—and one of Terry's subordinates—tapped on her open office door.

"So, Terry," Cresta said, "what are your thoughts about the new branch library, uh, I mean, Discovery Station?"

Terry shook her head. "Not today," she said and changed the subject.

Mika and Terry's first official meeting after the "announcement" of the new branch "Discovery Station" was set for eight-thirty in the morning—a time of day when Mika always thought everyone was at their best. Setting aside the inclination to debate the merits of Mika's (or was it the mayor's?) new vision, Terry hoped that the meeting could focus instead on the easier things, such as specifics, numbers, staffing, and budgets. Terry never thought she'd see those things as easy stuff.

"And what is the reaction from staff regarding the new branch?" Mika opened the meeting with a hardball.

"Well," Terry said, "we've not had a meeting about it yet."

"Why not?" Mika asked. "The mayor is insistent that we move forward as quickly as possible. I don't want it to look like we're dragging our feet."

"I think we need to slow down. Thinking strategically takes time," Terry replied.

Mika tightened her gaze on Terry. "Terry, I don't want to jeopardize my career and neither should you. This is important to the mayor. Change will be good for us all, and you can't take baby steps when a big leap is needed. Remember, you can't jump a chasm in two steps. It's what the mayor is continually telling me. Didn't you read that article I gave you? It went over all the red flags for our future. The mayor, and several of our library board members, have warned me that if people see us only as a place for books, we're doomed. We have to be able to show our communities that we are places for them to educate, create, partner, and enjoy. The statistics in that article are very good . . . all those studies it cites that show how playing soothing music not only lowers stress levels but can actually increase test scores; those can't be ignored. What better time to show the community that we are changing than right now with this new branch?"

"I'm not disagreeing, Mika. It's . . . " Terry paused. "I have concerns. First and foremost is that changing the lighting and playing music would increase the number of people who use the library as a napping place, not to mention the complaints from users who want to focus on what they are doing, especially during finals period. But let me drill back, Mika. Basically I'm not convinced of this whole new vision. I'm being honest. Did you realize that there isn't one bookshelf in all the artist's conceptions? Are we changing the mission of the library? Isn't this an awfully big leap? Couldn't we take smaller, incremental steps toward this vision of the future library?" Terry fought the urge to simply ask, *Where's the plan, Mika?*

Terry inhaled. "I read the article, and there is certainly a lot to think about. But, Mika, staff haven't even had time to appreciate all they have accomplished up to this point, and now we're asking them to switch gears! I'm just not sure that all of this will actually be useful in *our* community," Terry said, "especially at a time when so many patrons are using our library as a study space. Libraries have always been places of contemplation, and our patrons have always appreciated that. Despite decades of less-than-optimal physical surroundings, they've always used our facilities to the utmost. I think that piping in music would damage that."

Mika responded, "The mayor wants us to be leading the way for libraries and setting the tone for how users behave in libraries. He sees this new Discovery Station as a way to bring our library up to a level that no other system in the state has managed to achieve. I don't want to disappoint him. Terry, the board sees this as an opportunity to give ourselves a new start, and I need to completely capitalize on it. To show them I'm up to this. I thought I had an ally in you."

An ally, yes. A scapegoat, no, Terry thought but didn't vocalize. She knew this was a fight she couldn't—or maybe shouldn't—win. And, then again, there was the small matter of this project being a direct order. It was an order she perhaps didn't agree with, but it was also one she hoped had been researched, studied, and weighed by powers above her. Mika might not have the right view, but she had the authority to make this kind of decision, to expect her employees to deliver the programs as she had outlined them. Terry could do what she was told, or she could jeopardize her new promotion by telling Mika she was wrong. This wasn't a choice Terry was willing to make. She was being pushed into managing a project she believed wasn't right, but at the same time, she knew how she'd react if one of her own employees failed to deliver. Terry gave a resigned sigh and shrugged her shoulders a little.

"Okay," she said in as chipper a voice as she could muster under the current circumstances. "I'll see what I can do."

I HEAR MUSIC RESPONSES

Response 1
By Lyn Begraft, director, Bernards Township Library, Basking Ridge, New Jersey

The scenario in this chapter leaves the reader feeling the knot in the pit of Terry's stomach. Terry, the person next in line for a big promotion as the library's new special projects manager, is being left by her predecessor to implement a plan that was not communicated in full to her and not seemingly a good fit for the community of library users that it is being created to serve. The plans have been made, and the new bookless Discovery Station library branch has already been approved by the city's mayor. It should be an exciting time for Terry, but she is not sold on the design or philosophy of this "very different library."

Not enough can be said about the value of staff buying in to a new idea or innovative change when it comes to implementing these things in public libraries. Transparency and collaboration on projects leads to increased job satisfaction and a sense of ownership. Employees do not need to agree with the decisions that have been made, but if they don't find consensus it will be difficult to motivate them to put effort into the changes that you are trying to execute. The fact that Terry—and the rest of the library staff, it would seem—has no idea what the mayor and Mika (the previous branch manager and soon to be the new city librarian at City Hall) have been plotting in regard to new library service, or the Discovery Station, is equally troubling.

In this example, Mika is leaving Terry feeling as if her opinion and experience—particularly with her library's users—are not valuable. In addition, Mika's management style leads to confusion and self-doubt for Terry. What Terry needs from Mika is transparency regarding the new design and for her to listen to Terry's concerns about how these special projects will be received by the users of the library branch. Instead, she gets a magazine to read that will help her understand. So, in the span of one day, Mika has dumped an entirely new service model into Terry's lap and expects her to just read an article so she'll understand why a new service model was even necessary. It is assumed that Mika will expect Terry to translate all of this to the existing staff, and hopefully this new Discovery Station service model will just be an automatic success.

A critical management responsibility for a city librarian, or more commonly a library director, is to present ideas and innovations to staff. City librarians need to validate staff efforts and let them know that the previous service model wasn't wrong; it is just no longer practical in today's world. They need to explain why changing to a new service model at this particular time is critical. And they need to help create a critical mass among staff that drives support for the new model. The city librarian, or any library manager implementing change, must seek and listen to staff reactions and opinions. These can speak louder than any survey or article on library design and innovation. People who work directly with the public, day in and day out, sometimes know the community best. Their voices matter when it comes to decisions that will ultimately affect the user experience. Mika (along with the city mayor) seems to have decided on a new service model without any input from those who will be implementing the change and who stand to lose the most if this service model fails.

Things are moving very quickly for Terry with the promotion and this new service model innovation. This project is being left in Terry's lap with too little direction and not enough explanation. Ultimately, Terry will be the key decision maker once Mika has transitioned into her new position. Unfortunately, Terry is left in the dark, not knowing what decisions to make, why those decisions need to be made in the first place, or why decisions were made without any input from the staff.

Is it too late for Terry? Is there still a path for her to salvage this change management project? Yes, Terry does have the power to talk to Mika about what she is feeling. She can let Mika know how much she appreciates Mika's trust and confidence in her experience. But she needs to explain to Mika that she cannot guarantee successful change management without being more informed in the process and given the opportunity to explore how Mika and the mayor arrived at this new service model. Terry needs to help Mika understand why this particular change process is doomed and how she feels it can be better . . . maybe even recommending slowing down and considering a blend of library services to provide a better balance for everyone to enjoy. Continued communication with Mika is the best course of action for Terry. Terry's insight and expertise is something that Mika has relied on in the past, but Terry needs to communicate the heart of the matter: the needs of the library community. Terry could eventually be rendered ineffective in her new position otherwise.

A successful public library is a blend of many things. It can be the celebrated center of the community it serves. It can be a place for discovery and transformation. It must be a place that welcomes all people, a place that feels like home for those searching. I understand Mika's enthusiasm about new trends and discovery. A new service model may even be a perfect strategic plan. Many library managers have leaned toward a retail model of merchandising library materials and focusing on nontraditional library services like technology and maker-spaces. With these new products in mind, library managers and directors have been known to daydream about more modern design concepts for libraries that cater to these needs. But you can't retool an engine while the car is running. You have to stop, plan, and analyze. Terry can't do this in a vacuum.

This scenario resonates with a lot of library directors and managers, myself included. Libraries stand at a crossroad—yesterday's service model is showing wear and tear, and its expiration date may be approaching soon. Library managers should never expect 100 percent support from any individual who is not personally involved in devising a change that has an impact on their work. In order to be an effective and successful library director, include staff in the process—most especially the staff expected to implement change. Their opinions originate from hours of service to, and interactions with, patrons. They see what people are searching for, hear their requests and questions, and know what keeps them coming back as faithful users of the library. Mika has not given her staff, or her new special projects manager, a voice in the change. For this reason, I see nothing but confusion, low morale, lack of engagement, and a lowering of service standards at the city's new Discovery Station branch.

Response 2
By Carol Garcia, senior library assistant administrator (retired), San Jose Public Library, San Jose, California

I completely feel for Terry, the new special projects manager of the Axfall Public Library. There isn't a library manager around who can't recall the same gut-punch feeling Terry must have felt when her superior handed her an assignment and said something that can be interpreted as "Here! You do this; I don't want to." The alarm bells sound, the flags go up, and the general sense of regret can't be ignored. "Why don't they want to do it?" "If it's too hard for them, how am I expected to do it?" "Is this an unpopular assignment, and am I being framed to take the blame?" These are just a few of the questions I'm sure you will be asking if the same thing happens to you on the job. Sure, bosses will delegate lots of things to their subordinates. This helps an organization achieve collective success, save time, and increase employee skills. But, as this scenario certainly demonstrates, you have good reason to be concerned when you're being asked to do something your superior should be doing but doesn't want to—or can't—do.

After reading this scenario, I asked myself what the main issue was here. There were a few, actually, but the primary problem, I believe, is the lack of a clear and transparent strategic plan. The mayor of the city of Axfall has hijacked the planning process. We don't see what his goals are and what objectives are behind his strategy for the library. We don't know what the mayor's issues are with the current library operations or why he feels something drastic needs to change there. The only thing we know for sure is that there was a mysterious article called "Should Your Library Be More Like a Retail Store?" that the mayor seems enamored with for some unknown reason. It seems a bit dangerous for a city leader to want to change an organization's entire operation simply on the basis of reading one article. Perhaps after reading the article, the mayor saw a way for the library to position itself to his benefit. Does the article target a key constituent of the mayor's reelection? Does the mayor see a way for the library to "downsize" by doing less and therefore become less of a burden on the city's operational budget? We simply don't know enough about this article and why it is so appealing to the mayor. But if I were Mika, the city librarian, I'd be far more skeptical and probing before I'd be willing to take my department down such a dramatically different path.

Strategic planning should be a disciplined and thoughtful process. It should effectively link your organization's goals, values, and mission with coherent and consistently articulated purposes and objectives. It should also produce measurable steps, or specific action plans, to help the library achieve its strategic goals. What we see in this scenario is a mayor who likely has no idea what the library's goals and mission are and sees no problem with upending everything in favor of a completely different strategy. How, then, will Terry—who Mika has tasked with implementing the mayor's wishes—create strategies and tasks to achieve the library's goals when those goals haven't been clearly articulated? Furthermore, why does Mika pass this project on to a subordinate who she has just promoted but who has little—if any—proven experience in this area?

I have learned that there are three absolute essentials to ensure the successful implementation of any strategic plan. There needs to be complete and energetic involvement from top leaders within the organization's hierarchy. There needs to be effective and consistent communication from beginning to end. Finally, there needs to be involvement from any and all employees who will be expected to work within, and implement, the new plan. Ask yourself, "How successful are each of the three major characters in the scenario in meeting those absolute essential areas?" If I were grading them, they'd each get an F!

Let's start with Terry. While she is in charge of the plan's implementation, she certainly was not involved in its planning. To be fair, this isn't really Terry's fault. The plan was hidden from everyone—including Terry—to begin with. But now that Terry knows about the pending library change, she suddenly becomes concerned with her career. She mentions a few times that she doesn't want to jeopardize her career by challenging Mika. So, she resigns herself to just do as she has been told and tells Mika that she will "see what she can do." Not exactly the complete and energetic involvement necessary to successfully implement a strategic plan. Mika does no better in this regard. Rather than being involved in the implementation, Mika passes it on to her subordinate. Mind you, the plan she passes on is one that strikes at the core of traditional library service. If anyone needs to be involved, it should be the library director. Instead, Mika announces she's moving out of the library into City Hall, where she will focus on other things. She punts the ball. The mayor's involvement at this point is really unknown from what I see. Because the idea was designed in apparent secrecy without seeking input from anyone, I am doubtful the mayor has any intention of becoming a vocal and energetic participant in the transformation.

All three characters fail miserably at the necessity to effectively communicate a consistent message. In fact, there is no message whatsoever to communicate. "Here . . . read this article" seems to be the only messaging going on at Axfall. Even if we overlooked the fact that the entire staff wasn't involved in the planning process, the mayor and Mika should have produced a clear and concise written plan showing how this new strategic initiative they thought up would add value to their services. The mayor and Mika didn't produce any statement of strategy at all. Apparently, they got to a point where they had an artist's conception of the new Discovery Station created, but how they got here isn't clear. Where are the critical assumptions underpinning this strategic plan and architectural dream? Where are the initiatives required to meet the functional objectives that should have at least been established? These are the perfect pieces of a message that Terry and the staff should be expected to consistently communicate. But they are missing. The mayor and Mika apparently have only discussed this major change with the library's board. Other than that, they have been mum. Why? Do they fear their plan has no merit? Do they want to hide their idea because they anticipate resistance from the staff and users? Communication involves asking for input, talking about vision and purpose, having a message, and listening to the library's community of staff and users. The mayor and Mika should have been communicating with the staff and the public from the very beginning.

It's absolutely inconceivable that Mika wasn't insisting that all members of her organization be made aware of the plan, its importance, and how it might impact the staff. For any strategic plan to be successful—especially one of such magnitude as a complete change in the library's mission—it must involve all staff members. For top executives in an organization like the city's mayor and the city librarian to completely sidestep this important and basic implementation rule does not make me at all confident that this strategic transformation at Axfall Public Library will be successful.

It may be a controversial one, but there does seem to me to be a path for Terry to follow in pulling the mayor's and Mika's plan successfully across the finish line. Maybe she should go rogue and make this plan her own. It won't be easy, but she can certainly implement the vision in such a way that makes sense to her, that satisfies her superiors, and that doesn't jeopardize her career at the library. With Mika seemingly willing to divorce herself from the strategic transformation project, she has left total implementation up to Terry. The mayor is likely out of the project—save for an occasional publicity shot or media event—and won't concern himself with details that Terry will be involved with. Terry needs to better understand the purpose of the library transformation project. While getting a handle on this, she can also do her research and contact colleagues and libraries that have implemented similar projects. She can read other articles and talk to library strategic planning experts. Terry may even find merit in the original plans and become excited about the coming changes. Of course, Terry must begin involving staff immediately. She needs to begin communicating the new vision. She needs to survey staff and the public as well, including everyone in fine-tuning a new direction. Terry needs to stop stressing about small details she doesn't like and focus on the future. Once Terry stops worrying about whether music will be acceptable to her users, and stops obsessing over homeless people napping on the library furniture, she will likely learn that strategic plans—when they are created and implemented properly—are valuable tools. They are critical in keeping the library she loves so much relevant and useful to the community it serves. When she does this, she—and the Axfall Public Library community—will win, both personally and professionally.

Response 3
By Wayne Disher, San Jose State University School of Information, San Jose, California

Making change is one of the hardest things that managers will have to deal with in their career. It is never something that should be taken lightly or taken for granted. Change that is based on careful research and thought is hard enough, but making change based solely on fear of what you think might happen—or even on what you want to happen—is nearly impossible. And when that change comes without warning, planning, and participation from staff, the results are likely doomed from the beginning. Complicating matters is the fact that change is rarely acceptable to everyone—at least not at first. Even change that seems to benefit everyone will be looked at with resistance, resentment, skepticism, and/or ridicule by some—even if only by a few. Change makes people uncomfortable. It represents the unknown. To convince staff that change is for the good, they have to be a part of the strategic planning process. They need to be absolutely convinced that the place you want to take them is better than the place they are now. Managers need to make staff comfortable with the knowledge that the benefits they will gain far outweigh the risks. This is where the new city librarian, Mika Lorenzo, fails so miserably in this scenario. Mika wants to change the entire library mission in order to please her superiors—the mayor and her library board. But if there was any planning done at all in relation to this change, it certainly didn't include the very people who would be most affected by that change.

In this scenario, Terry seems to represent the entire staff of Axfall Public Library. She is reluctant—if not totally resistant—to take this change journey with her new boss. She has key questions: "Where are we going?" "Why are we going there?" and "How does the potential harm of moving from point A to point B personally benefit us?" If Mika and the mayor ever considered these questions, which is doubtful, they certainly didn't share the answers with anyone. The success of any change management depends on the leadership skills of the leader, and—at least in this scenario—neither Mika nor Terry show they have the proper skills to achieve success.

The key question that cries out for me in this scenario is "Why has Mika completely abdicated her authority to the wants and whims of the mayor?" The mayor's desires represent a serious change in service model and mission for the library. Why hasn't Mika taken control of this more professionally? My opinions here may be unconventional. Can it be that Mika sees the controversy she is about to create in changing the library's service model and mission as a means by which to show and wield power? I don't necessarily mean to imply that Mika is being vindictive or malicious. Some new managers and directors may feel that they need to show that they are powerful as a way to deal with insecurity in their own abilities or to solidify their place in the organization's hierarchy.

There are several clues that speak to Mika's insecurity. She continually says that the new "Discovery Station" is something the mayor wants; does this imply that Mika does not want the change? She doesn't want to "disappoint" the mayor and library board. Mika doesn't want the mayor to think she is dragging her feet. But, as city librarian, Mika should be a partner in setting the library's strategic path, planning how to achieve goals, and approving budgets that align with the new plans for Axfall Public Library. Mika already has the power to determine what the library does and when it does it. Of course, she will be held accountable for her actions, but it is Mika's responsibility to set strategic direction. Why has she let the mayor take complete control of her department's operation here? Would the chief of police let the mayor totally change that department's service model? Would the fire chief acquiesce if the mayor wanted that department to fight fires in a completely different way? Mika's actions reveal insecurities and lack of self-esteem. Her behaviors seem self-serving. She seems more concerned in showing her superiors that she is "up to this" and capable of being the city librarian they want. In doing so, she puts her own interests ahead of those of the staff she wants to lead.

Let's look more critically at Mika's behaviors. When we first see her, Mika is only acting in the role to which she aspires—in other words, she is the temporary leader only until a permanent leader can be selected. Mika seems to be overly concerned with how things reflect on her—and likely on how they may affect her being selected as the permanent leader. She has had secret meetings with the mayor and library board and seems to have handed over her responsibilities without question. She has let the research of one article on library innovation influence her actions. Maybe Mika should have contacted some of the libraries that were mentioned in the article and asked them what planning was involved in their own transformations. She doesn't seem to want to give the change in the library's mission any deeper analysis. Instead, she assumes the existence of disputed facts she thinks may lead her staff to arrive at the same decision she has already made. Mika has already decided where she is taking the library without really challenging if the transformation is necessary. Her critical failure was not insisting that her staff be a part of the planning process. Mika's lack of transparency shows a clear lack of respect and dignity accorded to her staff. It is clear to me, then, why Mika leaves Terry, the new special projects manager, in charge of this major service transformation and then abandons the library at this critical time. Mika wants someone else to implement a service model she has no faith in. Mika also wants to be able to take credit if the model is successfully implemented or place blame on someone else if it fails.

It may be difficult to do, but we need to get past whether the ends justify the means in this scenario. By this I mean, just because we might believe that Mika is correct in her desire to make Axfall Public Library a more customer-focused institution by changing service models and capitalizing on new trends, we cannot overlook her total failure in washing her hands of the change and walking away. Customer service, and customer-focused organizations, are key to remaining relevant and useful in today's information professions. But a better approach to changing the mission of the organization is to take control of the process and integrate it into a larger library strategic planning process that could involve all staff and major advocates for the library.

As mentioned before, Mika's process may be hiding some professional insecurities and self-esteem issues. Once she uses this tactic to make herself look good, she will most definitely use it again and again—all in the name of improving customer service. Power is a strong aphrodisiac, and Mika's power trip will likely alienate staff and destroy employee engagement. Even if Mika or Terry don't feel especially powerful, their self-protection behaviors do make them look like power-hungry amateurs who are only concerned with "how does this affect me?" Improving customer service is a lofty goal and should be high on the list of any library manager. But managers who are so insecure that they seek to show how great they are aren't really interested in customer service. Mika needs to trust her skills, trust her staff, and trust the change management process to allow for the entire Axfall Public Library staff to provide input.

By the end of this scenario, Terry seems to have given up. She is ready to run with the library transformation Mika and the mayor have dreamed up, even though she has little faith in it. She has a long and bumpy road ahead of her. As a new unskilled, unhappy manager, Terry (and the Axfall Public Library staff) will experience a lot of painful lessons as she learns from her own mistakes and the mistakes that others have thrust on her. The good news is that these types of managers don't last long. They eventually rise to the challenge, or they show their incompetence and insecurity in other ways that lead to their termination or departure. The library transformation described in this scenario is one so major, and one so in need of experienced and careful planning, that I'd just bet that both Mika and Terry will soon be looking for other jobs.

Part Two

Organizing

Chapter Four

Book Selections Can Be Challenged

An Organizing Scenario Using Skills

SCENARIO

The morning was as beautiful as Maureen had ever seen. It was almost a shame to be spending the entire day in the library, and worse, at the reference desk—a spot as far away as you can get from a single window. But that was her job as the newest of the reference librarians. She was ready for the day, but Maureen paused for a moment before going in the staff entrance to glance at the sky and make sure she had the image of the blues and pinks burned into her skull. It would help her keep a calm perspective.

The rest of Maureen's morning was as unremarkable as you could imagine. In fact, nothing was notable enough for Maureen to recall. She found herself almost dozily reading book review sources as she worked on some materials selection. In a week of short-staffing and time spent at various service desks, this was the repetitive sort of work she found herself favoring over just about anything.

"Excuse me, miss." A middle-aged woman walked up to the desk and handed a slim volume to Maureen. "I think this item needs to be removed from our library."

Maureen was not used to this sort of nonforceful demand. There was no anger behind the woman's voice, but there was also something emphatic in her tone that made it certain to Maureen that this was more than just a simple request.

Maureen took the book from the lady without taking her eyes off her.

"Is there a problem with it?" Maureen asked, somewhat befuddled. "Some sort of damage or something?"

The woman cut her off. "No," she said again, with the same quiet force. "It is a filthy book that needs to be removed. There are children in this library, and to think they could stumble upon this book at any given moment. We mustn't let that happen. Please see that you remove it right away."

Maureen looked down at the book. The title—blazing in a glaring, bold, hot pink screaming font across the cover—was *Smut-peddling*. The book was impressively made with a tight binding, and the covers seemed to be made of a faux leather. The title was embossed, and Maureen felt the depth of the letters before she made as if she was going to open the book.

"I wouldn't do that, miss," the woman said.

Maureen stared hard into the eyes of the woman and opened the book.

She had been warned, and she felt as if she had been hardened against any sort of content that might be found in a library book. She was wrong. Quite wrong.

"I told you so," the woman said, noticing the reaction on Maureen's face. "Can you imagine allowing this sort of filth to stand alongside all the other biographies on the shelf! It was actually touching the Pope John Paul II biography! *Touching it!*"

Maureen looked over the book's most shocking images—largely activities being engaged in by a tall man with a shaved head in all sorts of dangerous-looking scenarios. Some of the images featured unsavory materials—such as guns and knives—being used in highly violent and offensive ways. Were the images reenactments? Maureen couldn't tell for sure. She closed the book and looked at the back cover. There was an embossed image, a line drawing of the man, identified as Lennon Lennox. It also showed the dates: 1960–2015. Apparently, Lennon Lennox was no longer alive.

"Can you believe that someone would publish such undeniable sickness?" the woman went on. "That man was obviously a monster!"

"Do you mind if I ask why you picked it up?" Maureen asked.

"That title on the spine," the woman said huffily. "I had to make sure that it was what I thought, and it was so much worse!"

Maureen ran her hand along the book, feeling the recessed areas. She wondered what the patron meant when she had to "make sure that is was what I thought." What did the patron think it was? Was she familiar with Lennox's work for some reason?

"I . . . " Maureen was uncertain how to proceed. "I'll bring this to the attention of my supervisor."

The woman seemed unsatisfied.

"You're not going to throw it in the garbage?" she said.

"I can't do that, ma'am. There's a process the library goes through in removing a book. I have to follow that process." The images from the book had overtaken those of the beautiful morning Maureen had walked in the library trying to savor. "I need to show this to the branch manager. He knows the proper channels to follow."

The woman reached over and took a pen from the cup on the reference desk, then grabbed a nearby notepad, writing her name and phone number on it. She reached over the desk and slapped the note on the book.

"My name is Helen Lucase. I put my contact information on that note," she said, "and I would much appreciate a call about what was done. Thank you." The lady marched away, taking a handkerchief out of her bag and wiping her hands.

Maureen picked up the phone and dialed the number of her branch manager, Ravi Patel.

"This is Patel," he answered.

"Ravi, it's Mo at Ref," she said, using the nickname she'd allowed staff to call her. "Can you come by the desk here? I have a . . . Maybe it's better if I get someone to cover the desk for a bit and come there. This is . . . " She wasn't sure how to finish the sentence, and she saw Wendell, her colleague walking nearby. She waved him over. "This is something you'll need to deal with. I'll be right there."

Wendell agreed to take over at the reference desk, and Maureen made her way into the administrative annex, carrying the book pressed between both hands, as if trying to keep it from springing open and spilling all over the new carpeting.

She arrived at Ravi's office with the book slid up under her armpit, still clamping it closed. She knocked.

"Come on in," Ravi called out to her.

His office was practically bare. Just a desk and a few chairs. When they had completed the refurbishing, he had never rehung the commendations, certificates, and trophies that he had collected in his years at the library. Because of this, Maureen had the impression—perhaps incorrectly—that Ravi was leaving.

Maureen walked in and slid the book onto his desk.

"A woman"—she looked at the note stuck to the front of the book—"Helen Lucase, brought this to me."

Ravi nodded with a hint of recognition at the name. He pulled the book across the desk, then stared at the note on which Helen's name had been scribbled.

"Oh, yes. Helen." He stared at the note and turned the paper from side to side as if trying to read it. "That says 'Lucase'?" He chuckled.

"Apparently," Maureen responded. "Anyhow, she brought that book to me, very concerned. Very upset. She wanted me to throw it in the garbage."

Ravi didn't open the book. "All right," he said. "Then what?"

"Excuse me?"

"Then what?" he repeated. "Did she get belligerent?"

Maureen was slightly stunned. He didn't seem interested in the book at all.

"Not at all," she said. "Helen remained very calm, but she knew what she wanted, and she wanted that book removed. Now!"

Ravi leaned back, seeming somewhat relieved. "Whew, Maureen. You really had me scared there," he said. "From the look on your face, I thought there was an active shooter or something in the building."

Maureen sat there, slack-jawed.

"Aren't you going to look at the book?"

Ravi pulled the book back in front of him. He glanced down at it briefly.

"Ah, yes, the Lennox book. I wondered if it would cause a stir. Guess it was bound to happen eventually. Anyway, I know the book. I'd really rather not look at it again, Mo."

"Again? You mean you've actually read that before?"

"Not every word," Ravi said, "but I'm familiar with it. It was recommended to us by an important patron a while back, and I went over it, looked into the author, Lennox, and had it ordered."

"You know what's in that book?"

"I wouldn't have been doing my job if I didn't." Ravi smiled.

Maureen could not believe she was hearing this. "How could you order that book knowing what was in it?"

Ravi ran his hand along the embossing. "It's complicated. But after considering it, I didn't find it too much of a difficult question to order it," Ravi said. "It's a quality book, tells an important story about the life of a man who was a world-class dancer, who became one of the most significant figures in modern dance, and who is associated with the history of fetish pornography. There are two universities within twenty-five miles of this library, and both are well known in some respect for their significant dance programs. This Lennox guy sounds like an important figure, and one of interest to that community. Not to mention that the book's author is a local."

"That doesn't really sound like something that outweighs the content," Maureen said. "I mean, there are photos in there that I am pretty certain are against the law."

"Possibly at the time they were taken," Ravi said, "but there wasn't anything that seems to go against community standards, at least as I understand them."

"Against community standards?" Maureen asked.

"That's the standard we have to use," Ravi said. "Even if it is completely against everything we ourselves believe is good or decent, we have to follow the standards set by the community. Back in 1857, the US Supreme Court defined for us how to determine whether something is obscene. They said that obscenity could only be defined as whether to the average person, applying contemporary community standards, the dominant theme of the material—taken as a whole—appeals to prurient interests. Since the author is local, since students of dance may need to research this subject, and since our community member recommended it, I think it passes the tests of the Supreme Court's definition."

"You think those activities displayed in the book are sanctioned by our community?" Maureen asked, shocked.

"No," he said. "I didn't imply that. But it's safe to say that our community is interested in dance, that they are interested in notable individuals who participate in that industry, and they are interested in those dancers who have lived incredibly distinguished lives. They don't have to agree with the actions and beliefs of those individuals any more than they have to agree with the actions or beliefs of, say, Adolf Hitler. Yet we have Hitler's *Mein Kampf* in the collection, don't we?"

"But this Lennox book doesn't seem to be just a biography," Maureen said. "The things in there . . . well—granted, I didn't read it in depth—but I don't see much research value in it."

"I understand that the images in the book are not pleasant," Ravi said, "at least from where I'm sitting, but it's also not anything created for stimulation. It's a legitimate biography, with illustrations that are the dancer's simulation of real events."

"So, we would carry a book of murder victim photos?" Maureen asked.

"We have hundreds of true crime, nonfiction books on our shelves," Ravi answered, "and there are photos that are nearly as devastating as those in this book."

Maureen had to let that sink in.

"A member of the community brought this to our attention," Maureen said, working it out as she was speaking her words. "I briefly reviewed the book, and I believe that it is a work of extreme pornography."

Ravi gave a slight smile.

"Go on, Mo," he said.

"So, a community member raised the concern, and I find that it is pornographic. I'm not allowed to pull it, and I bring it to you, who I would assume has the right to pull the book. You don't find it to be pornographic, is that right?"

Ravi smiled. "Not quite. I'll get the policy out for you to review. But let's do an exercise," he said.

Maureen sat up in her seat as Ravi pulled a piece of paper off of a notepad and pushed it over to her, then grabbed a pencil, sharpened it, and moved that toward her as well. "Okay. Let's start by listing the requirements, in your eyes, that would make something worthy of being included in the library."

Maureen wrote down the following words: *significant, useful, informative, published, educational, entertaining, reviewed.* "Okay," Maureen said, "now what?"

"And, I think obviously, a list of things that would make a work unworthy of being in a library."

Maureen wrote another list, much more quickly. The words that came to her mind were *insignificant, self-published/unpublished, spurious, unverifiable, pornographic.*

Ravi waited until she finished writing and then motioned for her to hand over the list. Maureen handed it to him, and he scanned it and smiled.

"You're going to be excellent when you take over acquisitions," he said, smiling across at her. "These are very much within our guidelines. Very much like the things we use to determine the viability of buying a book. Published versus self-published is an important one, and one we're still arguing."

Maureen took that as a massive compliment.

"Now, rank your words from most important to least important with number one being most important in your mind," he said as he handed Maureen back the paper. She perused the words, then wrote a number next to each.

Significant	2
Useful	4
Informative	3
Published	1
Educational	5
Entertaining	6
Reviewed	7

She did the same with the other list.

Insignificant	3
Self-published/Unpublished	2
Spurious	4
Unverifiable	5
Pornographic	1

Maureen handed the paper back.

"Pretty strong ranking," Ravi said. "I might have gone very much that way myself. Now, suppose you only had your list of unworthy words to use, and a patron brought a book up to you and asked you to remove it."

"Well," she said, "I'm pretty sure that I'd review the work and then weigh it against those values I listed."

"And does falling into a single one of those categories disqualify a work?"

That had not occurred to her.

"I think the top two would certainly disqualify a book," she said, "but I think it would need two or more of those further down the list."

"All right," Ravi said. "Now, what about the inclusion list? Does a book need to meet more than one of those criteria?"

"Again," she said, "I'm pretty sure that the first two or three would be automatic for inclusion, but maybe two or more of the others."

Ravi smiled again.

"Now, what if something meets several criteria on both lists?"

Maureen's face took on a genuinely confused look, as if the two thoughts were fighting against one another, and her brain was placed into a holding pattern as it worked toward a conclusion that never became any clearer as she cogitated on it.

"All right," she said after a long period of quiet contemplation. "What's the point?"

"Well," Ravi said, "I wanted you to realize that removing a book is a lot more complicated than you think. For that reason, we have a process, a policy. We'll need to review that policy together, but there's more to it than just judging a book by one or two elements. I will look over the book reviews. Check usage. Discuss the item with the collections team. And, ultimately, the library board will need to be apprised. But I'll make the final decision. Once I do that, you can contact Ms. Lucase with our decision."

"Me?" Maureen asked, stunned.

"Absolutely," Ravi said. "You're the one the patron brought the book to. You're the one who has knowledge of the situation. So I can't think of a better person to make the call."

A month went by, and Maureen had nearly forgotten the Helen Lucase case. However, the whole sordid affair was brought instantly back to her mind with an email from Ravi with the subject line "Book removal decision." Maureen quickly opened the email. It read, "Maureen, the selection committee and I have discussed the Lennox book that was objected by Helen Lucase. Checking the usage statistics, we see the book has nearly three circulations annually. This isn't as high as some other biographies, but it does identify the work as moderately useful to the community. We contacted the author, who lives locally, and discussed the objections with him. The author provided us with several reviews of the book, which were all favorable. The reviews mentioned the stark images as relevant to the content of the dancer's life. Finally, we determined that—while some community members may indeed find the images objectionable—due to the scarcity of research on the author, the moderate use, and the fact that the author is local, we have decided that the book should remain in our collection. Please contact Ms. Lucase with our decision." The email included several attachments, including the American Library Association's Bill of Rights, the library's collection policy, and the appeal process if the patron wanted to take the objection up with the library board.

Maureen suddenly felt a deeper kind of conflict. She didn't feel like libraries should be censoring work, but this book went way beyond common decency. She just couldn't get past the pornographic content. If she couldn't get past that challenge, she knew Helen Lucase sure wouldn't.

Maureen spent a few hours digging through books in the library's stacks. She pulled a lot of the books she saw on a list of books that had been banned from other libraries. She held them up against *Smut-peddler*. There were many pictures in books of Maplethorpe that she found a little objectionable and that would raise flags for her, but ultimately nothing that would rise to the standard she'd set in her head to indicate removal would be worthwhile.

Why did she feel she needed to go through all this trouble? The decision to keep the book had been made. She couldn't (shouldn't?) change that decision. It was at that moment that a library page walked up to her and gave her a book that seemed to fall apart in her hands. "I found this while shelving," the library page said. "If you delete it from the computer, I'll process it for deletion and throw it out. It doesn't look like it can be saved."

Maureen took the book and thanked the library page. She could just as easily delete the Lennox book in a few months after things calmed down and people forgot about it. She could call Ms. Lucase and let her know that the library was getting rid of the book. Who'd miss the book anyway? It's not like it had as much usage as other books in the library. Books get deleted from the library all the time. Eventually even this Lennox book would need to be discarded. Was it wrong to do it now? Maybe so. She felt she was abandoning her professional ethics. But it was the easiest way to handle the situation. Or was it? She knew she could just as easily call Ms. Lucase and explain that the library manager had decided to keep the item. She could let Ms. Lucase know how to appeal, and she'd be done with the situation. Maureen thought about it for another hour before picking up the phone and dialing Helen Lucase's number.

BOOK SELECTIONS CAN BE CHALLENGED RESPONSES

Response 1
By Katherine Huddle, manager, Carmel Clay Public Library, Carmel Clay, Indiana

Maureen is experiencing quite the ethical dilemma! Book challenges, especially those based on explicit content, can bring up both moral questions and concerns for library staff depending on their own beliefs and backgrounds. That being said, Article VII of the American Library Association's (ALA) Code of Ethics states that library workers must "distinguish between our personal convictions and professional duties and do not allow our personal beliefs to interfere with fair representation of the aims of our institutions or the provision of access to their information resources."

It's a delicate balance to try to remain impartial when your personal beliefs are in direct contradiction with a professional situation. Telling the patron that the book is going to be removed and then not actually removing the book is a terrible idea. What if the patron followed up in a few months, inquiring as to whether or not the book had been removed yet, and found the book still on the shelves? Maureen risks losing her job or at least being written up for insubordination. How would Maureen feel if she did in fact weed the book and then a few weeks later a student requested the title for an assignment? If she is struggling with the decision to keep this book, I would urge her to consult the ALA's Office for Intellectual Freedom for further guidance on this issue. If I felt similarly to Maureen and disagreed strongly with the decision, I would reach out to my supervisor/director and ask to sit down and talk about the decision in more depth.

It can be extremely difficult to uphold a policy or decision that you do not agree with, but at the end of the day, you can't let it keep you up at night. If you made a list of every book that you didn't think should be in your library, the length of the list may surprise you. Remember, you're a patron at your home library too, and it doesn't hurt to try and put yourself in the shoes of the patron who voiced their concern about the material in question in the first place.

Let's say, for example, that you happen to be a librarian who thinks that books representing transgender children should not be in a library where children have access to them. You might sympathize with an angry patron who approaches the desk with Alex Gino's *George* in hand, wanting to know why "this *filth*" is on your shelves where any child can find it. It is difficult to imagine how you would actually respond in such a situation until it occurs. I recommend that library staff hold occasional role-playing sessions to practice responding to on-the-spot, in-person challenges. You can memorize your library's collection development policy, challenge procedures and processes, and the ALA Bill of Rights so well that you could swiftly recite them in your sleep; however, you can't really predict how you will respond when you have a screaming mother six inches in front of your face wanting to know why *you* ordered a book that uses the word *penis* on page thirty-two!

If the patron in this scenario does decide to appeal the decision, it should be made very clear to her that this requires her to read the book. Hopefully, doing so will help the patron better understand how the photos tie in to the purpose of the book, giving her a better grasp of their context. I think it is important to remember—as both a librarian and as a patron—that our collections are not endorsements of specific beliefs or values.

In *The New Inquisition: Understanding and Managing Intellectual Freedom Challenges*, James LaRue, director of the ALA's Office for Intellectual Freedom, writes that "the intent is to move the patron to a successful transaction and perhaps to underscore that the great value of the library is not what it doesn't have, but what it does." I would make an effort to ensure the patron understands that the decision to keep the book took into account that the title was requested by a community member, thoroughly vetted, met the library's collection development policy requirements, had been checked out several times, was written by a local author, had multiple positive reviews, fills a collection gap due to lack of other quality sources on the individual profiled in the biography, and is also of community interest due to the local college's dance program. I would also consider including a positive quote from a review in my follow-up with the patron so that they understand more thoroughly the many reasons why the title in question was selected in the first place and is being retained in the collection.

No one wants to have a book challenge go through a formal appeals process. It's time-consuming and can potentially bring unwanted and negative attention to the library. Trying to diffuse a potential formal challenge situation requires a delicate approach, and offering additional training to a point person on staff may be a good way to handle issues such as this—especially if, after being informed of the decision, the patron wishes to speak to the library director and/or pursue a formal appeals process.

One thing that is interesting in this situation is that the director asked a nonmanagement staff member (and someone who was not part of the review committee) to follow up with the patron who initiated the challenge request. I would prefer that all communications in instances of challenges run through one contact person in the library system, such as the chair of the review committee or a staff member in administration.

Maureen is right in feeling that she would be abandoning her professional ethics by secretly deleting the item at the heart of the complaint. However, she is also wrong in thinking that she should just call the patron and let her supervisor handle the fallout. Maureen needs to learn why decisions are made and how to address these decisions professionally—particularly if she ever sees herself promoting to a management-level position. Maureen, and others, should strive to learn from the many examples of excellent written responses to requests for reconsideration of library materials to be found online. Many of these responses are sent directly to the patron and include a copy of the ALA's Bill of Rights, the library's collection policy, and information on the appeal process. I would also include copies of the ALA's Freedom to Read and Freedom to View policies. These documents allow a patron time to read over the information and digest it—potentially allowing for a cooling-off period for both the patron and staff. Looking over examples of written responses—along with the discussions on censorship Maureen has with her branch manager, Ravi Patel—will provide Maureen with good insight into the thought process behind why disputed items should be included in a library's collection. At the same time, Maureen can hold true to the professional principles that make her a great librarian.

Response 2
By Amanda Broyles, manager, South Georgia Regional Libraries, Lakeland, Georgia

Patrons objecting to library materials, while not an everyday occurrence, is common in public libraries. In this case, Helen, a patron of the library, is perusing the shelves when she discovers the book *Smut-peddling* by Lennon Lennox. While Helen maintains a calm demeanor when approaching the reference desk, she is adamant in her feelings that the book should not be on library shelves.

The reference librarian, Maureen, seems unsure how to respond when Helen demands that the book be removed immediately. She does not know what the policies and procedures are for handling requests for removal. Since the scenario specifically describes Maureen as working on materials selection and reading book reviews, this is surprising. Someone who works on acquisition should be passingly familiar with a system's collection development and request for reconsideration policies, at the very least. As a library manager, I would expect all front-line staff to at least know enough about these policies to be able to respond to patrons.

Acknowledging Helen's distress, referring her to the collection development policy, and walking her through the process of library material reconsiderations would have been a more professional response than the one Maureen gave. It is possible to acknowledge a patron's feelings without agreeing with them. Everyone who works as a library professional should learn how to maintain neutrality while making patrons feel acknowledged and understood. Maureen's response could have suggested that she agreed with Helen about the book. Personal feelings have no place in a library's collection development. Materials should be selected (and defended) based on how they might benefit the community. This is why every library should have a collection development policy.

Maureen's hesitation and lack of knowledge about procedures could also leave Helen thinking that the library is staffed by unprofessional people who have no idea what they are doing. That is not the impression I would want to make on a patron. Maureen would have come across as more professional and in control if she had simply stated that she was not familiar with the procedure for removing materials and called her manager right then. Instead, Maureen let Helen control the interaction, taking away Maureen's agency.

After speaking with Ravi, the branch manager, Maureen learned that the book had been ordered on a patron's recommendation. Ravi also informed Maureen that the book was well researched and authored by a local person. The book was a biography of a world-famous dancer who later became associated with the fetish photography that had so scandalized Helen. Ravi also reminded Maureen that two universities with strong dance programs were within twenty-five miles of the library, meaning that books on dance and those associated with the dance industry would be considered of local interest.

Ravi also reminded Helen that other books that could be considered objectionable, such as Hitler's *Mein Kampf* and true-crime books with pictures of horrific crime scenes, could be found on their shelves. Almost every library has books that could be considered "smutty" in the adult fiction section; *Fifty Shades of Grey* certainly springs to mind. However, our job as library professionals is not to judge books from a moral standpoint. After all, everyone, library professionals and patrons alike, will have a different idea of what we consider "good" and "bad," morally speaking. That's why "every book its reader; every reader their book" is such an important thing to remember. By providing materials for an entire community, there will always be something on the shelves that someone disagrees with in some way or another. This is just a normal part of working in a library, which is why policies and procedures are so important. It is much easier to defend a controversial choice when you have a solid collection development policy to back you up.

If I had been in Maureen's place, I would have checked on the procedure for book removal if I was unsure of it. For example: "Yes, ma'am. I can see that this book does have some images that could be upsetting to some people. However, every book purchased for our collections undergoes a vetting process to ensure that it is up to our standards. We look for materials that are well written, well researched, and informative. However, if you do feel that strongly about removing the book, we do have a procedure that we have to follow. Would you mind waiting a moment while I contact the branch manager to ensure that I give you the correct information?"

I would then confirm the procedures for reconsideration requests and pass the information on to the patron along with a copy of the collection development policy. I would also remind the patron that our collection reflects the needs and interests of the community and that every book will not be for every person.

A significant objection from Helen about the book is that a child might find it. I would gently remind her that biographies are shelved in an adult area of the library, lessening the likelihood of a child finding it on their own. Many libraries have an unattended minors policy stating that any child under a certain age must be accompanied by an adult. Additionally, public libraries do not act *in loco parentis*—meaning that parents/guardians are responsible for overseeing the materials that minors choose to check out or use. All of this should help Helen understand that the library is simply not responsible for parenting every child that walks through the door.

I would also try to redirect the patron after giving information about the reconsideration procedure: "Now that our manager is informed of the issue, he will look over reviews of the book as well as the book's usage stats. Our collection development team will also be notified, and our board of directors will weigh in as well. The branch manager will be responsible for making the final decision. Would you like to leave your contact information so that we can reach you after a decision has been made? And is there anything else I can help you with today? Were you looking for a particular book?"

This response informs the patron of the procedure, assures them that they are being taken seriously, gives them the option to stay informed about the final decision, and hopefully redirects them to a more positive view of the library and the library's collections by giving the patron the option to find something more suitable to their personal tastes.

I find Maureen's reaction to the decision that the library will retain the book to be most alarming: she is considering going behind the backs of the library administration and deleting the book anyway. The reasons for keeping the book are sound: well reviewed, moderately used by the community, local author, and scarcity of research on the subject of the book. These are all solid reasons to keep the book in the library's collection.

When presented with the chance to just delete the book and lie to Helen, I would hope that Maureen would use her professional integrity and relay the decision that had been made by the library's administration. Maureen should let the decision stand, put the book back on the shelf, and help Helen understand why the manager ultimately decided to keep the book. She can also explain further options in regard to formally appealing the decision that has been made. While I'm sure Helen would be disappointed with the decision, with a good policy and staff that are educated on policies and procedures, any issue can be resolved in a professional manner.

Response 3
By Helen Palascak, director, Upper St. Clair Township Library, Upper St. Clair, Pennsylvania

While typically a rare occurrence, a challenge to an item in a library's collection can easily escalate into a publicity nightmare for the library if it is not handled with prudence and sensitivity from first interaction to final solution. Given the potential negative fallout on multiple fronts, decisions typically are both made and communicated at the highest administrative levels. Additional complicating factors (minefields, if you will) in this scenario are the purchase suggestion that was made by a resident, the fact that the author of the challenged book is "local," that the library manager actually approved the original purchase himself, and how the decision to retain the item was ultimately made. All these factors need to be explored as well. Then there is the curveball the library page throws near the conclusion of the scenario: finding the Lennox book as a potential candidate for repair, opening another serious collection management issue.

First, as the newest librarian, Maureen obviously did not receive adequate training on the policies and procedures of this library, or the library manager was remiss in not providing new employees with proper training in the library's policies. Or, perhaps, the library does not even have a formal process to follow if an item in the collection needs to be reconsidered. As described in the scenario, this library system is large enough to have several branches, a staff entrance, and an administrative wing; it should therefore have a standard process to orient new staff to not only all the unique technical training needed but also to how staff are expected to interact with patrons, especially in conflict situations. Instead of presenting uncertainty, Maureen could have responded that the library has a formal process to reconsider materials patrons deem inappropriate or objectionable for the library. She should have had easy access to the library's official Request for Reconsideration of a Library Material form to give the patron. Along with this form, there would have been a copy of the reconsideration policy that explained the process, an expected time frame, and who would be contacting her to follow up. Both parties would have had a "win." The patron made her point. Maureen did her job, professionally and competently. Instead, Maureen was caught off guard. She was sidetracked by the appearance of the book and even more flustered and upset herself by the images inside. The patron took charge, provided her contact info, and left unhappy. Maureen's subsequent interaction with the library branch manager, Ravi, leaves her unhappy as well.

As a branch library manager, Ravi has operational responsibility for all branch library services. He has been there many years and amassed awards and trophies for his work. Yet now his office is bare, as if he were not intending to stay much longer. Is he still as engaged in mentoring his staff as he once was? His responses to Maureen are curious. It seems he recognizes the patron's name and then dismisses the importance of the complaint because she was not openly hostile. He is self-righteous in his support of the book. He smiles and claims, "This Lennox guy seems like an important figure." He is condescending in his smarmy comment that she will be excellent when she takes over acquisitions. He is flippant making his final point that it is more complicated than she realizes, that there is a process. Unfortunately, he never gets around to helping her learn how to handle a similar situation the next time.

Maureen and Ravi's discussion on collection criteria leaves critical questions unanswered. The once black-or-white debate over "published versus self-published" is not as clear-cut as it once was. More importantly, who exactly is the publisher of the book being reconsidered? Given that this book sounds like it could be considered an "art book," is the publisher well known and reputable in the field? Reviews for the book are good, but who exactly reviewed the material? Selectors know that there are many types of reviews. There are reviews done by subject specialists and expert professionals or by time-honored review sources, and then there are reviews that are anonymous or have questionable authenticity. Ravi mentioned that the author had provided him with the positive reviews, but where were these reviews originally published, and what were the qualifications of each reviewer? They could have been the author's friends or colleagues. There is no mention of either Ravi or Maureen verifying the world-class proclaimed "significant status" of Lennon Lennox. Is he listed in any survey of dance history? Is he in a "who's who of modern dance"? Why is there a "scarcity of research" on him if he has world-class status? The quality leather-like binding with embossed letters is totally irrelevant. "Nearly three circulations annually" is also not too impressive and should be compared with other turnover rates in the collection.

Other important basic collection criteria are not addressed at all in the scenario. For example, if we assume this is a public library, what is its mission statement? Does it include any description of the role of the nonfiction collection—such as to support lifelong learning? What is the library's official service area? Does it actually include the two colleges twenty-five miles away? Public library collections typically do not have space for specialized research of any type, even if there are institutions of higher education nearby, and instead focus on subject matter of interest to the general public. Most collection development policies include a list of covered subjects (i.e., cooking, self-help, history, art) and the priority given to each based on community use. Is there actually a category for the Lennox book, such as "fetish photography," in this library?

Exceptions do happen, especially when a local author gifts their work or expects their library to purchase their work, regardless of how it is published or reviewed. In many cases it is simply prudent to be generous in your thanks, add the item, and see if it will earn its shelf space. Some will, especially ones of local interest. Those that don't are quietly moved to storage stacks or deaccessioned when enough time has passed. Another exception can be a request by a resident to add a title. Libraries actively solicit this type of request, with new publications forming the majority of these purchases. Interlibrary loan is available to bring in the older, more esoteric titles residents request. One wonders if in this situation the resident requesting the purchase was somehow connected to Lennox. What is—or was—the relationship between Ravi and Helen Lucase or the book's author? Is Lucase or the book's author connected somehow to community officials or major donors? Ravi is right; this situation is complicated. Therefore, it is even more puzzling that Ravi opts for escalating the situation with a flat "no," the book is remaining in the collection. Period.

At this point, Maureen really only has one choice: call the patron and communicate the decision as matter-of-factly as possible. She should not voice her opinion but rather explain the appeal process to bring the matter to the attention of the library board if the patron chooses. Hopefully the patron will push back, tossing it right where it belongs—back in Ravi's lap.

However, there are at least two compromise options that Ravi and his team could have considered. Most libraries have a closed stacks or storage section unavailable for patron browsing. Shelving the book there would keep it available yet not accessible to browsers of any age. Another choice might be to catalog the book differently, moving it to either the dance or art photography section (probably where it should have been) rather than in the general biographies area where it currently sits. Either of these options might have satisfied Helen Lucase.

Collection development is an art and is at the center of library services. The first word everyone associates with the word *library* is *books*. Acquisitions librarians hone their skill set through experience, data analysis, a thorough understanding of their community, and a willingness to explore and follow up hunches. Libraries that appreciate the work that goes into developing the collection have strict procedures for removing items. All items. No book should ever be deleted and thrown out without review by acquisitions. The book the library page turned up with could be a highly used item that should be replaced, perhaps with two copies. It might be on a high school reading list or be a cult classic. If it is out of print, there could be a way to rebind it. Falling apart is easier to fix than grubby or dirty. It bears repeating, all potential discards should be reviewed by a well-trained acquisitions librarian.

Maureen's foray into banned books is slightly off point. Community groups get books banned mostly when the ideas and words offend a group pursuing its own agenda. This is a different animal. We can't know if *Smut-peddling* is pornographic or not, but we can agree this situation was handled very poorly by Ravi. He intended Maureen to respond to the patron from the beginning but did not include her in the discussions with the acquisitions team. He sends her an email (an email!) with the decision! He does not offer to review with her the best way to communicate the decision. He apparently allows any staff to delete items without any review process. He is avoiding operational responsibilities critical to the success of the library. More problems will follow. One might also hope Maureen is looking for another position.

Chapter Five

My Time Is Valuable Too

An Organizing Scenario Using Problem Solving

SCENARIO

Peter Esquerre, assistant library director of the Point Park Public Library, had only been at his desk for ten minutes before the floor seemed to fall out from beneath him. Having already read two messages left on his desk from the library's circulation supervisor regarding three Central Library employees who had called in sick earlier that morning, he now was confronted by Gabriel Rojas, one of the library's delivery drivers.

"Hey, Peter. It looks like our backup delivery truck just bit the dust. I don't think we'll be able to make any deliveries to the branches for a while. I just called the city's central yard about repairs, but they can't get out here until at least tomorrow. This truck has been threatening to die ever since the first truck bit the dust two months ago. I thought we were purchasing a new one?"

"We had to wait for the new director to approve a requisition for such a large expenditure like a new delivery truck. I think she just signed it last week. I'll check with her . . . if she ever appears in her office." Peter didn't regret that last remark. After a nationwide search had been conducted, it had been over two months since Cindy Meyer had been selected as the Point Park Public Library director. And during those last two months, Peter had physically seen Cindy in her office maybe a dozen times. He felt that most of the new director's time was being spent hobnobbing with the city's officials at City Hall.

"Well, what should we tell the branches?" Gabriel asked. "There's at least twelve bins of return books, patron requests, mail, and—of course—the paychecks!" He smiled as he waited for instruction from Peter, his direct supervisor.

"Call the branches and let them know there's going to be a delay and that we're working on a backup delivery plan. We'll get back to them soon. I have a meeting that Cindy scheduled to start in about an hour, and I'll run it by her." The phone on Peter's desk rang. He ignored it, letting the call go to voicemail. "What ideas do you have, Gabriel?" Peter asked. "Does the city have a spare vehicle we can use for now? Even if it's smaller, we can still get some of the important stuff out to the branches."

"A request like that has to come from the top level of department administration. They won't approve it if I ask." Gabriel also volunteered to call each of the ten branch managers and ask them to come down to Library Administration and sign for the employees' paychecks.

"I don't know about that. Hold off for now. Let me get back to you." Peter's voicemail alert light on his phone blinked persistently. He ignored it and called down to the circulation supervisor to get a status check.

The circulation supervisor, Barbara Smith, answered Peter's call in two rings. "Peter, we're in a bit of a crunch here. I'm just about ready to open the library. What's up?"

"Barbara, what's the schedule look like with these three employees out sick?" Peter asked.

"I think we're good in the morning; it's our least busy time. But this afternoon I need approval to call in some of our relief staff to cover dinner hours." Barbara seemed to be waiting for some official agreement or approval.

"Let me get back to you. I want to check the budget and let Cindy know before you call anyone in. Stand by." Peter thought to himself as he hung up, *It's not even ten o'clock, and I've already potentially spent thousands of dollars.* The library's budget problems were well known, but the entire staff had done excellent work in curtailing spending until a new director had come on board. Peter had been on the wrong end of many budget decisions with the previous director, and he wasn't about to get into hot water with the new one. For now, he got all his morning questions, problems, issues, and approvals ready to run by his director before the start of this morning's budget meeting with Cindy and the staff.

Peter walked into the conference room and quickly looked around. Cindy was missing.

"Shall we begin?" said the reference librarian, Maggie Dom.

"Very funny." Peter smirked. "You know we can't do that without . . . What's her name again? It's been so long since I've seen her, I think I forgot her name." As he looked in the faces of the six Point Park Central Library department heads convened around the conference room table, he shook his head. Here they were once again awaiting Director Meyer's appearance at an important library budgeting meeting. His anger quickly showed on his face. He blurted out, "Cindy spends nearly fifty percent of her time outside her office. It sure would be nice to get some direction from her every now and then. She scheduled this meeting nearly two weeks ago, and she's not even here. Her absence is really beginning to bother me!" Peter jumped up and retrieved his phone from his jacket pocket. He dialed the director's office.

"Point Park Public Library Administration. Can I help you?" answered Pam Sheppard, the administrative secretary.

"Pam? It's me, Peter. Is Cindy there? We're waiting to start the budget meeting over in the conference room, and she's missing in action."

"Oh, hey, Peter. No, Cindy called about two hours ago to let me know she'd be out of the office for a special meeting the mayor convened. I just left you a voicemail. Cindy wanted me to tell you that she'd moved this morning's meeting to four o'clock this afternoon," came Pam's nonchalant reply.

"It's been a busy morning, Pam. I haven't had time to check my phone." He felt his blood pressure rise. "Now I have the seven of us here and no leader. Our time is valuable too!"

"Sorry for the miscommunication, Peter, but don't kill the messenger. I'll let her know that this afternoon's meeting is on." Pam hung up the phone.

Peter turned to the others with a sneer. "Looks like we need to reschedule this meeting until this afternoon, folks. Cindy is at some City Hall meeting. I guess that outranks us."

Among a chorus of groans, Maggie Dom exclaimed, "Not again! I guess we shouldn't be surprised. This isn't the first time we've been left in the lurch. Look, let's just continue this meeting and make some decisions and give Cindy our thoughts." It was something that Peter had considered. He could conduct this morning's meeting, create a list of alternatives, rank them, and discuss some possible next steps. He'd meet directly with Cindy at the four o'clock meeting and update her on some of the staff's ideas.

The previous director, however, had been very hands-on and wanted direct input on everything. *Perhaps*, Peter thought, *I'm putting the cart before the horse.* He remembered one time several years ago when he had coordinated a meeting with his Central Library staff and created a Central Library collection budget spending plan. He and his direct staff had been so proud of the work they'd put in to ensuring there was collaboration and consensus in spending the dwindling collection funds for Central Library. When he'd presented that plan to the previous director, she'd gone ballistic, accusing Peter of trying to usurp her power. Was he putting himself in the crosshairs of another target? Even though he was sure his job specifications didn't preclude him from making decisions with his direct staff, Peter thought for sure that meeting without Cindy could likely be considered as some form of circumventing established lines of authority. He decided against meeting without the new director present.

"You know we can't do that, Maggie," said Peter. "Budget decisions can't be made without the director. She holds the purse strings and therefore the power."

Maggie felt Peter needed to remember he held power within the organization too. "You're well within your authority to make budget decisions for Central Library. Isn't that your job?" she said. "Of course, Cindy can override your decision, but who knows better about our library than we do? Anyway, Peter, it's your call. But whatever you do, you need to bring this lack of respect for our time up with her face-to-face this afternoon. We all made time for this in our schedules and adjusted staffing to coordinate with this meeting. It seems disrespectful to me that she cavalierly tosses that all aside to attend a meeting with her superiors. What about us? Our time is valuable too!"

As the group left the conference room, Peter saw Gabriel Rojas hovering around the door, waiting for him to come out. Peter walked over to him with raised eyebrows.

"So, I called the central yard," Gabriel said. "They have a small utility van we can use for the week. But you're going to have to call over to set this in motion. They won't do it on my order."

"I'm on it!" Peter returned to his office, walked over to the phone, and dialed the central yard. As he waited for someone to answer, Peter noted the blinking red voicemail alert light. *It's as if it's ridiculing me*, he thought.

"Central Yard. This is Eddie."

"Hey, Eddie. Is Ahmad there? This is Peter Esquerre over at Library Administration."

"Yeah, let me transfer you to his office." Eddie put him on hold. After about ten rings, Ahmad Amari, public works assistant director, answered the phone.

"Oh, hey, Ahmad. I was just about to hang up. Sounds like you're having about the same type of day I'm having," Peter said, playing up the "misery loves company" angle. "It's Peter Esquerre over at the library. I need your help." Peter had been to several city meetings over the years and knew Ahmad fairly well. While the two certainly didn't share the same duties, they did share similar titles.

"Yeah, Peter, I heard the library might be calling. We have a utility van that you can use for the rest of the week. There's a charge back to the department for operational costs. Not sure how much you'll use the van, but charge back averages about two hundred dollars a day. Hey, that's cheaper than a rental." Ahmad laughed. "Of course, the more you use the van, the more it could cost the department."

Resisting the temptation to say he'd have to get back to him, Peter told Ahmad, "That's fine. Email me the paperwork, and I'll send it over with Gabriel when he comes to get the van. Thanks again." The requisition appeared in his office within five minutes. Estimated costs were listed as $1,500. Before he could talk himself out of it, he signed the paperwork, called Gabriel up to his office, and set the process in motion. It felt good to have a least *one* problem solved this morning, even if it wasn't his problem to solve. Or was it? Before he could think on that question, the circulation supervisor, Barbara Smith, appeared at his door, somewhat out of breath.

"Peter, I jogged up here because I'm working the desk on my own, so I need to jog back quickly. We need to call in relief staff for this evening. I leave at five o'clock, and we have nobody to work the circulation desk this evening. If we wait much longer, the available staff pool may be empty. Can I have your approval to call now?"

"How much will it impact the Central Library budget to call in some relief?" Peter asked.

"About two hundred dollars if we can get two. But at this point I'm not sure we can round them up." Barbara was clearly stressed out and backing away to get back to the desk.

"Okay," Peter called out, feeling somewhat empowered all of a sudden. "Start calling in some relief." He felt bad that his lack of decision making in this issue may have cost Barbara time in getting adequate support. "Sorry it took so long!" he called out—not even sure Barbara could hear him as she rushed back to the circulation desk.

Later that afternoon, Peter and his group of Central Library department heads reconvened as scheduled. At 4:15 p.m., Cindy strolled in and was immediately confronted with a feeling of discontent. Peter rose, but before he could speak, Cindy offered a half-hearted apology—at least Peter felt it was half-hearted.

"Sorry, folks. It's been a crazy day. The mayor called a special meeting with the school superintendent and the education task force, and it ran way longer than expected. And then there was lunch. Before I knew it, four o'clock crawled around, and I jumped away—even though the mayor was still speaking! Anyway, let's get going here," Cindy said with a long exhale.

Peter finally broke in and spoke for the group: "Before we do that, Cindy, we wanted to bring this up with you. I think this is the fourth time that we've all been left waiting for you. We feel you're putting your professional priorities elsewhere and not valuing our time. Every time an important decision needs to be made, you're out of the office, and no decision can be made. Now, don't get me wrong, I know you're still fairly new in our city administration, and you are still trying to strengthen your coalitions, but we think it's time you place more focus on running the library."

Cindy was surprised. She looked around the conference table as the department heads averted their eyes. "Well, that's certainly out of the blue, so I have to admit you've caught me off-guard." She turned and directed her comments to Peter. "I didn't realize my absence was so problematic for everyone. Peter, you're the assistant library director. When I first started here, you told me that part of your job was 'making decisions' and 'managing the department heads.' If I have to do that for you, why do I need an assistant director? Now, I'm not trying to incite an argument, but I don't know where you got the idea that I needed to be involved in every decision. Remember, I was hired by the mayor and library board, and I report directly to them. Part of their specific direction when I was hired was for me to work to improve community partnerships and increase the potential for grants and outside sponsorships of library services and programs." Cindy took a deep breath to calm herself and then continued. "I promised the library board that I'd work my butt off trying to increase the library's profile in the city—especially in the eyes of those who hold power and money. The board felt the library was significantly underappreciated due to the previous director's unwillingness to 'get involved' in the city's business."

Peter listened respectfully but finally blurted out, "We get that, Cindy! And it's admirable that you've taken on that role. But what good will it be to increase the profile of your department if your department is unable to run effectively? It's like buying party favors for a party that's already over! And isn't increasing our profile and marketing the library really the role of the board?" Peter was on a roll now and decided it was time to lay it all on the line. "There are certain decisions that only you can make, Cindy, and those decisions are *not* getting made. Sure, I'd be happy to make those decisions for you while you're out rubbing elbows with the mayor, but I'm not sure the decisions I make would be the same ones you'd make."

Cindy threw up her arms. "Is that what you think I'm doing—'rubbing elbows' with the city's power brokers? I'm trying to increase our library's relevance not only to the community but also to the city because, frankly, the city's impression of the library—up until now—has put our continued operation at risk. Do you seriously want our library to miss out on the opportunity to participate in major city projects and initiatives in order for me to stay in my office and answer the phone? Do you want the library to continue to be an unimportant component in this city's service to the community? Frankly, I have heard some in the city's management team groan about the library being nothing more than a drain on the operational budget. I have heard others whisper about saving the city money by outsourcing library operations to a private vendor. Do you want that sort of talk to continue so that I'm available on site to go to our library meetings and run our day-to-day operations? How does that accomplish anything for our department?"

Just then Cindy's phone rang. "Look, I'm sorry. I have to run. This is a serious matter, and we will talk about it more. I'll clear my schedule tomorrow so that we can resolve this issue. But right now, the mayor is on the phone. I have to take this." She rose and left the conference room, leaving Peter and the group shaking their heads. Peter clasped his hands under his nose and put his elbows on the table. "So, let's all pull out our job specifications, and I guess we'll meet tomorrow to figure out where we go from here," he said. "Unless the mayor calls between now and then."

MY TIME IS VALUABLE TOO RESPONSES

Response 1
By Lisa Richland, director, Floyd Memorial Library, Greenport, New York

Communication is key to the success of an organization. Library management problems—like many portrayed in the scenarios in this book—usually boil down to someone's failure to communicate effectively. In this case, both the Point Park Public Library's director and assistant director's failure to communicate their expectations of each other's roles have created an untenable situation.

Many students do not realize that even the head of a city or county department has someone who acts as their manager. This manager holds them accountable to specific goals and expectations. Cindy Meyer, the new director of Point Park Public Library, had been given specific goals by her superiors—the city mayor and the Point Park Library board. Unfortunately, Cindy did not communicate these goals with Peter Esquerre, her assistant director, or any other library management team subordinates. Therefore, these staff members are left on their own to wonder what she is doing. Cindy missed the boat on letting her direct reports know what her expected role within city government was to be. She assumes that Peter will act as the library administrator in all ways while she spends time building relationships with City Hall and other agencies.

Without clear strategic direction or specifically communicated expectations from his new boss, Assistant Director Esquerre chooses to operate under the same expectations he had under the previous library director. The previous director was unwilling to cede any authority at all and penalized her subordinates when they made decisions without her. Can we blame poor Peter, then, for not wanting to act in situations like the broken delivery truck or the staffing problem? When employees are faced with decision-making and problem-solving uncertainty—such as trying to operate under the conflicting management styles of his past and current directors, as Peter is doing—they need to be given clear instruction and be provided clarity in terms of expectations. In this instance, Peter lacked this communication. Compounding the problem, Director Meyer has abstained from gaining any knowledge of her subordinates' communication needs, and she shouldn't be surprised at what her ineffective communication has produced at Point Park Public Library. If Director Meyer and Assistant Director Esquerre had taken the time to clarify their expectations and voiced their needs, they could have avoided the crisis they are in now.

Peter spends too much time feeling aggrieved, and Cindy becomes far too easily irritated. Unless they both take deep breaths and sit down calmly to set up expectations and new procedures, the library and staff will continue to suffer. Their situation isn't insurmountable, but changes need to be made right away. First, Cindy needs to understand Peter's communication needs. She needs to identify how Peter has been trained in the past and empower him to make decisions going forward. Cindy needs to find out what Peter needs from her. Is it written instructions he prefers? Or is he more comfortable with oral instruction followed up by a written memo? Identifying and using subordinates' preferred communication styles will empower them to be more proactive and far less uncomfortable about making decisions. Cindy should certainly set aside time every week to consult with Peter and review decisions he has made during her absence. Cindy should not do this with a sense of punitive malice but instead with the intent to support decisions he's made that she agrees with or to help him understand how and why she would have made different decisions.

Peter is undermining the library's leadership and must stop criticizing and verbalizing his dissatisfaction with Cindy to his staff. Instead he needs to cultivate a more positive and productive leadership style with his team, perhaps empowering them in the same way Cindy needs to empower Peter. She was not absolutely correct when she confronted Peter about his job specifications. As Cindy asks Peter, if she has to make decisions for him, why does she need him? The reader of this case understands why Peter is reluctant to make decisions, but Cindy has no clue. Peter hasn't made any effort to help Cindy understand his fear in this regard.

In many public libraries, or in libraries funded by public money, managers are—by policy—authorized to make budgetary decisions up to a specific dollar amount. If there are larger budgetary expenditures, the manager will usually need to take time to consult with a superior. In this case, if the budget decisions Peter needs to make fall within the parameters of the financial policies, he shouldn't hesitate. If the issues fall outside those boundaries, he will know that he needs to wait. It seems as if Peter and Cindy need to review this policy in order to clarify their responsibilities. It is more than likely, considering Peter's position on the organizational chart, that he should have had no hesitation to call in staff when needed and use the motor pool as necessary.

Communication is the key here. Right now, the Point Park Public Library is in shambles due to lack of proper communication at the top. If both Peter and Cindy want to correct this situation, they need to learn to communicate properly to each other, to their staff, and to the public.

Response 2
By Tammy Garrison, executive director, Ross Library, Mill Hill, Pennsylvania

The key issue here is the lack of clear expectations. The assistant director, Peter, does not know what to expect from the library director, Cindy, nor does he know what Cindy expects from him. Peter is still working on the expectations of his last director, who was a micromanager. Cindy is working on the expectation that Peter will be a decision maker, as Peter told her in their initial meeting. These expectations are not only vague but also incomplete. At what point does the director need to step in? When will the assistant director make decisions unilaterally? Will he have the support of the director if he makes a decision she would not have made? Based on previous experience, he does not believe so.

Lack of team building is probably what is causing the lack of clear expectations. The new director has not taken the time to get to know her team and establish those expectations. She is not available at the office enough for those expectations to be addressed organically, and she has never set a time for a meeting to discuss expectations with Peter and her other staff. This can leave staff feeling like they are waving in the wind, without direction.

Before making any decisions regarding this issue, there is some information that must be taken into consideration. Managers must have thorough knowledge of what the actual job descriptions and responsibilities are for their subordinates, and clarifying these could certainly benefit both Peter and Cindy. It would also be beneficial to have a list of what each party finds essential from the other in order to do their jobs. Job descriptions are important because they detail exactly what each party is supposed to be doing. A list of what each party expects or needs from the other is essential in identifying where actualities and perceptions may be out of sync. No one is an island at work; we all need things from each other: assistance, permission, authority, and, sometimes, for the other person to do the job they are required to do. Realigning these with what is actually going on is part of a larger puzzle. The person most involved in resolving this issue is the library director, Cindy. She is ultimately in charge of what happens at the library, and issues with staff and process flow are within her purview to solve.

Cindy has several alternatives available: one is to demand from on high exactly what she wants Peter to do in her absence. This is not a preferred option because Cindy would be making assumptions about what the actual problem is (keep in mind, the actual problem and the stated problem may be two different things). By resolving the problem on her own, she is producing solutions in a vacuum, without Peter's input as to what would actually help him. Peter does not feel empowered to make decisions. Ordering him to make decisions he's not comfortable making will only make the situation worse, as he's not comfortable doing what Cindy wants him to do.

A second option available to Cindy is she can stop going to external meetings and being involved in the larger life of the city. While this will put Peter at ease, because he won't have to make difficult budget-involved decisions anymore, it puts the library at a disadvantage when it comes to having a seat at the table with the city. This may endanger the library's existence, since it is not seen as a viable city resource by some decision makers. Additionally, one of Cindy's stated objectives from her own superiors is to be more involved in city activity, and this option prevents her from doing so.

Cindy can also work toward a more compromised solution that puts her in the office more often while empowering Peter to make the decisions she feels he is able to make, and should make, in her absence. Having the important discussion regarding her expectations for Peter, and also learning about Peter's expectations for the type of support he expects from Cindy, will make this possible.

It is this last option that makes the most sense for resolving the issue presented in this scenario. As assistant director, Peter will understand clearly the decisions that the library director, Cindy, empowers him to make. He will understand how much budget leeway he has before he absolutely needs to have her sign off on a decision. He will understand how she feels about making decisions without her direct supervision, and he will know how she would like him to report those decisions to her. He will also know that, if he acts within the parameters of her expectations, he will not face negative backlash like he did when taking initiative under his former boss. Cindy's style of management is different, and Peter needs to be made aware of what that new style is through the setting of clear expectations.

In a discussion of expectations, Peter should express what he currently feels empowered to do and how he feels about going past his previous director's expectations to fulfill Cindy's requirements. He can make clear what he needs from her in order to feel confident that he is making the best decisions for the library that he can make, within his authority. Cindy, then, will have the opportunity to reassure Peter about any misperceptions.

If I were in library director Cindy Meyer's situation, I would take several steps. First, I would ask myself why might my employee feel this way? What have I done that may have contributed to this feeling? What good-faith steps can I take going forward? Second, I'd hold a meeting with Peter. I'd apologize for unclear communication and unclear expectations but also make my expectations clear. This would involve reviewing job descriptions and responsibilities together and explaining specific examples of how I see those items being acted on. This would also involve a review of my own job description to explain how and why I plan on carrying out my duties. This would involve explaining the expectations I have been given from the library board and mayor. Third, I would block time in my schedule to be in the office more. The thing about a schedule is that if you don't purposefully carve out time for important things, other commitments will quickly fill those voids. By not attending a few city events, I would be showing my staff I am committed to them, and to their success, and that I am present to assist them. Cindy might also consider sending Peter to city events she plans to miss so that the library is still being represented and so that Peter can gain experience at this level too.

I would set regular meetings with Peter and other subordinates. These would help keep me aware of library issues and challenges and reveal how my staff resolve or manage them. If I learn of a decision that I wish hadn't been made, I would not focus on making it an immediately punishable action. Instead, I would give clear feedback as to why I would have done it differently.

Finally, I would look for ways to become more a part of the life of the library and the staff. This involves being present and participating. Getting to know employees better, attending social functions like office birthday parties, celebrating small achievements (like surviving a day without the broken library delivery van!), and listening regularly to employee feedback would bring me into the fold. Building better interpersonal relationships will help the library staff operate as a team more effectively.

Response 3
By Deborah Hicks, faculty member, San Jose State University School of Information, San Jose, California

This is an interesting case for many reasons. First, it's told from a perspective that many of us can sympathize with. It can often feel like leadership isn't there when we need it. And, as in this case, when we have to deal with incidents like those the assistant library director, Peter, and some of the department heads were confronted with, we end up feeling resentful and overlooked. Second, it pits management and leadership against each other. Peter is very much concerned with the day-to-day running of the library. The problems he is facing are practical and immediate. Library director Cindy, in contrast, is facing leadership challenges. She is not only advocating for the library with city officials but also attempting (and failing) to gain the trust of her new staff. Third, the case asks the reader to make a choice: side with either the assistant library director, Peter, or the library director, Cindy. In other words, the case is asking you to consider what it is you value: the smooth running of the library in the day-to-day or a library that is valued not just by clients but by powerful stakeholders as well. Fourth, it demonstrates how entrenched organizational cultures can become—even after a change in leadership. Many of the problems Peter encounters are not necessarily because his library director isn't around when he needs her to be but because the past Point Park Public library director was much more controlling. However, what is the key issue in this case? I would say it is a breakdown in successful communication. There appears to have been miscommunication between Cindy and the library staff from the beginning. Cindy clearly believes that she is fulfilling the requirements of her job. She was given a clear direction for her position from the mayor and library board when she was hired (i.e., improve community partnerships and increase potential grant funding). Given Peter's frustration with this situation, it's easy to assume that this direction and focus wasn't shared with the department heads at any point. Cindy just dove into her new role without taking the time to build relationships and establish goals with her own staff. Relationship building, in which clear and consistent communication is key, is the first thing any leader should do when they start a new position. By getting to know staff, the leader can identify organizational priorities, find out who is the unofficial go-to person for problems, "diagnose" the organization's culture, and determine where changes need to be made. In many ways, the ideal first meeting with staff would look much like the "Band-Aid" meeting we see staff scrambling to put together after the big blowup: a meeting where everyone comes together to clarify job expectations and roles. The problem with holding this meeting two months after starting the position is that Cindy has now allowed resentment, distrust, and ill will to build up among the staff. This will make building trust and establishing rapport much more difficult going forward.

However, Cindy isn't the only one at fault here. Peter might have legitimate complaints and concerns about Cindy's leadership style, but he is also in a leadership position. Complaining and making snide remarks to his own direct reports only serves to undermine Cindy and, ultimately, himself. Instead of airing his dissatisfaction with Cindy, Peter should have taken the initiative and asked Cindy how she would like day-to-day problems to be managed. Some of these communication issues might have been avoided by simply saying to Cindy, "Your predecessor was really hands-on when it came to financial decisions, so I'm used to checking in with the director when those issues come up. Is that how you'd like to continue handling things?" It is interesting to note that Cindy clearly regards decision making and managing department heads to be Peter's role as assistant library director. At the meeting, she isn't upset that he took the initiative to make decisions—only that he ambushed her with accusations that she wasn't doing her job.

So how might this issue be satisfactorily resolved? Peter and Cindy need to have a meeting to discuss each other's roles, responsibilities, and authority. Each one of these individuals needs to lay out precisely what they understand to be those roles and seek concurrence with that understanding—or clarification if there are any discrepancies between what each believes. Ideally, this meeting would be done in an open-minded manner with space for both parties to express themselves and listen, and both need to remain focused on the library's mission and vision. As noted above, this case asks the reader to make a choice between Cindy or Peter—or, more specifically, choosing between two goals: having a library that's valued or having a library that's well managed. Approaching problem solving from a "who's right and who's wrong" perspective will sabotage the resolution—someone is certainly going to be left unsatisfied with how things turn out. This does not have to be an either/or choice! In fact, it sounds like Peter and Cindy have the skills between them to ensure that both goals are achieved. But, in order to achieve those goals, Peter and Cindy must come to a shared understanding of the library's mandate and their respective roles in ensuring that mandate is met.

Chapter Six

The 38 Percent Reduction

An Organizing Scenario Using Supposition

SCENARIO

Paula O'Neil, director of the City of Fairmont Public Library System, sat with her forehead perched on her fingertips, eyes open, staring at her laptop screen, or more specifically, the subject line of the email she had just received from the city manager. When she saw the email subject line, which read "Recommendations for Reduction in Staffing," Paula felt sick in the pit of her stomach. Now—upon seeing that email in her inbox—that pit had turned into a bowling ball.

This is going to be bad, she thought. *Real bad.*

Paula had fully expected something like this to come through her inbox later in the year, but the timing was off. The city's budget process usually started with a budget message from the city manager sometime after the first of the year, or maybe as late as February. Department heads would then use the city manager's instructions as a starting point to amend or enhance their budget needs for the coming year. But today was September 10. The city council had seemingly just passed an operating budget a few months prior, and a new annual budget *normally* wouldn't need to be proposed for five or six more months from now. Why was this message appearing now? Adding to Paula's anxiety was the fact that the font of the email's subject line was in red. Paula didn't even know that was possible to do. She took a deep breath and clicked on the email to open and read it.

> To all department heads,
> As we have discussed at nearly every department head meeting for over a year now, you should already be well aware of the fact that our city has reported a fourth straight year of failing to meet revenue income projections—those funds necessary to sustain department staffing levels. Until this point, departments have been able to use a combination of staff attrition and retirements—both planned and unplanned—to manage budget shortfalls and allow us to avoid drastic cutbacks in staffing. Unfortunately, this year our city's coffers have been hit so drastically by loss of revenue resources that we no longer have such a luxury. In fact, the revenue projections for our current operating budget have come so far under expectations that we will need to reduce our expenditures immediately in order to end this fiscal year with a balanced budget. As such, each department is required to submit a proposal within the next seven working days for a reduction of

38 percent in your staffing budget. Obviously, due to the sensitive nature of this request, I am asking that you not discuss it with any staff at this point.

Paula had to admit, the city manager had a way of being both succinct and brutal in equal measure. This was devastating. She kept reading the reduction figure over and over in her head: 38 percent! How many actual people did that mean? Paula was director of a public library system that included ten branches and the central library. In total, the Fairmont Library System provided jobs for 142 full-time-equivalent employees. She did the math in her head as best she could, and—depending on the salaries of those eliminated—found that a cut as deep as 38 percent could mean letting go of between forty and fifty employees! Paula knew that there were a couple of retirements already in the library pipeline, and she knew of at least two employees who had already given notice that they were leaving within two weeks, but that wasn't going to help. While those staff departures would certainly make the cuts a tiny bit less painful, it still meant that dozens of library employees would soon be losing their jobs. Thinking about the cuts even further, Paula wondered about the long-term effects to the city's library system. It would mean a severe talent drain for years to come, as some of the library system's brightest and most productive workers would most certainly be lost. Paula kept rereading the city manager's email, hoping she had simply misread or misunderstood something. Unfortunately, her eyes were not playing tricks on her. She was, in fact, seeing the reality of a very dire budget picture. What the heck was she going to do? She didn't even know where to begin.

Paula quickly opened a program on her office computer that showed the entire organizational chart for the Fairmont Libraries. The resulting image was a big, confusing bundle of boxes and arrows showing lines of reporting and levels of responsibilities. Paula hadn't realized, until now, just how big her organization actually was. As she stared at the large chart on the computer, she noted the things that immediately jumped out at her. One thing she saw right away was the fact that the system's ten branch libraries accounted for the largest amount of space on the chart. The branch libraries were obviously where most of her personnel budget was going. She was, however, quite proud of that fact. The branch libraries accounted for the majority of the system's business, and they were the primary method of extending library services to the many various communities in Fairmont. Next, she noted the top of the organization chart, where she herself resided. The administration unit included herself and four other people. Marcy, who had dutifully served as Paula's administrative assistant for the last ten years at the library, was pregnant and would soon be leaving to raise her baby. The other three individuals in her administrative office were allocated to the library's business office and processed payments and payroll and the like, so Paula figured she couldn't cut there. Looking down the chart at the rest of the central library staff, she noted a facilities team, responsible for janitorial and building issues such as plugged toilets and broken lights, and the acquisitions/cataloging unit, responsible for purchasing and processing the library materials the public used. With a budget as dire as the one she was facing, Paula thought she could push most of the library facility problems to the city's public works team. If need be, she'd even buy a plunger and take care of any clogged toilets herself. Additionally, since there'd be little, if any, money to acquire library materials for the collection, the need for acquisitions/cataloging staff would be greatly reduced. She made a mental note to return to that idea later. So, in just ten minutes, Paula had already identified places she could look for potential cuts. However, in referring back to her organization chart, she could easily see that cuts in those two units accounted for *maybe* ten people. That left potentially twenty to forty *more* staff members to cut. Paula almost laughed out loud.

It was right then, as she was looking at that organization chart staring back at her from her computer screen, that something jogged loose in her mind. The thought came to her that if she focused on cutting staff who made the most money, it would mean fewer people overall would need to go. She could eliminate one librarian who made $60,000 annually or three library clerks who made $20,000 each—the savings were the same, but the cuts were far less drastic. Paula clicked a few keys on her keyboard, and the program quickly ranked staff by annual salary. The results were interesting. At the top of the list were all the managers at Fairmont Public Library. Leading that group were each of the ten branch managers, classified as librarian III. Below the librarian IIIs were librarian IIs, of which there were fifteen: one at each branch library and five others dispersed throughout the central library. The central library's librarian IIs acted as managers in the children's unit, the periodicals unit, the reference unit, the acquisitions/cataloging unit, and the adult services unit. The salary ranking after the librarian IIs showed a fairly significant drop in salary from the librarian Is to the paraprofessional library assistants. At the bottom of the ranking were, of course, clerical staff. There was something there in those rankings that she thought she needed to explore, but she just couldn't put her finger on it. Maybe if she kept looking at the chart, she'd figure out whatever it was that she was missing.

The organizational chart program Paula used allowed for various views. However, the default view was always with job titles. Maybe if she clicked the key that put employee names in boxes rather than job titles, she'd get a clearer picture. She regretted doing it the moment she saw the names of staff members who'd potentially be cut. So much talent. So many incredibly motivated and dedicated employees, all of whom brought their own skills and personalities to the library. She couldn't imagine looking at them with anything other than sadness if she had to tell them they were being laid off. Paula quickly wanted to change computer views again, so she clicked on the salary ranking view. She checked the salaries again and again and then did some math in her head. And there it was! If central library units were being managed by librarian II classifications, why couldn't the librarian IIs at the branches serve as on-site managers? Paula thought she was on to something big. She had a path toward her goal that might look bad, but it was better than catastrophic!

The next day, Paula spent the entire morning going over job specification and duty sheets. She knew the duties well, but looking at the list, she began to find many areas and responsibilities that overlapped within the librarian II and librarian III classes. She needed to know if workload at each branch was identical. Or, perhaps there were ways they could divvy up the work responsibilities, consolidate duties, and eliminate nonessential tasks. Paula took out her notepad and drew two lines, defining three columns. She labeled the first "Maintain," the second "Redefine," and the final "Reassign." She went through each duty performed at branches by either the librarian III or the librarian II, then allocated it to one of those three columns. It was clear that various duties were lighter in some branches than others, but at the same time, she could easily see that most of the librarian III tasks at the branch level were purely administrative work that could easily be consolidated or taken on by the other librarians.

Paula liked it, but she knew she would have to look deeper at the "Redefine" column. There were labor rules and compensation considerations she would have to carefully consider there. Managing schedules was one duty she had placed in that column. She could take the idea of a broader scheduling methodology, as if the library system was a single library, with each branch schedule managed as units within a larger whole. There were even online scheduling programs that she had seen at a library conference that could help manage the entire library system's schedule from one location. Paula found other purely administrative duties—

such as writing policies and training employees—that branch librarian IIIs were performing. These, too, could be easily consolidated to one place and one person. Paula was feeling energized, if not positively giddy, at how impressive this was turning out. She was interrupted when her office phone rang. She would need to continue to look for ways to make the librarian III positions irrelevant and unnecessary later.

"Hello? This is Paula O'Neil. How can I help you?"

It was Judy Sheppard, branch manager (librarian III) at the Fairmont Public Library, West Valley Branch.

"Paula, we have a revolution brewing here," said Judy. "The morale at the branch is sinking fast—you know the rumor mill—and I've been trying my best to keep energy high and focus on the customer. But you'll likely be hearing from a very upset West Valley customer soon who felt she was being treated very rudely by staff. I won't go into the specifics, but it's indicative of supervisory issues popping up all over the system, I'm sure. I think we're forcing change on staff too quickly, and customer service is failing. I've noticed it, and other branch managers have been telling me similar stories. We need to get on top of this quickly."

"Thank you for your candor, Judy," Paula offered, her mind on more serious issues, "but now is not a good time to talk. I promise we'll get together soon to discuss these, and other, issues further," Paula said, knowing that Judy may very well be out of a job soon. Paula hung up the phone and continued looking at her librarian III data analysis.

Several days later, Paula had her 38 percent reduction plan in hand as she headed to City Hall to see the city manager. Poking her head into city manager Phil Levy's office, Paula said, "You got a minute, Phil?"

"Of course," Phil said, putting down a small but delicious turkey sandwich he'd been eating at his desk. "I assume this is about the reduction notice."

"It certainly is," Paula said, but she sounded positively chipper about things.

"Well," he said, "let me have it. Convince me your department is so important that we can't cut a single position. But I'll tell you what, the police chief and fire chief were unsuccessful in doing that, so I suspect you'll be as well."

Paula smiled, an expression that had not been seen in the city manager's office for several days.

"I'm not going to do that at all," Paula said, "because I've got it locked down."

"You do?" Phil's eyebrows shot up.

"Yes," Paula said triumphantly. "I do. I figured out a way to make the necessary cuts to staffing. Now, I won't lie. This is going to kill us as a library family. Morale is already in the gutter. But I've got a plan to cut thirty-eight percent while not significantly damaging patron services or operating hours."

"It sounds like you have found a miracle," Phil said.

"Not a miracle. A slight reorganization."

She let that hang in the air for a moment, until she caught the look of impatience from the man who had obviously had a devastating few weeks.

"I want to move one librarian III branch manager position into the administration and eliminate the others. We'd just have one librarian III for the entire library system."

Phil looked somewhat stunned. "Explain how that works."

"Simple," Paula said. "We eliminate branch-specific managers, instead consolidating branch operations within the administration layer, so they'll be able to more closely align with my administrative staff and our work at the central library. Librarian IIs at the branch can act as on-site managers, referring issues to the librarian III if necessary."

"And how would that one librarian III position differ from your own?" Phil had asked a very good question—one Paula had not anticipated. She thought a moment.

"Well," she said, "I will realign a bit as well. I will focus on policy, coordinating with the library board, budgeting for the system as a whole, interacting with city government, applying for grants and such, while the librarian III—our new manager of branches—will handle the schedules, hiring, which I doubt we'll see much of, and many of the supervisory and performance issues faced at the branches. Day-to-day branch operations can be pushed down to the librarian IIs. It will free up an incredible amount of funds, and combined with attrition for positions we're losing in the next few weeks and a planned retirement in the department, we'll make our target. Oh!" Paula quickly added, "There will also be the closing of the Hartlove branch, so those positions will be temporarily eliminated or reassigned as needed."

"Hartlove goes dark next year?" Phil asked.

"Remodeling, yes."

"It's an elegant solution," he said, "but you'll need to flesh it out with HR a bit more, get further into the specifics of how duties fall and reporting chains. The last thing I need right now is labor strife. I'm already getting pushback from the police and fire unions. But, overall, I think this could work." Phil picked up his turkey sandwich and kept nodding approvingly. Paula, feeling a bit proud of her accomplishment, smiled and then walked out the door.

After leaving the city manager's office, Paula headed over to Hartlove—the branch she had managed years ago when she herself was a librarian III. Hartlove was the last of four branches to receive remodeling—approved from funds set aside in a capital budget a few years ago. Paula walked in and found Bev, Harlove's branch manager for the last three years.

"Morning, Paula," Bev said. "I imagine you've got a lot on your mind. I've been hearing rumors about the reductions." Knowing that the city manager had asked that the reduction not be discussed with staff, Paula simply smiled and changed the subject. But, darn it, other department heads were obviously spilling the beans because the news Paula was hearing from the rumors was actually quite accurate.

She decided she'd talk as vaguely as possible about the topic. "Yes, the budget is horrible. And there's a lot on my mind, of course," she answered. "I'm starting to firm up some plans, but we can't talk about it just now."

"How many of us are getting the axe?" Bev asked.

"A few, for sure," Paula answered. "It's the nature of us having to close the Hartlove Branch for the six-month remodel project. We'll shift some folks around, but some will have to go."

Bev wasn't letting on about what she knew, but from the question she asked, Paula knew Bev had heard something. "You're looking at doing something more drastic, though, aren't you?" she asked.

Paula looked away for a moment.

"What would you say is irreplaceable about your role as branch manager?" Paula asked.

"I manage the team," Bev answered, "and make the plans that they execute based on the inputs from you and the administrative team."

"That sounds about right. It's certainly what I was thinking."

Bev thought she could tell where this was going.

"Are we just not going to reopen the branch?" Bev said, terror edging in around her normal countenance.

"No," Paula answered. "We've got to reopen. We opened Hartlove because it was the most important neighborhood on this side of town. We need it." Feeling she had perhaps let out more than she should, Paula turned the subject to remodeling timelines and design ideas.

The following morning, Paula headed over to the Dennison branch and set herself up for lunch with Chris Hammon, the branch manager who had been with the system longer than any of the others. If they only kept one branch manager, it would be Chris. If Paula's plan materialized, Chris would be the new manager of branches.

Paula arrived in the lunch room, where Chris was already enjoying his lunch.

"You started without me?" Paula said, bringing her sack lunch in with her.

"Sorry," he said, chewing a leftover sausage from the night before. "I got hungry."

Paula took her seat.

"So," Chris said, "who are you kicking to the curb?"

Paula should have been prepared for this blunt-nosed question, knowing how Chris tackled even the most sensitive of scenarios head-on.

"Not many," she said. "But that's where you come in."

Chris leaned back.

"Bev called. We talked," he said, "and she thinks you're looking into the role of the branch managers?"

"I am," Paula responded.

"A branch manager is the segment of the branch library administration whose hand you can shake," he said. "We are the part of the team that understands the needs of our branches and the communities we serve. We manage that sort of understanding of our needs through three things: interaction with our staff, participation within the branch, and a full understanding of the needs of those higher up the chain."

Paula listened patiently.

"We," Chris said, "are the voice and advocates of our branches and our communities and to our individual staff—the plow that breaks the ground for the strategic plan's success within our individual locations. We are the ones who enable our community to experience the greater benefits of the higher-level plans."

Paula nodded, a bit stunned.

"Ultimately," Chris said, "we are the ones who bring your vision and the vision of the library board and city manager to our part of the world. Who else could bring all that out?"

"Don't you see the duties and the duties of the librarian II as a bit redundant?" Paula asked.

"Of course," Chris answered, "but every restaurant in the franchise has a chef, no?"

Paula laughed at that.

"Seriously," Paula said. "I went over job descriptions, and I found so much overlap."

"Sure, but at the same time, we're so many different libraries. Sure, we're a library system, but we're a system made of individual specialized parts. Hartlove needs to provide facilities for after-school programs that the rest of us don't. I need to make sure we're staffed most heavily on Wednesday afternoons since we get a flood of kids when the Catholic school across the street gets out early that day. We are fine-tuned machines, not blunt instruments, Paula."

"Okay, but don't we have that institutional knowledge captured already?" Paula suggested. "We know the paths each of our branches walk, wouldn't you say?"

"Paula, this is not a static universe. My branch is not the same branch this year as it was last year; and it will certainly be a different branch a year from now."

"I've got to cut. I've got to make the hard choices."

"Yes, and I hate that you have to do that. But the reality is that there have to be better ways than removing the interface between the motherboard and the components. We interpret and deploy, and that has to count for something."

"Of course it does. But weighing salaries and numbers, it's one of the least devastating of all options."

"Is it?" Chris asked. "I'm not saying that we're the most important aspect in this system, but we have a role, a role that wasn't created arbitrarily. There is a reason for our role. Has that reason been eliminated? You may find a way to shift some of the work we do down, or across, or up the organization, but you'll be sacrificing the ability of each library to settle into its community, to react appropriately and quickly to user changes, and to handle staff personnel issues. You're basically saying that there is a one-size-fits-all library service template. That might be true, but that template will be adequate at best and will soon push our branches—if not our whole system—into irrelevance."

"Well, isn't adequate library service better than *no* library service at all?" Paula asked somewhat roughly. For the first time she was beginning to question the validity of eliminating her entire team of branch managers. "That's why I came to you," she continued. "You get the ideas and never shy away from admitting there are no-win situations."

"Well," Chris said, "I'm hoping I'll be able to convince you that my insight is enough to keep giving me a paycheck."

Paula stared at the budget reduction forms. They had been couriered to her office from City Hall an hour ago, and she still hadn't done anything more than open the package. She had known that this would not be easy; she had the future of many families in her hands. She realized that she had been far too glib in her mirth at discovering the path to eliminating the librarian III branch managers. Even with that plan, Paula would still be required to lay off a batch of people—but only ten at most. Any other route would mean forty staff members would be out the door. Nearly 70 percent of her entire budget was staffing costs. Without the librarian III plan she had created, dozens of employees would be laid off, branches would need to close, service hours would be reduced, and expenditures on materials and databases would be cut 75 percent or more. Looking at the numbers that way, Paula knew there was a lot to be said for eliminating the librarian III branch manager positions and creating a manager of branches position instead. In fact, that would allow for far fewer people to lose their jobs, it would keep each branch open, and hours could stay the same. Whichever way she went, it wasn't going to be a kind set of cuts, but what cut is truly kind?

Paula had stayed up the night before, crunching numbers, reevaluating duties, looking at other options, and, ultimately, she kept coming back to the idea of eliminating the branch managers. But she could not forget what the branches had done for their communities in the time she'd been director of the Fairmont Public Library System.

Paula knew the options. She also knew that the 38 percent budget reduction forms had to be over to City Hall within the hour. She quickly wrote down her plan. She envisioned the calamity that would erupt when she told the staff. It was a no-win situation and a decision she would have to shoulder. She put the forms back in the envelope and walked them over to the city manager's office before she could change her mind.

THE 38 PERCENT REDUCTION RESPONSES

Response 1
By Mary Grace Flaherty, assistant professor, University of North Carolina School of Information, Chapel Hill, North Carolina

The Fairmont Public Library System director, Paula O'Neil, has a challenge on her hands, that's for sure. Her initial response and approach to the request for the 38 percent reduction of the library budget to be enacted within just a week, while seemingly expedient, does appear to demonstrate tunnel vision. It seems once she landed on staff reduction as an option for enacting the reduction, she didn't see a need to explore possible alternatives or gather more data before coming up with and submitting her plan. In her zeal to immediately address the city manager's unreasonable request, the library system director may have made some missteps.

First, as soon as she received the email, Paula should have requested an immediate appointment with the city manager (rather than "poking her head" into his office several days later and interrupting his lunch). If she has any allies in other departments, or on the city council, she should contact them as well. For the meeting with the city manager, she should be well prepared, with a clear agenda. The main points she needs to cover include why this *sudden* reduction, why the need for secrecy, and whether all the agencies are facing the same (thirty-eight) percentage of requested reduction. Surely the city agencies would be better equipped to handle this loss of funds if they worked together and there was a clear and transparent communication process. Is there a mayor to whom the city manager reports? If so—and depending on the outcome of the meeting with the city manager—Paula should make an appointment with the mayor to address these points. It is unclear from the scenario whether this library system has a governing board; if there is one, Paula needs to apprise them (or at the very least, the board president) of the situation as well. As active residents in the community, board members can be powerful advocates for the library, and they may be able to influence key players. Paula should also turn to trusted colleagues in her professional network for advice; perhaps other directors have faced this situation and can offer support and suggestions.

Before the meeting, Paula should equip herself with more data in a number of areas, starting with, if the library budget is passed or voted on by a library or school district, is it legal to enact such a reduction in the middle of the fiscal year with no warning and without voter consent? She should also collect data on services across the libraries within the system (i.e., What are the hours of use across the system? What are the rates of database usage? Besides the upcoming retirements we learn about in the scenario, is anyone else planning on leaving?). Surely, the more data Paula collects, the more alternatives she may find, and the better her decision-making process will be. After she meets with the city manager (and hopefully is given permission to share this information with senior-level staff, especially as it seems rumors about the reduction are already rife), Paula should schedule a meeting with all the branch managers to discuss the looming reduction and brainstorm options and solutions (e.g., Would staff be willing to take pay cuts in order to keep everyone employed?). They may have suggestions that she hasn't considered, given they know their facilities, communities, and service provision better than she does.

Additionally, Paula should try to buy time so that she can explore ways to increase revenue across libraries in the system (e.g., grants, help from donors, friends' groups, local foundations and nonprofits, opportunities for collaboration with other library systems, book sales—some, such as the Tompkins County Public Library in New York, have been known to raise hundreds of thousands of dollars) that can offset and/or minimize the needed reduction.

There are other details that bear examination. For instance, until she had to think about reducing the budget by eliminating positions, it appears that Paula was unaware of the larger structural organization of the library system. It seems that she was blindsided by the request for the 38 percent reduction, but the flailing budget issue has been discussed regularly at department head meetings for over a year. Over that course of time, Paula should have been making preparations by gathering data about library services and asking senior staff to prioritize those services, with suggestions for where they might be able to make budgetary adjustments if necessary.

Her interaction with her staff seems problematic as well. For example, when branch manager Judy Sheppard contacts Paula to discuss "a revolution brewing" with failing customer service and low staff morale, Paula is somewhat dismissive and exhibits an extreme lack of support. Even if Paula is busy and knows that "Judy may very well be out of a job soon," her job as system director still currently dictates that she support her staff and be responsive to their concerns for supervisory issues "popping up all over the system." If this example is an indication of her communication and management style, it will be even more difficult for her to unify staff for the tough path ahead.

Paula was given a mandate to create a plan for reductions and to keep it a secret. She very quickly compartmentalized the reduction and acted as if she was fulfilling a request rather than using the opportunity to start a conversation, examine organizational priorities, and galvanize her community and staff. While transparent communication, preparation, and anticipation may not have averted this catastrophe, they would have left Paula in a better position to respond to the city manager's request.

Response 2
By Julie Todaro, director, Austin Community College, Austin, Texas

Obviously, a primary issue of this case is the budget cut with which the director, Paula O'Neil of the Fairmont Public Library, is suddenly faced—and how to operate the library effectively with such a large budget cut. There are a number of other, perhaps less obvious, issues Paula faces, though, and they contribute to a difficult budget year. Adding to the complexity of the problem are some conflicting points the scenario presents. First, the budget figures are unclear. On the one hand, the city manager's directive states that cuts should come from each department's *staffing* budget, which is typically the largest portion of an organization's operating budget; however, at the end of the case, a number of other budget line items outside the staffing budget are listed, including both operating and capital cuts. Director O'Neil should advocate to have the latitude to include cuts from these other areas if they accomplish the required reductions the city manager is requesting. She should determine which budgets she will cut and in which variety of areas she will look for reductions. This should be the department's choice. It is more than likely that Paula will not be able to avoid cuts in the staffing budget—owing to the fact that staffing costs are the operating budget's largest expense—but she needs the latitude to determine what is best for the department while she strives to meet the city manager's request.

We are told in this scenario that all department managers were aware of the budget problems as they were discussed in every city management team meeting. Why, then, is it that Director O'Neil is so unprepared? Situational management practice dictates that a manager needs to prepare for a variety of contingencies. If Paula had paid attention in meetings throughout the year, she could have already enlisted the assistance of her management team in making this decision. Paula acts as if she operates alone. Even if she doesn't have an assistant manager, she has a large team of leaders in her library system. They could have created scenarios for the system. Paula should never have been caught unprepared. Budgeting the public's money is a serious responsibility of the director, and Paula seems to have been caught off guard.

There are other troubling aspects we see exhibited at the top of the organization chart as we read this scenario. Director O'Neil clearly identifies as having been at the library for some time, but from her knowledge of her system, she is unaware of so many things! For example, Paula seems to have no working knowledge of the position responsibilities of her librarian IIIs and the fact that the job description for this position is apparently outdated. Paula tends to believe that one person can do it all and appears to have a lack of knowledge and appreciation for managing a facility. She has no sense of the value of her middle managers to their branches and the communities they serve. Finally, Paula's blasé attitude toward the low morale, as well as the performance issues, at the branches points to a director who has truly lost touch with what her responsibilities are. While one can view all these troubling issues as the reasons for her cutting these positions, it doesn't make sense. These issues need to be dealt with, not swept away.

As noted earlier, it is not clear why Paula is making her cuts solely in the staffing budget, but it's a safe assumption that her lack of knowledge of the variety of other ways she could cut is a contributing factor. She certainly has not considered all the factors she could have considered. For example, are there any labor union issues associated with erasing an entire classification of her management team? Has she or the city manager solicited or included ideas or suggestions from the labor unions in meeting the budget shortfall? What about including the ideas and suggestions of other librarian IIIs? She could easily have asked some oblique questions of some or all IIIs, and, frankly, the questions she did ask in the scenario weren't all that oblique—especially if she was asked by her superior to keep the cuts quiet at this point.

So, given all of Library Director O'Neil's faults in approaching this problem, and her general lack of awareness of her library's and organization's operations, where does she go from here to get the cuts that her city manager is requiring? First and foremost, Paula needs to find out just how flexible is the city manager's request to get cuts from only the staffing budget. She needs immediate clarification of how much latitude she has in determining where the cost savings are to come from.

Second, Paula needs to quit acting as if she is alone. While there has been an expressed desire to keep the pending cuts quiet, it is clear that this is not happening and that the rumor mill has already started. Paula needs to seek help from whatever library system leadership or management team there is. The same is true for any library advisory boards or commissions representing the library. These citizens are usually community members appointed by city council members who can become strong advocates and ambassadors in helping the library better position itself within the budget negotiations and discussions.

Third, Director O'Neil needs to remember the benefits of making data-driven decisions. She needs to do much better in pulling appropriate data that gives her a more complete picture. She hasn't looked at performance data, branch usage, program inputs/outputs, nor position audits of the librarian II and librarian III classifications. She needs to evaluate expenditure data from previous budget years to determine how effective they were in meeting the organization's objectives. Paula needs to identify how her colleagues in other departments (police, fire, public works, etc.) are handling the city manager's difficult budget request. Finally, Paula can explore what other libraries have done to cut budgets and what benchmarks and strategies they used to make sensible cuts. They may recommend closing some library branch facilities based on data or investigating the feasibility of staff salary/benefit reductions rather than complete elimination of positions.

If I were in Library Director O'Neil's shoes, I'd have resisted the knee-jerk reaction to cut an entire classification—thinking someone else can do the work they were doing. Instead, I'd estimate just what a 38 percent cut represents in the library's budget; I'd need a dollar amount of what 38 percent means. With that number in mind, I'd gather as much of the data mentioned above as I could, and I'd call an immediate meeting with my library management team in a closed-door planning session. We'd discuss various scenarios based on data, such as "What if we close four of the ten branch locations? Does that get us to the dollar amount of cost savings we need?" or "What if we lay off x number of certain employees in the system.

Does that get us to the dollar amount of cost savings we need?" or "What if we do both?" Once my team and I had identified the appropriate path forward, I'd begin to build coalitions with community members and partners to help advocate and educate around the rationale behind the pending cuts.

Library Director O'Neil has taken a lot for granted in this scenario. She needs to begin to take her job a lot more seriously and implement a more participatory management style. These pending cuts will be drastic and will decimate a lot of what the library system has done in the past. As Paula O'Neil continues the day-to-day operations of her library system, and becomes more engaged in what is happening around her, she needs to start to design a method for continuing to offer one level of service while building the justification for future expansion of levels of service when her city's budget situation improves.

Response 3
By Jennifer Hovanec, digital and maker services manager, Indian Trails Public Library District, Wheeling, Illinois

In the scenario "The 38 Percent Reduction," the library director, Paula O'Neil, finds herself in a very challenging situation. She struggles with a decision that does not seem to have a correct answer or positive outcome. As the reader follows Paula through the decision-making process, flaws in her system arise. There are strategies and actions that Paula could have employed along the way to ease the burden of making tough cuts.

Paula missed an opportunity to proactively employ strategic change by not mobilizing and fact finding early enough. Now she's been caught off guard and unprepared. The city manager's email mentions that this budget shortfall has been discussed at a majority of department head meetings during the year. Yet, when we meet Paula, she is in a state of disbelief. Why wasn't Paula preparing her workforce in anticipation of the budget shortfall? As a leader, acting proactively exhibits long-range planning skills and results in reliability for your employees. Pacing changes efficiently over time is going to be more work for Paula than making sweeping cuts, but doing so is in the best interest of the organization as a whole. Applying strategy much earlier in the process would have helped Paula when the time did come to make her final decision. It would also have drastically changed the landscape in which the library was working, potentially making the final cuts more understandable. The first rumblings of budget reductions were a call to action to gather information, mobilize the existing workforce to collect data, and start making small changes that would not destroy library services or negatively affect morale. Paula could have prepared her organization for efficiency alignment over the course of a year or two instead of coming to a decision within a few days.

Paula, when she does take action, is operating from the most baseline amount of information. She looks at duty sheets and job descriptions, which are factual. But a list of activities and her personal perception are not really providing the broadest view of the organization; they lack nuance. In a normal situation, Paula would not necessarily need to have this view. She works in a large system, so she does not need to deep dive into the minutiae of each employee's day-to-day work. However, when making a systemwide decision, a broader understanding of what happens in each job classification and knowing the activities expected of those jobs at individual library branches would provide usable data. Paula could have invited the library branch managers into the process of reviewing duty sheets and job descriptions and gotten the necessary scope of information. Paula is not blind to the fact that there are redundancies. In the scenario, both Paula and library branch manager Chris acknowledge that there is overlap between some of the job classes. In fact, she directly mentions that the organization chart is a "big, confusing bundle of boxes and arrows." If it confuses her, how must it look to those who are inside the jumble?

The library branch managers are, in fact, Paula's greatest resource for gathering the necessary information. It is clear that Paula values their input when necessary. Though the email from the city manager explicitly asks department heads not to involve staff at this point, Paula does it anyway. She speaks in thinly veiled terms about library branch manager positions with Bev and Chris. However, these inquiries come too late. Had Paula brought alignment activities to her branch management team earlier, they could have had honest conversations about finding ways to unify duties across the organization, which is a much more reasonable solution than eliminating an entire job position across the organization.

The library branch management team could have executed a common task for each job classification in their library system: a time study. A time study allows a manager to take a sample of the real work being done for a defined amount of time. Then, the results are compiled and compared to give percentages of how labor hours are being allocated. Doing this activity for just a week would provide Paula and her management team a real idea of the work that is being done and provide data to assess how each position aligns itself within a branch library, within a job classification, and even within the library's priorities. Redundancies would surface, and there would be opportunities to streamline processes that even library branch managers may not be aware of. Trimming away redundancies and sunsetting services or realigning/reassigning job positions would have been a natural outcome from conversations with her library branch management team. Budgetary needs would have been assessed and contributed to the bottom line rather than draining from the city's overall personnel budget. Jobs may have been lost or adjusted in this process, but change would have occurred in smaller, easier-to-justify portions.

Early action and management team involvement could have also helped Paula to have a firmer handle on the morale and culture of her library organization. Her people are on edge about their jobs. Readers witness a call from library branch manager Judy that talks about staff feeling restless and low on morale; this is affecting customer service. Paula brushes it aside. Library branch managers are calling each other about looming cuts being made; it is clear that the rumor mill in Fairmont has been churning. Had Paula started acting earlier, being honest and open about evaluating the library's current operating situation, she could have better controlled the optics of the impending budget shortfalls. Addressing an issue, in whatever way that you can, rather than avoiding it completely provides a strategic approach to getting your desired outcome. In fact, approaching an issue with honesty may very well have the opposite effect; instead of lowering morale, it has the potential to boost morale. By approaching the budget shortfalls in a more political and timely way, Paula could have acknowledged the work being done by her staff, made thoughtful changes to align services to the community, and had more control of the messaging around the survival of library services being the top priority.

In the end, while Paula is handing in her final decisions, she knows that this is going to destroy her library staff. As a library director, Paula clearly cares for the organization, the constituency, and their place in the neighborhood. She is focused on talent and refers to her staff as bright and productive. Let's not pretend that any strategizing or collaboration would make the actions of more systematic downsizing any easier; to do so would deny Paula's humanity. Yet, what preparation and slow and steady change would have provided was evidence to her organization that these decisions were made from the best information available with an abundance of care and consideration. Paula could have addressed this situation more successfully by employing more timely and strategic change, gathering information with the help of her team, and controlling the messaging and optics of the library's current situation.

Though this difficult, unpreventable situation loomed, the best course of action would have been to exercise pragmatism and simply work to prepare the whole organization for the best possible outcome.

Part Three

Leading

Chapter Seven

The Mean Girl

A Leading Scenario Using Problem Solving

SCENARIO

Virginia Miles was nearly skipping as she entered the Bellview Library of the Genoa County Library System. She had had a wonderful morning. She'd gotten her kids to their school, picked up her dry cleaning, done some grocery shopping, and managed to get home to put everything away before starting work that day. *These are the benefits*, she thought, *of working only part time.* As a part-time employee, she had time to finish little chores and still be able to put her professional skills to use for part of the day. It was why Virginia had given up full-time work at a much larger—and certainly more progressive—library in a nearby urban community. She had been a part-time library assistant at Bellview Library for about two years, and she'd grown accustomed to only working three or four days a week for half the day. And today was just one of those wonderful days where she had accomplished so much prior to getting to her library that she was humming as she entered the building. Her mood wouldn't stay that way for much longer.

"Hi, Carol," Virginia said. "How's it going?" Carol, the full-time children's librarian at Bellview, waved back and greeted her coworker.

"Oh, gosh. Hi, Virginia. Is it noon already? Where does the time go?" Carol called back as she zipped over to her desk to retrieve her purse. "If you're here, it means it's lunchtime. And I've got a hundred things to do when I get back. See you in an hour. Oh, and, Virginia, be careful. 'You know who' is on a real tear." Car keys in hand, Carol exited out the staff room door with a wave.

Virginia knew exactly who Carol was referring to. Even if she hadn't known, she found out almost immediately when she saw Karen Black, Bellview Library's one full-time library clerk. Karen had the most unwelcoming scowl on her face as she glanced out at the library from her chair at the circulation desk. While this was certainly not unusual for Karen, Virginia noted that today Karen's scowl had an acute animosity behind it. She looked mean.

Virginia approached Karen with caution. She put a pleasant tone in her voice and quietly said, "Hey, Karen. How's it going?" Karen nearly jumped out of her seat, being jarred out of her intensity.

"Oh my god. You scared the daylights out of me!" she said loudly, causing some of the nearby library patrons to look up. "Hello." But Karen's reply wasn't a pleasant one.

"Is there something wrong? You seem upset. What happened?" Virginia asked.

"Mr. Peterson is back," Karen replied with venom in her voice. "I can't believe he's here. He was just here last night, remember?"

Indeed, Virginia did remember. The previous night, about five minutes before the library closed, Mr. Peterson, one of the library's regular users, had wandered through the library's door.

"We're closing, sir," Karen snapped at him.

"I thought you closed at eight o'clock," Mr. Peterson said. "I have some books being held for me. I just need to pick them up."

Ten minutes later, Mr. Peterson was heading back to his car, and the library staff were finally able to go home. As they were gathering their personal belongings and heading to the staff exit, Virginia had heard Karen telling Carol that maybe she should request overtime pay for the ten minutes extra she had to stay while Mr. Peterson got his books checked out. She didn't say goodbye to anyone before she got in her car, slammed the door, and drove away.

"See, he's back here just to rub it in our faces," she said now. "If he knew he was coming to the library today, he could have checked out his books now. Why did he need to inconvenience everyone last night?" Karen scowled out at the library stacks, watching Mr. Peterson. "He does that just to make our lives hell. He knows we want to go home, and so he shows up right as the library is about to close so we'll stay open and serve him."

Virginia had to admit that she thought Mr. Peterson was perhaps taking out a little vengeance on Karen. Maybe he thought it was all a funny game. She thought she even noticed a bit of a grin on his face as Karen looked out at him. "Don't let it get to you, Karen," Virginia said. "Remember, our posted hours are on the door. We can't close earlier than that." Virginia knew this wasn't going to satisfy Karen.

"But, Virginia, if you show up at a store three minutes before closing, you don't get served. We shouldn't have to stay late just to serve one person!" Karen glared at Mr. Peterson for a few more minutes and then returned to her backroom desk while Virginia took over duties at the circulation desk. Mr. Peterson walked up to Virginia, greeted her politely, and placed some books on the counter for checkout.

"Well, you certainly look happier than the mean girl," he said in a conspiratorial tone. "She's always so mean."

Virginia smiled and greeted him, but she didn't acknowledge the comment about Karen. She just asked him about his day, and they chatted a bit about a few of the books he'd checked out. Virginia wished him a good day, and Mr. Peterson left quietly. A few moments later, Karen walked up and asked why Virginia had been so nice to Mr. Peterson. "Why shouldn't I be? That's my job. You choose an attitude every day, Karen, and I choose to be nice. It just makes my day easier. Being angry takes a lot more effort."

"Thanks for the support," Karen said, then grunted and walked away.

Two hours later, Virginia noticed that Karen had returned to the checkout desk. "Oh, are you relieving me?" Virginia asked.

"Well, I'm not here to 'support' you." Karen chortled sarcastically. Virginia didn't acknowledge the comment and just said she'd be back next hour.

Virginia returned to her backroom desk to start processing some of the library's books when Carol, the children's librarian, came in off the public floor. "I'm glad it's quiet out there. It gave me a chance to catch up a bit. How's Karen doing?" Carol asked.

"I don't get it. I mean, I understand her frustration sometimes, but she can be so rude. She's been an employee of Genoa County Library System for years. I know that she's been assigned at the main library and some of the county's other larger and busier branches. Surely she couldn't have displayed this kind of attitude at those libraries. If she'd been this unhappy her whole library career, somebody must have noted it and tried to correct it. Over the few years I've been working here at Bellview, her attitude has only gotten worse. Bellview is a smaller community, with much fewer patrons. She should be happier, I think." Virginia looked over at the circulation desk. "And this is probably the third time I've seen her looking at the week's daily schedule. What is she doing?"

"Oh," Carol said, "she told me once that she likes to make sure that the 'on desk' and 'off desk' time is evenly distributed between her and the part-time library assistants. And if she feels it's imbalanced, she just pushes the schedule aside and pouts the rest of the day."

"Well, if she feels things are not equal, she needs to discuss that with Riley. She's the branch manager, and she assigns the hourly duties. We have nothing to do with it," Virginia said as she placed a label on a new book. "It all seems so childish. Karen needs to get a grip. She's bringing the whole team down. Not to mention the branch users. You know I actually overheard one of the kids leaving your story time tell her mother that she didn't want to check out a book because 'the mean girl' was there. The part-timers walk on eggshells around her because they don't want to make her mad."

"Really?" Carol exclaimed. "Maybe she has something personal going on. Have you asked?"

"Yes. I've asked several times," Virginia said, shaking her head. "She always says she's fine. She often says that she just doesn't appreciate being taken advantage of by the patrons. Or she'll find a way to blame it on something else. Once I was at the checkout desk and put some pencils out that hadn't been sharpened yet. I thought Karen was going to explode. She was so mad, grabbing them out of the pencil holder and taking them back to the staff room to sharpen them. The whole time she was saying how useless the pencils were at the front desk if they weren't sharpened first. When I came up to her and apologized, saying that it was my mistake, I guess she realized that she'd overreacted. She just said, 'I'm sorry I got so upset. You know I'm OCD about these kinds of things.' Thirty minutes later she's off on some other tirade."

Carol nodded in agreement. "One time before you were here, Riley brought some cookies in to share with everyone because it was my birthday. Karen came into the staff room and instantly threw a fit, saying that she had started a new diet regime and had asked—very pointedly—that no one bring in anything unhealthy as a courtesy. She said we all shared the staff room, that it wasn't just for one person, and that perhaps we should all respect each other's wishes. I mean, really? No one can bring in anything because Karen doesn't want to spoil her diet? Uh, that doesn't work for me, so I just ignored her."

"Maybe it's time I bring this up with Riley?" Virginia suggested. "I know this is a small library, and Karen will know that it was me that reported her, but I don't see any improvement, and I don't think it's best for the library and our community to have Karen acting this way."

"Well, I feel bad for her," Carol said. "I know she tries. I've seen her be very good with some patrons."

"Sure. She has her favorites at the library. But if she has to help other people in the building, she feels put out. And if the same person asks for help more than once, she thinks they're dumb or just purposefully trying to make her job difficult," Virginia countered. "She doesn't work harder than any one of us here, but sometimes I feel like Karen believes she's the boss. She wants to take charge when Riley isn't here, and she'll sit in the back room and crochet. If I bring it up, she'll say she's finished all her duties so she's just keeping herself busy until she gets back to the desk."

Carol glanced at the clock and started to put her supplies away. Before going back out to the children's desk, she remarked, "Well, I'm not sure Riley will be much help. She's talked to Karen before. Karen gets better for a while, but in a few months she's back to her old self. Riley doesn't seem to see the low level of customer service you—we all—do. But maybe you should bring it up again."

Virginia put her work supplies away as well and went back to relieve Karen at the checkout desk. On the way, she looked over at Karen's area of the office and noted a box full of glue sticks stashed in the corner. She went over and counted nearly forty glue sticks, brand new, just tucked away on a back shelf. It angered Virginia a bit because several weeks prior she had been assisting Carol with a children's craft time and had run out of glue sticks. When she went to the supply closet to retrieve more, there were none there. When she asked Karen if there were any more glue sticks left, Karen merely said that if there were none in the supply closet that they'd have to order more.

Virginia got to the checkout desk and alerted Karen that she was there to relieve her. "Oh, Karen, I noticed you have a whole box of glue sticks. We were looking for some the other day. I thought you said they were all gone?"

"No. I said if there were none in the supply closet that you'd have to order more," Karen said. "I need those glue sticks for my craft hour."

"But, Karen, your craft time isn't for three more months!" Virginia was astonished. "We needed those glue sticks."

"Oh, I'm sorry, Virginia. You know I'm OCD. You just have to be patient with me," Karen said as she left the desk and went into the staff room.

That was the last straw for Virginia. She'd had enough of this foolishness. Not only was Karen being rude to library users and making the part-time staff miserable; she was also hoarding library supplies for her own use. Virginia decided to meet with Riley the next time the two of them were scheduled to be working together.

Riley called Virginia into her office two weeks later, after receiving a note saying that Virginia wanted to talk to her about an important personnel issue. Riley assumed it was regarding Karen but wasn't sure. When Virginia knocked on her door, Riley motioned for her to come in.

"What's up, Virginia? How can I help?"

"Riley, for the few years I've been here, I've been increasingly distressed with the poor level of customer service that Karen has displayed. She's rude to many users; she seems unwilling to help them more than once; when she does help, she acts as if she's being bothered; and she continually has problems with the daily schedule." Virginia went on to discuss several instances as examples. "She actually confronted me once about the amount of vacation time I was taking. And when I got back to the library, she spent every minute telling me about how bad it was working with a substitute and that it's so much easier for her when I'm here."

"I've been aware that she's unhappy, but I want us all to work as a team. We should make it easy for one another." In Virginia's mind, Riley was clearly trying to avoid confrontation. *But sometimes it's worse to avoid confrontation than to just face it head on*, she thought. So Virginia recounted several of the most recent transgressions Karen had inflicted on the staff. She ended with the glue stick incident.

"I mean, don't you find that passive-aggressive behavior, Riley?" Virginia asked. "Here we were in the middle of a craft time with the children and in desperate need of those glue sticks. Karen obviously knew she had some stashed away, and yet she chose to keep quiet so we couldn't have them. How is that working as a team?"

Riley nodded her head in tacit agreement. "Well, couldn't you just order more glue sticks or consider a craft that uses something else? Make the job easier for everyone." Riley smiled. "If we order more glue sticks, we'll have enough for everyone."

"Sure, that would perhaps have helped for future craft programs. But in that moment, we were stuck in the lurch. But glue sticks are not the big issue, Riley. Karen's lack of teamwork and her customer service outlook are definitely what I see as problematic. I just wanted you to know about Karen's attitude and what it's doing to the patrons and the rest of the staff," Virginia said. "If you haven't noticed, the morale here is pretty bad, and Karen is most likely the issue, not the glue sticks."

Riley listened for another hour as Virginia explained several recent problems. She also was a bit surprised to hear Virginia tell her that Karen was being somewhat negative in regard to library innovation.

"Yes!" Virginia said. "You know I came to this library from a bigger library. We had much less restrictive policies and rules. We had staff that seemed to embrace change and productivity. But when we bring these ideas up with Karen, she immediately shoots them down, saying they're too expensive, or too messy, or that they wouldn't work at our library. She thinks library service is about books and only books, and she puts everyone else down for trying to think of ways our library can be more attractive or useful to our community." Virginia could see Riley nodding.

"Well, thank you, Virginia. Let me think about this for a while. I'll talk to some of the other staff and see what they say." Riley promised she'd do whatever she could to make it better. She walked Virginia to the door and said she'd talk to other staff and meet with Karen. But as she left the office and heard the door close behind her, Virginia didn't really believe Riley had a good idea of how to get the library to a better place. She'd wait and see what happened and take it to a higher level if there wasn't any improvement. She'd give Riley the benefit of the doubt. She just hoped that Riley had it in her.

THE MEAN GIRL RESPONSES

Response 1
By Rachel Fuller, adult and youth services director, Urbana Free Library, Urbana, Illinois

In this scenario, two main problems need to be addressed:

- library clerk Karen's interactions with patrons and colleagues
- branch manager Riley's avoidance of this specific situation and of conflict in general

Karen's interactions with patrons and colleagues are based on her perceptions of the library as an institution and the role she plays as an individual employee. Unfortunately for Karen, her behavior is at odds with that expected by colleagues and (at least some) patrons. At the same time, Riley's unwillingness to hold Karen accountable for her behavior has produced an environment that is at times unpleasant for everyone. To move forward in this situation, I recommend that branch manager Riley consider the following suggestions.

Riley needs to reflect on her tendency to avoid conflict and recognize the incompatibility between that tendency and the ability to provide effective leadership in this situation and others. How can Riley become more comfortable with confrontation in general? And what actions does she need to take in this case, specifically, to address the issue?

Riley may find that she needs to prepare thoroughly for her meeting with Karen. What evidence can Riley provide to demonstrate that Karen needs to change her behavior? What expectations for Karen's interactions with patrons and colleagues will Riley set? And, if Karen opts to ignore these expectations, what consequences are appropriate (and which ones will Riley be willing to follow through on)? Since Riley and Karen's past conversations have resulted in no long-term change on Karen's part, what will Riley do differently during this conversation? And what will Riley do differently in the weeks and months ahead?

Riley may find during her reflection that the library as a whole lacks clarity regarding patron service standards. Does every staff member know what constitutes good patron service? Are all staff providing consistent patron service in terms of programming, circulation, reference, and reader's advisory? If not, what tools and systems can Riley call on to develop and implement training that will enable everyone to know what good patron service is and how to deliver that service? Riley may also want to check in with her fellow branch managers to see whether other branches (or even the whole Genoa County Library System) may be interested in training.

I recommend that library clerk Karen consider the following suggestions. When Riley and Karen meet, Riley's message is likely to be a difficult one for Karen to receive. When Karen leaves the meeting, she should know both the immediate actions expected from her as well as the actions expected from her in the long term. In other words, Karen should know what success looks like moving forward. Karen should also know what to expect if she chooses to ignore the expectations Riley has set. If Karen is unclear on expectations or consequences, she needs to ask about them promptly and directly.

Assuming Karen is interested in rising to Riley's expectations, she will need to reflect on how she has seen her role and the role of the library over the past years. What, specifically, about her perceptions may have contributed to her treating patrons and colleagues discourteously? How can Karen meet Riley's expectations while also repairing her relationships with patrons and colleagues?

Since Karen's behavior has been discourteous—at least at times—over the past years, she should plan, specifically, how she will begin anew. What will she say, and how will she conduct herself? And when she falls into old behavior patterns, how will she acknowledge the pattern and self-correct? Karen may find it helpful to consider the parts of her work she finds most fulfilling and rewarding. How can she embrace these parts of her job and use them as fuel for the parts she finds less fulfilling?

To prevent a situation such as the one we see in this scenario from happening again, the library as a whole will need to develop an organizational culture in which everyone in the library is focused on providing good service to patrons and respectful interaction with colleagues. A culture such as this one is built on clarity of mission, trust, and accountability. As the library's manager, Riley is tasked with implementing and leading this type of a culture shift, and each staff member must be held responsible for shifting the service they provide individually to patrons and colleagues. Once the culture shift is underway, the entire team should meet regularly to reflect on—and continually work at—providing good service. In short, providing good service will become a "practice" and a norm of the library's culture.

Response 2
By Theresa Mai, patron services manager, Fort Lupton Public and School Library, Fort Lupton, Colorado

A Systemwide View

There is something wrong with the organizational culture of this library, and it's likely not limited to the branch library that is the focus of the scenario. Branch manager Riley needs to work with the library system's director and other branch managers to ensure that the culture of each library—including her own—is positive, empowered, and supportive. It is time for this management team to evaluate each library's working environment and identify issues that are counterproductive to the library's mission. This will reduce the negative chatter, backstabbing, and gossip about coworkers infesting this branch library. If the sort of things described in the scenario are happening in the branch, it is very likely that the entire system team is not working together successfully. Having quarterly or semiannual team-building events will help to support all staff. These programs allow teammates to see each other as people, friends, and partners rather than as just coworkers. These sorts of events can also help uncover festering issues and find ways to correct them in a positive manner. Team-building exercises do not have to be expensive, all-day events. There are many resources available in print and online that offer games and projects that can be done in an hour or so that support building a more cohesive team. If the issues affecting the team are serious enough (as they seem to be in this scenario), and if resources allow, it might be even more productive to seek the assistance of a professional outside training consultant to help the library managers tackle, and resolve, tougher conflicts in this regard.

Sticking to the Actual Events at This Branch

Branch manager Riley needs to be far more proactive in engaging in what is happening with her staff and patrons. She needs to ensure that customer service is a top priority. She needs to make sure that her staff know that everyone who walks in the library's door is a customer—that includes patrons *and* coworkers.

Courtesy and consistency are paramount when dealing with the public. Situations that are seen or overheard by others are impactful, even if they are not reported to management. Anyone who sees or hears an altercation between staff—for example, the one we witness in the scenario—would begin forming negative opinions about what they've witnessed. The three employees presented in this situation are not being professional. They are rude to customers and to each other, and they spend far too much time gossiping about each other. Riley would (and should!) know this if she was more engaged in what was happening with her staff. Riley needs to spend time on the library's public service desks with the staff and patrons, modeling the exemplary customer service she expects and correcting or redirecting any poor behavior she identifies.

Looking at Specific Incidents

Carol does not allow Virginia to form her own opinion of Karen's mood when we first meet them. Instead, she colors Virginia's mind by saying "you know who" is in a mood. This sort of petty talk should not be tolerated. Next, we are offered a detailed backstory involving Karen and a male patron who may (or may not) be arriving late at the library to make Karen angry. We are only hearing one side of a potentially lopsided story. Working in a library, we are seldom privileged to backstories, nor do we always completely understand why some staff react the way they do. Library staff have to work with each situation as it arises. Carol and Virginia need to be more professional and refrain from evaluating others' mood. Instead, they should look to support the patrons and even support Karen by helping her deal with, and maybe improve, her work-related behaviors at the circulation desk. It would be easy and cliché to say Karen is the culprit here. She is not. Instead, she is just one character reacting to something happening within a far more complex, and toxic, work environment.

Talking about the Minutia

If Virginia wanted to talk to Riley about her issues with Karen, she should have done so immediately. Waiting two weeks dilutes the impact of any behavior redirection. The fact that Virginia has waited so long leads to a suspicion that Virginia does not trust or respect Riley as the branch manager. This is further demonstrated by the gossip about Riley and the closing comments: "She'd give Riley the benefit of the doubt. She just hoped that Riley had it in her." Both of these thoughts illustrate a lack of trust and respect.

Another incident to consider in the scenario is the trouble with the programs, crafts, and supplies. There needs to be clearly documented expectations regarding library programs. The lack of documented expectations and policy is another indication that there is a systemwide problem within this library. Staff at this library seem to have no direction or purpose in planning their programs. The incident regarding counting the glue sticks seems designed to manipulate and trap Karen. We are privy to some backstory here, but not all of it. Has this branch library had issues of running out of supplies for crafts in the past? Is there a policy regarding when and how early to order supplies? How are the library's supplies organized, and who can access them? Did Karen order the forty glue sticks specially for a program of her own? Why would anyone order and set aside supplies for a craft three months early? These are all logistic issues that need to be addressed and that point to a library system in need of policy and planning.

In the incident involving Karen and the gentleman who arrives at the library just before closing, we see an indication that patrons are not completely aware of staff expectations. Library staff must always ensure that our patrons know how to use the library correctly and outline the best way to meet our expectations. Some libraries sound a gong or make an announcement ten to fifteen minutes before closing. If a patron comes into the library within that closing timeframe, they should get a polite, gentle reminder of the library's operating hours. They should also be clued in to why it is necessary to come prior to certain times if they expect certain services. As staff assist a patron to complete a task at the last minute, a simple reminder of why it is important to meet certain expectations should be offered. Staff members, for example, could state that "in order to allow staff to secure the building and put cash away, we have turned off our computers. Therefore, we ask that you keep this in mind the next time you come to the library." Offering good customer service in this way lets the patron know you are paying attention to their needs while at the same time outlining the proper way they can meet library expectations in the future.

As noted earlier, it is often too simple to look for a single villain in scenarios such as this. Clearly, the reader is expected to see Karen in this way. She is not completely wrong. Nor are her work colleagues completely right. It is the collective team that shares the real burden of fault here. However, a properly trained library staff, and one that has been given the tools to embrace customer service at all levels, will take personal ownership of what happens in their work environment. Branch manager Riley and her colleagues at the system level need to take control now to build a more effective team and make this library a more supportive one for all its staff.

Response 3
By Cari Rerat, director, Pryor Public Library, Pryor, Oklahoma

I'm the director of a rural library serving just about ten thousand people in northeast Oklahoma. With our small staff (six full-time and five part-time employees) in such a small community, we cannot afford to have a staff member who is consistently giving poor customer service or who drags staff morale down the tubes.

There are two key issues needing to be addressed in this scenario. First, there is the fact that customer service appears to be lacking from library clerk Karen Black; second, Karen's attitude toward her coworkers is harming staff morale. Each is equally serious.

A first step in problem solving requires that we look at the context/influences of the problem. Unfortunately, context/influence for the problem described in this scenario isn't really clear and requires some investigation. Library clerk Karen mentions twice in this scenario that she is "OCD," so perhaps there is a diagnosis that library branch manager Riley needs to be made aware of and make reasonable accommodations for? What might be going on in Karen's personal life? Riley doesn't need details but should be aware of any major personal issues (e.g., divorce, death, financial struggles) that might be influencing work performance. Karen's work history seems problematic. She has apparently been moved several times around the county's library system, and she seems very unhappy at her current library assignment. Karen constantly checks the library's daily desk assignments and seems unwilling to be at public desks. All of this context seems to point to the fact that Karen's library clerk assignment at this branch library is not a good fit for her.

In addition to Karen's own situation, the library branch's manager, Riley, should address how and why the rest of the staff perceives Karen the way they do. The part-time library assistant, Virginia, clearly doesn't like Karen (she spent more than an hour complaining about Karen in Riley's office). We can assume the children's librarian, Carol, feels similarly. The staff may have already passed final judgment on Karen. So, the main question to answer here is whether the rest of the staff can support Karen even if/when she is able to adjust her attitude and customer service. Has it gotten so bad that Karen will be seen as a "mean girl" no matter what she does? Or will the other staff members allow Karen the benefit of the doubt if/when she works to provide better customer service and display a better attitude? This is a balance Riley will need to seek to achieve.

If I was managing this issue in my library, I would approach finding a balanced solution from several angles. First, I would start spending some more time on the floor—either working the desk or working on a laptop where I can observe the interactions between staff and patrons. I need to know what's actually happening and not just what one employee says is happening. Riley has abandoned her staff by staying in her office and not seeing or reacting to things happening around her.

Second, assuming I can confirm what the library assistant, Virginia, has expressed, I would formally speak to Karen. The conversation would start with the question, "Is everything okay, Karen? I have observed, and some staff members have expressed concern over, your interactions with patrons and other staff, so I want to make sure you're okay." Then I'd look for Karen to be the primary driving force for whatever change is going to occur. But I'd forcefully impact on Karen that a change will need to happen since the current behavior is unacceptable. This would all be documented and subsequent steps articulated.

My job as a manager is to let my employees know what I expect from them and then to give them the tools necessary to do what I've asked. I expect my staff to deliver good customer service to our community, and I expect them to behave professionally toward one another.

Everything we do in the library is customer service oriented. Whether it is frontline staff interacting face-to-face with patrons; behind-the-scenes staff selecting, cataloging, preparing, and mending materials; or managerial staff overseeing the entire operation, we are here to serve our communities. Every job within the library has that same goal. Riley could do well to adopt and model this same behavior. But she can't do this by squirreling herself away in her office.

Chapter Eight

Challenging the Challenged

A Leading Scenario Using Difficult Professional Topics

SCENARIO

"There's some psycho lady in the parking lot!"

The library assistant, Karyann Miller, looked up from her task of checking in returns at the check-in desk to see an elderly woman staring at her. "I'm sorry," Karyann said. "What was that?"

The lady, who Karyann recognized as one of the Midtown Branch Public Library's regular patrons, repeated herself. "I said, there's some psycho lady in the parking lot. I was just driving into the library's lot and noticed her walking up and down the rows of cars, waving her arms in the air, and checking to see if any car doors were unlocked. Earlier this morning I saw her over by the market standing on the sidewalk just screaming. So, when I saw her in the parking lot, I wasn't sure I wanted to get out of my car. Now she's just walking around muttering to herself and trying to open car doors."

Karyann picked up the desk phone near her computer and called the reference librarian, Brian Smith. "Brian?" Karyann looked across the library to make eye contact with him. "One of our library patrons just told me that there's a crazy person in the parking lot trying to open doors. It sounds like Trash Bag Lady is back." Karyann was referring to the nickname they'd all given a person they were quite familiar with. As she looked over at Brian, she watched him rise out of his chair and look—as best he could—through the library's windows toward the parking lot.

"I don't see anything," Brian said. Just then, they heard a commotion coming from the library's lobby. "Never mind. I think she's inside now." Brian hung up the phone, and Karyann did the same. Brian left the reference desk to check what was happening and noted to himself how the commotion was getting louder. He arrived in the lobby to see a black woman entering the library's restroom carrying several large garbage bags full of what he assumed were aluminum cans. Another library patron approached Brian and told him, "Wow, she's a real nut case. She started yelling at me about trying to take her bags." The patron went into the library, shaking her head and vocally complaining about the "nuts" that come into the library all day.

Brian stood in the library lobby and kept his eyes on the restroom door. He heard the woman inside, presumably moving her bags around and flushing the toilet. He turned back to look inside the library to check the reference desk and noticed the patron who had just passed him was now standing at the desk. Brian left the lobby to go see how he could help the patron. The patron needed some stock market information, which Brian was able to retrieve from the internet. About ten minutes later, he returned to the library's lobby only to see that the restroom was still locked, and the woman was still inside. He heard the faucet turning off and on and the garbage bags of aluminum cans shuffling from side to side. Brian knocked on the restroom door and identified himself.

"Hello? This is Brian on the library staff. Is everything okay? There are other patrons needing to use the restroom. Do you need help?" He waited for a response. When none came, Brian knocked again and this time loudly said, "Hello? If you don't answer, I'm going to have to send a library staff member in to check on you. Hello?" Again, there was no answer. Brian walked back inside the library and went to his branch manager's office.

The Midtown Branch Public Library manager, Cindy Magyar, was sitting in her office when her door opened. Brian Smith poked his head inside. "Hi, Brian. What's up?" she said.

"Cindy, I need your assistance out in the lobby. There's a homeless lady in the public restroom, and she has the door locked and isn't responding. I've called out to her several times. I told her that someone was coming in to check on her."

Cindy slammed her hands down on the desk. "This is getting out of hand!" She grabbed her master keys and followed Brian to the lobby. When they arrived at the restroom door, Cindy knocked loudly. "Hello! I'm coming in," she called out, and she put the key in the lock and opened the door. Brian stood just outside the door. As Cindy opened the door, it hit one of the lady's bags of aluminum cans, and the contents spilled out.

"What are you doing?" the lady cried. "You're spilling everything!" Cindy saw the black woman sitting on the baby changing station, leaning over the restroom sink, holding a wet wig, and pulling clumps of hair out of it, letting the hair fall in a mound on the floor.

"No, what are *you* doing?" Cindy yelled back. "You can't sit on that table. You'll break it! And you're making a mess in this public facility." Brian entered to offer support, adding that he had called in to ask her if she was all right and that she had been in the restroom with the door locked for nearly fifteen minutes. "This is unacceptable!" Cindy said. "You need to leave this building immediately or I will call the police to escort you out. I've talked to you about this sort of behavior several times. I'm not letting you take over this library."

"Why are you picking on me?" the black woman said, staring daggers at Cindy and Brian. "Oh, you're racist. You're trying to get rid of black people. Ain't this a public building? I can be here. I'm part of the public. You just don't like black people."

"You need to leave now!" Cindy said as forcibly as she could. "All day long I'm getting complaints about people harassing library patrons. You need to get out, and take this mess with you!" Cindy instructed Brian to go and call the city's police.

The black woman started screaming obscenities, but she gathered her detritus, pushed past Cindy, and left. "You are all racist!" the lady screamed as she barged out the library's doors.

Cindy caught Brian as he was dialing the police and told him that the woman had left. "Let them know she has left the library. They might want to keep an eye on her. She's belligerent and likely dangerous." Cindy went back to her office to resume her day.

It wasn't even a month later when Cindy was confronted with a similar episode. Library assistant Christopher Garcia was working at Midtown Branch Public Library's registration desk and issuing a library card to a new user. As he was entering the user's data into the library system, he noticed out of the corner of his eye that there was someone standing nearby. He turned to look more closely, and he saw a tall, slender man dressed all in black and wearing a hoodie. The hoodie was tightly tied around the man's face so that only his eyes and nose were clearly visible. Christopher finished issuing the new card to the person in front of him, gave them some library literature, and welcomed them. The person left the desk, and the man wearing the hoodie approached Christopher.

Feeling a slight sense of panic, Christopher smiled and asked if he could help the man. The man said nothing but instead slid a piece of paper across the registration desk toward Christopher. Christopher picked the paper up and saw that the name Tyrone was written on it. Christopher glanced up and focused more closely on the man's face. "Oh, Tyrone, I didn't recognize you with the hoodie on. Are you cold?" Christopher had recognized Tyrone as one of the users who came into the library just about every day. Tyrone usually kept to himself, sitting at a library carrel reading an anime book or resting his head in his arms. Tyrone was acting a little stranger than normal today, so Christopher asked if there was something Tyrone needed. Tyrone just stared back, not saying a word. Christopher pressed Tyrone again.

"Tyrone, what do you need? Did you leave your card at home again? Do you need to know your library card number?" Christopher asked. Tyrone just nodded. Christopher said that he'd do it "one last time" but reminded Tyrone that he needed to bring his card in with him and that they had told him this several times before. Christopher wrote Tyrone's card number down on a piece of paper and handed it to him. Tyrone walked away toward the public computers, and Christopher returned to his registration desk duty of checking for data entry errors on library cards issued the day before.

About an hour later, Christopher heard someone at the computers exclaim loudly, "No! Get away from me, freak!" Several other people said the same thing: "No." When Christopher looked up, he saw that Tyrone was going from person to person, and he was asking them if he could use their cell phone. The last person Tyrone asked jumped up from his chair, knocking it over, and yelled, "You touch me one more time, dude, I'll knock you down."

The loud noises and yelling had brought Cindy out of her branch manager office. She walked swiftly over to the desk to see what was going on. Christopher had gone over to try and calm everyone down. Cindy came over to take charge. Seeing Tyrone, and noting how he was wearing his hoodie, she turned to him and commanded, "Sir, you'll need to keep quiet. This is a library!" Christopher helped the other gentleman pick up his chair and apologized. "Are you two fighting?" Cindy asked. "You'll need to leave the library."

"I want to call my mother," Tyrone said. "I just asked if I could use his cell phone."

Hearing this, Christopher said, "Tyrone, you know you can use the library's phone to call your mother. You've done this before. Come over here and I'll show you how to dial her." Christopher led Tyrone over to the registration desk and pointed to the phone. Cindy followed behind, making a mental note to remind staff that the library's phones were not for public use.

"Do you remember how to dial your mother?" Christopher asked. "You have to press the number nine first and then your phone number."

Cindy stood next to Tyrone and added, "You need to make it quick."

Cindy overheard Tyrone's conversation as he told his mother that the reason he was late was because he was at the library and nobody would let him use the phone. Cindy heard Tyrone's mother tell him he needed to get home now. Tyrone yelled into the phone that he was coming and that she didn't need to yell. Tyrone slammed the phone down hard enough that it caused several library users to look up.

"All right, that's enough! You've disrupted people trying to study in this library, and you're harassing people and causing a scene." Cindy lifted the phone to her ear. "You'll need to leave the library right now or I'm calling the police," she threatened. Tyrone just walked away toward the front door. Cindy followed and watched, telling Tyrone that he wasn't allowed to come back to the library if he didn't follow the rules.

Thirty minutes later, Tyrone walked back into the library behind an elderly black woman. The woman asked a staff member where the library's manager was and said she needed to speak with her immediately. When Cindy finally came out of her office, the woman asked, "Are you the library manager?"

"Yes, I'm Cindy Magyar."

"I'm Tyrone's mother. He tells me that you banned him from the library. Is that correct?"

"Your son was harassing library customers and threatening them. I told him if he couldn't follow the library's rules then he wasn't allowed to come back."

"My son," the woman said, "has mental disabilities, and he missed his medication today. But he was treated unfairly. He uses the library every day, and he tells me that your staff know him. He never causes a problem. He misses his medication one day, which causes him to behave poorly, and now you're banning him from the library? Doesn't that seem unfair? Is it because he's black and wearing a hoodie? I'm going to speak to your supervisor. Can I have that person's name?"

Cindy wrote "Jane Loughtry, city librarian" on her business card and jotted down Jane's number. "I look forward to telling Jane what really happened," Cindy said. "I'm merely looking after the safety of all my library's users." Tyrone and his mother left the library, and Cindy returned to her desk to make notes of what had happened, just in case she needed to refer to them in the event that Jane called her on it.

Cindy never heard from Jane Loughtry, her supervisor, regarding the Tyrone incident. She figured that Tyrone's mother had become occupied with other problems, or realized that Tyrone was at fault, so she'd left the matter alone. She was glad to have plugged up that problem. Unfortunately, her satisfaction was only temporary. The dam really broke for Cindy and the staff at the Midtown Branch Public Library several months later. Neither Cindy nor her staff were prepared, and it showed.

Billy Riley, an eighteen-year-old man with Asperger syndrome, entered the library with his father on a bright June morning. The two men walked through the library, looked at the online catalog, and searched the bookshelves. Christopher and Karyann were once again stationed at the library's circulation desks when they heard loud crying coming from the stacks. Karyann looked over at Christopher, and Christopher shrugged his shoulders. Again, some cries were heard from the book stacks. Christopher finally left his desk to go investigate.

He noticed Billy Riley sitting on the floor, crying. Billy was rocking back and forth and thumping his knee. Christopher approached Billy's father, but Billy's father motioned that it would be all right. "He's expressing his unhappiness after I told him he had to do something he didn't want to do. This is normal." Christopher acknowledged him and returned to his desk. The cries subsided after several tense moments. Eventually, Christopher noticed that Billy and his father finally came out of the stacks carrying books to the checkout desk.

"Hello," Karyann said. "Checking out?" Billy slid the books across the desk for Karyann to check out for him. Billy looked down at the ground and rocked back and forth. His father stood behind him, ensuring that Billy did what was asked. "Do you have your library card?" Karyann asked.

"Library card. Library card," Billy repeated, continuing to rock. Billy's father helped him give Karyann his card. "Library card."

"Thank you," she said. As she was checking the material out, Karyann noticed that the books were marked Reference. "Oh, I'm sorry. These books can't leave the library." Karyann told Billy's father that the books were for in-library use only and apologized.

Billy's father told Billy that they'd need to go find new books as the ones he wanted could not be checked out. Billy became extremely upset. He started crying and hitting his head.

Billy's father tried to quiet him, with no luck. The more his father tried to calm him, the more Billy flailed and screamed.

Cindy came out of her office rolling her eyes. "What's going on? What's happening now?"

Karyann apprised Cindy of the situation. Cindy said, "Sir, you'll have to leave. You're disrupting our library's users."

Billy's father, who was obviously doing his best to calm his son, said that Billy was having a tantrum and that he would be okay momentarily. He told Billy they'd go find some better books for him to check out.

Billy's cries grew louder. "Want these! No!"

"Sir, this disturbance is unacceptable. You'll need to take your son from the library," Cindy commanded. "If you can't remove your son, I'll have to call the police to remove him."

"Nobody is laying a hand on my son," Billy's father said. "I'm handling this the best way." He returned to convincing Billy that there were better books for him to find. Billy's cries, while subsiding, were still disturbing library users around the desks. Many of them came over to watch what was happening. Billy continued to whimper, and he fell to the floor, once again beating his legs. "Want books! Want books!"

Remembering where Billy and his father had first been when he approached them, Christopher went to the library's shelves to find some books that would circulate that might be just like the ones Billy had chosen. Christopher found several and brought them to Billy's father. Billy's father used them to help diffuse the situation and told Billy to check out the "better books."

After about ten minutes, Cindy once again threatened to call the police. However, just as she was about to summon them, Billy's crying stopped, and his father was able to get his son to check out and leave the library. Cindy figured the confrontation was over. She'd later find that the confrontation was, in fact, far from over. It had only begun.

A week after Billy's breakdown, city librarian Jane Loughtry called the Midtown Branch Public Library and spoke to her branch manager, Cindy. "We have a major issue, Cindy. There has been an Americans with Disabilities Act compliance complaint filed against the library by a gentleman who visited your library recently with his son who has Asperger syndrome. Do you remember this?" Jane asked.

Cindy recounted the whole situation and proudly said she'd done the best she could in light of the commotion that the man's son was making. Jane alerted Cindy that the Americans with Disabilities Act's definition of a disability included people with mental disabilities. "Cindy, the act protects people with a mental illness. I've discussed this at several of the branch library manager's meetings. This Midtown branch user may very well have a valid complaint, saying that you discriminated against him by demanding he leave. I need you to come down to speak to our attorney about what we can do. I think there was a much better way for you to have handled this situation, Cindy. Let's discuss. Can you come down here now?"

Cindy said she'd come down to the city's administrative offices. As she was driving to her boss's office, she recounted the several situations she'd resolved over the last few months. Maybe there was a better way to handle these types of situations. Or did her staff now need to be social workers rather than library employees? Cindy pulled into the city administrative offices parking lot and headed inside to hear what her city librarian and attorney had to say. She felt she was in the right. Wasn't she responsible for the safety and well-being of her library users? How far should she have gone to open her library to those who are seemingly unfit, or unable, to use it?

CHALLENGING THE CHALLENGED RESPONSES

Response 1
By Carol Garcia, senior library administration assistant (retired), San Jose Public Library, San Jose, California

At first look, this scenario seems to present a fairly logical dilemma: How does a public institution—one that prides itself on the principles of providing services freely and equally to everyone—actually try to limit access to users it sees as problematic? But a deeper investigation of this scenario reveals a different, more immediate problem. There is a leadership vacuum at the Midtown Branch Public Library, and it has boiled up to create a maelstrom of resentment, harassment, and legal troubles.

There isn't a public library in existence that hasn't had to deal with challenging patrons. From physical disabilities to mental disabilities to social disabilities, public libraries provide services to all the users in their communities without judgment. When Cindy Magyar, the branch library manager at Midtown, makes the sarcastic statement questioning if her staff must now "be social workers rather than library employees," she is voicing a sentiment that I'm sure many in our profession have thought (if not voiced). As public facilities, we are expected to provide the same level of service to mentally challenged individuals or homeless patrons that we give to any other citizen who enters our library's door. I have known library customers who have "special names" for people they see as different: "Oh, here comes Trash Bag Lady" or "hoodie guy is out at the phone again." Or, if we find these users to be disruptive, we escort them to the door or call the police. A large portion of library staff just turn away and pretend they don't see them, hoping they'll just disappear without our having to interact with them. But, as the staff at Midtown Branch Public Library have realized, their mentally challenged library users are not going anywhere. In fact, these types of users are likely to grow in number. According to an often quoted statistic from the National Council for Behavioral Health, at least one in five Americans has a mental illness. It's long past time for the Midtown branch staff to stop ignoring this "problem" and take a more proactive, humanistic approach to helping this underserved population.

If you are looking for a leader who shows exactly the *wrong* skills and qualities necessary to inspire and motivate employees, look no further than Cindy Magyar. She apparently sits in her office most of the day and has no idea what is happening at her branch library until she is disturbed by a scream, an uproar, or an intrusion by a staff member pleading for her assistance. Under the pretext of looking after the safety of her library's patrons, Cindy seems to be practicing a selective policy of who gets to use the library and who doesn't. People who don't disturb her (she's not really worried about her library's users), or who don't require her to come out of her office, are welcome to come in. But be quiet, sit down, and don't cause a disturbance!

Cindy states that "all day long I'm getting complaints about people harassing library patrons." If this is true, and she's only seeing the complaints that come directly to her, what must her staff members be seeing? Let me just say this: it is impossible to solve a problem without seeing the problem for yourself. Cindy is hearing complaints. She needs to get out and lead. She needs to see the problems that her staff are seeing. By coming out of her office, and being a part of the staff, Cindy can build better relationships with her staff and users. By joining her staff and evaluating library activity for herself, she will see how things are going and when (and how) things begin to deteriorate. She can begin modeling appropriate skills (if she indeed has those skills!) and showing a more approachable and engaged management style.

There isn't a template that one uses to handle every mentally ill patron. Perhaps the staff could have enlisted the advice of a local shelter or mental health facility in recommending proper methods of handling the homeless. Perhaps the staff could have worked with Tyrone's mother in setting up a procedure for communicating with her son. Perhaps the staff can work with Billy's father in selecting material ahead of time and ensuring books that his son wants to check out are available. This staff has the skills and capabilities to offer suggestions and to work more effectively with their mentally challenged patrons. But Cindy needs to get on board first and lose her punitive philosophy.

Once Cindy is ready to lead, and once she sees library problems for herself, she can begin to enlist her team in creating better strategies to handle them. Cindy's staff members, particularly Brian and Christopher, showed some excellent skills in relating to patrons like Tyrone and Billy. Cindy should capitalize on these skills and promote teamwork in handling library problems. Rather than banning users from the library, or calling the police on users, what strategies can this staff employ to make their work lives easier when dealing with mentally challenged users? For this, I turn to the other leadership issue this scenario brings up—if only indirectly. That issue is with the city librarian, Jane Loughtry.

I'd be amazed if the Midtown branch was the only library branch in this system that was having issues with mentally challenged and/or homeless users. Why isn't Jane aware of them? Surely Cindy and her colleagues have brought up their issues at systemwide meetings and performance conversations? In fact, Jane mentions that the issue has come up at several branch library manager's meetings. Could it be that Jane is also to blame for not proactively tackling this issue? I'd say yes. Had Jane been a better leader, she would have looked to assist her branch managers and offer training and staff development that targets how staff can help users experiencing mental issues. The American Library Association, state library associations, state and local social service organizations, and others provide excellent resources, consultants, and trainers who can assist library managers and staff in working more effectively with mentally challenged library users. Our professional literature is filled with inspiring stories of how libraries have successfully partnered with organizations to offer social services at the library, or who have offered unique training programs that benefit staff's efforts in working with mentally challenged users. I suspect that Jane, much like Cindy, spends too much time in her office with the door closed, trying to ignore what is going on around her.

Now that Jane has called Cindy to her office to discuss the legal problems created at Midtown branch, what can be done? This is a serious issue that is best left to the city's attorney—that's why we see him included in the meeting that Jane has called Cindy to at the scenario's conclusion. Make no mistake about it—this will be a difficult issue for the library department, and it likely will not end well for Cindy. Jane is quite right in acknowledging that the Americans with Disabilities Act protects people with mental illness. Much of that law deals with discriminatory practices against mentally ill individuals in the area of employment, but there are also several sections that provide protections in government services and activities. Cindy was wrong to handle the situations at Midtown Branch Public Library in the way she did, and the city will likely need to rectify this in some way.

So how *do* library employees walk the fine line between providing services to everyone equally while at the same time protecting the safety of library users who have the right to use the library without disturbance? One particularly relevant case comes to mind that most library directors are aware of—*Kreimer v. City of Morristown Library*. While the case is relevant to this scenario, this isn't the space to properly examine its implications and meaning (students should certainly research the case for a broader depth of understanding). In short, a homeless man was banned from a public library in Morristown, New Jersey. The man sued the city for violating his First Amendment rights. The homeless man won the case, and the court instructed the library to change its policies. A higher court later overruled the lower court's decision, establishing libraries as a *limited public forum*—or a facility that is open to the public only for a particular use or purpose, like a courthouse. The court decided that the Morristown Library, which administered the facility, was only obligated to allow those First Amendment activities that are consistent with the nature of the forum, even if the facility is open to the public. I bring this case up because perhaps this is an area in which the Midtown Branch Public Library and its parent institution could consider limiting access to those users who violate the limited public forum definition. But does this supersede the protections given to the mentally ill by the Americans with Disabilities Act? Once again, it's best to leave that argument up to the legal experts. What is sure is that the library is walking down a slippery slope if it seeks to limit its services to people it doesn't like. Who would be next on the library's list? A much better approach is striving to understand this underserved population and find the best way possible to provide our valuable library services to them. Connecting all users to the information they want and need is a primary role of a library professional. It benefits society in so many ways. Isn't that the reason we entered this profession anyway?

Response 2
By Samantha Sednek, children's library services, Medford Public Library, Medford, Massachusetts

Continuing professional development is a real and necessary thing. It strikes me that this library's staff may need a little extra support. A workshop on de-escalation techniques, racial sensitivity training, and staff/caregiver burnout might have made these situations less difficult for all involved. Also, there needs to be a fresh look at the library's behavior policy. It should be reassessed with support from a member of the town's diversity and disability commission or office and, if available, someone who works with the town's social support systems (homeless shelters, social work, etc.).

The first incident we read about in this scenario is tricky because the patron is guaranteed to be breaking some of the library's rules. Many libraries have restrictions on the size of baggage someone can bring in as well as rules about using restrooms for bathing. Additionally, the fact that the homeless woman was spotted trying to open car doors in the parking lot of the library, and has locked herself in the library's restroom for a long time, all point to the fact that this person has no intention of following established rules. These rules are in place for many reasons (such as to discourage people from camping in a library's space) but, depending on how they're enforced, they can disenfranchise some of the most vulnerable populations that a library serves.

The Midtown branch, however, seems to be particularly inhospitable to potentially homeless individuals. If the library did have a bag restriction, the patron should have been met upon entry by a staff member willing to check her bags so that she could pick them up when she left. Or a staff member could have told the woman where she could safely leave her bags until she was finished in the library. Instead of a friendly redirect, she was met with hovering and suspicious staff. Her willingness to comply with any directives is going to plummet.

When Cindy was called onto the scene, she started her interaction with this patron by walking in on her in the restroom and shouting at her. While no one is perfect, and such situations are stressful and can bring out our worst, Cindy's reaction was not going to de-escalate the situation. The library staff should have been proactive. Greet incoming patrons, politely remind patrons of rules as they enter if it looks as if the patron isn't abiding by them, and ask if they need assistance. Much like classroom behavior management, proximity and opening a dialogue can counteract a lot of negative behaviors. If the Midtown branch has a large homeless population, staff should know where they can direct folks who need assistance, whether that is for access to housing, food, or just hygiene facilities. When enforcing rules, staff should keep their tone low, firm, and conciliatory. Shouting only leads to more shouting.

Finally, know that calling in the police shouldn't be a first step unless there's a clear and present threat of danger. There are many circumstances in which a police presence can, again, escalate an interaction—race, for one. That's not to say a library should never call the police for support, but it is important to weigh the risks. Also, getting to know your local police force can help alleviate some of the circumstances that might cause a worse encounter. For instance, some police forces have officers or teams that are trained to better handle individuals who may be dealing with mental health issues. If Midtown is struggling with myriad interactions of this caliber, getting to know if the local force has a crisis intervention team could be helpful. However, in this particular instance, calling the police would have been over the top.

The second and third library incidents portrayed in the scenario are much simpler to deconstruct because there's an obvious "bad" actor and a "good" actor in both. Let's start with the positives. Christopher seems to understand that people with differing needs come into the library, and it is clear that he is trying to assist, even if it means bending the rules. Again, most libraries will have an "our phones are for staff use only" rule, but it is important to be flexible and remember that (a) not everyone has access to a phone, (b) children and teens often don't have reliable access, and (c) sometimes letting a patron make a quick call saves everyone a larger headache. If your library's mission is to serve a diverse population (whether that diversity includes socioeconomic status, age, race, or ability), then knowing when to bend rules is important.

Cindy, again, started too angry to make an uncomfortable situation less fraught. Another staff member was already assisting and handling the scene. By adding herself to the mix, she escalated the tension. By following Christopher and Tyrone as they called his mother, she, again, made the situation more stressful for the others involved.

When Tyrone's mother came in, Cindy had an opportunity to recover the situation a little bit. She could have explained that some rules weren't being followed, acknowledged Tyrone's medication might have been at fault, and said that he wasn't banned forever—just that he has to know what the rules are and the library's expectation to follow them. Since he had such a good rapport with Christopher, she could have asked that Tyrone check in with him or another staff member if he feels like he's having a bad day. In this way, you can acknowledge the rules and establish a path for Tyrone to meet expectations and still use the library. Instead, she's cut Tyrone and, likely, his mother out of the library.

In the final situation, Karyann might have been able to prevent the situation if, instead of starting with "no," she'd offered another course of action. She could have mentioned that these are special books, but the copier or scanner over there can help you get the pages you need to take home. Or she could have asked for help because it appears that Christopher also had a perfectly fine method of assisting this patron. Good customer service doesn't always mean you get to say "yes" to people, but it does mean trying to find a way to get them to the "yes" or, at least, a close proximity. Still, tantrums happen in libraries. It is difficult when tantrums happen, but they *will* happen. It is a situation that's hard for everyone: the staff, the parent/caregiver, and the child. Christopher's quick thinking to try to appease Billy's need for a particular item with similar books might have calmed the situation if Cindy had enough patience to let it play out. Again, Cindy starts out in a manner that seems accusatory, that escalated tension for all. Using "you" statements also tends to increase tension. Offering alternatives and providing a space for the family to safely (and with less disruption to others) come down from their meltdown would have been helpful ways to have tried to soothe the issue. Instead, Cindy almost immediately starts her interactions by threatening to bring the police in, and her ability to contain and ease the situation rapidly disintegrates.

Cindy seems to have preconceived notions about who should and shouldn't use the library. Her final self-question of how far should she have gone to open her library to those who are seemingly unfit or unable to use it suggests she thinks there are people who are unfit and unable. She is the one creating barriers to use, and her interactions suggest she, at the very least, needs some sensitivity training.

Library behavior policies are important because rules are there to keep people safe, but rules can also create inequity. Question why certain rules are in place, and, if you can, choose kindness and flexibility, and try to meet people where they are instead of expecting them to be paragons of exemplary library patrons.

Response 3
By Kelly Bohannan, assistant branch manager, Seminole County Public Libraries, Seminole County, Florida

Every situation seems to have a target word or phrase that—when it is heard—does not bode well for where the conversation is about to go. Once you hear someone use the phrase "psycho lady" or "nut case," for example, you know that the situation is going to immediately escalate. It is obvious from this scenario that the staff at the Midtown Public Library has not had sensitivity training—or any other classes—in the best way to go about dealing with differently abled patrons. In fact, the staff at this branch seemed to see any sign of mental illness as a disturbance that needs to be removed from the library. From the several incidents described in the scenario, we see the staff become instantly wary and uncomfortable before even approaching the patrons they disapprove of. This staff needs to become aware of the fact that some individuals who visit public buildings will not always display behavior with which others are comfortable. For this reason, basic education in dealing with patrons of diverse backgrounds and abilities should be the first recommendation for all staff. Library managers and other library staff who work in public facilities need to recognize that serving the public means serving all kinds of people—including people who are different from ourselves.

One of the major issues presented in this scenario is the behavior of the branch manager, Cindy. Her responses to each situation were immediately negative and showed no real attempt to defuse the situation. Cindy obviously has taken the phrase "homeless person" (as her staff member, Brian, calls the lady in the bathroom) to mean something very negative. She slams her fists on her desk and exclaims that "this is getting out of hand," which seems to indicate that Cindy has been confronted with similar issues in her past. Because of past experience, Cindy has already assumed the homeless lady to be guilty of wrongdoing, even though no rules were actually being broken. Cindy often expressed that she was protecting the safety of other library users, but it never seems that anyone in the building is in any actual danger. When library patrons showed any signs of possible mental illness, they were immediately labeled "problem persons" and asked to leave. While Cindy offers limited warnings—often delivered in anger—she does not offer any clear options that might help the patrons. She couldn't even muster basic politeness for any of the individuals. Cindy must remember that, as a manager, she should be modeling good behavior. Is this the way Cindy wants her staff to handle future situations?

The final incident involving the father and son is almost painful to read. Cindy's staff were already handling the situation well, and, if left alone, they would have gotten the family checked out and on their way. For example, the staff member Christopher remembers which shelves the father and son were browsing when he first saw them in the stacks and runs back to retrieve some similar circulating material that may have calmed the child. This was a smart choice and one that showed some concern for the user. Instead, Cindy's interference did nothing to improve the situation and set a bad example for her staff. Her unsympathetic behavior has alienated these patrons—and likely those library patrons observing the situation.

Library managers who work in public facilities are not operating in a bubble. They are operating not only under certain library and organizational policies and procedures but also under the auspices of state and federal laws—like the Americans with Disabilities Act—meant to protect the public. Cindy's actions in this scenario have potentially sparked a lawsuit. It is not surprising to see why. If these types of situations at the Midtown Public Library are as regular as Cindy seems to believe, she needs to immediately plan for appropriate training and guidance that both she and her staff can benefit from and avoid costly lawsuits and poor public perception in the process.

Chapter Nine

Budget Woes

A Leading Scenario Using Problem Solving

SCENARIO

Molly Dunphy, supervising librarian of branch services at the Forked Run Public Library System, ducked out of her car and quickly looked around the library parking lot to make sure none of her fifteen branch library managers were within earshot. She would be meeting with them later to give them their collection budget allocations, and they constantly tried to waylay her before meetings in hopes of convincing her to give them more money. Ascertaining that the coast was clear, Molly darted toward the staff entrance to the library without incident.

It had been a challenging budget year. Her library director had reported that a structural deficit in the city's budget meant another year of cuts. In fact, the city had cut funding to the library in a big way—to the tune of 14 percent! With the realization that a majority of any library's budget burden came from personnel costs, the library had managed to handle most of its previous reductions by not hiring new employees to fill vacant positions and even eliminating some positions. But it was clear that these reductions would need to cut deeper—like into the library's collections and resources. In preparation for her meeting today, Molly had determined each of the total collection allocations for each of her branches. The easiest way to allocate her funds was to take her entire budget and divide it equally between the fifteen branches. She then checked the most recent circulation statistics to find her top three circulating branches and her bottom three circulating branches. Molly then had her assistant determine the average percentage difference between the top and bottom circulating branches, which was 10 percent. So, Molly took 10 percent of the collection funds from each of the bottom three branches and added it to the top three branches. She wasn't exactly sure that this was the best way to allocate, but she knew it sounded fair, and she could "sell it" if she needed to. Once Molly had the total collection budgets for each branch, she then needed to divvy up each branch's total collection budget into the individual collection categories—children, teen, adult, reference, and so on. This is where the process became messy! The branches' children's selectors wanted more money for their kids' books, the branches' adult services selectors wanted more for their books, and so on. She saw the process as a lose-lose prospect. No matter what she did, someone was going to get upset at her. So, the best thing she felt she could do was just seem equitable and fair.

Molly had to admit that she didn't quite understand structural deficits, and she despised dealing with accounting and budgets. However, she had made it a personal goal to improve her budgeting skills and had even attended a night school accounting class a few years ago to learn more. Even with her improved skills, Molly had chosen to adopt the simple budget allocation plan of taking the pot of money she'd been given for branch library collections and allocating those funds using the same allocation percentages that were used the previous year (and the year before that, and the year before that). Now, in preparation, she had retrieved last year's branch library collection budgets from her files and had her staff assistant calculate what allocation percentages had been used for each collection category. She planned to apply those same percentages to the branch collection category allocations this year. Whatever worked last year would work this year too, right?

Unfortunately, Molly hadn't figured on what would come next. She opened several emails and checked through her inbox for messages marked "Important." There were two. Somehow, she knew this wasn't going to be good. The first email flagged "Important" was from Molly's library director. It said: "Hey, Molly. I thought I'd alert you to something I overheard at the library commission meeting last night. I was getting coffee during our break, and I overhead two of our library commissioners discussing—well, 'complaining' might be a better word—about our DVDs and digital movie subscriptions. In fact, Commissioner Roberts said she thought the library had become a free DVD store, and she wondered if the library should look toward purchasing more books rather than movies. I didn't want to take up the topic right then, but I will call Roberts to ask her a little more about that. I'm passing this on to you just to give you a heads-up that it's on the radar of the library commission and could be a major topic of debate in the future."

The second "Important" email came from one of Molly's continual "headaches"—her colleague Grace Liu, supervising librarian of foreign-language services at the library.

Like Molly, one of Grace's duties was coordinating material collections—but only for foreign-language material. Molly would calculate the amount of money Grace could spend on branch foreign-language materials, but—because selecting foreign-language material required expert knowledge—Grace would decide the best ways to spend that money on foreign-language material and what foreign-language material would go to each branch. Molly knew that Grace was a forceful advocate for those foreign-language collections, and she was relentless in her pursuit of more funding. Molly clicked on Grace's "Important" email and read: "Molly, I'm sure you have noted the increase in the population of Chinese immigrants in most of our branch library communities, right? I know the increase seems small, but check the circulation statistics for each of the branch's Chinese collections. It's way up over the previous years. However, the branches' collections of Chinese material are all relatively small. That's because I can only buy so much material with the little money you give me. I'm sure circulation would be huge if there were more Chinese books for the community to check out. As selector for all the branches' Chinese-language material, I beg you for more money this year. I'll see you at the allocation meeting soon. We can talk more at that time if you want."

Feeling stretched in two different directions, Molly was sort of tired of hearing Grace make this case to her over and over. She'd been thinking of augmenting Grace's funds this year just to shut her up. But from where would she take those augmented funds?

Molly's budget woes only got worse as she prepared to meet her branch personnel later in the day. In preparation for that meeting, Molly began combing through her files of collection-related notes and observations she'd made over the course of the last year. It didn't make her allocation problem any easier. In fact, it seemed to complicate her task even more. There were some important—if not troubling—observations in those files. She wrote down the following eight items to share at the allocation meeting as rationale for her allocation decisions:

1. Don't forget! We discussed in our September system management meetings that a core value of the library system's mission is services to children, and before making any decisions, we must ask ourselves, "How will this effect children in our community?"
2. I think that adult fiction systemwide may be overfunded and underused, as reflected in our annual stats. Look for ways to increase circulation before increasing allocation. Seaside branch did their big marketing and display program, and look at that branch's circulation of adult fiction. It is used well and exceeds the use ratio of the system's use in the adult fiction area. Is there a way to report this success systemwide for other branches to use?
3. Chinese DVDs are one of the highest-circulating items at each library, but don't forget that users from this community demographic also use popular entertainment DVDs in English.
4. In the annual branch library walkabouts, I noted that children's picture book shelving units at every branch are packed. Although demographics show the population of children holding steady (if not growing ever so slightly), I wonder if books for children are not circulating as often as before.
5. Don't forget the library's new mission: "The Forked Run Public Library is an integral part of the educational process for youth and a venue for continuing education for adults. Our public library supports a sense of community within the population it serves. The specific collections and services of our public library are designed to meet the specific needs of your community."
6. At least five young adult material selectors have told me (and circ stats confirm) that teens are clamoring for anime and manga books as well as popular music. These collections at each branch are very small—in some cases just a few dozen books. Has the system ignored materials for teens for too long? It's been almost a decade since there was any concerted effort to improve services to teens. Is it time to address this?
7. June's collection management retreat was so interesting. Some items of note: the recent Census projections claim there are 154,000 people in our community, and 48 percent of these people are families with children. Seventy percent are affluent white families. There are several Asian communities (Vietnamese, Chinese, Korean, and Japanese) represented locally. This community is expected to grow by 9 percent in the next decade. Also showing a strong presence is the Russian-speaking community. The most heavily circulated collection in our library is children's books of all types, including children's paperbacks, hardback fiction, children's nonfiction, media, and picture books. The most heavily used single collection in the library is the DVD collection, which out-circulates any other collection by a ratio of two to one—but remember the loan period for DVDs is one week rather than three weeks. The average age of the population is forty, and that average age is dropping as more and more young families and immigrants move into the area. The population here speaks mostly English, but more than half speak a language other than English at home.
8. There were four branches that did not spend all their collection funds in the previous year. This can lead to rush buying and a possible decline in selection standards at the end of the year.

Molly was exhausted. She kept thinking that this systematic approach to fund allocation she was taking was too subjective. Were there things she was overlooking? How would she incorporate all the important collection issues she'd identified over the last year? Should those even be addressed at this point? If only there were some standard formula that all libraries used. That would certainly help her in this case. But it was time for Molly to do the math and put numbers in the fund allocations for each branch collection. As she readied herself to begin her traditional allocation methodology, she suddenly had a better idea.

"Why am I doing this alone?" Molly asked herself. "Couldn't I make someone else do it? Why should I bear the weight of solving this problem year after year?"

Molly wondered if maybe the answer to her problem was somewhere in the collective knowledge of her selectors. She could announce at the upcoming meeting with her branch library selectors that she wanted their help in making this year's allocations. Using the same previous year's figures they'd been given, she could ask them to complete their own allocation worksheets, listing how much money they needed for each collection category. This would give them each an opportunity to walk a mile in her shoes. She also needed a way for them all to reach some consensus regarding the entire library system as a whole. This might actually help them loosen their grip on their own personal collection agendas. She would read them each of the eight issues noted above and find a politically appropriate way to convey information in the two important emails she'd received. Then she'd ask for them to complete the allocation worksheet. She'd then work together with her team to listen to any alternatives they had and hope they would reach consensus.

As Molly walked into the branch collection allocation meeting later that day, the chatter and buzz immediately ceased. All the managers and selectors looked to her and waited to hear what she had decided they could spend. Molly decided the best way to do this was to jump right into the fire.

"I know you're all anxious to hear my branch collection category allocation decisions. But this year we're going to do things a bit differently. I'm asking each one of you to help me develop options. Instead of me telling you how much to spend in each collection category, let's think of some options and come to a consensus on the best way *as a system* to approach this year's allocations. As you already know, the city is in a budget crisis once again, and we've had to reduce expenditures by fourteen percent across the board. I also want to point out some important considerations we must consider." Molly listed the eight issues already discussed above and then briefly relayed the information from her two emails. "Additionally, because selecting foreign-language material requires special skills, our library's foreign languages selection expert, Grace Liu, will once again select all your branch library foreign-language materials. Because her allocation for foreign-language materials has also been reduced by 14 percent from last year, we need to figure out what to do about the foreign-language books purchased for the branches this year.

"Ladies and gentlemen, let's roll up our sleeves and get to work. Who's got the answers?" Molly's mouth dropped open as the hands of nearly everyone in the room shot into the air. She was amazed. What had she overlooked? Could the options on how to allocate funds be that simple?

"Okay." She pointed to her first manager and readied herself to write the first alternative on the whiteboard. "What's your plan?"

BUDGET WOES RESPONSES

Response 1
By Jason Grubb, director, Sweetwater County Library System, Green River, Wyoming

Unfortunately, scenarios like this are not uncommon. Most county or city library systems in the United States are 100 percent funded by their parent organization. Most of the public funds that allow a public library to operate come from tax revenue. When tax revenue decreases significantly, it will likely result in a decrease in library funding. All areas of the library will likely be affected—including the funds budgeted for the library collection. When a library system finds itself facing many of the same issues outlined in this scenario, the collection budget is the obvious first choice for substantial cuts. Circulation reports are run, individual collection categories are analyzed, and meetings with managers are held. It is a team effort to decide which categories will decrease and which will increase slightly. The library's mission statement and circulation statistics should guide the decision-making process.

One element that is missing from the scenario is a date for the collection budget to be finalized. This could certainly affect the decision-making process. Does the collection budget need to be finalized at the same time that Molly is meeting with the fifteen branch managers? Or does the team have more time to discuss options and then decide? A majority of library systems operate on a fiscal year—meaning that the budget is adopted during the first part of July and runs through until the end of June. Consequently, public library managers work with their county or city officials to prepare budgets between April and June. This gives them several months to address any decrease in funding. Obviously, decisions that can be made without the stress of time are often better than those made without having time to adequately prepare.

While having adequate time to make a decision is helpful, it is not always possible. Sometimes decisions have to be made immediately. This is why library systems often look first to the collection budget. In order to gain immediate savings, the library simply needs to stop purchasing items for the collection. This can be a quick way to respond to a decrease in funding. It is also less complicated and more popular than laying off staff. Eliminating staff hurts morale, costs in unemployment benefits, and, in some communities, can hurt the library's image if the public perceives laying off staff as more detrimental than not purchasing new items for their collection.

Assuming time is against Molly, and a decision must be made in her meeting with her managers, the quickest way would seem to be to allocate the exact same amounts as was done the previous year—minus the 14 percent. Facing an immediate time constraint, it may not be possible at this time to give consideration to the important emails Molly has received and the eight observances Molly had noted in her file. She probably should have been discussing these items long before this point, but if she is facing a deadline, she'll likely have to wait with those issues.

A 14 percent decrease is a difficult amount to manage. It takes time and conversation. If Molly can spare the time, it would be far more beneficial for each of Molly's fifteen branch managers to weigh in before making any changes to how the collection is funded. Because Molly decides that this is a good approach as well, it seems as if there is indeed some time to make the final collection allocations and there isn't a pressing deadline. However, Molly is overlooking something important. Her library system has a culture of fear and not a culture of trust.

In a culture of fear, people are motivated by self-preservation. They act in ways that protect themselves from emotional harm. Molly is the perfect example. She views colleagues as a headache who should get what they want so they will shut up, tries to avoid uncomfortable conversations, and hopes to act in a way that won't upset anyone. She seems to want to make decisions without input from others and hopes to avoid any criticism with carefully constructed arguments for why she decided the way she did and with a nontransparent decision process that she knows she could sell if needed. These decisions are motivated by an effort to avoid criticism and bad feelings. But the culture of fear underlying this scenario does not originate with Molly. It comes from the director. This is demonstrated in the email that the director sent to Molly.

The director emails Molly with information overheard in a conversation between two board members. Why is the director willing to act on an opinion that was not brought directly to the director? What does the director fear? The director says the concern is on the radar of the library commission. It is not. It is an opinion shared by one commissioner in a private conversation. And why would it be a problem if this particular concern was on the radar of the library commission? These two commissioners were privately discussing a difference in opinion on what materials the library should purchase. Does the director fear being questioned on how the library is run? Does the director fear losing her job as a consequence? The director states the concern "could be a major topic of debate." The tone suggests this is something negative and should be avoided. What is feared about topics being debated? Clearly there are several things the director fears and—by sending an email to Molly—the director has shared her fears with her staff. Doing this maintains a culture of fear. Molly now acts out of fear of how the library commission may respond to how she decides to allocate the collection budget.

Molly's behavior provides possible insight into the reasons why a culture of fear exists. There is a lack of transparency, communication, and teamwork. Up until her meeting, it seems Molly has not involved the branch managers in the budget process. She herself decides what the budget for each branch will be and what the budget for each collection category within the branch will be. The staff working in the branch who oversee the day-to-day operations are left out of the decision-making process. Molly observes that the branch managers each have "their own personal collection agendas." From what is portrayed of this library's organizational culture, it is far more likely that the branch managers fear giving up their agenda and/or not having the resources to carry out their agenda. This is why they always try to waylay Molly "before meetings in hopes of convincing her to give them more money." More transparency in the entire process and with the funding challenges facing the system may help the branch managers better understand how their branch fits into the needs and priority of the entire system.

A lack of teamwork and transparency is rooted in a lack of communication. Molly is anxious she might run into a branch manager on the way to the meeting. If the channels of communication were working better, she would not have any concerns. Processes would be in place that would have allowed the branch managers to communicate their needs outside of a chance meeting in a parking lot. This would help everyone—the supervising librarian of branch services and the branch managers. If Grace was brought into some of the budget conversations and the decision-making process, she may be more willing to accept and understand why more funding is not provided for the Chinese-language collections.

A culture of trust is built over time. It requires operating with transparency, teamwork, and communication. Leaders set the tone by listening. The director listens to the library commissioners. Molly listens to the branch managers. The branch managers listen to each other and

Molly. Staff value one another as colleagues working together toward a common goal rather than as individuals working independently.

The fact that Molly is making the attempt to gather input and be more transparent by meeting with all her managers at this point is a good sign. However, in the absence of a culture of trust like the one presented in the scenario, the meeting will likely result in each person advocating for their own area of responsibility. While this information will be helpful to Molly in prioritizing how to allocate the collection budget by bringing awareness to specific needs, it is also a reminder that, going forward, more will need to be done to foster a culture of trust so her team is better equipped to address future budget challenges together.

No library can successfully be all things to all people—especially with limited resources. Finite resources require decisions to be made solely by focusing on the mission of the library. The mission of this particular library focuses on children's services, and this is precisely where Molly and her team should focus to ensure that they are funded at the same level as the previous year—adding the increase for anime and manga books as well as popular music. The library's mission statement in the scenario guides this decision. Will everyone be happy with this approach? Probably not, which is why it will be necessary to hold budget conversations throughout the year and continue to try and come up with a way of funding the collection that best serves the needs of the entire community. It is safe to assume that next year's funding will either be the same or reduced again. It takes time for funding to be restored. Molly and her team need to prepare now for how to approach future cuts or how to deal with multiple areas of need when revenue increases.

Two problems in the scenario have been explored: an immediate problem with a 14 percent decrease in funding and a bigger problem with a culture of fear. Both problems are representative of what a library manager might face during their career. Both problems have multiple solutions. The important thing to remember is to not lose sight of the mission and purpose of the library in the community. As long as everyone knows why they do what they do—even if they disagree on how to do it—the library will continue to move forward. It is when staff stop doing things for the patrons and start doing things for themselves that libraries become less effective.

Response 2
By Wayne Disher, San Jose State University School of Information, San Jose, California

I often tell my friends that there was a reason I became a librarian: I don't like math! The idea of balancing checkbooks, tracking expenses and revenue, and monitoring a budget was unappealing—if not downright scary—to me. Little did I expect that, like most any management or supervisory position in the workforce, math would be an incredibly useful tool to library staff. The higher up you climb on the organizational chart, and as problems become more complex, the need to employ math skills becomes more important. This is even more so as cities and counties struggle to deal with shrinking revenue resources that are passed down through an organization and require libraries and other departments to make tough budget decisions like the ones exemplified in this scenario.

Molly Dunphy, the supervising librarian of branch services at Forked Run, has a tough problem to solve: How does she make fifteen of her library branch supervisor subordinates happy about absorbing a 14 percent cut to the library system's annual budget? The short answer is, it's impossible! She can't make everyone happy. This doesn't mean Molly can't make everyone agree on a course of action and agree to live with whatever the ultimate decision is. This she can do. Molly certainly has made the right decision to gather her team together and ask them to assist her in reaching consensus about the cuts—together, as a team.

At first, Molly stumbles on the path she travels before we see her arrive at a proper destination at the scenario's conclusion. She does what many managers tend to do at the start of a budget season. They take whatever was done before and then adjust it whatever way is necessary to meet their needs. Last year, perhaps Molly took the previous year's budget and tweaked it a few percentage points up or down as was required to meet her budgeting target. This year, she readied herself to take last year's allocation again and adjust it as equitably as possible to create the least amount of resentment among her staff. If everyone receives as bad of a budget allocation as their colleagues, at least they can't accuse Molly of being unfair. Misery loves company! Molly seems to be caught up in a common budgeting philosophy: "You get what you get, and you don't throw a fit!" You wait to see how much money you will be given, you decide what that amount of money can buy, and then you conclude "Here's what you get with that money you've given me." This reactionary form of thinking has no bearing on the library's ultimate mission. There are better approaches to get ahead of the budget decisions by thinking more proactively. Think about the library's mission and how you and your department are expected to participate. By doing this, you can propose a different type of budgeting philosophy: "Here's what you want our department to achieve [the library mission]; here's how we plan to achieve it; so, this is the amount of money our department needs to accomplish this." Regretfully, Molly has missed the boat on this possible budgeting proposal and instead is stuck with using old formulas.

The problem with this method, as perhaps Molly figures out, is that it perpetuates her (or her predecessor's) previous budgeting mistakes. You have to remember that a budget is based on a set of assumptions. Assumptions made in the past may have been inaccurate—if not completely misguided. Assumptions made about expected expenses or resources two or three years ago are then just carried over again and again. Molly mentions that she doesn't "quite understand structural deficits." It is therefore likely her previous budget allocations will bolster that claim. If Molly had understood structural deficits, she'd realize that she has been allocating an amount of money that represents more than she is projected to receive year after year—whether the economy is performing well or not. Eventually, Molly will find that this budgeting method is unsustainable—even if she incorporates a single year budget cut.

Molly gets back on the right track when trying something new with this year's budget. She decides to let everyone "help" her in her allocations by making them recommend their own branch collection allocations. A team approach is indeed a bright idea because it allows everyone to have input and share ideas. Brainstorming and employing group decision making is an excellent process in problem solving. But looking back at the events in the scenario, it's important to note why Molly decides to relinquish control of this process. She has at least eight competing pressures and observations that represent many different agendas and demands, and it scares her.

While each of the eight collection-related issues that Molly has observed over the year—as well as the two important emails she receives regarding the library's collection—are important to deal with, they shouldn't be a part of the budget allocation yet. She needs to set them aside for the moment and focus on a wider goal: What is best for the entire system as our library strives to meet our mission? There will always be outside interference when you are dealing with a problem. In the communication process, this interference is commonly called "noise," and it often prevents the problem solver from making effective decisions. Molly shouldn't be tripped up by this noise right now. Allocations must be made without favoritism or influence. Molly can then prioritize these collection issues and deal with them separately after allocations have been determined. If too much weight is given to one of the competing observations or emails, Molly may be accused of playing favorites or giving tacit approval to something she doesn't really intend to give.

So even though Molly has reached a team decision-making approach for slightly dubious reasons, I think she's latching on to an approach that will not only help her solve her collection allocation problem but also likely increase buy-in to whatever allocation the team decides to make. So, what's the magic here? It's called reaching consensus, and it's the best problem-solving method I would recommend managers use when trying to make potentially unpopular decisions. Some people incorrectly assume that consensus means everyone agrees with the decision and that someone has to compromise in order to reach a solution. But I see consensus as a process that takes note of everyone's most important concerns and everyone's best ideas and weaves them together. I've seen consensus building result in surprising and creative solutions that inspire both the individual and the group as a whole.

Contrary to what you might think, consensus isn't about floating an idea out to the group and then voting on it to see if you can get a majority of the group to approve. Instead, reaching consensus in the problem-solving process means each person is committed to finding a solution, or solutions, that everyone can actively support—or at least live with. At the scenario's conclusion, we certainly see some commitment to resolving this problem, as each person in the group that Molly has convened thrusts their hand in the air when she asks, "Who has the answer?" This is very promising. The more ideas that can be generated by the group, the more they can synthesize alternatives and create consensus. Having a respectful dialogue between equals will also go a long way in helping Molly deal with the eight or so collection-related observations she has made. If Molly can help everyone work with one another (instead of against each other), she may reap other team-building benefits as well, such as fostering openness and trust among the staff. Given that each of Molly's staff members is willing to drop personal agendas and work toward a common goal, and given the time it could take to reach consensus, Molly may solve her allocation problem. She has provided her managers with the opportunity to decide their own course in this process and the right to play an equal role in creating a common goal. By listening closely to each other, the group can come up with a collection allocation plan with which everyone can agree to work.

Response 3
By Terri Pilate, collection management librarian, Placer County Library, Placer County, California

When a library suffers a cut in its materials budget, library staff have a huge challenge to keep the programs and patrons satisfied with the books and information they've come to depend on. A library system must find ways of working leaner and more efficiently to meet its goal of serving the community effectively. When the budget is larger, a library can afford to spend resources without needing to be specific about statistics. When the budget has been cut, a good way to keep pace with both patron desires and the library's goals is to know specifics about all relevant circulation statistics, such as what are the most popular materials versus what material is sitting on the shelf unused.

Molly Dunphy is on the right track in finding ways of collaborating with the branch managers in determining how to spend 14 percent less in funding. Branch managers know what patrons ask for and what they check out. Asking the managers to divide their branch's allocation into collection categories is a smart beginning. I recommend the next step for Molly in order to help them reach consensus is to have the team figure out a 14 percent reduction for each of their branches from the figures used last year. The librarians could then allocate their funds into each collection category. Molly should gather these worksheets and total the amounts for each collection category—for example, a systemwide dollar amount for children's nonfiction, for adult mysteries, for teen fiction, and so forth. Molly should then assign a collection category of selection for each librarian to select for the whole library system. This will help the team focus on the health of the *whole* library system rather than on their own specific branch and agendas. As a professional library staff, they need to remember they work for the benefit of the whole library community. They are one library collection housed in several library branches.

As a selector who has been employed in a system that uses this sort of centralized collection management, I have seen the benefits to a system approach. By using internal circulation statistics, selection tools, vendor resources, and feedback from branch staff, it is easy to ascertain and calculate what are the popular topics, popular authors, and most heavily demanded subjects—even without working in a specific outlet. Additionally, Molly and her staff should be well aware of the system's weeding reports and deselection activities to help allocate the collection budget throughout the year.

Using collection statistics also helps provide justification and rationalization on collection spending. Furthermore, it assures both the professional staff and stakeholders that decisions are based on solid evidence. This will help address concerns brought up in the scenario by Commissioner Roberts and her fear that the library is becoming somewhat of a DVD rental store. By showing these collection statistics, Molly and the Forked Run Library director can demonstrate the popularity of DVDs within the community and how important it is to buy users what they most want—particularly when the available funding you have to spend is being reduced.

Another way to work with a smaller budget is to have some collections float between branches. Just as interest in one small collection of material at a branch is waning, that material is sent on to another branch—whose users will see that collection as new to them—even though it may have been in the library system for a while. This practice may be something for Molly to consider in order to help her and her staff cope with a 14 percent cut in the materials budget.

Molly's observation of packed shelves of children's picture books in her annual branch library walkabouts may not be because of lack of use or interest in picture books. It could be statistically based weeding would solve this problem. If a book has not been checked out in many months, it is time to delete the book from the system. It is a widely known professional observation that books circulate more when librarians weed often. Weeding helps to increase circulation by refreshing the collection and ridding the shelves of tattered, outdated books. Buying new picture books and marketing them effectively will also help the use statistics go up.

Since the Forked Run Public Library staff are not familiar with the systemwide approach to collection development, Molly may still need to use her perspective as the supervising librarian of branch services to make the final spending decisions. But if she can reorganize selection into a systemwide approach as described above, having the librarians select for the whole library system, this will help bring the professional staff into making material selections as a whole instead of concentrating on their own home branch.

Chapter Ten

The New Guy

A Leading Scenario Using Supposition

SCENARIO

Library staff Miles and Harriet took their seats in the back row of chairs they'd spent the last hour helping to set up for the pending "Big Event." Harriet had actually thought it kind of funny that they were calling this the "Big Event." They knew that the new director of the Shiloh Public Library System would be introduced to the staff at this event, but other than that, they really knew nothing else about what would be going on.

"You think there'll be snacks after they formally announce the new guy?" Harriet asked.

"If you've seen the poor budget numbers for the last year," Miles said, "you'd know the answer to that question."

"Well, let's just hope this goes quickly, because my stomach is growling. Oh, it looks like things are getting started," Harriet said to her colleague as they settled in to watch.

The city of Shiloh mayor, Al Siroe, took the podium on the small dais they'd erected in the courtyard in front of the Shiloh library.

"Welcome, welcome everyone, welcome," he said. "Thank you all for coming this morning as we introduce the community to our new library director, Michael Todd. Michael has a thirty-year career working with some of the largest companies in the United States. He started as a manager at DigitalActive Computer Company, and he is often credited with being a driving force in bringing the company into the library world, helping to deliver the BookData integrated library system that revolutionized automated circulation control. After leaving DigitalActive, he joined AnaLogistics as their director of data sciences, leading the team that brought about the revolutionary AMS-Data tracker, which allowed businesses to collect and analyze hundreds of different productivity and performance metrics. After they were purchased by Bilderberg, Michael continued to lead the business industry in the areas of data collection, analysis, and presentation."

Faith Pine, the library's fairly new IT manager, leaned toward Harriet and Miles and whispered, "It looks like the mayor has gone back to his retail business roots. If they can afford this paragon of American business and industry, why can't they afford donuts for this event?" Harriet and Miles chuckled.

"For the last four years," the mayor continued, "Michael was the chief information officer for a major league baseball team, where he was in charge of introducing the most incredibly complex statistical tracker ever put online."

At that, there was polite applause, and Miles whispered, "Did I miss hearing his actual library management experience?"

The mayor went back to reading from his notes.

"Michael has been a significant force in the nonprofit world as well. He sat on the board of the American Museum of Industry for twenty years, serving as its chairman for nearly a decade. Michael serves today on the boards of the American Data Scientists League and the International Association of Online Sporting. He told me earlier that he is an avid collector of twentieth-century art books, which I'm sure you all will appreciate. He plays piano in the annual children's charity pageant, and he helped that charity raise nearly one million dollars using his metrics and data analysis. But the one thing Michael says he is most proud of is the fact that he has won his fantasy football league for the last seven seasons."

At this, there was significant laughter. Even the usually stone-faced Miles cracked a slight smile and mumbled, "I guess he can't be all bad then."

"Please join me in welcoming our new Shiloh Public Library System director, Michael Todd."

There was applause as the mayor stepped back. Michael Todd, all six foot nine of him, stood and walked to the podium. He waved to the staff and reached into his pocket for some prepared remarks.

"He's really tall!" Harriet said.

"Really tall," Miles added.

"Thank you," Michael said. "Thank you all for such a great welcome on such a beautiful morning."

Miles pulled his phone out of his pocket and took a picture of the man looming over the top of the podium.

"I'm so incredibly lucky to be a part of the Shiloh team. So many people have said wonderful things about this staff," Michael continued, "about your dedication, your extreme skill, your empathy, and your enthusiasm. I certainly plan to take full advantage of all of these as we make Shiloh's library the best library in the world."

"Wow! Talk about setting goals," Harriet noted.

"As we all begin working together," Michael said, "my plan is to hone the library's methods, to develop clear and effective new programs, and—most importantly—to allow the library's most valuable resource, its incredible staff, to make the best use of every minute they have. In short, we will bring the library blazing into the future."

There was loud applause as the mayor, the library commissioners, and the other city of Shiloh dignitaries on the dais stood up and gave him their ovation. The mayor walked up to the new director, shook his hand, and took the podium again.

"Thank you so much for coming," the mayor said. "Please stick around and introduce yourselves to Michael. Donuts and coffee will be delivered shortly."

Miles, Harriet, and Faith exchanged pleasantly surprised looks and offered their own cheers—more for the pending donut delivery than for the new director.

The next morning, just before opening, Michael held his first "all hands" staff meeting, and this time there were no donuts.

"Thanks for coming," he began, "and for not missing the donuts."

Friendly laughter followed.

"I want to start by saying that it is an absolute honor to be here, to be the new library director," he continued. "I meant what I said in front of the mayor yesterday. You all should be commended for your incredible work here in Shiloh. You know, I've had quite a few people ask why I'd move away from the tech field, and especially major league baseball, to take a position like this. To be honest, I've asked myself the same question. But, while there are many reasons, there are two that stand out. First is the fact that this is the library where I used to study for my tests when I was a kid, sitting right back there, where an old potted plant would provide the perfect cover for my youthful shenanigans." Michael pointed to a corner of the library as more laughter rang out. "And, as I said many times in the interview process, I'm here to bring this amazing library into the modern age. When I came back to Shiloh last year, I immediately got myself a new library card, and I saw that there were so many places here that new methodologies could improve."

"*Methods*," whispered Harriet to Faith, who was sitting to her left. "*Methods* is the proper word, not *methodologies*."

"I'll be meeting with many of you over the next several days," Michael said, "and we'll begin looking at your processes, how we can bring new support to you, and how to alleviate some of the grunt work. Every moment of your workday is precious, and we'll be looking into the ways that you work, looking at every step, and how we can apply new techniques to improve every aspect of your job. It won't be easy, and many of you may think that looking at metrics is crazy. But it works, and I'm here to show you how." Many staff members looked a bit confused—if not overly concerned.

"So, I'm all in if the *numbers* he's talking about means giving us all huge raises and longer breaks," Miles mumbled to nobody in particular.

Michael continued quickly. "I fully understand that it will take many of you some time to get comfortable with my affinity to measure benefits and outcomes. But if you're not looking at the numbers, you're pretty much driving blind. Staff may have a gut feeling that a library program or service is successful, but gut feelings are sometimes—if not often—wrong. Now, I have some auditing and metric evaluations to go through. I'll look over the preliminary results and then contact most of you to come in and help me design some performance goals. For now, let's get to work."

For the next few days, the Shiloh Public Library System staff observed the new director as he walked through the staff workrooms. Always quiet and in the background, Michael was constantly scribbling in his little notebook. Occasionally he'd ask a library clerk a seemingly obscure question like, "How long does it normally take you to put that sort of label on a book?" or "Why do you walk across the room to a computer three different times during a single process?" At one point, Michael pulled a staff member over to him and gave them a diagram of the first floor of the library and a pencil and said, "For the next three hours, I want you to stand at the front doors and watch every user who comes in the building. As they move through the library to where they are going, I want you to chart each user's path here on this diagram."

The staff member looked dumbfounded and replied, "Okay, but I'm supposed to work at the circulation desk for the next two hours." Director Todd assured the staff member he'd alert the supervisor that he'd reassigned her. Something else caught Michael's eye across the room, and he took out his notebook and headed over to investigate it.

Faith was the first on the schedule to meet Michael, and she was waiting alone in the small meeting room for her director and who knew who else to join her. As the head of information technology, Faith was the newest arrival at the library, having started at Shiloh Public Library only about a year earlier. Her main job had been the library's website, updating it to incorporate HTML5 and transitioning away from a website that had been built during the previous century and had rarely been updated since. Faith was glad to know that someone with an understanding of technology was on board and that her and her team's concerns would be understood on a technical level.

Of course, the other 35 percent of her job was restarting public computers for patrons, replacing frayed cords, updating software programs, and getting projectors and printers to connect to roaming laptops.

Director Todd finally walked into the meeting room, ducking his head to make it through the door. "Morning, Faith," he said. "I've been reading up on your time here. Just over a year, right?"

"Yes," she answered. "I used to be at Baylor, working in database maintenance."

"And doing a great job, if your recommendations are to be believed."

Faith had to admit, she liked that Michael had done some homework.

"You've been working on our website mostly, no?" he asked.

"I have been," Faith said. "It's been an interesting experience, basically growing the traffic month over month. It's been impressive growth, but some of that might have to do with the redesign the entire city did."

"And what are the numbers?"

Faith had anticipated this question and had printed out all the information she had collected. It fit onto a single page. She pushed the document across the table to the director.

She wasn't sure she needed to help him interpret the data, so she just offered a brief, "About two hundred forty impressions, or hits, each month—forty-nine thousand unique."

"And dwell time?" Michael asked, looking over the document, turning it over as if to see if there were any data he might be missing.

"Average, three minutes, twelve seconds, accessing two pages."

Director Todd was quiet for a few moments, glancing through the document, looking at the numbers. "Graphs would be nice," he added. Faith found the comment odd.

"And what's the dwell-per-unique?" he finally asked.

"Excuse me?" Faith asked.

"The dwell time per unique visitor a month," Michael said. "And do you have demographic breakdowns for all of these?"

Faith was confused. "I don't really see how that would be useful to know. We don't typically collect any of that," she said. "It might actually run afoul of our data privacy policy."

Director Todd looked up and asked, "And these are the numbers for only the in-house computers? Or is this data inclusive of data from users at home?"

"I've always assumed it presents data from only the computers in the facility, but now that you ask, I suppose it could also include hits to our servers from outside the library. I'll have to dig around the user manuals for an answer," Faith said. Michael pulled a small reporter's notebook from his inside suit pocket, pulled out a pen, and started jotting down things as he spoke.

"Faith." The director sighed. "I'll need you to get me the following metrics for the website: dwell-per-unique, access types, uniques by physical location, devices used to access, and I really want a series of day-time graphs for all those. It's the only way we can know about our web commitments."

Michael slid the paper he'd jotted on across to Faith, who picked it up and looked it over. For such a tall man, he had incredibly tiny handwriting.

"Now," Director Todd said, "more about internal use data?"

"Excuse me?"

"The use of the internal computers, databases, and computer training," Michael elaborated, "usage times, and the peaks for usage, number of individual accesses, and the most popular sites, how often the catalog is being used versus the number of external sites. We need to do some cost to benefit analysis, and this data is the only way."

Faith gave him a bemused look, and Michael began writing in that reporter's notebook again. This action aggravated her for some reason, and she snipped, "Getting all that data is a bit out of my wheelhouse. I'm not even sure it can be done."

"Really?" Michael replied. "I'd think a stellar Baylor student like yourself would have had tons of training in that regard. At any rate, trust me, computers can collect almost any data. You just need to know how to ask for it. Why don't you Google it?"

Faith's mouth dropped open.

"I'm joking, Faith. Lighten up." Michael chuckled. "We can certainly hire some programmers who know how to extrapolate that type of data, but if we did that, then why would I need you?" Michael held up his hands. "Again, I'm joking!"

Faith wasn't convinced that he was. But she stood up and assured the director she'd look into it.

Miles, the circulation services manager, knew that he was the last person on staff to sit down with the director. He'd heard from dozens of his colleagues who'd met with the director over the last week that he was somewhat demanding but generally a nice guy. The thing was, Michael seemed to be asking for some of the most esoteric—if not useless—numbers. Why was he asking for this sort of stuff? It didn't seem to make sense. But Miles had anticipated that this "numbers guy" would be wanting lots of statistics, so he'd spent most of the morning running reports and gathering circulation and collection statistics. He was actually running a bit late to the meeting with Director Todd as he waited for the last report to print. Once it was done, he grabbed it off the printer, put it in his folder of other reports, and sprinted to the meeting room.

Director Todd was already sitting at the table when Miles entered the room.

"Come on in," Michael said, friendly as could be. "Looks like I saved the best for last. I've been so interested in all your numbers! I just met with Lydia about her teen programming, and the lack of attention to numbers in our programs and services alarmed me. It will be good to see some concrete numbers from you, and judging by the size of that folder you're holding, I'm not going to be disappointed."

Miles took a seat and grinned in response.

"Well," he said, "I know Lydia and the staff like to give our kids the best possible time at the library . . . especially since it's so difficult to get them to come in at all."

"That's what I like to hear. So, Miles, let's talk circulation numbers." Director Todd reached into his pocket and pulled out his reporter's notebook. "So, let's see what I need to know from you about our circulation services and programs."

"I'm happy to help. I've brought you the most recent reports I could find," Miles said, and he handed his folder across to Michael.

"So," Michael said, consulting the notebook instead of the circulation reports, "how many teens do we serve in an average month?"

Surprised by the question, Miles had to think.

"Honestly, I can't say. I can show you the circulation numbers for the teen collection. It's there in that folder. But we don't track ages of our users when they get a card—well, not exact age, just whether they are a child or adult. But the circulation numbers will help," Miles said. He'd taken the time to print all the stuff and, darn it, the director was going to look at it!

Again, Director Todd ignored the folder. Instead, he referred to questions he'd written in his notebook.

"Miles, I've written down some questions here the answers to which will be extremely helpful in getting a full picture of our performance success." Michael waited a dramatic beat, then added, "Or performance failure." Director Todd handed a list to Miles. "I know there is a lot on that list I need answered, but if you'd please start with the ones on top of that list. First, what has been the year over year percentage change in user traffic by various hours the library is open? Second, what are the total number of circulations as related to total user traffic patterns? Third, what are the total number of users in a time period compared to the number of staff members on the library floor in the same time period? Do you think you can pull those metrics together, Miles?"

Miles's head was spinning, and he wasn't really sure why he blurted out what he did: "No. Does any library collect this sort of stuff?"

Director Todd replied, quite sternly, "We're not interested in being 'any library,' Miles. We are interested in being *the* library. The Shiloh Public Library System will set the standard."

"But—" Miles couldn't finish his statement before Director Todd pushed on.

"Look, I know you and your staff collect a vast amount of data." Michael held up the folder Miles had given him. "But performance success is more than just counting. I need help to develop a coordinated, systematic, data-driven approach to this library's key decisions. I need help in our ability to forecast more effectively. I need help in showing staff how to design a plan for growth and expansion. Yes, many libraries collect usage statistics. The problem is that they then erroneously report them as successful performance indicators."

Miles shook his head. "I'm lost. I really don't follow what you're saying."

"Let me give you an example, Miles." Michael opened Miles's folder of statistics and pointed to a number. "Okay, here. You report the number of adults who attended computer training sessions last year. Or over here. Here's a number for how many children's nonfiction books were checked out. But, Miles, these types of statistics, without any reference to an outcome, are simply measures of usage or busyness. Now I could find a use for this type of data if I were, perhaps, making a case for increased funding. But how does it help us measure the library's performance?"

Miles tried to turn the discussion back to the first question the director had asked regarding the teens. "Well, as far as teens in the library, I know there are a couple dozen who are regulars, here just about every day, but total numbers I don't have."

"You don't collect data on users?" the director asked.

"Not for the teen room."

"Well," Director Todd said, "we're going to have to change that."

Miles was getting frustrated and felt a bit like he was being attacked. He tried to remain positive but couldn't let his frustration go unattended. "Mr. Todd, I am more than willing to help you get whatever data I can. But you need to understand that we are trying to operate a library here. It's hard to build a bridge as people are walking over it. I need my staff to focus on what they are trained to do. Just a few days ago, I had a missing staff person at the circulation desk, and come to find out he was drawing on a library map for you as library users moved around the building. I had no one at the checkout desk for thirty minutes, so I had to spend time checking out patrons myself. Surely there are more important things my staff can do than drawing lines on a map for you, sir."

Director Todd took a deep breath. "I apologize for that, Miles. I had promised to let you know about that but got distracted. But there was a very strategic purpose to my request. I plan to use that drawing to help us identify 'power aisles' in the library—those areas that get the most exposure to our users. Places where we can feature important promotional displays and collections. Miles, there is much we can learn from metric analysis and performance evaluation. But there is an equal amount we can learn from the retail world and its use of merchandising and marketing. For example, I've learned from research that shoppers usually prefer to move right and walk counterclockwise around the store. The same is most likely true for libraries, and we could easily capitalize on that knowledge in laying out our collections and services. The map I had your staff member draw on could certainly help validate that research. Do you see what I mean?"

Miles agreed that there was much to learn, but he couldn't agree that numbers collection was the best way to do it. He told Director Todd that he'd talk to the staff and come up with some methods to collect data that would be more useful. Until then, he said, he needed to get back to the circulation desk. They were consistently short-staffed, and Miles needed to relieve a library clerk who was due for a lunch break.

The following Friday, Harriet, Miles, and Faith found themselves all together in the lunchroom. It was the first time they'd all been together since the "Big Event." They each managed to share their week's difficulties. Instead of eating in the staff room, the three of them decided to head across the street and enjoy some Chinese food and have a more private conversation. As was usual, the first portion of lunch was reserved for conversation of what they'd been streaming at home and the various meals that had disappointed them over the previous week. After the final plate was made clean by the scraping of Miles's fork, the conversation turned quickly to work.

"So," Faith said, "the new guy, right?"

"You have no idea," said Miles, shoveling the final mouthful of sweet and sour pork into his mouth. "He wants me to start tracking attendance at programs by time of day and wants circulation data cross-tabulated with staffing levels! What's the point? Whether it's two or two hundred people, we're still serving the community!"

"There would be a problem if it were two hundred," Harriet noted. "I think that room is only coded for seventy-five people max."

"Whatever," Miles said. "I mean, we do that annual survey where the kids all say they want more anime and the parents say we're the best in the world. Why waste time just collecting that sort of garbage dump information? We know what we're doing!"

"He wants data on how every terminal on the network is used by patrons!" Faith said.

Harriet tutted. "That probably doesn't fly considering our new privacy policies," she said. "We don't delve into what our users are looking at."

"It might," Faith added, "but barely since he doesn't want specific sites visited, just what programs are being used and for how long. He wants to know how many different users are on each one, for how long, and whether they're using the net to interact with our catalog or whatever. I don't get it. I don't even know why we need to know that level of detail."

"That seems excessive," said Harriet.

"What about you?" Miles asked Harriet. "What duck does he have you hunting in collection development?"

"Mostly he's looking for top titles," she responded, "but he wants the top five hundred, and then he wants it broken down by genre, and then how many of them were checked out by the same user, and how many times they were renewed, and how many generated fines, and on and on and on."

"What will any of this accomplish?" Faith asked.

"Even if we know exactly what everyone who comes to a program in the teen room thinks about every single minute of every single program," Miles said, "it's not like we're going to change what we do fundamentally. We're not in the entertainment business; we don't live or die by the number of kids who come through and see our programs."

"I can see wanting some of it," Faith said, "like knowing which PCs we're going to need to replace first, but really, dwell time by day of the week and hour of the day? What's that going to tell us? That people are home in the evening, that's what!"

"I mean, he's got a pedigree," Harriet said. "He obviously understands the world of business, but he arrives at the library and then starts working to get us providing all of this data. It just seems like he's punting on addressing the big stuff but making us all dig hard for—and stare hard at—the small stuff."

"If it turns into something bigger," Miles said, "like a five-year plan, or actually addresses our concerns, that's one thing. He didn't even ask me what I thought the library should be doing; he is entirely focused on datapoints, inputs, and outputs."

"We're understaffed and overworked, but what library isn't?" Harriet said. "And, really, what library director absolutely *needs* to know who prints out the search results for *The Tempest* from the computer by the back stairs?"

"Oh," Miles added, "that printer needs ink. Message came up this morning."

Faith made a mental note of it.

"We're growing faster than ever before," Harriet began, "and this guy who has all sorts of business experience wants to break everything we do down into meaningless numbers instead of seeing the bigger picture."

"What did we expect?" Faith said. "The guy's greatest achievement is working as a data collector. And, apparently, he's quite successful at using that data."

"I get that," Miles said, "but there's a limit to data analysis when that data is useless or serves no greater purpose. Speaking of numbers, lunch is over. We should get back."

The trio walked back to the library, and as they walked through the doors, a very bored-looking library clerk pressed the button on a hand-counter three times as they walked by. Miles, Harriet, and Faith looked at each other and rolled their eyes.

THE NEW GUY RESPONSES

Response 1
By Kathy Parker, consultant and director (retired), Glenwood-Lynwood Library, Lynwood, Illinois

Whenever a new library director comes to a library, staff are often trepidatious and have lots of questions. "What will they be like?" "Will they like me?" "What education and experience do they have?" "What are they going to change?" "How will my job be affected?" "Will I still have a job?" Other than the fact that the person has been hired as the new library director, the staff have no prior knowledge of their new boss. It is to be expected, then, that staff are anxious to know more. It is obvious by the accolades the mayor extols on him that the new library director, Michael Todd, comes to his position at Shiloh Public Library System with impressive credentials. However, Michael does not have formal library training nor has he ever worked in a library setting.

Michael comes into his new position with a lot of prior knowledge, some great new ideas, and a penchant for data. The primary library staff, clerks Miles and Harriet, have been working at the library for a while, while Faith, the new IT person, is relatively new. These library staff members have established routines and processes and believe the library has been running smoothly. Miles, Harriet, and Faith all believe that they are already providing good library service to the community, and they are therefore perplexed with the "new guy's" credentials.

Lack of communication to and from all parties is a theme running through this entire scenario. The first indication of minimal communication is seen when we learn that the city's mayor and library commissioners have released absolutely no information about the new library director to the library staff prior to his introduction to the community. We note even more communication problems later in the scenario when the new library director walks the library floor, taking notes and observing staff and processes without letting them know what he is doing and why. He asks for data from key staff without really explaining how and why he will use it. Library Director Todd appears to have a grand plan for improvement and forward movement for the library but does not ask for input or share his vision with staff.

While the library staff are communicating with each other, they are merely reacting to the situation and Michael's actions, not discussing their thoughts with the one person who needs to hear from them—their new boss. Library Director Todd is moving full steam ahead, trying to gather data for his plans to move the library forward. The library staff feel that their new boss does not appreciate all that they have accomplished before he became library director and that he is a bit condescending to staff when he meets with them. This is creating some resentment and a level of distrust toward Michael—not a positive way to start a new position.

One piece of information missing from this situation is the motivation of Library Director Todd. He has mentioned that he knows the library can be brought into the modern age. But he hasn't been at all clear in this scenario on how that can be accomplished or why that is beneficial. Library staff only know that their new library director has no formal library training or experience and is asking them to do a lot of data gathering for some unknown reason. Why is he doing this? What is his motivation? Michael may have a directive from the mayor and library commissioners to bring the library into the modern age, but the reader does not know this for sure. The mayor introduces Michael as a "paragon of American business and industry." If so, Michael should be well aware of the need for a chief executive to share their mission and vision before they start to transform their organization. What would help resolve this situation is if Michael would communicate more clearly with the staff. He has the complete power to turn this situation around by being more communicative and transparent. He needs to inspire and motivate the change he desires by articulating why it is necessary, explaining how it can be achieved, and listening to the staff's concerns.

It's unfortunate to note that this entire situation could have been avoided from the start. Ideally, the mayor and library commissioners should have involved key library staff in the hiring process in some way or—at the very least—shared some basic information about their new boss. Many institutions involve staff members from all levels of the organization in the screening and interviewing process when filling executive positions. Some city organizations even include fact-finding discussions with community members and stakeholders—as well as all library staff—to identify what type of candidate to look for that would best fit the organization. While that did not happen, a successful path forward for the library is still possible.

Library Director Todd should sit down with all staff and acknowledge the good work that they have done thus far and explain that he hopes to learn from them how the library runs. By doing this, he is validating the prior work of the staff and acknowledging that—while he does not have formal library training—he wants to learn all that he can so he can use his skills to enhance the work they have already done. He should then meet again with key staff individually to ask about their departments and positions, asking them what works, what doesn't, and how they think things can be improved. Michael should also ask these key library staff members to tell him what would help them give the best services possible and what they need from him to accomplish that.

Once he has met with the key staff, he should create a plan of what he wants to accomplish to move the library forward and how he plans to get there—including what he needs from his staff to meet these goals. Once that plan is finalized, he should meet with key staff again in a group to present the plan, discuss the best way to implement it, and get staff buy-in. Since he is a numbers guy, he should discuss with them how data can help form and drive decision making and what types of data will be required to make those decisions. He should articulate how data-driven decisions benefit organizations by taking emotions and assumptions out of the process, thereby leading to more effective services. By being more communicative, transparent, and inclusive of all library staff in this way, Library Director Todd will have created a feeling of goodwill, enabling his staff to feel some ownership of the inevitable changes along the way.

Response 2
By Jenn Carson, director, LP Fisher Public Library, New Brunswick, Canada

When I am presented with any challenging interpersonal situation, either at the library or elsewhere, the first thing I do is appreciate how complex human interactions can be. Many management tools and experts will guide you to a "simple" solution, a one-size-fits-all sort of shorthand you can use as your "management style." I don't have a management style. I adapt my actions and directives based on the staff or patrons involved and their unique personalities and challenges. While my general off-camera personality is fairly open and easygoing and would prefer to let people handle their own issues unless they request help—or I really see them flailing around—I have come to realize that some staff members actually prefer to be micromanaged. They *want* me to give them step-by-step details, check in with them often, and provide continuous feedback. These types of employees often flounder, directionless, if left to their own devices. Others, like Michael Todd, the new director of Shiloh Public Library in this scenario, are more than happy to step in and take charge—confident in their abilities—and expect others to see that their way is the *best* way, after all. They require a completely different approach. Therefore, in every situation, I am prone to first step back and see if I can understand all the variables at play and their influences. I like to look at the situation from as many perspectives as possible, as objectively as possible, trying to keep my own personal biases and triggers to the periphery (no easy task!). I try to understand the environment the conflict is taking place in. For example, Todd's behavior may have been received by staff very differently in a manufacturing plant than at the public library. I also examine the psychological makeup of those involved and any external stressors, given the information I have at the time. For example, if Todd just moved for this job and is also in the process of settling his family into a new house, new school, new routine, and so on, that may make him more high-strung than he would normally be. Most importantly, I try my best to approach each individual involved, including myself, with compassion, knowing that for the most part we are all doing our best with the tools we have.

So, by stepping back and taking a broad, compassionate view of the recent appointment of Michael Todd as the director of the Shiloh Public Library, we can look at the following components.

Environment

Michael comes from a for-profit, analytical, statistics-based background where soft skills such as relationship building and community engagement are valued less than producing hard numbers and measurable results. A not-for-profit public library is a place where a pleasant atmosphere, teamwork, and meeting the informational as well as emotional needs of the patrons is highly valued. In order for the staff and Michael to meet halfway, they are going to need to see how his methods are in the best interest of the public and their own workflow, and Michael will need to appreciate that not every success in a library is something that can be easily quantified. He will also need to come to realize that a library is not a retail environment and that while some ideas in libraries are borrowed from bookstores (eye-catching displays, for example), our marketing and merchandising budgets (and staffing allocations for those departments) are not the same.

Priorities and Motivation

Michael appears to be extrinsically motivated by numbers and efficiency. For him, productivity is a top priority. He wants to observe and manage "every step" because "every moment of your workday is precious." Most of the staff appear to be more intrinsically motivated; they got into library work because they like helping people and because their work feels good to them. That doesn't mean they don't take their work seriously, as the circulation supervisor Miles wasn't pleased to be short-staffed at the desk without notice, and Faith was initially hopeful to have someone else as invested in technology as she is. The employees and Michael are going to have to work together to make sure their priorities get into closer alignment, and this is going to require some good communication and active listening on everyone's part.

Personality Conflicts

Clearly Michael is intent on micromanaging the employees at his new workplace—at least until he feels like he has the situation under control. If he's feeling uncertain about all the changes that have taken place, this is more than likely going to make him double down on his controlling ways. Likewise, the staff, feeling threatened that their daily operations and long-term work habits are being challenged, are likely to become more entrenched in "the ways things have always been." Anyone trained in change management will tell you that the worst thing is to go into a new environment and start making huge changes right away. Michael isn't doing that—yet; for now he's just (perhaps overzealously) observing and recording information, but he's threatening to make changes, and this is making everyone uncomfortable. On top of that, Michael's poor use of humor to try to add levity to the situation is making things worse. The staff are, understandably, reactive and finding themselves getting defensive.

Goals

From what we read in the scene, there doesn't appear to be a lot of long-term goal setting on the minds of the staff at Shiloh. The staff are just trying to get through the next program, the next shift at the circulation desk, the next software update. Michael, on the other hand, has the overly ambitious goal of making Shiloh "the best library in the world," which places an enormous amount of expectation not only on the staff but also on himself. It is also potentially setting him up for an "overpromise and underdeliver" sort of disappointment with the city of Shiloh shareholders and citizens. Again, there needs to be some halfway point of balance where Michael creates a realistic and achievable three-to-five-year strategic plan with specific goals for each department. The staff need to be clear on these goals, how they will be measured, and what the consequences are for meeting or not meeting them.

So, given what we know, what are the staff and new director of the Shiloh Public Library to do to solve their problems? Well, first they need to accept that they will probably never solve all of them. The nature of human interaction is that it will always involve some amount of conflict. Then, they will need to examine the situation clearly and decide what they personally can control and be brave enough, and willing enough, to have some hard conversations with each other. Sharing perspectives and resources with one another will broaden their knowledge of what is happening around them and allow them to accept it with a lot more comfort. For example, Michael may consider sharing insight and inspiration from an excellent article or book he values. One such quote—from Peter Block's *The Answer to How Is Yes: Acting on What Matters* (Berrett-Koehler, 2003)—seems more than appropriate in this case:

> No one is going to change as a result of our desires. In fact, they will resist our efforts to change them simply due to the coercive aspect of the interaction. People resist coercion much more strenuously than they resist change. Each of us has a free will at our core, so like it or not, others will choose to change more readily from the example set by our own transformation than by any demand we make of them.

Response 3
By Barbara Kerr, director, Medford Public Library, Medford, Massachusetts

The Shiloh Public Library finds itself in the middle of a library culture clash that has been going on for several decades. Before the internet, libraries didn't have any competition to speak of, so librarians didn't have to work very hard at promotion or merchandising. When you have no competition, and people have no options other than to come to you, then you don't have to reach out and draw them in. Unfortunately, the age of "no competition" is long over, and librarians can't just sit around anymore. There must be a concerted effort to reach out, merchandise, promote, forecast, and understand who uses the library and who needs to be pulled in.

At first, the fact that the city of Shiloh has hired a nonlibrarian seems a little shocking. However, it really isn't odd to appoint an administrator who comes from outside the profession. A nonlibrarian may be able to see the big picture and resist the temptation to respond to the underlying conditions that have given rise to some of the problems our organizations face, unclouded by preconceptions, unproductive professional traditions, and that long history in which libraries existed without competition.

As this scenario unfolds, the reader sees that the new director, Michael Todd's, "outsider" point of view has revealed a lot of holes in the library's procedures. The library staff are very complacent and uninformed about their library. They have no idea who comes to the library or why; they don't know what the top titles are or what genres are most popular. They don't think beyond the same static circulation and attendance numbers they've used over and over. They don't even know how many people fit in their library meeting room! Shiloh Public Library's staff are stuck in the old-fashioned idea that they don't have to make an effort because people will come to them. This attitude must end! This library must start caring and moving forward—not just sticking in the same rut. Otherwise, they risk losing relevance within the city and community they serve.

The "new guy," Director Michael Todd, has his work cut out for him. Michael's data-driven approach is a good one and necessary given the lack of staff initiative. However, there *are* some issues with a nonlibrarian being in charge. Businesses are often too focused on the bottom line. In getting too caught up in that business-minded point of view, Director Todd is not evaluating the human interaction of staff and patrons. Those interactions and relations, like those between Lydia and her teens, can't be easily quantified. There are elements of library success that are driven by relationships, not just data. Performance measures often overlook the value library users place on relationships and programs, and the value programs and services add to the overall mission of the library. Director Todd is wise to measure critical success factors, but "increasing numbers" is only one factor in showing success. Michael must also include performance measures that integrate satisfaction and value to library service measurement and show the overall impact that these relationships result in meeting the library's mission and goals.

Michael also needs to take a serious look at the staff's attitude. His data gathering certainly brought a lot of staff issues to light. Something is wrong if everyone on the staff is so disinterested. Was it the previous administration? Is it the pay rates or physical facility or the way library staff are treated by the city? These are questions that the new director needs to investigate as well. In particular, library clerk Miles's attitude is terrible, and he seems to influence his coworkers. He seems to be in poor control of his circulation department in terms of scheduling and supervision. The staff can't be allowed to continue as they are—Michael has to gather data about them as well and make some changes. Hopefully, Director Todd can inspire his staff, but he may also have to begin the disciplinary process, and eventually terminate some, if they cannot embrace change.

There is hope for the Shiloh Public Library as both the "new guy" and the old staff have great potential. Although the staff are blasé, they do have good credentials, skills, and experience. And while Library Director Todd currently seems more focused on data than people, his experience with nonprofits is significant. There must be changes at this library—whether it be in staff attitudes, library merchandising, or performance measurement outcomes. Librarians cannot accept the status quo—they have to embrace constant change and bring it home. If they all come together—with the new guy's numbers and the old staff's experience and reputation—they will make an incredibly effective team.

Part Four

Controlling

Chapter Eleven

The Cops

A Controlling Scenario Using Skills

SCENARIO

"Um, Kyle, you're gonna want to listen to this," Cynthia said, pressing the button on the phone to call her branch manager over to her desk.

The library branch manager, Kyle Resotrepa, walked over and took the phone from Cynthia.

Cynthia hit the 6 button to replay the message.

"Hello. This is officer Jason Peters from the city of Freer's police department," the voice said, sounding tired but firm. "We have a couple of questions that we hope you can help us with in a case. So if you could return my call, we can quickly run this over. It is sort of a pressing issue, so call us back ASAP." Officer Peters left his phone number and quickly hung up.

Kyle reached over and replayed the message. "Well, this is a new one. What the heck can the library do to help the cops? It's usually the other way around. Ha!"

"I can't think of the last time that our police department called us with a reference question," Cynthia said. "What do they want to know, the address of the local donut shop?"

"This doesn't sound like a reference request," Kyle said. "It sounds more official than that." Kyle replayed the message. This was the kind of message that required a full understanding of all the variables in order to know how to respond. Cynthia didn't seem to see that this might be a serious matter, or at least she didn't understand the matter as thoroughly as he did. Kyle feared there was a nuance in the officer's request that they were both missing.

"You want me to call him back?" Cynthia asked.

"Actually, Cynthia, forward that voice message to me," Kyle said. "I'll give them a call after I listen to it about fifty more times. Oh, and if Officer Peters calls again, have him call me first. I want to know what this is all about."

Kyle listened to the voice message again and again. He wasn't sure he found anything new after that first listen, but now he was focusing on the officer's use of the word "case" and the reference to "pressing issue." Yeah, this was serious. He quickly gulped down the last of the coffee that had lingered in the cup on his desk for almost three hours, then picked up the phone and dialed Officer Peters's number.

Half a ring and the click announced the answer.

"Peters," the officer said gruffly.

Do all cops have to sound that way? Kyle wondered.

"Hi." Kyle was exceptionally nervous, and there was no way to hide it in his voice. "This is Kyle Resotrepa from the Freer library returning your call."

There was the sound of shuffling and a gentle click that sounded as if it was a recorder turning on. This only made Kyle more nervous, and he could feel a bead of sweat rolling down his forehead.

"Thanks for returning my call," Officer Peters said. "I'm calling about an investigation I'm involved in at the moment. We're trying to confirm the identity of a young man we picked up last night."

Kyle was wondering which of his employees had gone off the rails, but there was something in the officer's voice that said this was going to be something a whole lot more complicated.

"The young man has refused to identify himself to us, and the only ID he had in his wallet was a Freer library card," Officer Peters said, a stiff exhale after the last word.

"Okay," Kyle responded.

"We noticed that there's no name on the card, but we have the card number," Officer Peters said, sounding like he was reaching across the desk to pick it up. "The guy somewhat matches the description of a suspect in the recent burglary over at the hardware store. We just need to confirm. Can I read you his card number?"

"All right," Kyle said, stunned.

This was nothing that had ever happened to him before. With the little information he had been given, it would seem that he should at least attempt to help with the identification. After all, he had heard that the theft at the hardware store had involved not only money but also supplies that could be used in bomb making. If this person was a thief, and if this person had even more sinister ambitions, shouldn't the library be willing to help? Wouldn't it be best for the community to help Officer Peters? Yet, at the same time, there was a major tickle at the back of Kyle's mind that this was not nearly so cut and dry.

"I'm g-going"—Kyle stammered, and that lone bead of sweat now seemed to have a friend traveling with it—"I'm going to need to do a bit of research on our . . . our . . . patron privacy policies first."

That was the best that Kyle could manage at the moment, and he thought that Officer Peters gave an exceptionally huge, and expectant, sigh to accompany his exacerbated response.

"Understood," Officer Peters said, "but we have policies too. We can't hold this individual without cause very much longer. Look, would you mind if I bring the squad car over in a little while? It might be easier to go over this face-to-face."

Kyle panicked, but he took a moment to center himself, to bring himself into a place of quiet, peaceful calm. He took several deep breaths, felt those drops of sweat meet their terminal absorption into his eyebrows as a new one seemed to form.

"Hello?" barked Officer Peters over the phone. "Are you still there?"

"Oh," Kyle said, "sorry. Okay, I guess that would be fine. I mean, sure, come on down. Do you need directions?" Kyle was not doing well.

"I think I've got it," Officer Peters said. "Plus, it'll give me a chance to return the three le Carré novels I've got out. Give me about an hour." Kyle was immediately impressed that there were police officers who read library books. The officer hung up the phone, but Kyle continued to hold the receiver as if he was expecting there to be more.

Sensing he didn't have much time, Kyle zipped over to the reference desk. "Cynthia, I'm heading over to admin. I've got to talk to Director Palentina about this police matter."

"Oh! What's it about?" Cynthia asked.

"I don't have time right now. I'll tell you all about it later," Kyle called back over his shoulder, car keys in his hand, as he sprinted out the staff door.

When he arrived at the central library administrative offices, Kyle didn't even stop by the desk of the director's secretary. He headed right to her office door and knocked. He could see through the side window that she was on the phone. She signaled to him through the window to come in. He opened the door and walked through, and Palentina pointed to the chair across from her desk.

Kyle remained standing. He didn't know why he was so frazzled about this situation, but he was just too nervous to sit down. He simply loomed over the director's desk, waiting for her to finish. She could tell Kyle was agitated for some reason, so she tried to disengage from the caller.

"All right, Mr. Mayor," Palentina said. "I'm happy to oblige. Talk to you next week."

She hung up the phone, then noticed the look on Kyle's face.

"What's wrong, Kyle?" she asked.

"We got a call at the branch," Kyle started, forcing himself to sit down. "From the Freer police. They want us to give them the name of one of our library card holders."

"They want us to give them the name of a card holder?" Palentina repeated, confused.

"Yeah," Kyle said. "They picked someone up who matched a suspect's description, and this guy won't identify himself to the cops. The only thing he had in his wallet was a card for Freer library."

"Really?" she asked.

"Really," Kyle responded, thinking about that fact as strange for the first time. Who in the world carries nothing on them but a library card? Well, maybe a criminal. That was something that Kyle hadn't thought about.

"So," Palentina began again, "they have the person, they have the card, and they want us to confirm his identity?"

"Yep."

Palentina was known for her steady head, for never showing any visible signs of being shaken, but here some cracks were showing. It was the rarest of expressions on her face, and that rocketed Kyle's anxiety into overdrive.

"There are privacy and confidentiality laws here, aren't there?" Palentina asked, somewhat oblivious to the fact that not two feet above her on the wall behind her desk was a framed copy of the American Library Association's Library Bill of Rights.

Kyle pointed to the wall. "It's right there! Article VII of the Library Bill of Rights." He quoted, "All people, regardless of origin, age, background, or views, possess a right to privacy and confidentiality in their library use. Libraries should advocate for, educate about, and protect people's privacy, safeguarding all library use data, including personally identifiable information."

He pulled out another page he had gathered quickly on his way to her office. "The library board based our own privacy policy on that statement from the ALA." He began reading, trying to be as even as possible. "The Freer Library System, in its role of providing information services to the citizens of, visitors to, or those working within Freer, Indiana, is dedicated to preserving the privacy of patron data. The library will collect only what data is deemed necessary to allow for the operation, maintenance, and internal analysis of patron services. Data, including registration, circulation records, reference inquiries, and financial transactions, will be held in confidence by the library only as long as is required by local, state, and federal statute, and not be sold or distributed to third parties without notification."

Kyle stopped reading, put the paper on the desk, and pushed it across to her.

"And?" Palentina sighed. "But after nine-eleven didn't the government pass the USA Patriot Act? I believe I talked to the city attorney about it way back then. I remember him telling me how the Patriot Act gave law enforcement agencies broad powers to investigate terrorists in our country. Doesn't that policy negate this policy?" she asked, picking up the Freer library privacy policy. Then, as if arguing with herself, she said, "I'm sure this guy isn't a terrorist though."

"Who knows," Kyle said. "The officer said the guy somewhat matched the description of the hardware store burglar—and that theft involved potential bomb-making supplies."

"Oh, jeez!" Palentina exclaimed. "Okay, so we're basically in the position of violating one or the other policy no matter what we do. So, isn't it best to help the community first at all cost?"

"Are we?" Kyle asked.

"Our own policy has that odd note about not selling the data to third parties," Palentina said, "and there's the phrase stating that we only keep the data as long as we deem necessary."

"I don't follow. Are you saying that *giving* the data is okay as long as we don't *sell* it and as long as we deem it's not necessary for us to keep it any longer?" Kyle asked, somewhat incredulously.

"Well," she continued, "it does seem to be within the library's purview to provide the data *freely*. And since the library and the police department are of the same city entity, we wouldn't be giving data to a third party. We're merely sharing it within our city."

"That seems pretty slim," Kyle said. "And what about our own professional duty. Ethically we'd be violating the Library Bill of Rights, right?"

"Fair enough," Palentina said, "and if my data was transferred to another division, I'd be looking for the number to my lawyer's office."

"So, we shouldn't give the cops the name?" Kyle asked.

"That's not clear either," Palentina said as she tapped at her laptop for a few moments.

Kyle walked around to see her pulling up a section of the library webpage. It was the same section the privacy policy had come from. She pulled up the library safety policy.

"Here it is," Palentina said. "'The Freer Public Library is dedicated to maintaining the safety of all patrons.'"

Kyle waited for her to continue.

"And?"

"That's it," she says, "and that's all it needs to say. If there is a patron of the Freer library who is caught committing a crime, isn't it in our statement to inform the police of the identity of someone who might be a threat to the safety of the rest of the patrons of the library?"

Kyle looked at Palentina, amazed at how a human mind could so thoroughly weigh two contradictions with such powerful conviction to both.

Or maybe she was simply really good at playing devil's advocate.

"So, how do we choose which is the right way?" Kyle asked.

"Well." Palentina looked at Kyle with a steady gaze. "What exactly do we know? Fact: the police called the branch library saying they wanted us to confirm the name of the library card holder." Palentina was quickly adopting that level, steady head for which she was so well known. She went on. "Fact: they asked for that information because they had picked up someone who won't talk to them. Fact: the person who won't talk to them has a library card that will tell the police who the person they picked up is. Correct so far?" Palentina asked.

"There's no way to know if the library card belongs to the person holding it. The guy may have stolen that library card too, and now we'd be giving the police private information about a person who has nothing to do with this whole situation," Kyle responded. "So, all we really know is that someone was holding a library card," he said, now thinking he had a clearer view.

"Now, the only thing we know about the person they are holding," Palentina said, "is that he *somewhat* matches a description of a suspect."

"Isn't it also possible," Kyle said, playing the devil's advocate himself, "that they've got someone who was lost or having an episode and the card is the only way to confirm his identity and allow for finding his family or figuring out if he needs medication? Surely helping out the police in this instance would be beneficial even if we were breaking our own ethical standards."

"Or maybe this person is trying to run away from someone trying to harm him, and he doesn't want to be identified," Palentina said.

Kyle paused. "There is no good answer, is there?"

Palentina shook her head. She then opened up her email program and sent a quick message to the city attorney. "Call me immediately regarding police matter" is all she wrote.

Kyle drove back across the courtyard and was glad to see that there were no police cars in the parking lot yet. Palentina had said that they just had to let the matter go to the city's legal team and that all he should say is "the matter was referred to the city attorney, and he'll be calling you" and send Officer Peters on his way. It would be quick and clean and hopefully would lead to them getting the information they needed without a nasty incident. He'd get right on pushing Palentina to work on an improved privacy policy as an annual goal. That would prevent this from ever happening again.

Or at least that's what Kyle hoped.

He walked into the library, the automatic doors opening immediately before he would have walked right into them. Cynthia was waiting for him just in front of the circulation desk.

"How fares the library?" Kyle asked cheerfully.

Cynthia frowned.

"Officer Peters is waiting in the Hopkins Room," she said.

"What? Why is he here already, and why in the Hopkins Room?"

"He had people with him," Cynthia said as she turned and started walking toward the room typically reserved for use by small study groups, "and I wanted him out of sight."

Kyle probably would have done the same thing.

"I'll talk to him."

In the Hopkins Room, there was a small cadre of people standing behind an obviously tall man sitting at the table in a white shirt and tie. Kyle didn't have to guess which one was Officer Peters.

Kyle entered the room.

"Hello. I'm Kyle Resotrepa."

Officer Peters stepped out from the crowd standing behind the taller gentleman at the table.

"I'm Jason Peters, Mr. Resotrepa," he said, walking over to Kyle and offering his hand.

Kyle shook it.

"I brought the team," said Peters, "since I figured you'd have questions they'd be able to answer for you."

Kyle took a seat at the table.

"Well," he began, "I discussed this with the library director, and she said that this is a matter to discuss with the city attorney."

The gentleman sitting at the table spoke up. "I'm Harold Young, the department's legal liaison," he said. "I've already contacted both Mitch and Davina, and they've said that whatever decision you make, they'll back you on it, so there's no worry on that front."

"I'm Linden Faros, community relations officer," a young woman standing in the back row said. "I'm not allowed to go into the specifics of why we're holding the young man, but it is crucial that we get the name of the gentleman we're holding."

"I'm sure you're aware that the library card might not be his. I mean it could be stolen or something he just picked up out of the trash," Kyle said.

An older gentleman from the back spoke up. "We can't know that for sure until we know the name associated with that card."

Kyle had expected to walk in, take a seat at his desk, have Cynthia walk Officer Peters in, deliver his line, and that would be that. He had not expected the full-court press, and he certainly had not expected to have to rehash all the thoughts he'd had over the last hour with a significant chunk of the Freer police department, but there he was. He basically replayed the entire conversation he'd had with Palentina, only performing both sides as if he were in a one-man show playing multiple characters.

The entire half of the room occupied by the police were either pinching the bridge of their nose or rubbing at their temples.

"Look," Officer Peters said, "you can give it to us now, and help us resolve this, or we can get a subpoena and a court order that will compel you to do so."

"May as well save yourself a little time, and save us a lot of effort and goodwill, and just give us the name," said Harold Young.

At that moment, the *Freer Dispatch* news reporter walked into the Hopkins Room. Kyle knew immediately what he *wanted* to do. He also knew that what he *wanted* to do was far different than what he *had* to do. He just wasn't exactly sure what he *would* do.

THE COPS RESPONSES

Response 1
By Patricia Wong, president-elect, American Library Association; director, Santa Monica Public Library, Santa Monica, California

Branch manager Kyle Resotrepa's good library antennae are activated. This scenario is something that most library leadership will experience at least once in their career. It's best to be prepared. Kyle knows to lean in to all of his prior skills and knowledge as a leader and library practitioner. He was reminded of the Library Bill of Rights, and Director Palentina has some good instincts as well.

Kyle needs to ask to get back to the group to allow him the time and space to handle this in the most appropriate way. He has a relationship with his colleagues in law enforcement. When I am confronted with such requests, I express that I always want to support the efforts of my colleagues on the police force or the FBI, but in order to do so I have an obligation to make sure that my actions are in accord with legislation pertinent to the privacy of library records. I remind them that I appreciate their work, our relationship, and their duty. I have one too. And I need to check in with my superiors. That usually seems to work.

Education

Kyle should do a little bit of research before his next steps. He should contact his director, and together they should work on a process. The library has guidance with local policies. Some states have created legislation that protects patron privacy in libraries and expressly prohibits sharing of customer records and information related to those records without court order or subpoena.

The Library Bill of Rights is the underpinning of the library's commitment to community trust and confidentiality, so Kyle has the American Library Association Office for Intellectual Freedom to support his efforts. ALA staff is available to assist on the steps and the communication with law enforcement. There are also guidelines available online regarding law enforcement and privacy of library records.

Relationships and the Communication Chain

Some in law enforcement are not familiar with the privacy protections issued by local, state, and federal statute. If information that is protected is obtained without appropriate subpoena or court order, the data may be deemed inadmissible, and any investigation will be thwarted by how the information was obtained.

Kyle and his director also have support from their city attorney for legal advice. And sometimes calling on the leadership of other local library jurisdictions on what they have done, without revealing details, can be reassuring.

Once Kyle and his director have a strategy supported by research, data, and advice from their respective leadership, they should get back to their local colleagues in a timely way, with support from the city attorney. Officer Peters's first offer to get a subpoena or court order was the right move. The police require such documentation to appropriately request information. Once they receive the proper documents, the library can provide the information as requested in consultation with their attorney.

The library wants to maintain a good relationship with local law enforcement. There is an opportunity here to have a positive conversation about any future needs from the police department and to arrive at a common understanding and establish a process for actions moving forward.

Policy

That privacy policy that Kyle remembered is a perfect example of how to best prepare for a future request. If there is no policy in place, the ALA Office for Intellectual Freedom has many examples of such policies and can assist with developing one. They can provide training for staff on how to implement the policy and develop processes to ensure that frontline staff know how to respond appropriately when law enforcement comes calling again. This kind of policy is meaningful if drafted with the assistance of several supervisors so they have a firm understanding of its value in the organization. The state library can also be a good resource.

Process and Practice

It's important to set up a regular practice with frontline staff on what the policy means and how staff should interact with law enforcement at all levels when they request information. The policy will optimally identify the precise steps for staff and law enforcement and library leadership's role to inform local counsel. It is a good opportunity to review these steps annually with staff at all levels and to share any training with governing boards. When there is a new seated or appointed counsel or a new city manager or library board member, I include this policy review in their onboarding as they become familiar with their respective roles. The next time Kyle and Palentina and all of their staff encounter this situation, they will all be better prepared.

Response 2
By Lisa Rosenblum, director, King County Public Library System, Issaquah, Washington

The city of Freer has a problem, and it isn't only about an alleged theft from a hardware store. It all starts with a profound lack of leadership at the library. Prior to this incident, all staff—from the library director to the library page position—should have been well versed and trained on what to do if law enforcement requests information about library patrons. Clearly, from the staff's reaction, they were not at all trained on what to do and were not familiar with any library policies. This situation put the library in a reactive position and potentially compromised the ethics of the library when it came to protecting the privacy rights of its users.

In this scenario, Kyle seems to be the one person who has a sense of what is proper. Kyle was right to be wary and to question the police officer's request. Ideally, however, he should be familiar with all library privacy policies as well as state law protecting the privacy of library users *prior* to calling back Officer Peters. Not only the branch manager but all staff should know this.

However, worse by far was Library Director Palentina's reaction to the incident. The library director seems to be clueless regarding how the library should respond. At the library director level, this is unacceptable. Kyle gets high marks here for knowing the American Library Association's Bill of Rights and having the guts to recite it back to his boss. It was equally commendable that Kyle reminds Palentina that the library board had approved a privacy statement for the library. He also gets high marks for concluding that the library's current privacy policy is ambiguous. This shows that Kyle not only has knowledge of the applicable policy but has also seen its shortcomings. However, none of this should be happening in the middle of an incident. All of Kyle's concerns should have been vetted and resolved prior to the policy becoming the center of a potential publicity nightmare.

When Kyle returns to the library after meeting with the director, he must *by himself* handle three law enforcement officials pressuring him to give up information. Once again, there is a clear failure of leadership here. Why hasn't the director offered any support or taken control of this situation herself? Not only has Palentina seemingly abdicated all her authority to her subordinates; she has also shown staff that she is not willing—or able—to make important decisions. The library director is responsible for protecting the privacy rights of the library's patrons, not in making things easier for the police. The library director is also responsible for protecting and supporting the staff. Poor Kyle is doing his best, but the key decision maker is not in the room. She should have immediately dropped what she was doing and accompanied Kyle to the branch.

But Kyle has some blame to share in this scenario as well. Putting aside the fact that he obviously didn't pursue the problems he was having with the privacy policy when it was originally adopted (he should have detailed his issues and suggested how those could be resolved), he allowed the city's police to bully him. Although it must have been scary to be in a room with police pressuring him to provide information, Kyle should have stopped the conversation right at that point and left the room to call the director and get some backup. To add to the chaos, the media show up. The police and media should be held off until the library figures out what they are going to do. This means including the city's attorney, public relations staff, and possibly the city manager. This illustrates why it is so critical for Kyle to step away from this situation and throw it back into the lap of the library director where it belongs. Palentina can contact the appropriate personnel listed above, discuss with them how the library will respond, and receive guidance on how to handle the situation. This will show that the city is reacting as a united front.

In this particular scenario, the major problem can be traced back to the ambiguity in the library policy regarding sharing data. This should be tightened up to align with the American Library Association's and the state library's privacy policies. These clear and well-informed policies concerning privacy need to be adopted by the library board, communicated to the public, posted to the library's website, and thoroughly discussed with all library staff. Good, clear policies are a library's armor against significant problems like those presented in this scenario. If a library does not have adequate policies, or if their policies are too vague, the library will certainly find their operational environment a whole lot more difficult.

And although the case study ends with the media showing up, there should also be policies and procedures on what to do when the media calls. This may not be a big enough library system to have a public relations expert on staff, but certainly the city of Freer has a person on board trained to handle media requests, and they should be contacted whenever the media shows up. In summary, don't wait until the worst-case scenario happens and be caught unaware.

Ever since 9/11 and the Patriot Act, libraries have been increasingly challenged regarding their core principles of protecting the privacy of patrons and promises of confidentiality. Public libraries are being increasingly pressured in some communities to agree with the idea that to be a good American is to become partners with law enforcement, and in many cases the ask means providing library records and patron activity to police. In fact, the very day I reviewed this case study, the FBI showed up wanting the library to provide information about a patron's computer use!

As a student of history, I am often reminded that everything old is new again. The Library Bill of Rights was written back in 1939. It was written because it was needed during a time of increasing intolerance in Europe and suppression of free speech both here and abroad. Its importance and our understanding of its importance still holds true today.

Response 3
By Philip Williams, local history manager, South Georgia Regional Libraries, Valdosta, Georgia

There are several problems with the scenario faced by branch manager Kyle Resotrepa, but they all ultimately revolve around the concept of individuals having the right to privacy. In the United States Constitution, this right is loosely codified in the Fourth Amendment and has subsequently been confirmed by a multitude of United States Supreme Court cases. Librarians have expressed the importance of that right, as far as library services and patrons are concerned, in article VII of the American Library Association's (ALA) Library Bill of Rights. That article reads: "All people, regardless of origin, age, background, or views, possess a right to privacy and confidentiality in their library use. Libraries should advocate for, educate about, and protect people's privacy, safeguarding all library use data, including personally identifiable information."

Branch Manager Resotrepa and Library Director Palentina are both familiar with the Library Bill of Rights, but neither is absolutely aware of the appropriate response to an inquest by law enforcement. The fact that they are both seeing the scenario as a dilemma is a problem in itself. They are uncertain of where their system's privacy policies stand post–Patriot Act. It seems that the policies of the library system have not been reviewed for a number of years. Conducting an audit of the policies of a library periodically is highly important and prevents dilemmas like the one in the city of Freer. While conducting a policy audit, consulting a lawyer (such as the city of Freer city attorney's office) to ascertain if library policies outright contradict any federal, state, or local laws and to discover legally problematic sections is recommended.

The ALA's website has a variety of resources pertaining directly to the Patriot Act. "Libraries cooperate with law enforcement when presented with a lawful court order to obtain specific information about specific patrons" is what the ALA has to say on the matter of legal inquests of library records under the Patriot Act ("USA Patriot Act," American Library Association, accessed March 30, 2020, http://www.ala.org/advocacy/advleg/federallegislation/theusapatriotact). Ethically, as a librarian, Kyle should request that the Freer police come back with a court-ordered subpoena if they want the information. This action also protects the Freer library as an institution from any potential lawsuits that the unidentified man could bring against the Freer library for providing the information to law enforcement in violation of his Fourth Amendment rights.

If the library did consult with an attorney about the matter, or consulted the ALA's website, they would find that section 215 is the relevant part of the Patriot Act that allows law enforcement to have access to library records while pursuing investigations into potential terrorist activities. With further investigation, they would find that section 215 is limited as to who can make a request for such information. The relevant part of section 215 reads, "The Director of the Federal Bureau of Investigation or a designee of the Director (whose rank shall be no lower than Assistant Special Agent in Charge) may make an application for an order requiring the production of any tangible things." Local law enforcement, such as the Freer police, are not able to make use of that section of the Patriot Act. The exact procedure for state and local law enforcement to procure library records varies from state to state but usually requires a court-ordered subpoena. The ALA's website has compiled a list of state privacy laws regarding library records and how law enforcement are able to properly obtain library data ("State Privacy Laws Regarding Library Records," American Library Association, accessed March 30, 2020, http://www.ala.org/advocacy/privacy/statelaws).

Kyle and Palentina also question if the library's safety policy takes precedence over their privacy policy. This is another question that they should consult with a lawyer about during an audit of library policies. Given that the known crime occurred off of library property and that no threat had been made specifically to library patrons or to the library itself, it is doubtful a lawyer would consider that library safety policy to be relevant to the situation. If the unidentified man in this scenario was actually making bombs, and the library did give the information requested in the scenario over to law enforcement without a subpoena, a mistrial could be declared due to evidence obtained illegally, and the man could potentially be released from custody. Following the letter of the law regarding the release of patron information is effectively also protecting the long-term safety of the library and the community it serves.

Chapter Twelve

Story Times Can Be a Drag

A Controlling Scenario Using Difficult Professional Topics

SCENARIO

Megan Kennedy, director of Oregon Trails City Public Library, had barely managed to let the dust settle after an emotional few weeks before it was kicked back up like a desert sand storm. Her phones had finally stopped ringing nonstop, and she was seeing fewer and fewer vehemently nasty emails crowd her inbox. She took a deep breath, ready to relax again, when her administrative assistant opened her office door with bad news.

"Uh, Megan," the assistant said hesitantly, "you're not going to like this. I just opened a bill from the Oregon Trails police department. It's charging back costs of eleven thousand four hundred and fifty-six dollars for managing those protesters at last week's event."

"Eleven thousand dollars!" Megan screamed as she jumped up and grabbed the bill out of the assistant's hands. "This can't be right," she said, looking over the bill. Apparently, the police chief had designated twenty-two personnel to the event. Of those people, eighteen had received some sort of overtime pay ranging from $71 to $200 for nearly eight hours of overtime. Then there were the charges for barricades, riot gear, additional equipment, and signage. "It was only a story time!" Megan said, raising her gaze to the ceiling. "How did that rate such a police response?" Megan let the bill slip to the office floor. Her assistant quickly retrieved it and left the room.

Megan shut her office door, turned out the lights, and sat in her chair as she contemplated just how insane this whole event had become. In just a few short months, her job had turned from something she loved into something she dreaded. *How did this happen?* she mused, falling into some sort of deep meditation as she recalled the long sequence of events that had led to a bill charging her department for over $11,000.

Things had actually begun quite excitedly several months earlier, when Megan and her children's librarian, Carol Garcia, had attended their state's Library Association annual conference. Megan and Carol were sitting at lunch at the start of the conference, going over the programs being offered and mapping out a strategy to attend as many worthwhile programs as possible. There were the typical programs one sees offered at Library Association conferences—such as career planning, new technology, and literacy management—but Carol had circled one program in particular that caught Megan's interest immediately.

"What's this one all about?" Megan asked as she pointed at a program listed in the calendar titled Queen for a Day: Drag in Libraries.

"Oh, doesn't that sound interesting?" Carol replied. "It's a trend rushing around the country recently. Drag queen performers reading to children in libraries. I have a friend in Brooklyn who was telling me how popular the program was in her library—sometimes getting two hundred or three hundred people! Wouldn't that be phenomenal?"

"That does sound fascinating. Do you mind if I come along with you to that? I'd really be interested in hearing about the program and what it offers kids," Megan said, thinking she could skip the diversity lecture and customer service program offered during the same time. The two of them finished their lunch and headed to the program.

"Gosh, I'm glad we came a little early. Looks like a popular program," Megan said as she perused the packed room. The two of them found their seats and waited for the program to begin.

After about the fourth announcement imploring attendees to "please fill in empty seats beside you to allow others to join us," an announcer entered the room and called up two panelists. They were Joan Byers from the "trailblazing public library in Brooklyn, who pioneered the idea of bringing drag queens into the library as readers," and Lucas Reiter, chairman of the state library's Office of Intellectual Freedom. Megan wasn't quite sure why the Office of Intellectual Freedom was a necessary component to this program, but she figured it had something to do with handling potential complaints.

The announcer then pointed to the last chair at the panelists' table. "And there's one more person we'd definitely like everyone to meet. She participates in the library's drag queen story time program and has firsthand knowledge of these events. Please welcome Kitty Glitter!" Megan was transfixed as she saw Kitty walk onto the stage and sit down at the table. She wore nine-inch platform shoes covered in what looked like Swarovski crystals. Covering her sequin-festooned red dress was a glorious chartreuse cape. The cape was embroidered with the words "Always Sparkle!" in shiny black satin across the back. Kitty's shoes glimmered in the glare of the room's spotlight. Megan smiled at the magical transformation of Kitty's face. She had glittery blue eyeshadow, sparkling eyelashes, and wonderful cherry-red lipstick that framed the biggest and widest smile Megan had ever seen. But what really impressed Megan about Kitty was the incredible poise, confidence, and self-acceptance that exuded from her with every step she took across the stage as she made her way to the panelists' table. *There isn't a child in the world who couldn't benefit from acquiring that sense of composure*, Megan thought.

The program began with a wonderful PowerPoint presentation full of colorful slides featuring the drag queen story times held at several libraries. There were loads of smiling children, happy parents, rooms overflowing with children wanting to hear books read to them. Megan had never seen so many kids at her own library's programs. Joan Byers then began to talk about the positive effects the story times had made in attendance and circulation. Increased attendance had driven up the library's numbers in all regards. Megan was impressed. As her city's budget allocation process would begin in a few months, she was looking for ways to increase her library usage statistics in order to show how popular the library was with the community. *Getting numbers like these libraries are getting*, she thought, *might even allow me to ask for* increased *library funding!*

After Joan had finished her presentation, she passed the program over to Lucas Reiter from the Office of Intellectual Freedom. Lucas took some time to explore several issues libraries were confronting with their drag queen story time programs. As Megan expected, there were those who opposed the idea of drag queens reading to their children. In Megan's mind, these individuals presented themselves as small-minded, intolerant, and prejudiced bullies who wanted everyone to think and believe as they did. She didn't listen too closely to Lucas's portion of the program, feeling that the good obviously outweighed the bad in this case. *Besides*, she thought, *libraries are far too familiar with complaints like this with the occasional censorship attacks on books we receive every year*. As Lucas talked about the potential controversies libraries could expect when offering unconventional story times such as the ones they were discussing today, and explored how public libraries from Brooklyn to Los Angeles were dealing with the controversy, Megan let her imagination wander to the huge crowds and happy children she'd seen in the slide presentation earlier.

Megan's attention was brought immediately back to the moment when she heard loud, infectious laughter on stage. Kitty Glitter stood up from the table as she laughed, thanking Lucas for such a fabulous introduction.

"Let me assure you," Kitty began with that immense poise and hyper-exaggerated persona, "I've never met a child at one of these story times who didn't leave the library with a huge smile, an appreciation of togetherness, a newfound energy and joy, and—of course—at least two or three library books!" The crowd laughed. "I know Mr. Reiter may have scared many of you with his stories of controversy and protests associated with drag queens in libraries. And, yes, that will occur. But when it's explained how important it is to introduce children to the idea of diversity and acceptance, many of those naysayers will scurry away," Kitty said, using exaggerated hand movements to emphasize her point, as if she were pushing away an unwanted plate of food. "Drag represents a lot of things to a lot of people in our society. We queens like to think of drag as a way to show children how to embrace whoever and whatever they want to be. Remember, children are not born to hate. Hate is a learned behavior that children usually acquire from someone important in their lives, such as a parent. Isn't it important for children—no, for *all* of society—to understand that 'different' doesn't mean 'bad'? Being different—and accepting that difference is not something to be ashamed of—can be represented in many ways. It can be represented by having two moms, or by having lost the use of an arm or leg, or it can be represented by a giant glitter and glamor queen sitting down and reading a picture book to a room full of transfixed children looking for acceptance and assurance in their world. Drag queens relating in a fun, relaxed way provide just a glimmer—or should I say 'glitter'—of hope to every child told they are too girlish, or too boyish, or too flamboyant. These children are looking for someone who is able to show them that being different is something to be proud of rather than scared of. I'm proud to be able to do something so positive for our children, and you should be too." The room erupted in applause, and Megan joined them in rising to her feet. "Now, if you'll allow me," Kitty cooed, "I'd like to read you a story, just to give you an idea of what an average drag queen story time looks like."

Kitty and the crowd sat back down, and she read a charming picture book about a young girl who was ashamed because she was poor and couldn't dress like the rest of the kids in her school. The story was filled with engaging interaction and lots of energy. It was obvious that Kitty Glitter knew how to tell a good story. When she finished, Kitty explained that most of the drag queens would end the story time with some sort of simple craft—usually helping the children make a crown or a magic wand using, of course, lots of glitter!

When the program was over, Megan and Carol could barely contain their enthusiasm. They spent the entire conference thinking about how their library, too, should offer such an inspiring and fun series of programs like the drag queen story time. However, Carol was just a bit hesitant. "This could cause quite a stir in Oregon Trails City, couldn't it, Megan? I mean, we don't live in a very liberal city like Brooklyn or Los Angeles," she cautioned. But Megan was caught up in the excitement and knew that she could sell the program because of the amazing benefits Kitty Glitter had promoted.

"Don't worry, Carol. Leave that to me. I'll run it by the library board when we get back, and I'm sure they'll be as excited as we are. Oh, I'll see if Joan Byers will share her slides with us so I can show the board."

Carol and Megan spent the next two days at the conference attending dozens of other programs, but it was the drag queen story time idea that kept infiltrating their conversations until they headed back to Oregon Trails City when the conference was over.

About a month later, Megan received the packet of slides in Joan Byers's PowerPoint presentation. She called Carol into her office, and the two of them looked at it once again. It brought back the smiles and excitement. Megan asked Carol to take care of the logistics in contacting the drag queen story time resources that had been distributed at the conference. "You take care of finding a drag queen to be our reader, and I'll start getting the library board's approval," Megan said. "Having the library board's support will help mitigate any backlash." Megan proceeded to add the issue to the next board agenda. Not even an hour later, things started to crack.

"Megan? I'm looking at next Wednesday's board meeting agenda." It was Connie Right, president of the Oregon Trails City Public Library board on the phone. "One of the action items just says 'drag queen.' Is this a mistake?"

"Oh, hello, Connie," Megan said with excitement in her voice. "No, it's an event I wanted to share with the board that I learned about at the recent library conference I attended. I'll have a whole presentation about it."

"Okay, but it would be nice to have some heads-up going into the meeting. Is this something I should prepare for?" Connie asked. "I mean, I don't think this community's ready for drag queens."

"I'm sure it will be fine. I'll go over everything next Wednesday. Once you all hear about how wonderful these events are, and what they can add to our service, the library board will have no problem." Megan ended her conversation with Connie, but as she hung up the phone, Connie's words about the community perhaps not being ready for drag queens rang in her ears. Suddenly Megan felt a slight feeling of doubt creeping into her otherwise positive exterior.

The library board meeting had gone worse than Megan had ever expected. Rather than enthusiastically embracing the drag queen story time idea, the board seemed to be recommending abandoning the thought altogether! Even after viewing the PowerPoint slides and reviewing the positive increases in measurement statistics other libraries had seen and the potential benefits for children—in terms of self-worth and acceptance—that Kitty had talked about, the Oregon Trails City Library board wasn't ready to give the drag queen program their blessing.

"Megan," Connie began, "I don't reject any of your points regarding the positives associated with your program idea. My concern is with the negatives. Didn't we undergo a thorough community analysis a few years ago? I believe it classified—although in general terms—our community as fairly conservative and family oriented. Bringing a drag queen program into our library will surely cause an uproar among the religious right and 'family values' element in a community such as ours. Why ask for that sort of negativity if it can be avoided?"

Several other board members concurred with Connie's thoughts, nodding and adding their own warnings. One board member even asked whether children could become confused by seeing men dressed as women. Another felt it was sending the wrong message to "normalize sexual abnormalities like this" and thrust it onto four- or five-year-old children.

But it was library board member Julie Smith who had one of the more alarming requests. Raising her hand, she spoke with assurance and composure. "This controversy will stain the library's reputation. I fear that the autonomy we have given staff in choosing programs without our input has gone too far. We need to strengthen the library's policy in programming. The library board needs to be able to provide direction to the library staff in regard to children's programming. Since the item isn't on today's board agenda, I know that we can't address it right now. But shouldn't we adopt some sort of policy for future consideration? Something that prevents this controversy from happening again? I'd suggest adopting a programming statement that future programs be chosen on the basis of suitability and safety of the children attending." Julie then looked at Connie for her reaction.

"You're right, Julie. We can't vote on items not on our agenda. And I'm not sure the library board should step in and disrupt professional autonomy. But let's put that on our next agenda for further discussion." Connie jotted a note to herself.

"Despite the potential for controversy," Megan responded, "it is clear from everything I have seen and read that these programs are not only popular in the community but also provide incredible intrinsic value to children. I believe that those who support the library will see how amazing these programs are, and once they understand what the benefits are, they will be very supportive."

"Well," Connie interjected, feeling that Megan was getting a bit defensive, "you don't *currently* need our 'approval' for any programming. You're the expert and know what is best for the library and the community. We've all given you our opinions. Do with them what you will. We are all well aware of the strong intellectual freedom principles to which public libraries adhere. In this case, the one principle that seems more than applicable is that libraries do not act in *loco parentis*—that is, in the place of the parent. Parents will decide what programs they want to bring their children to, just as they will decide what websites their children visit and what books their children read. Megan, if you decide to offer a story time program such as this, it doesn't mean that the library board is supporting or advocating a drag queen lifestyle. It simply means we are supporting another entertainment outlet for Oregon Trails City's children. Now, let's move on to the next agenda item."

As she stepped out of the meeting, children's librarian Carol Garcia ran up to Megan and asked, "How'd it go? Are we on? Did the board like the idea?"

Making an instant decision that she suddenly seemed to regret, Megan told Carol, "Yes. We're on. The board wasn't really in favor of the idea, but they don't want to hold us back either. Carry on and develop the program."

"Great! I've been put in contact with several drag queens in the area who are associates with the drag queen story time organization. I'll nail down some dates and start times, check for room availability, and create some publicity flyers to get the word out. I'm so excited!" Carol ran to her desk to make some follow-up calls and to create a flyer.

Several days later, Carol knocked on Megan's office door. "Here's the flyer for the Oregon Trails City drag queen story time program for approval, Megan." Carol handed Megan a colorful flyer announcing four dates for a children's event that promised "unique" fun, lots of laughter, and tons of glitter. There was a cute photo of a drag queen hugging a child with a princess crown on her head. The first of the four programs would be in just two weeks. Megan studied the flyer. It was definitely cute and seemed fairly benign. She didn't see how it could generate any discomfort in the community.

"Okay. Go with it, Carol. Ask the web master to get the flyer on our website, and we need them to open the story time reservation system so folks can reserve a spot. We need to keep track of the number of people who are attending," Megan said. "But, Carol . . . Let's not do a press release just yet," she added. "I'm not sure we need to get too much publicity." It was the first time Carol had noted some reluctance from Megan in regard to this program.

"I'll get copies made and post them tomorrow and distribute them to the regular places," Carol said as she sauntered away. "I'd do it sooner, but there's a note on my desk about a lady who wants to talk to me about a book she objects to being shelved in the children's collection. Don't worry, I know how to handle these. We get stuff like this pretty frequently," Carol said as she walked out of Megan's office.

It wasn't even twenty-four hours later when Megan walked into her office and checked her voicemail. "Thirty voicemails! What the heck?" She pushed the Play button.

"This is Louise Brach. I'm a patron at the library, and I bring my kids there all the time. I am absolutely appalled that our library is allowing a drag queen to read to children! Having these perverts and sexually confused people in a public facility that is *supposed* to be family friendly is insane! I can't believe the library would expose our kids to perverted lifestyles at such a young age. I will encourage all good Christians in our community to show up and let you know what we think of this disgusting use of our tax dollars." Ms. Brach ended her call by slamming her receiver down with loud bang.

Megan's blood drained from her face as a series of voice messages just as vitriolic as the first played from her phone. There were callers who let loose a string of curses and threats that made Megan's skin crawl. There were threats to sue the library, to crowd the city council chambers, and to disrupt the program. The last caller was especially troubling to Megan. An unidentified man spoke calmly and slowly. He said, "I don't have children, and I don't live in your city, but when I first heard that your public library was being used to teach teenage boys how to become drag queens, I thought it had to be a joke. But the joke is apparently on Oregon Trails City taxpayers, who fund your library. With all the wonderful heroes and role models you could have chosen to read stories in your library, you chose *these* people? This is one of the most bizarre breaches of the public trust I've ever heard of, and I will make it my goal to prevent it from happening."

Megan opened her email to shoot a message to Carol regarding the backlash she was receiving, and she was stunned to see over a hundred emails. Most had subject lines objecting to "drag queens in the library." She saw emails from two of Oregon Trails city council members asking her what was going on. *This is bad, really bad*, Megan thought.

It was at that moment that Carol rushed into the room. "Megan, it's amazing! Three hundred people have signed up for the drag queen story time program. There's another two hundred people on the waiting list. I announced the program at this morning's story hour, and the parents were so excited. It looks like you were right. I wonder if we need to use the large community room for the drag queen program. It holds a lot more people, doesn't it?"

Megan threw up her hands and said, "Listen." She tapped the Play button on her phone, and the string of voicemails replayed for Carol to hear. When those had finished playing, Megan shared a couple of her more vitriolic emails.

Carol fell into the office chair. "Oh my gosh. I can't believe it. I thought we were on to something good. But all the reservations are full, and the parents seemed so supportive. Now what do we do?"

"We can't back out now. Let's just go with the first program and see what happens," Megan said, shrugging her shoulders. "Let's hope these people are all bark and no bite."

The days leading up to the first of the four planned drag queen story time events were a blur. The city manager, mayor, council members, police chief, library board president, and even the drag queens had called asking about the complaints, wondering about the potential for riots and protection, crowd control, and more. There were repeated demands from community leaders for the library director to "make this right" and "clean up this mess." Megan did her best to assuage their concerns and promised that all would be fine once they saw the program and how popular it was with the children. Megan was glad that she had received nearly three hundred letters and calls in support of the event. She was also glad that the requests for reservations to the program had been overwhelming. These votes of confidence had buttressed her claim that the program would benefit the library in the long term. Once the program was over, people would see how wonderful it was and how silly the fuss over the whole thing had been.

On the day of the first drag queen story time event, Megan drove up to her regular parking space near the staff entrance and was absolutely floored by what she saw around her. There were crowds of thousands of people. Many were carrying signs of protest and shouting "Save our children!" and "Down with drag!" The Oregon Trails city police had set up a parade of police squad cars flashing their blue-and-red lights, and she noted a sea of police officers keeping crowds from crossing established barrier lines. Megan also saw at least two media vans from local network news stations, each with reporters making live broadcasts. Along the side of the library was an entry line for parents and children who had tickets to attend the program. Four police officers and library staff were checking tickets and verifying attendance lists to ensure that no one who wasn't registered to attend the story time entered the venue to disrupt it. There were already at least a hundred people standing in that line, many of them children who not only looked terrified as they held tightly to their parents but some of whom were crying in fright. One television reporter had actually elbowed her way to that line and was interviewing the attendees. Megan parked her car and saw the television reporter gesture toward her. Megan ran to the library's staff entrance as quickly as she could to avoid having to make any sort of statement.

Once Megan entered the library, she went immediately to the community room to talk with Carol, the children's librarian. Megan found Carol sitting in the staff lounge with the drag queen as the two readied the program.

"Carol! Have you seen the crowds? They're protesting out there. I've never seen such a huge crowd! Oh my god. This isn't what I expected," Megan said with alarm. "Should we just cancel this event?"

"Oh, this is to be expected," the drag queen said. "If you cancel the event, you'll be seen as very weak. Libraries need to stand up for freedom of speech. Some people are very small-minded. I'd bet that three-quarters of the people out there don't even have children. We see this all the time at these programs. But, trust me, it will pass. You've already 'lost' the support of the protesters—if you even had it to begin with. If you cancel our program now, you'll risk losing the support of those who support you."

"Well, the library is opening now, and the program starts in thirty minutes. I better get out there and help direct the commotion," Megan said as she left the room.

Megan actually missed the entire children's program; she had gone to her office to meet the library board president, mayor, and city manager, who were waiting there for her. For the next hour and a half, the four of them met with reporters and protesters and helped with crowd control. Before Megan knew it, a stream of people was leaving the program. Most of the kids were wearing glitter crowns, and many of the parents were giving interviews to the reporters, letting them know how fantastic the program had been.

By all reports, everyone who actually attended the library's first drag queen story time program—those who were actually in the room—had had a fabulous time. They told how inspiring the stories had been and how happy the children had been to meet the drag queen after the story. One news reporter had a parent on camera saying how much she had appreciated what the Oregon Trails City Public Library had done. "My daughter has always been so withdrawn and shy. She told me she feels different from the other kids. In today's program, my daughter was laughing, singing, and standing up with the other kids. I've never seen her look so happy and confident," the lady said.

By and large, however, the media had focused on the negative reactions. A week later, the daily protest crowds had shrunk, and the backlash had calmed down. Unfortunately, Megan's anxiety certainly had not. She faced three more drag queen story time programs. And, now, with the receipt of a bill from the city's police department for over $11,000, Megan was considering canceling the remaining drag queen story time programs. She certainly couldn't afford more bills from the city's police. Then she remembered the request from library board member Julie Smith. Julie had advocated the possibility of the library board adopting a policy that would seem to allow the board to assume future responsibility—if not total control—for the library's programming. This could certainly help take the decision about canceling the other drag queen story time programs out of her hands and place it squarely in the hands of someone else. She'd sleep on it and make a decision tomorrow. There's always tomorrow.

STORY TIME CAN BE A DRAG RESPONSES

Response 1
By Katherine Huddle, manager, Carmel Clay Library, Carmel Clay, Indiana

Megan Kennedy, director of the Oregon Trails City Public Library, has a problem—one that I dare say has happened to many librarians who have sat in an exciting conference session or webinar about some innovative library program. She is imagining hosting such a program, service, or fantastic new idea at her own library and making a positive impact on her library community. She makes a knee-jerk decision to implement that program without first following basic protocols to determine if such a program is really a good idea. Professional conference programs often excite and inspire us. Hearing heartwarming presentations of how a new program or service has changed a community for the better inspire us to facilitate something similar in our own communities. But we sometimes find—upon pitching this plan to our coworkers, administration, and boards—that their response is "thanks, but no thanks." This can be extremely disappointing, especially when what we are proposing is something we feel passionate about. When this happens, do we let the idea sit in a drawer until it's dusty and long forgotten, wait until someone who objected to it moves away, or do we go ahead and do the program anyway? Megan Kennedy decided to give it a go and now finds herself in over her head. She has learned some lessons that are important for all library managers to remember.

As inspired as Megan was by the drag queen program at the conference, she neglected to listen to the part of the presentation that surely must have addressed the planning and implementing process of such a program. A drag queen story time involves a significant amount of work behind the scenes and should be part of a larger, overall effort to offer diverse and inclusive library services, collections, programs, policies, and more. Before planning such a program, seriously ask yourself why you want to host this program. Do you want to increase program numbers or present programs that more appropriately align with your library's mission, values, and programming goals? Or are you trying to offer programs that will benefit the community you serve by increasing diversity awareness? It is important to establish your program priorities and goals *before* implementing new programs. This is where Megan Kennedy's train started going off the tracks. She may have been excited and motivated by the conference program she saw, but she neglected to go back to the basics with a programming proposal and community analysis and needs survey. Megan needed to give more attention and due diligence to her inspiration before closing her eyes and jumping in the deep end.

Megan held her first drag queen story time, and hundreds of patrons turned up—along with even more protesters. There were many positive reviews. It was a truly rewarding experience for those who attended. However, she's left with a bill of $11,456 in security fees for a single program. (We have no idea how much of her total programming budget that is, but for some libraries, it would be everything they have for the entire year!) The complaints have begun to die down, but she's concerned about the potential costs and security risks for the next three programs in this series. She's also now concerned about her library board gaining too much control over her library's future programming. What should she do? What should she have done differently in the beginning?

If Megan Kennedy's library budget has the money to cover the existing police overtime bill, Megan could authorize payment and move along. But what if the library needs security for the next programs? There will likely continue to be community protests and security needs. Megan will need to work out a plan for programming security and staff training for future events. She'll likely need the assistance of the police department to ensure the safety of staff and patrons without an excessive police presence.

There are other options Megan could consider as she makes plans to pay for future programs if necessary. The library's friends or commission groups may be able to offer funds. Megan can seek the help of her library supporters by asking for donations. Or she could seek out a possible community sponsor for these programs. If the drag queen story times had as much enthusiastic community support as we are led to believe, there may be lucrative opportunities for the library to raise funds via social networking and other avenues.

Suppose the library isn't capable of paying the bill presented by the police department. While it may seem prudent to just cancel the remaining programs, it's not actually that easy. The library would be facing a new group of protesters who would be justifiably upset that the library caved in the face of mounting pressures and canceled the program. The library could also be in breach of contract with a paid presenter. The programs should go on. That being said, at this point Megan needs to think through how to proceed and work with city administrators and staff to find funding options to reimburse the city's police department.

How could Megan have been more successful in implementing this program? First, she needed to slow down and involve others in the process. She needed to get staff prepared and trained, letting them discuss their expectations, and produce talking points in order to properly address patron concerns. Megan could have used this time to call on the experience of other libraries that had already implemented such a program (the scenario seems to suggest that there are resources and websites for libraries considering the program to use). Megan needed to learn what worked for them and what went wrong and why. She needed to reach out and use her resources and other professionals and staff. There is no such thing as acquiring too much knowledge.

When thinking about implementing a new service or program—particularly one like a drag queen story time, which is sure to be controversial—don't make the same mistake as Megan Kennedy in this scenario and forget the normal analysis, planning, and vetting process that all library programs need to go through. Carefully construct and clarify the messaging behind your program (e.g., "This is not a drag performance; this is an early literacy story time and craft for families with children of all ages" and "The library is not promoting a political or religious position and wishes to celebrate the diversity in our community"). Mention other children's programs the library has scheduled as well to offer options to those who are not interested in a drag queen story time event. Having messages ready that show the library still has something to offer everyone will be critical. Partner with your police department well in advance to alert them to potential security issues. Plan how to react to possible disturbances. If the police department can be brought into the planning stage, managers can work to avoid costly surprise bills.

Megan Kennedy's experience in this scenario highlights a key element she completely mishandled: involving her network of city and library stakeholders. Library managers cannot ignore this network when planning to offer a controversial program or service. A manager needs buy-in and support from library board members, city council members, and key library stakeholders. Library managers should never put their library supporters and city leaders in a position that makes them look uninformed, uncaring, or unsupportive. Instead, it's beneficial to tap stakeholder expertise in a proactive way. By doing this, a manager can build agreement and buy-in that ultimately leads to more effective programs. Involvement begins with understanding the interests and needs of key library stakeholders. Once we know the positions of key players, we are better equipped to determine what decisions need to be made, who should participate in making them, and how to appropriately involve these players going forward.

Several Oregon Trails City Public Library board members voiced concerns around children becoming "confused by seeing men dressed as women" and felt the library would be sending the wrong message to "normalize sexual abnormalities like this and thrust it onto four- or five-year-old children." As director, I would have suggested that we seek out a local lesbian, gay, bisexual, transgender, queer plus (LGBTQ+) advocacy group (if available) to provide training and education for the board and library staff. Board member Julie Smith expressed an interest in the board voting on having a more hands-on, controlling presence in future library programming. This is to be avoided, and Megan will need to work hard to prevent the library board from gaining such control and to prove how this program serves the library's mission, values, and programming goals.

This scenario illustrates that libraries are in a unique and difficult position when it comes to programming—especially children's programming. Due to this unique position, it is even more important not to implement something you think is cool or innovative before you first think about why your particular library needs to implement it. What are you trying to accomplish and why? You should complete some appropriate planning and discussion and avoid an explosive reaction for which you weren't prepared. Megan Kennedy could have saved herself a good deal of trouble had she followed that advice.

Response 2
By AnnaLee Dragon, director, Kinderhook Memorial Library, Kinderhook, New York

When reviewing this scenario from the point of view of a library director, there are two areas that need to be addressed. First is to consider how handling the situation differently from the start may lead to a more positive outcome. Second is how to deal with the outcome that has already occurred in the most productive and positive way possible.

In examining the series of events, the first action that might have improved the outcome is gaining consensus and support from the library's board members before the program launched. While the day-to-day operations of the library, including programming, are under the purview of the director, instances where there is potential for controversy and split public opinion justifies a broad conversation with library leadership so they may present a united and coherent message to the community.

It appears in this scenario that the director and board would mutually benefit from further clarification as to their respective roles and responsibilities. This kind of training is often available upon request from either a professional association or within the library system. Director Kennedy's board members need to understand and trust that it is her job as the director to plan and execute library programs that are responsive to community needs. A board should be proud to hire an individual who considers the community's needs and strives to reflect the whole spectrum of their diverse population.

Director Kennedy and the board could collaborate on creating a programming policy, if one is not in place already, to help shape the vision of the library and build consensus on mission and purpose. This policy would serve to inform the selection/creation of programs for the library while also providing support for the director should programs receive public criticism. Another suggestion is to a create a one-page document with talking points and responses to frequently asked questions surrounding programs. This tool can provide a clear and concise message that would be a useful resource for any library representative talking about the program.

The $11,000 charge from the police department described in the scenario is another critical point that might have been addressed before this situation occurred. All libraries should develop an effective and responsive working relationship with their local police department. Having a healthy relationship with local law enforcement is beneficial for several reasons, such as making them more aware of how the library impacts its community. More importantly in this scenario, having a more effective interdepartment relationship could have prepared the police for the potential issues surrounding this program. An earlier conversation would have supported advanced planning for officer staffing, they could have provided guidance on dealing with situations that may cause controversy, it would have given officers an idea of the type of support the library may need in the future, and could have allowed the opportunity for these two organizations to foster a stronger partnership. Not to mention the fact that touching base beforehand would have ideally resulted in not having a surprise bill and a contentious situation between police and library administration.

Planning a series of programs without testing the waters can also prove problematic. When developing a new program, especially a controversial one, it is helpful to begin slowly and build from there. If the first story time is a success, then the library can easily plan more. If it does not work for any number of reasons, the library has not committed to a multiple session series and does not face the problem of whether to cancel or continue.

While there are a number of things that could have been done differently to alter the outcome of this scenario, Director Kennedy is now in the thick of it. Focusing on what actions she can take to minimize the public relations damage and decide on a course of action should be the priority. In the position of library director, things can go sideways at any moment, and it becomes less important to figure out how you got there and more important to resolve the situation.

A good first step would be to reach out to the head of the police department before any other action is taken. Communicating the importance of the program, the fact that the public library is a not-for-profit organization with an extremely limited budget, and the wonderful turnout of attendees at the program might encourage some understanding and flexibility on the part of the police department. Should that effort prove ineffective, this could be viewed as a fundraising challenge. With over three hundred people attending and hundreds of letters in support of the program, it is clear that there is community need and desire for the content. By starting a fundraising drive online, and explaining the unexpected costs of police presence, the library might be able to make up at least a portion of that $11,000 and avoid putting the entire burden on the library budget. Looking to future sessions, there may be potential donors in the city who would help to financially support future efforts in this vein. Having a donor underwrite the program is helpful in both showing public support for the subject matter and removing the argument about taxpayer funding being used. Furthermore, it provides the library with the opportunity to advocate for its civic importance and brings attention to the good work that Director Kennedy and the board are supporting.

As to the issue of whether to cancel the future sessions or continue, the story times should go on as planned and advertised. Canceling a program like this due to backlash can lead to a larger outcry than hosting it in the first place. The library made a commitment to these programs and to those patrons and community members who wish to attend. There is very clearly a demonstrated need and desire for drag queen story time, and the director might possibly be exploring future LGBTQ+ programming possibilities. As a public library, the mission is to have the entire community feel seen, welcome, and represented in the collections and programming. LGBTQ+ youth suffer from significantly higher rates of attempted suicide and depression than the general youth population due to many factors, including bullying and lack of acceptance. Programs such as drag queen story times serve to signal the library as a safe space for all and teach messages of love and acceptance. These are not silly, frivolous programs. They are powerful examples of inclusivity and should be treated accordingly. There is also the matter of data-driven decision making. Any program that draws a crowd of over a hundred people is a program that should likely be repeated or expanded. The community has more than shown its interest and enthusiasm for the content.

Finally, libraries should be cautious in allowing a vocal group of upset patrons to have the final say in what programs are offered. If the library acquiesces to this group now, there is no telling what other programs they might take issue with. By canceling future sessions, the leadership sends the message that the library can be controlled by a small, outraged group of citizens. It would be no different from removing a book from your shelves due to a patron complaint.

The heart of the matter is making everyone in the community feel welcome and represented in their library. For all of the negative press, complaining citizens, and stress that can be leveled at the director and the library, the power and meaning of the message should not get lost in the mayhem. In whatever community your library resides, the library can and should be a leader in creating a sense of community and inclusion. This means making tough decisions about collections and programming and using the library's position of power, influence, and privilege in the community to stand up for those who are more vulnerable and underrepresented. If the library faces flak and complaints about hosting this program four times, imagine what the performer or anyone in the LGBTQ+ community deals with on a daily basis.

As a community leader, the library should not engage in negativity surrounding this program or work to convince anyone who is not interested in participating. The beauty of library programs is that they are voluntary; no one is forced to attend. The library does not make those decisions for the public. Each person has a right to decide what is best for themselves and their family. No one individual, however, has a right to determine what is best for anyone else. The library's job will always be to represent its community as it is, not as it was or as some may wish it to be. Library directors and boards face challenging situations every day, but as librarian Jo Godwin famously said, "A truly great library contains something in it to offend everyone."

Response 3
By Lauren Comito, branch manager, Brooklyn Public Library, Brooklyn, New York

The library hosted its first drag queen story time! It went great. Attendees were happy, they supported part of the community that often feels neglected, and they upheld the ideal of what a library is—a place with something for everyone. So why does the library director, Megan Kennedy, feel so stressed out? Well, she is stressed out because she didn't plan ahead, a bunch of stuff happened that she wasn't expecting, and her actions are both going to cost the library a lot of money and make inclusive programming more difficult in the future.

Drag queen story time is a great way to make people feel welcome and "seen" in the library space. It can also bring out the worst in a community. In this scenario, it has done both. When we are introducing inclusive programming that we know is likely to be controversial, we have a responsibility to our patrons, staff, and institutions to do so thoughtfully and in a way that allows the community to discuss the issues without devolving into abusive behavior. Library Director Kennedy in this scenario did not do this, and her lack of care, planning, and communication resulted in a number of problems for the Oregon Trails City Library.

Let's break this all down a bit. As a result of the lack of communication about—and planning for—the new drag queen story time program, the following problems occurred:

- The library incurred $11,000 in security costs for the protests.
- Library staff were exposed to abusive phone calls, emails, and voicemails.
- Members of the board are looking to have direct control over the content of library programming.

While there was always the probability that patrons and the public would be upset, none of these problems or issues were caused by the drag queen story time. These problems were created or exacerbated by a lack of planning and coalition building.

So, what do you do to prepare for a library program that you know will be controversial? Start by thinking ahead. Don't ignore that feeling that there may be problems. Furthermore, don't discount the feelings of the people who are telling you there will be problems—as was the case in this scenario. Slow down and take the time to consider how you can host the program or service in a way that is prepared for blowback. As you are thinking about how best to approach any new service or program, ask yourself (or your staff) some questions. Rather than ignore input from your peers or colleagues regarding potential snags, solicit their input and listen to it in order to make better decisions going forward. It can help to write down and log what you find out so you can continually check yourself and refer back to your data.

Ask yourself, "Why do we want to have the new program or service?" You should have an idea of why you want to implement a new program or service and should be able to articulate your reasons. The fact that a program is new and cool is not enough of a reason. How does the program tie in to your library's mission? What service or value does it provide to the community—either as a whole or just part of it? Does it fit in with the library's other offerings or collections, and how? Asking these sorts of questions helps a manager eliminate much of the knee-jerk reaction borne out of an emotional desire to do something and rely instead on data as the determinative factor.

Managers shouldn't forget to consider the library's stakeholders in the decision-making process when considering new programs or services. What reasons might they have for objecting to a program or service? Why would they say no? Think broadly at this point. You might get objections from board members, elected officials, patrons, or staff. Consider why different stakeholders might object; it's not always certain to be an objection to the idea itself. A board member might be concerned about financial implications, elected officials may be worried about reelection, and staff might not want to do the extra work involved in a huge program. A staff member may also be concerned about crowd control, and the board member may be worried about the press reaction. Some people just say no at first and then need a while to consider it fully. Thinking about objections before they happen helps you identify problems or weaknesses in your plan and address them early on.

How can a manager address those concerns while still providing the program or service? Once you have fully fleshed out why the program is important and what objections or issues your stakeholders may have, you are ready to think about how to address the potential roadblocks. Match up the reasons for doing the program with the relevant objections and come up with solutions for the problems that are pointed out.

If Library Director Kennedy of Oregon Trails City Public Library had gone through this process, she may have picked up on some red flags. She may have considered the conservative nature of her community and planned for the protests better. If she had prepared for protests, she could have negotiated the amount of security needed and given the police department time to schedule regular hours for the officers at the protest instead of overtime. They would also have been able to plan to separate the protesters and counterprotesters ahead of time and made better use of the outdoor space. If Megan had considered the question "What if a board member has a concern about negative press?" she could have prepared and distributed a press release, shaping the narrative about the story time from the outset instead of letting it be controlled by the protesters and media.

When planning a controversial program, it's important to communicate with the board and community before the program. In this scenario, Library Director Kennedy had a chance to talk to the board president before the board meeting, but she skipped it! She could have gone into that meeting with an ally but hadn't thought through the possible objections and didn't realize she would need to. Be prepared for questions and have answers ready, and be clear about the program, its purpose, and the library's stance on equality and freedom of speech. Accept the feedback you receive, and modify your plans if necessary. Then move forward with your library board as partners. Having talking points and communicating your vision to your library board allows each of your stakeholders to speak from a united front and send a consistent message. The same thing goes for staff. Have a discussion about the program with library staff. This gives managers a chance to get their input and help organizing the program and provides the opportunity to discuss talking points and set boundaries around patron conversations.

None of the things mentioned above has happened in this scenario, and now there are some problems that need to be addressed and three more drag queen story times to plan! While the previous steps would have been helpful to complete before the program, it would still be helpful to start them now. Library Director Kennedy needs to talk to the library board president and have a debriefing meeting to discuss what happened, its effect on the library and staff, and the security costs. She should discuss the positive things too! Three hundred patrons at a story time is a massive success, and the two hundred people on the waitlist are ready for the next one. It's not appropriate for a library board to approve specific programs. The library manager wants library board members on their side, but members of a governing board are there to set direction for the organization rather than get involved in day-to-day operational decisions. For this reason, Megan needs to prepare a response to the idea floated by a library board member that the board should have the power to veto library programs based on content. Her response could possibly include some education on how freedom of speech works in libraries, appropriate governing board responsibilities, and the dangers involved in setting a precedent like that.

Megan then needs to turn to her city's internal department management team. She'll need to negotiate with the police department for lower security costs based on what happened at the first event. Obviously overtime costs were the culprit there, and they should be able to lower costs considerably by preplanning the response to the next few events to prevent using overtime in the future. Megan will need to work internally with the city's manager and finance department to work out a solution to cover the costs already incurred by the police department.

Programs like drag queen story time are great, and their popularity demonstrates that they reach a part of our community that wants to be seen and belongs in our libraries. It's important to remember that libraries have a responsibility to make sure that we are providing services to the whole community in a considered way that keeps everyone safe. This requires exceptional planning ability and effective communication. By employing these qualities to more effectively make the Oregon Trails City Library drag queen story time program happen, Megan could have saved herself a lot of headaches and instead saved some glitter to share at the next program.

Chapter Thirteen

A Sticky Situation

A Controlling Scenario Using Problem Solving

SCENARIO

The way Lizbeth Brockledge saw it, nothing was as unfriendly as a sign that said "No!" Seeing the "No food or drink allowed" sign at the entrance of the library raised her hackles as she came in to work. As the new dean of libraries for Prince College University Library, Lizbeth was a bit embarrassed to admit that her library was so restrictive in this policy. To her, the large white decal letters that stated "No food or drink" communicated some unintended perceptions. *They might as well just hang a sign that says "Unfriendly and unprogressive staff inside,"* Lizbeth mused. It didn't quite matter that the policy was frequently overlooked anyway. Library staff were constantly finding evidence that the policy was not appreciated by the community. As staff made "the rounds" in the library, empty snack bags, water bottles on the tables next to books and library computers, and candy wrappers were a frequent sight. Additionally, carpet stains under tables and chairs seemed to be appearing in locations where library patrons were hiding food out of the sight of watchful library staff. Lizbeth didn't understand why library users felt a need to "hide" their booty, since the library's staff rarely confronted users who had food out on the desk in plain sight. More than likely, a librarian would just walk right by a user and overlook a small bag of chips or nuts sitting on the table in front of them. As long as it wasn't smelly, and there was a sense of plausible deniability, staff normally tended to let it go—regardless of what that unfriendly sign at the library entrance commanded. Lizbeth wondered why the staff wasn't being more diligent in calling out patrons who ignored the posted sign—that was, until she actually heard a staff member comment that they hadn't taken a job as a librarian to become the food police. So, what good was the unwelcoming signage posted at the library entrance? Staff were just ignoring those who abused the policy, which she found to be passive-aggressive. What other policies might her staff be choosing to ignore? Policies were put in place for a reason. If her staff was picking and choosing which policies to enforce, she'd need to address that someday.

Lizbeth squirreled this thought away to pursue at a later time—she first needed to focus on finding her footing as the new library administrator and understanding the library's weaknesses. She knew that revising the collection development policy was a very high priority to the library—as it had been the one question each of the seven people who interviewed her had asked in one form or another. She would tackle that first. Then she would work on what she considered to be her greatest calling: making the library feel more comfortable for all patrons. She wanted to create a library patron environment that was comfortable rather than punitive. When she was ready to implement those types of changes, maybe then it would be the appropriate time to revisit the library's existing food policy.

Over the course of several months, Lizbeth was able to concentrate on collections as she had wanted. She got together a team of library staff to help enhance, if not completely replace, the twenty-year-old collection development policy. At Lizbeth's request, the staff designed a collection assessment program to identify collection strengths and weaknesses. Additionally, the staff created an impressively aggressive weeding program that was included in the new policy. In fact, the new policy required that collection assessments and maintenance be conducted on a continual, routine basis. All in all, Lizbeth was quite proud of what she was able to get the staff to do in regard to the collection. She felt she could check this box off her to-do list and move on to her other task. That policy, she knew, might not be as easy to implement.

By the following week, Lizbeth had generated a plan to approach this food and drink issue from a more general customer service standpoint in which she'd drill down and target more specific issues—like food and drink. She now felt she knew the staff well enough and had enough experience and confidence under her belt to assemble her team for a brainstorming session wherein they could tackle the problems hindering library customer service. She announced to the staff that they'd be meeting the next morning for a "customer service at the library" discussion.

That morning, Lizbeth walked to her office, placed her bag just inside her office door, and then marched over to the library's conference room, going over in her mind all the things she needed to remember to say. Dylan, one of the library's paraprofessionals, was already there, opening the meeting room's door.

"You ready for this, Dylan?" Lizbeth asked.

"I wouldn't miss it for the world," Dylan said, a slight yawn betraying his enthusiasm.

Lizbeth had brought together the seven people at the library who she believed had the broadest view. She hadn't just looked to include the employees who had been there the longest. She wanted the ones who had given her the best unasked-for advice that turned out to be correct. As she put out coffee for the meeting, Lizbeth went over the members of this team she had compiled. There was Dylan, the youngest person on staff who had worked as a volunteer while in middle school. Then there was Dessie, the prototypical reference librarian, who had been at this library for almost a decade. She had included Assistant Dean Lou, who wasn't the most outspoken member of the staff but who had stopped Lizbeth from making awkward missteps in her early days, such as pointing out key faculty members and telling her who sat where at the academic senate meetings. Next, Lizbeth had the periodicals librarian, Misty, join the group. Misty had been a student at the same high school as Lizbeth back in the day. Although Lizbeth hadn't spoken to Misty since then, she remembered that Misty had been a cheerleader, and this team would certainly need one. The last member of the team was the library's circulation supervisor, Jose. Jose had been at the library since the day it opened, and Lizbeth appreciated the fact that all the other staff members seemed to respect him and look to him for almost everything.

Once the entire group had arrived at the meeting room, Lizbeth made her way to her seat, dropping off a small packet in front of each of the participants on her way.

"Here's this morning's agenda and a few things I'd like to go over with you," she said. "I've got a few things I'd like us to address." The participants took out the pages and started flipping through the content. Other than the agenda, which focused on customer service at the library, there were articles on wayfinding and signage, statistics from customer service surveys, and images from library cafés around the world.

Lizbeth began, "Since I'm all about the user experience, over the last several months since I started here, I have noted some of the more challenging customer service failures at our library. You'll see them documented in your packet."

The group members glanced around the room at one another and then looked at the packets of papers, trying to determine which of them would be singled out for reproach.

"Lizbeth," Jose said, "we're not a retail store; we're a college library. What does customer service have to do with academia? And I'm not sure what to extrapolate from all this data you've handed us."

Lizbeth squirmed a little with the natural discomfort of a person having to present controversial ideas. She'd start with some low-hanging fruit before proceeding to food and drink.

"Well," she said, drawing it out to buy even a microsecond, "I would like to see us address the, um . . . the need for a place for the students to work on more expansive projects."

Jose looked at Lizbeth with a touch of confusion.

"Art projects?" he finally asked.

"Well,"—she returned to the tactic of stalling—"yes, but slightly more. We need a place for architecture and urban planning students to spread out large drawings, stagecraft students to work on diagrams, and the like."

"So, that sounds easy," Jose offered. "How about one of the rooms with the large tables by Misty's office? It has some lighting issues, and it's not exactly a quiet space, but it could be easily retrofitted."

Lizbeth was impressed that Jose had grasped her idea so quickly. "Exactly. I like that kind of thinking, Jose."

"It would need to be a space they can access after hours, so first floor might be a better choice since security can monitor that area twenty-four/seven," Lou contributed.

"Especially since students will need to come in and out so frequently," Dylan added, "to head over to the campus store for sustenance."

Lizbeth nodded, secretly knowing how this entire scenario would play out. She moved it along.

"How about you, Misty?" Lizbeth asked. "Thoughts?"

"I've got a few," Misty began. "I think we need to provide better lighting between the tables on the side of the building and the main entrance."

Lizbeth nodded.

"Late at night," Misty continued, "students are always making the trip out there."

"Usually to smoke," Dylan added as slyly as his sleep-deprived brain would allow.

"And to eat, grab a Coke, listen to music or whatever," added Misty.

Lizbeth started to smile. "Okay, then, we have our first few action plans to investigate the use of that first-floor room for after-hours study. Now, any other customer service ideas? How about you, Lou?" she prompted.

Lou leaned back in his chair.

"We need more water fountains," he said. "The number of people I have to reprimand for having water bottles in the stacks is ridiculous."

Lizbeth smiled once again. This was her moment. She needed to strike while this iron was hot.

"So, it would seem that many of the customer service problems involve lack of food and beverage." Lizbeth was glad to finally let that cat out of the bag.

There was laughter. Lizbeth had expected such, but she steeled her eyes as if she were taken aback and annoyed. She had practiced this move, planning on using it at board meetings when they didn't take her seriously enough.

It worked here. The laughter stopped immediately.

"Let me draw this picture for you," she said. "We keep giving warnings to folks walking the stacks carrying water bottles, but I think that's a waste of time. We hang rude signs about food and ignore those who bring it in. And to muddy the water, you've all pretty much agreed that food and drink are the things most students want to bring in. So why are we wasting our time? We could be doing pretty much anything other than being food and drink police." Lizbeth thought that using the same allusion she'd heard other staff members use some time ago about not wanting to be food and drink police would earn her some credibility.

Jose looked concerned. "So, we should simply not give a damn anymore?" he said.

"No." Lizbeth went on. "Instead of wasting our time policing the stacks like kindergarteners on a field trip, we accept that our students are adults, that they know how to handle food and drink. It's clear they are bringing it in anyway, so why fight it? Why don't we update our policy to reflect the new realities of the day?"

Dessie looked stunned.

"Libraries don't allow food," she started, "and they certainly don't put their collections in danger of having soda poured all over them."

"Don't they? Look at these pictures of library cafés I included in your packet," Lizbeth asserted. "Clearly other libraries have taken stock of new user behaviors."

Lou was silent, but as he looked through the photos in the packet, he took a position that seemed to indicate he was thinking deeply on the matter. Dylan, on the other hand, seemed to be coming alive.

"I like it! In fact, I have been asked by many students to help them smuggle food in," Dylan said. "I guess many of them see me as a student rather than a staff member. But let me play devil's advocate. Suppose a student comes in, he's carrying a pizza, he takes a study desk on the third floor, sits there for a few hours, someone comes up, complains that it smells. What do we do?"

"That's a clear question," Lizbeth said. "If someone complains, we go to the person, ask them to get the pizza out of there."

"And then we have to deal with the grease stain on the desk?" Jose asked, more than a touch of sarcasm coming in around the edges.

"Yes, there will be some of that, of course," Lizbeth said. "And yes, we may have to deal with a grease stain or two, some spills, but aren't we doing that already—even *with* the policy as it is? Haven't you all had to clean a few spills? And if we're worried about someone getting spaghetti stains on our books here in the library, how is that different from someone getting spaghetti stains on our books when they check them out and take them home? And perhaps we are causing spills by being so unaccommodating. Since patrons are worried about getting caught and in trouble, they hide food and drink on the floor, or under a jacket, or someplace where they are far more likely to spill it."

Lou's face indicated that he was taking that in with a fair deal of weight.

"We're just going to let a student walk in to the special collections room carrying a sandwich?" Dessie asked.

"Obviously not," Lizbeth said. 'There will always need to be places—like the special collections area—where we need to be more diligent. But these are easier to control since access to these rooms is monitored closely."

"We should also become a fragrance-free facility," Jose noted.

Everyone in the room nodded at that.

"We can post some guidelines, of course," Dylan said, seeming to be thinking out loud. "No eating in the open space, special collections, maybe the listening rooms."

"Why the listening rooms?" Lizbeth asked.

"They have sound-absorbing panels," Dylan said, "and they hold smells and amplify noise like chewing and paper rustling."

Lou made that *you're right* face again at that.

Lizbeth realized that the group had already moved past the "No way" phase and were now moving into the "Well, it's possible, but how can we implement it" phase. This was a good sign.

"The upsides of doing this are pretty clear to me," Lizbeth said. "It allows for longer study times, since students won't need to leave to eat; less wear on our internal resources, since we won't have to at least pretend to police people eating and drinking; and it would just make the place feel a little less stiff."

"But you're not supposed to eat in the library, and you're certainly not supposed to eat in one of the finest college libraries in the state!" said Dessie, resistance returning to the conversation.

"Many libraries allow food," Lizbeth noted. "Even a few major research libraries allow bottled water."

"Hightower allows you to drink bottled water, but only if you buy it in their little shop," Dylan stated.

"Well," Lou said, "that's a revenue stream."

"Let's get real," Jose said. "You allow food in the library, especially with the stuff these kids are grabbing, we'll be dealing with amazing amounts of spills, smells, stains, and damage to materials."

"I have been over damage surveys for the last three years," Lizbeth said, "and almost half of the damage noted was from normal wear and tear, and about thirty were writing in the books, but about twenty percent was staining or water damage. I honestly don't think saying that you can bring in food will make any difference in how much food ends up in this place," she continued. "The kids all have snacks in their backpacks, and they're drinking in the stacks; they're just doing it undercover. It's not going to end up with spaghetti being flung around the stacks; it'll just make the library feel a little more like a place a student would *want* to come and spend more time in, to work with a little less strictness. It will make the library a friendlier place."

Misty tutted severely.

"You keep talking about making the library a 'friendly' place. But don't we support research here? We're not trying to be a living room. We serve a community that includes respected researchers and those serious about academics. Are we demeaning, devaluing our library going this way? Last year alone, we had three *New York Times* best-selling authors on faculty, and we graduated a student who was named Shakespeare Scholar of the Year. This library has played a role in all of that success. Why would we want to be a 'friendlier' place? We shouldn't strive for friendly; we should strive for serious, studious, and empowering."

Lou had on his *nope* face.

"Misty," Lizbeth said, "friendlier doesn't mean less serious."

"In fact," Dylan said, "there are studies that show that information presented in a convivial manner has a higher rate of retention. It promotes creative thinking and application, plus it makes people feel more secure in their environment."

"We're building a new library idea," Lizbeth said, "and it's important to realize that the role of a library within research is changing, but more importantly, that the buildings themselves are changing. We're working in a building built in 1954, with all the good and bad aspects of the libraries of those times, but we don't have to be stuck in the 1950s when it comes to policy. We can, and should, expand what we permit in response to the role we should be serving in the community of the moment."

Misty gave her a look that seemed to say, *We're from the same school, lady! Where did you go wrong?*

"I think," Lou said, finally leaning forward to speak, "we need to look at all the different angles on this one. First, and most importantly, there is tradition. The Prince College Library has never allowed food or drink and has managed to achieve remarkable success supporting research. We're an institution that has never fully understood its role in the community it serves. We focus on the tent poles and often fail to see the fabric running between them. We are not merely a resource for scholars but also a site for regular college student interactions. For every professionally recognized scholar, there are many kids just scraping by who need a place to study, to relax, to meet other students. We're not merely a site for academic excellence; we are a building block of campus life.

"That said, we are also not a recreation center. We are a site where that serious research can, and will, happen. If we allow the aspects of campus life that can be distracting, we may endanger the function of enabling top-quality research. We cannot allow that to happen." Lou was on a roll here, and the entire room was listening with intent.

Lou took a purposeful breath and continued. "There is the idea that providing a place where a student can execute all their needs in a state of comfort actually promotes excellence and, on the flip-side, also promotes the extended use of the facility, putting a greater stress on those maintaining it. So, overall, it is a question of the past, up to and including the present, and the future. We must understand where we have been while not losing sight of where we would like to end up." Lou finally rested.

"I think Lou has actually provided a great perspective and lots to think over," Lizbeth said. She seemed to be chewing something over. "I think we can call this meeting done for now. You've all been great. Let's meet next week to continue the discussion and make some final decisions at that time. Thanks, everybody."

The group got up and began walking out. Dylan lingered behind.

"So, Lizbeth," he said. "What's your takeaway?"

Lizbeth smiled broadly. "You always cut to the chase, don't you?"

"It's why I'm here," Dylan said mischievously.

"I've got an idea," Lizbeth said, "but either way, we're still the library, still doing what we do. That won't change."

"But what're you going to do?" Dylan asked a bit more insistently.

"I've made my decision, Dylan," she said playfully. "My job next week will be to bring everyone else to the same one."

A STICKY SITUATION RESPONSES

Response 1
By Helen Palascek, director, Upper St. Clair Township Library, Upper St. Clair, Pennsylvania

Library policies generally range from basic regulations (behavior, attire) to more complicated ones reflecting state and federal laws (firearms, service animals, nondiscrimination) to unique library issues (study rooms, computer use, reserves). Each sets standards for patrons with the expectation that staff will uniformly enforce the policy and apply consequences. Thoughtful library administrators committed to improving patron services will regularly review policies with an eye to reducing pain points between patrons and staff wherever possible. What was regulated in the past may not be necessary or appropriate today.

The real issue here is not whether the library should review their food and drink policy but how the new library administrator for Prince College University Library went about pursuing a change. Lizbeth Brockledge apparently did not first check with the central university administration offices. Is this a campuswide policy, enforced in all university classrooms and computer labs? Does she even have the authority to change the policy? Has she read the actual policy, or has she only been spurred to action by seeing the sign on the library's door?

Brockledge also has watched students and staff ignore the policy in question for months but evidently never mentioned her misgivings over the unfriendly messaging and secretive environment it produced. It's not clear why she seems to feel that staff will be resistant to a change in policy, since most are already ignoring it. No one that we know of has come to her complaining that other staff are not enforcing policy. Her attitude when she finally decides to bring up the issue with her staff is confrontational. First, Brockledge's choice of staff members is a curious mix—not the senior staff or the public service staff. At least the circulation supervisor is there.

At the time of her meeting, Lizbeth Brockledge marches into the room, provides a stack of articles and data with no explanation, and immediately accuses the meeting attendees of customer service failures. Understandably, they are confused and defensive. She backs away from the controversy she has created and pretends to be open to ideas for a new study space and other service improvements. Brockledge may not realize it, but she has started the meeting with unfriendly messaging and a secretive agenda, the very things she dislikes about the food and drink policy and its effect on the staff and students.

Once Brockledge opens up about her real purpose, the staff respond more positively than she expected. Even though there are reservations, they move fairly quickly to walking through specific issues of implementation: not this room, not this kind of food, how to deal with complaints about smells or messes. No one, however, refers to the actual wording of the current policy, and Brockledge apparently did not include it with the other documents she provided. One would think this a quite critical step in the process. Instead, Brockledge stops the meeting and pretends to be unsure of how to proceed, but she has made it extremely clear she wants this policy to be less restrictive. Everyone at the meeting, and everyone they tell (and that means everyone who works there), most likely will be feeling frustrated and manipulated by the end of the day.

Lizbeth Brockledge could have taken a much better approach for a more productive meeting. A more transparent approach that looked to gain better staff consensus could have been considered. First, Brockledge needs to remember that this is an issue impacting *all* staff; they all should have been invited to participate in the decision-making process. Second, the meeting agenda should have clearly stated that the customer service issue to be discussed was specifically the library's food and drink policy. Third, the current policy should have been included in the agenda for everyone to review beforehand. All the data and research that Brockledge had collected, along with a set of questions for staff to consider, could have also been distributed *prior* to the actual meeting. What policy changes could be implemented with the least chance of damage, messes, policing, and argument? What creates the most friction for staff? How to communicate changes to students also needs to be discussed. Other considerations, such as cleaning the library, replacing carpet, and planning for ease of student trash discards, should be discussed and could help to create an environment where a new policy is respected by all.

As it stands now, staff will be buzzing like bees around sticky tables.

Response 2
By Kelly Bohannan, assistant branch manager, Seminole County Public Libraries, Seminole County, Florida

I could empathize with Lizbeth the library administrator in this scenario. One of the biggest pet peeves of managers I have known is having rules that are impossible to enforce. "No food or drink allowed" is one of those rules. It is a definite signal that bureaucracy—and all of the negative connotation that comes with that word—is in place at this organization. Signage outlining the rule is unwelcoming and often ignored. Staff (even those who agree with the rule) hate policing or telling patrons about the fact that food and drink are not allowed, and so staff don't consistently remind patrons about it. Staff see the rule being broken and turn their eyes away, not wanting to get into any sort of confrontation. Patrons, too, often blatantly ignore the rule—even if they may have been told about it before. They recognize the simple fact that there are not usually any significant consequences for being caught with food or drink, so they don't need to worry. Muddying the situation for users is the realization that many other institutions they frequent, like coffee shops and bookstores, *do* allow food and drink, sometimes selling it themselves. Why wouldn't the library be just like those places? These users expect to be considered as responsible, conscientious adults who are able to safely use the building without making a mess or damaging property. This "no food or drink" rule rightfully seems outdated and arbitrary to library users and often discourages return visits.

Lizbeth, therefore, seems to have the right idea about the need to bring about positive change to this policy by having staff be involved in the change. Many times, supervisors and managers go into a new workplace and immediately try to change things. While these changes are usually well intentioned, the action often seems arbitrary and unnecessary and is implemented without proper explanation. Therefore, the change alienates staff. They feel their opinions and experiences were not solicited. There is no background, no context. It seems to staff as if change has been enacted merely for the sake of doing something different. This, then, creates resentment and trust issues that can lead to even more difficult issues later on.

People tend to be naturally resistant to change. It's therefore heartening to see Lizbeth's strategy of researching and looking for possible roadblocks before meeting to discuss concerns. This is a sound idea. Doing so shows staff members that you have given a complex issue some significant thought. This food policy change is definitely going to be a controversial one, so Lizbeth definitely needs to show that this decision is not just a random one that will be rolled back in a few months. The packet Lizbeth hands staff members seems to contain excellent data, survey information, illustrations, and articles. At the "customer service at the library" meeting, Lizbeth seems to want to listen to everyone's input, and she allows everyone to express their concerns. This is an indication that she values staff input. It was also good for Lizbeth to emphasize what an inconvenience the food rule is to both her staff and their patrons. Empathy is an excellent quality for managers to exhibit, and Lizbeth gets high marks for doing this. Finally, Lizbeth shows good judgment by giving some of her staff time to think her proposal over. Giving the staff a week to think over the pros and cons of the issue can deflate high emotions and knee-jerk reactions and can help bring people around in the long run.

Where Lizbeth trips up, however, is that she does not involve *all* staff members and only selects certain staff in her efforts to change a major policy. Furthermore, she only seems to be interested in involving this group as a way to validate a decision she has already made. Those involved in the execution of the job should all have direct input in decisions made by the one in charge. Most good managers solicit this input after they have done appropriate research regarding the change and by soliciting feedback and considering everyone's opinions. From what the reader is presented in this scenario, the only resemblance of any due diligence on Lizbeth's part seems to be represented by a pile of magazine articles she plops in the lap of the select staff members at a meeting and expects them to read and comprehend on the spot. As Jose, one of Lizbeth's employees, states at that meeting, staff do not seem to be sure what to "extrapolate from all this data you've handed us."

What has Lizbeth done to ascertain why the food rule even exists in the first place? Does she know if there are valid reasons for the library's food policy? Maybe the university at large has a food policy that all departments are expected to follow. Maybe the "no food or drink" rule fits into a larger policy concerning student behavior. Maybe the university's faculty has requested the policy as an attempt to preserve certain materials. We simply don't know. All we see from the scenario is that Lizbeth—for sound reasons—does not approve of the rule she sees posted on the library's front door. She has charged forward to change the library policy but seems to involve staff as an afterthought. Lizbeth needs to understand that there are reasons managers ask staff for input before making a decision that will affect everyone. She needs to be open to different perspectives. Lizbeth, as the head of the library, has the overarching vision, the "big picture," of what constitutes her business. But her employees are in the day-to-day trenches. Her employees work more directly with library users, so they may better know what users need and want. Her employees may better understand user behavior and what the driving factors are behind those behaviors. But she hasn't solicited this information from them.

Lizbeth must be open to the fact that staff may well arrive at a valid, yet contradictory, conclusion about the "no food or drink" rule. Managers must avoid falling into the decision-making trap in which their own bias leads them to seek out only information that supports some existing point of view while avoiding or discarding any information that contradicts it. It's easy to make a strong argument that leans in favor of your own. It's much more difficult to figure out why we want to do something before we decide what we want to do. Lizbeth has decided what she wants to do well before deciding why it should be done.

Response 3
By Bridget McCafferty, dean and university librarian, Texas A&M University, Killeen, Texas

As the dean of a university library, I get mired in a conversation about some aspect of our food and drink policy about once every eighteen months, despite the fact that we have a fairly open and permissive approach that I thought would take care of the problem once and for all. I instituted our policy years ago because I, like Lizbeth Brockledge (the new university library administrator in this scenario), have a strong conviction that allowing food and drink in academic libraries is essential to attract students and provide them with a supportive place to study. I have also worked in both types of facilities—those that allow food and drink and those that don't—and my informal observation is that you get less mess when you allow it, because you can enforce limited, reasonable, well-thought-out restrictions instead of trying to catch people hiding it everywhere. Also, when you have an open policy, you can plan for appropriate refuse receptacles and janitorial services to keep trash under control. My experience has been that people will eat and drink regardless of your policy.

That said, Lizbeth made a fairly large mistake in this scenario. She obviously came to a decision about this policy before she met with her staff. Therefore, she is trying to lead them to the conclusion she wants so that they think it's a grassroots change. Lizbeth doesn't even give her staff an accurate idea of the topic for the meeting when she notifies them about it, saying only that it will concern "customer service at the library." She is trying to act out a participatory management style, but she is only acting—it is not authentic. Lizbeth is making a mistake that I think is common with new chief librarians: she has already made a unilateral decision, one that is totally appropriate in this situation, but she is allowing her staff to think that they have a real opportunity for input. This is a waste of time and will ultimately lead to resentment when her staff realize that she was always going to overrule them. New leaders sometimes do this as a way to build buy-in with the decision, but there are other, more honest ways to achieve the same result.

There is a time and place for managers to use a participatory management style, a style in which managers allow staff the opportunity to participate in organizational decision making. It is a great overall approach that works well for many kinds of decisions, but it doesn't work every time. For example, in an emergency situation or time of organizational stress in which an immediate decision is necessary, it could be disastrous for the organization to wait to form a group or committee and attempt to reach group consensus. Additionally, there are decisions where staff are too deeply invested in the outcome and may not be able to let go of personal or emotional bias. For instance, I recently heard a story of a library that still had a card catalog to "back up" their online system. When a new librarian wanted to stop updating the card catalog to save staff time, several other longtime employees became upset. In this case, the director gave in to the longtime staff, in deference to participatory management and despite the fact that a card catalog is a terrible waste of resources—it isn't even a real, viable backup to an online catalog system. The staff were invested in the card catalog because they had worked on it for years and because it represented something about the library, and by proxy, about their own identities. They couldn't make a rational decision.

I would argue that Lizbeth's staff are invested in this food and drink policy in the same way. They view the library as a noble institution in support of high-level research. Allowing food and drink might cheapen that, metaphorically, and also literally if they end up swimming in trash and damaged materials. This policy ties in to their sense of what the library is and what it does as well as their own identities as employees. In my opinion, Lizbeth's staff aren't thinking rationally. Enforcement of this policy is already erratic. This is important for two reasons. First, my hunch is that the library staff aren't enforcing the "no food or drink" policy because they've realized how it represents poor customer service, and that means it feels wrong to confront people who disobey it. In other words, the staff know it is bad customer service, to a degree where they are informally changing the policy by letting food slip by unchallenged. Second, there is already a food and drink problem in the library; Lizbeth cleverly draws this out of her staff at the meeting. Lizbeth has shown the staff members the reality of the current situation, regardless of what they believe the ideal should be.

The real choice here is between striving for certain ideals or planning for the reality on the ground. Keeping the policy, but continuing to selectively enforce it, is not an option. In general, policies have to be enforced, uniformly and consistently, because erratic enforcement means that people are being treated differently, and that is both wrong and a liability. This library can either start to strictly enforce their food and drink policy to strive for their ideal, even though everyone recognizes that this is contrary to what the patrons actually want, or they can change the policy to one everyone can enforce, since food and drink in the library are already a reality. This arithmetic might change in a different type of library, such as an archive or special collection, but in *this* library, one wonders why holding the line against pretzels and granola bars is equated so strongly with some ideal of what a library should be. One would hope we stand for more. For this reason, both Lizbeth and I think the obvious solution is a change. She isn't helping anything by pretending there's another option so that her staff believe they have input.

To fix this, Lizbeth needs to hold another meeting. She needs to tell them that she is going to change the policy, and she needs to explain why. She has already made up her mind, and there is no reason to pretend she hasn't. She should then reassure everybody that she understands this is a big change, and she wants to create a taskforce to determine the appropriate implementation and scope for the new policy. This approach will be much more authentic; people can always tell when a manager isn't actually open to their input. The staff will likely resist, but at least everything will be out in the open, which will show that she respects them enough to tell them the truth. The taskforce will allow her to take advantage of their hard-won understanding of the difficulties in implementing a new approach. After all, her staff have voiced some very valid concerns.

Ultimately, telling people that they have agency in how something is implemented, and then ensuring that you respect that agency, goes a long way to building trust and buy-in when you have to make an unpopular, unilateral decision. That's what this really is. Head librarians make these all the time. They aren't fun, but they're necessary. The big mistake is pretending that this is anything else.

Chapter Fourteen

Transitioning to a New Job

A Controlling Scenario Using Difficult Professional Topics

SCENARIO

Richard Berman had been to a lot of job fairs in his long career as human resources specialist at Hartwell Technical College Library. He had found that meeting candidates face-to-face, talking about the school, and explaining the various programs the college offered was an excellent way to perform a cursory first search for qualified candidates to fill positions for his library. While Hartwell Technical College had attained a fairly good level of familiarity within the educational community, Richard had found that many candidates approaching his table at these job fairs were actually quite unfamiliar with just what a "technical" college was—let alone what Hartwell's values and educational philosophy were. So, Richard spent a lot of his time at these job fairs explaining to visitors that Hartwell offered its students practical, hands-on coursework in subjects like information technology, applied sciences, and technical skills. He would also discuss Hartwell's unique approach to education, which stressed a mixture of religious, cultural, philosophical, and aesthetic experiences and perspectives. He would then explain how the Hartwell Technical College Library provided services and resources that best helped its students successfully achieve their educational goals and that best promoted the college's values. Most of the job fairs Richard had been to were unextraordinary—small events with a few hundred people milling about the room, many not even interested in working in the information sector. He'd normally greet only a dozen or so candidates, and—if he was lucky—he maybe found one potentially qualified person interested in filling a library position. But today was different. Today was the first time Richard was attending the job fair at the state library's annual conference held in the state's most populous city, Miami. Here, there would be thousands of people, all of whom would be interested in working for a library, if they weren't already doing so.

Richard was glad that there would be a larger pool of potential candidates to meet, since Hartwell Technical College Library had a number of entry-level positions to fill, and these annual state conferences were filled with candidates just entering the profession and looking for employment. The college library had recently received a number of large endowments from several well-known Christian foundations, which had allowed the college to expand many of its services and hire additional personnel at the library. There was even talk of expanding the library's facility sometime in the near future.

As Richard began to set up for the onslaught of library professionals looking for employment opportunities, he placed library brochures and applications around the table. He was inundated almost immediately by a number of people looking for paraprofessional and entry-level library positions. So, Richard did his best to shepherd the crowds around his table, gather employment applications, and set up impromptu face-to-face interviews for later in the afternoon. It looked like Hartwell Technical College Library would get a terrific response here at the conference, and Richard would have little trouble helping the library fill its open positions. He knew that the college's human resources director, Aliyah Andrews, would be equally pleased.

During one of the few lulls in the crowds gathering around the table, Richard greeted a prospective employee who introduced herself as Stephanie Smith.

"Hello there, Stephanie. Are you interested in working at a technical college library?" Richard asked.

"I'm very interested," Stephanie said. "I've been looking at technical libraries as an outlet for employment, since I've got lots of experience with information technology and web design. I would be happy to look over one of your brochures and take an application."

Richard began gathering appropriate materials and explained some general information about the entry-level jobs for which he was recruiting.

"I'm wondering, though," said Stephanie, "what management opportunities your library might have available—either right now or in the near future?"

"Well, as I said, a majority of our available positions are for entry-level library positions, and we have quite a few paraprofessional and clerical library positions," Richard offered. "But I'm only aware of one management position that will be opening soon at the library." He hadn't really planned to recruit for that position, knowing how much experience and knowledge was needed. It would definitely require a higher level of recruitment beyond what could be offered here.

"Do you think you'd be more interested in a starting position? We do offer competitive wages and benefits—even for entry-level positions," Richard said, raising his eyebrows and looking at the table for an information sheet outlining the wage and benefit packages for the lower-level positions. "Since there are so many more of those, your chances of being hired would be far greater." Richard found the information sheet he'd been searching for, and he handed it to Stephanie. She took it from him and looked it over.

"Well, those are certainly excellent benefits, but my skills and technical experience would be far more useful to the library at a management level. What was the management position you mentioned earlier?" Stephanie asked.

Richard had to think about it a moment, then he said, "The library is looking for an information technology specialist with a minimum of ten years' library-related experience, five of which should be in IT."

Stephanie asked if Richard had a job specification sheet that she could take with her, assuring him that she had twelve years of experience. She told him that she had taken a brief professional break but was ready to get back to what she loved—helping library users. Stephanie asked a bit more about the hiring process for the specialist position. Richard had to admit that he hadn't prepared to do any recruiting at that level and asked if Stephanie would mind coming back in the morning after he had taken an opportunity to chat with the human resources director and college library director about the position later that day.

"Oh, I don't mind at all. I'd be happy to come back tomorrow. I'm here at the conference until Tuesday. I have a couple of diversity programs I'm attending in the morning and an alternative lifestyles workshop, but I'd be happy to swing back here, say, at one o'clock tomorrow?" Stephanie offered. "And, in the meantime, I'll look over the information you've given me about the job and fill out the interest application. How would that be?"

"That's perfect," Richard said. The two continued to chat a bit more about the library and the college. While chatting with Stephanie, Richard was happy to discover that they were from the same hometown. "Oh, really? Fort Lauderdale? I was born and raised there! I worked at Broward University for a few years. Where did you work there, or were you going to school at the time?" Richard was certainly sounding friendly and interested, but his question was clearly intended to assess Stephanie's viability as a high-level management candidate.

"Oh, really? Broward? What a great school. I actually did undergraduate work there, but I worked at the City College of Lauderdale for about five years before . . . " Stephanie paused, curiously, before she added, "before moving on. I took a brief hiatus, and now I'm relocating to Miami," she said.

Richard was clearly impressed. "They have a great training and development program there at City College," he said. Although he didn't tell Stephanie, Richard was also quite familiar with Shane Billet, the City College of Lauderdale's human resources manager. Richard and Shane had worked closely together about two years ago on a regional task force addressing recruitment challenges. They had stayed in contact over the last few years and occasionally ran into each other at professional events. In fact, he thought he had seen Shane somewhere in the immense conference hall as he was setting up his table earlier that day. He made a mental note to try and find Shane . . . just to chat.

As more conference attendees began to crowd around the Hartwell Technical College Library table, Richard needed to return to his regular business of greeting and orientating others. He disengaged from his fascinating talk with the potential new information technology specialist by telling her that he looked forward to seeing her the next day at one o'clock. As they parted, Stephanie handed Richard her résumé. He quickly glanced at it, then tucked it in his briefcase. He promised to have more information tomorrow regarding the management position in which she had expressed an interest.

Late that afternoon, as the job fair concluded, Richard Berman gathered up his materials and returned to his hotel. He had an opportunity to take a closer look at Stephanie Smith's résumé, which included high marks in project management and web design. It also revealed a great deal of progressive managerial responsibility during her time at the City College of Lauderdale. He had to admit, Stephanie Smith looked like a viable candidate, and he wanted to ensure the college took a closer look at her. He just needed to ascertain the library's needs and timeframe so he could pass this on to Stephanie the next day when they met.

With Stephanie's résumé in hand, Richard placed a conference call to the Hartwell Technical College human resources director and the college library director. Once the conference call had been established, Richard updated the two on the progress and success at the state conference job fair. "I think we have quite a few qualified candidates in the pool for just about every position," Richard offered.

"That's great! Don't forget to collect their interest applications so we can follow through when you return. Oh, and you informed each candidate about our college philosophy and values, right?" Aliyah, the human resources director, asked. "We're not like the average college library, and we need to be transparent."

Richard replied that he had indeed done a thorough job of orientating prospective candidates and said that each person received the college brochure and information sheets. "We have a few face-to-face interviews scheduled for tomorrow. In fact," Richard said, "I have a potential candidate for the information technology specialist position we were talking about last week, Caroline." That got the attention of Caroline Grady, Hartwell Technical College Library's director.

"Really, Richard? That's great. The vacancy needs to be filled soon. I think Randy is scheduled to retire next week, and we've exhausted just about all avenues in recruiting a capable person for that position," Caroline replied. "It sure would be great to find someone with a lot of management experience. With the library technology upgrades, new web design, and some other major tech projects in the pipeline, we're going to want to fill this position as quickly as possible, and fill it with a quality candidate. We have not had much luck yet."

Richard looked at the relevant experience he saw on Stephanie's résumé. "Well, she has a wealth of experience in all of those areas and more!"

"She?" said Caroline. "Wow, that sure would be great to have a female candidate in our IT department, particularly in a management position. I look forward to hearing more about her when you get back to campus."

The human resources director thanked everyone for being on the call, and the three of them ended the phone meeting. Richard continued to make notes on Stephanie's résumé and tried to think of a series of questions to ask her at their scheduled meeting the next afternoon. He included the standard questions: "Tell me about yourself and why you think you're qualified for this position" and "What are your proudest accomplishments in the profession?" But at the last minute he remembered Aliyah's remark to him earlier about Hartwell not being like the "average college." He assumed she was referencing the college's strong religious foundation. So, Richard composed the following question: "The idea of integrating faith and learning is pretty important for our school *and* our library. How would you say your faith informs your decisions and judgment?" If Stephanie Smith was uncomfortable with a question like that, he'd be able to discuss the school's philosophy and values further and decide where to go from there.

At one o'clock the following day, Richard Berman welcomed Stephanie Smith to a reception room at his hotel, where he was holding impromptu interviews over the next few hours with all the candidates that he'd met throughout the conference over the last few days. Stephanie was dressed professionally and had a pleasant demeanor. She shook hands with Richard and took a seat.

"Thanks again for meeting me. I did look over the materials you provided me, and the job specifications for the information technology manager position look like a perfect match for me. I'm interested to hear more. Were you able to talk to your library personnel about the pending position?" Stephanie asked.

"I sure did! And let me tell you, Stephanie, I looked over your résumé, and you sure get high marks for all the progressive managerial responsibility you've acquired during your time at City College of Lauderdale. I'm really impressed. It shows you have the experience we need." Richard smiled and told Stephanie about his conversation with the human resources director and the library director. He let her know the position was opening within the next few weeks, and the college was hoping to fill the vacancy quickly. He went over the expected salary and benefits package and proceeded with the list of questions he'd prepared. The ensuing conversation was going quite well, so Richard felt it was time to pop his question regarding the college's philosophy and values.

"Stephanie, as I'm sure you ascertained from reading all the material in our brochure, integrating faith and learning is pretty important for our school and our library. How would you say your faith informs your decisions and judgment?" Richard anticipated some reluctance but was surprised when Stephanie quickly replied without any outward sign of discomfort.

"Well," she said, "I was raised in a very conservative and religious household. I wasn't always the model child my parents expected, but their religious upbringing at least taught me not to judge people harshly and to leave that to a higher power. I firmly believe that those who are highly religious are more contented with life, and we can all learn something from that faith. They are often more involved with family and often look for guidance through prayer. That can never be a bad thing." Stephanie took a deep breath as she considered the question a bit more carefully. "I also look for guidance when faced with tough decisions. I meditate, and I always seek answers that best serve the individuals and organizations I work for." Stephanie wasn't completely satisfied with her answer; she herself wasn't a religious person, but she respected those who were. She felt she had done the best she could with a tough question like that—especially on the fly.

Richard felt the answer was good as well and was glad to hear that Stephanie had been raised in a religious household. The answer didn't raise any red flags, and he didn't see a need to question her more about the Hartwell Technical College Library's religious foundations and principles. "Well, I've got a series of other interviews scheduled here in just a few minutes, so let me just end by saying that—at least from your résumé and from what I hear—I think you'd be an excellent candidate, and I really want to encourage you to apply for our management position. I can let you know when the position officially opens, and I will contact you regarding the next steps." Richard shook Stephanie's hand again and told her she could expect to hear back from him in the next few weeks. "Until then," Richard said, "I have your résumé, and I see that you prepared our standard interest application. Would you like me to take that with me? It's likely there will be another application you'll need to complete once the position becomes vacant, but I'll take this one to get your information into our system."

Stephanie was extremely excited. She handed Richard her completed interest application and told him that Hartwell Technical College Library was a terrific opportunity for her to excel at what she did best. The position seemed like an almost perfect fit for her skills and experience. Stephanie said goodbye, left the conference, and waited for a call from Richard.

Several days after Richard returned to Hartwell Technical College, the information technology manager position officially opened. Richard began entering Stephanie Smith's information from the application form he'd collected at the conference into the college's candidate screening and tracking system. Stephanie had provided the name of Roberta Cliff as her former immediate supervisor at City College of Lauderdale. She had also indicated that Roberta Cliff was a professional reference. Richard knew that standard practice at Hartwell Technical College was for him to receive résumés, conduct a preliminary interview, and then proceed to check only the references candidates provided. Richard decided to deviate a bit from that practice. Before contacting Stephanie to initiate the formal employment application process now that the job was open, he decided to skip Roberta Cliff and instead informally check in with his friend and colleague Shane Billet—the human resources manager at City College of Lauderdale. Unfortunately, he had been unable to connect with Shane at the job fair, but since Shane was the human resources director, he seemed like the perfect person from whom to ply information about Stephanie. It seemed harmless to get Shane's informal take on Stephanie's performance while she had been at their library. He picked up his office phone, dialed Shane's work number, and waited for him to answer.

"Shane Billet. How can I help you?"

"Shane, it's Richard Berman out at Hartwell. Long time no see. Sorry I missed you at the conference. We were absolutely swamped at the job fair."

"Yeah, we were as well," Shane answered, and the two of them spent a few moments catching up on things. Finally, Richard decided to get to the point.

"Look, Shane, the real reason I called is because we have a big management position open now, and I may have found the perfect candidate at the conference. And I know I'm asking this a bit out of turn, but I wondered if you might help me by giving me some idea of how this potential candidate did while she was at City College or if we are way off base in even considering her. Her name is Stephanie Smith."

"Hmm. Doesn't ring a bell. Let me look here on my computer." Richard could hear Shane tapping on his keyboard. "No, we don't have a Stephanie Smith in our records."

Completely surprised, Richard explained a bit about what Stephanie had listed on her résumé. "That's so strange that she's not in your records when she obviously knew we'd check on her experience."

"Oh! That's not Stephanie," Shane finally exclaimed—as if a light bulb had just turned on. "You're talking about *Steve* Smith! I completely blocked that out of my mind. That was quite a situation here. I guess if you like drama in the library, then Steve—I mean, 'Stephanie'—would be great."

"I'm not sure I'm following you, Shane," Richard said, obviously confused.

"Way back then, Steve told many of his coworkers here that he was 'transitioning' and wanted to be called Stephanie. He was doing a good job, but the whole thing caused quite a commotion among the staff, and there was pressure from all over the place for me to deal with it. At some point, however, Steve just resigned and left. It sort of made my job easier. I didn't know how to handle a case like that one. Hey, Richard, I'm expecting an important phone call. Can I give you a call back later?" Richard thanked Shane and said they'd talk again soon, and they ended the conversation.

Putting Stephanie's application aside, Richard decided to talk to his human resources director about his discovery. As he entered Aliyah's office, he noticed she was talking to the college library director. Richard signaled to Aliyah by putting his finger up to interject. "If that's Caroline, I need you both to hear this." Aliyah put Caroline on speaker phone so Richard could talk to them both.

"The candidate with all that experience that we were considering for the information technology manager position—well, she is . . . or was . . . well, she's transgender. Her name used to be Steve."

"Whoa!" said Aliyah. "How'd you find this out? Oh my gosh, it sounded like that was the perfect candidate. I knew it was too good to be true. Can you imagine what would happen if our foundations found out? We'd jeopardize our grants."

"I was more worried about staff responses and how that would work," said Richard.

It was Caroline Grady, the college library director, who played the devil's advocate. "Maybe this person isn't 'out' at work. If you didn't detect her previous identity, Richard, maybe no one else will. You told the candidate about the college philosophy and values, so she knows this isn't the best environment to let that sort of information be made public. She might come to work, do her job, and go home without anyone ever knowing. Are we jeopardizing losing an incredible candidate if we don't consider her? And what about legal ramifications if we don't consider her? Are we opening ourselves to discrimination lawsuits?"

Richard thought about this for a second, then said, "As far as I know, there isn't a federal law that protects an employee from being fired because of their gender identity."

"Actually, Richard, there is. The US Supreme Court just decided a relevant case," Aliyah corrected. "And I'm certainly aware of several state and local ordinances that prohibit discrimination based on gender identity and expression. But, as a private college, a lot of the law is interpreted differently when applied to us. At any rate, I'm more concerned with how the college's benefactors and student body would react if we hired this person and the information came out that we had a transgender employee. It's too risky, even if the person does have excellent skills. I'm sure there are equally qualified individuals out there. We'll just have to find them."

Richard returned to his office and thought about how he would go about notifying Stephanie that she was being dropped as a candidate for the position. It would be tricky, especially as he realized that he hadn't *really* followed established protocol in discovering the information he had learned from Shane. But he was glad he had discovered it nonetheless. Maybe he wouldn't notify Stephanie at all. But she would surely be expecting a call, and she might see the recruitment posting elsewhere. No, he'd have to face this. But how?

TRANSITIONING TO A NEW JOB RESPONSES

Response 1
By Brenda Robertson Spencer, university librarian, University of North Texas, Dallas, Texas

The prevailing issue is, will Richard Berman, the human resources specialist at Hartwell Technical College Library, decide to hire Stephanie Smith, who is (as far as we know from the information given in the scenario) one of the best qualified candidates for the position and whose skills and experience are so much above and beyond the demands of the job that Richard felt confident enough to encourage her to apply for the position, or will he not hire Stephanie because of surreptitiously obtained information that revealed she is transgender.

The situation is compounded because Hartwell Technical College is founded on strict religious principles, and there is a legitimate concern that the decision to hire Stephanie will offend the college's benefactors. The risk of financial loss must always be taken seriously and weighed carefully. There is also the possibility that Stephanie's presence may disrupt an otherwise analogous workplace environment.

While there does not seem to be an easy resolution to this dilemma, there are some steps that Richard Berman should take to understand how he should proceed here as well as how to avoid similar problems in the future. The first step is for Richard to produce the Hartwell Technical College statement of hiring practices. The human resources departments of most organizations—either private or public—have crafted some sort of generic statement outlining the principles and processes under which hiring for the organization is conducted. Such a statement typically mirrors the Equal Employment Opportunity Commission ruling that discrimination based on sexual orientation violates Title VII of the Civil Rights Act of 1964. A direct conversation with human resources director Aliyah Andrews and Caroline Grady, the library director, about the responsibility of the organization to uphold the statement of hiring practices in this case is in order. This dialogue would be a good starting place to discuss decisions that have been motivated by fear and find inspiration that considers best-case scenarios versus potential worst outcomes.

It is important to note that in the initial interview at the job fair, Richard perceived Stephanie as the ideal candidate who could fulfill the needs of the job and also satisfy future plans for growth in the library. Library director Caroline Grady added her support by expressing excitement that Stephanie—being a *she*—would be "great to have in the IT department." In fact, Richard made several direct statements to Stephanie, extolling her skills and professional match for the library's future management position. He actually said, "I really want to encourage you to apply for our management position." But since Richard has found information about Stephanie that normally should not have been asked for or obtained prior to offering employment, he has introduced fear into the decision process and may now have set the library up for a potential lawsuit. It must also be noted that the information he obtained was gathered outside the boundaries of acceptable hiring practices. There is a reason that this information cannot be gathered as a part of the hiring practice—and Richard should have known this. Having obtained the information, however, it has done exactly what the law fears it will do: it has biased Richard from hiring the best candidate.

Are lawsuits something that really should be considered in the hiring process? Yes! According to the Society for Human Resource Management (SHRM), the number of workers filing lawsuits claiming discrimination based on religious faith or sexuality is on the rise in the United States. Additionally, there seems to be legal precedent for Stephanie to pursue here. The US Supreme Court in 1989 recognized that discrimination against a female who didn't conform to female stereotypes was a form of sex discrimination in *Price Waterhouse v. Hopkins* (490 U.S. 228) (SHRM). The Hartwell Technical College Library might very well become the next in a long line of cases.

To help counter the potential for legal repercussions, more institutions are including clauses in their hiring policies that restrict the hiring manager from things such as checking an applicant's social media accounts or conducting background checks without first getting a candidate's approval. These sorts of restrictions are put in place to lessen the potential of legal trouble, but they also prevent bias when considering hiring an otherwise qualified candidate. Such rules represent the shift away from allowing fear, stereotypes, and systematic trends to alienate persons who exercise their legal freedom to express themselves outside what has formerly been the norm.

The genuine concern of losing the institution's benefactors is another matter. The second step in resolving this issue, then, could be for Aliyah and Caroline (and perhaps even Richard) to seek a transparent and straightforward discussion with the college's highest administrators about the issue. In this discussion, the library director and human resources director can begin to assuage the likely fear-based reactions to potentially hiring Stephanie Smith. They should start presenting the facts and logic in a way that clearly explains that if Stephanie is not hired now, there will most certainly be more Stephanie Smiths to contend with in the future. Candidates like Stephanie (as well as many others on the fringes of society) will continue to present themselves because they are more quickly becoming a part of society. They can explain why it is best to choose to voluntarily hire the most qualified candidate currently being considered by the college versus being forced to hire a less qualified applicant as damage control. It would also be important to acknowledge that funding from benefactors could potentially be at risk, and there could be a loss of tuition from potential students—which is the lifeblood of an academic institution—following the humiliating public and widespread announcement of a lawsuit that depicts Hartwell Technical College in a most unflattering and unwelcoming way.

The last step to consider—while perhaps not immediately helpful in dealing with the prevailing issue in this scenario—would be more than beneficial to Hartwell Technical College Library going forward. As mentioned above, nondiscriminatory hiring policies are being firmly established and embraced by administrators and managers. There should be simultaneous efforts to construct an in-house culture with zero tolerance for discrimination and harassment and to create training programs that guide employees toward not simply tolerance but inclusion. Most important is to lead from the top down. Having been confronted with this latest issue, it is clear that this organization and its managers have ignored most—if not all—of those efforts.

Stephanie Smith is being hired for her qualifications to do the job. As long as she is meeting the demands of the job and performing at least at the level of the standard required for other Hartwell Technical College Library staff members, her personal beliefs and gender expression should not be the reason she is hired, or not hired; nor should it be the reason she is made to feel uncomfortable in the work environment.

Response 2
By Wayne Disher, San Jose State University School of Information, San Jose, California

As a public library employee most of my career, it's hard to believe that there are institutions that are governed by academic senates, provosts, and deans rather than city councils, city managers, and library directors. It's a bit strange to think about an institution that has only students and faculty as their primary client rather than the diverse community of young and old that a public library serves. But regardless of the library environment in which a library manager works, we do share one common interest. We each exist to connect people with the information they need. The means by which we connect people and information may differ, but our ultimate goal of sharing information is the same. Still, it is hard to detach myself from how one might resolve the problem presented in this scenario from a public library perspective. Like me, the first thing that might come to the reader's mind is, "Are there differences between public library employment and private library employment that might affect my perspective in this case?" The answer is a complicated "yes."

Those employees who work for businesses and nonprofits—such as a research library at Microsoft or the American Heart Association—are considered private-sector employees. Those who are employed to perform official duties for a government or public service—such as a public library or public university—are considered public-sector employees. As you might guess, individuals have different employee rights dependent on the sector in which they are employed. For example, most private-sector employees are granted certain rights that are not available to those in the public sector. Conversely, public employees have certain rights that private-sector employees do not. This fact seems to be pertinent to this particular scenario, so it needs to be explored a bit more. It might help us answer why the human resources specialist, Richard Berman, and his Hartwell Technical College colleagues are so concerned with the troubling information that has been surreptitiously obtained about a prospective employee.

Many private-sector employees are considered "at will." This is simply a legal term used in US labor law that implies a contractual agreement in which an employee can be terminated by an employer for any reason—provided the employer can establish a reason, or "just cause," for the termination and as long as the reason is not illegal. "At will" employment is even more common when an employee is hired for a management position. In this case, I believe Richard has discovered a controversial personal fact about a prospective employee that could jeopardize the college's ability to legally terminate that employee. So, rather than put the college in that legally dubious position, he decides to stop the employment process altogether.

It is not explicitly stated as such in this scenario, so we cannot be certain of this fact, but I would assume that Stephanie Smith would have been hired on an "at will" status. She was applying for a management-level position at a private-sector business, so this seems like a relatively safe assumption. Stephanie's employment on an "at will" status means she could have been terminated for any reason—that is, any reason other than race, gender, or sexual orientation. Since Richard Berman, human resources director Aliyah Andrews, and college library director Caroline Grady are concerned with Stephanie's gender and sexual orientation, they've come to the realization that they'd be legally trapped if they tried to terminate Stephanie for the fact that she is transitioning genders. For this reason, it is likely a professionally smart, if not ethically derived, decision.

Richard and his colleagues cannot change the past. The way they have discovered the information was wrong, but they cannot now ignore that information—nor do I believe they should. The decision to abandon Stephanie as a candidate allows them to protect the college from a legal tempest as well as steer the college clear of a likely negative public spectacle. We see some indication of the potential "drama" Stephanie's sexuality is likely to cause at a religious institution like Hartwell when Shane Billet—the human resources manager at Stephanie's previous employer—reveals that Stephanie used to be Steve. Apparently, it was Stephanie herself who publicly announced she was transitioning, and we know that it apparently caused "quite a commotion" with staff there. Past behavior is the most reliable indicator of future behavior, so I'd expect Stephanie to be just as honest and up-front about her transition with the staff at Hartwell. Therefore, when Shane confides to Richard that he had no clue how he would have handled the problem, and that he was lucky it went away on its own (due to Stephanie's resignation), it's not surprising that Richard suddenly becomes hesitant to proceed with Stephanie's recruitment and potentially have to handle this tricky situation himself.

I do not pass judgment in any way on Stephanie Smith's sexual orientation or personal qualities. By all indications in the scenario, she is incredibly composed, uniquely skilled, and completely capable of becoming Hartwell's information technology specialist. Had she been offered the position, accepted it, and officially assumed the position, I'd be right at her side in protesting her dismissal on grounds that she is transgendered. I'd be steadfastly encouraging her to find the closest attorney and sue Hartwell Technical College for wrongful termination. But the truth is, Stephanie has not been hired or even officially interviewed for the position. I can't fault Richard and the college for retreating and starting a new search.

Letting the Hartwell Technical College off the hook for its decision in regard to Stephanie, it's time to put my public-sector library hat on and look at this from an ethical perspective. Richard Berman crossed the line in circumventing proper hiring procedures. Additionally, Aliyah Andrews showed herself to be more interested in the college's reputation as it appears to potential funders rather than how her actions might violate any of her professional and personal ethics. Finally, library director Caroline Grady seemed far too willing to give up on the opportunity to have an incredibly talented employee on her staff—especially since she had apparently been having issues recruiting someone even remotely capable for the position up to this point.

While I reluctantly let Hartwell Technical College off the hook for making the decision they did, I cannot in any way excuse the unprofessional conduct of Richard Berman. He crossed the line in calling up a colleague and casually asking them about a prospective employee. While this sort of thing might routinely happen in a private-sector environment, I can't believe it would happen—even infrequently—in the public sector. The mere thought of not closely following the established hiring protocols would cause a public-sector human resources department to go nuts. Rules and regulations in a public-sector bureaucracy are often so rigid and inflexible that compliance is often impossible to avoid. For this reason, Richard should be reprimanded immediately. He crossed the professional line, put the college in legal jeopardy, and deprived the university of an excellent prospective employee. If I were Aliyah Andrews, and if Richard is an "at will" employee himself, I would likely terminate him for such unprofessional conduct.

There is sadness rooted in this scenario. Stephanie Smith represents a neglected population faced with constant ridicule, bullying, and profound personal challenges. Businesses are changing and becoming more and more diverse, and it's sad to think that organizations like Hartwell Technical College have not become flexible enough to look past gender and sexuality and instead respect the talent and skills a person brings to their employer. In an ideal world, the library staff room (like any office) should be a place where transgender people feel welcomed rather than judged. Unfortunately, as this scenario shows, businesses have quite a long way to go and a much higher bar to set in celebrating diversity and respect for employees of all types. Stephanie Smith has incredible skills, and she should have no problem finding an employer who can look past her difference and see the incredible diamond hiding just beneath the surface.

Response 3
By Kristin Whitehair, director of library services, St. Luke's Hospital, Kansas City, Missouri

In reading this scenario, we see that Richard Berman, the human resources specialist at Hartwell Technical College Library, has two primary issues that require deeper analysis. First, we should look at would-be employee Stephanie's status as a potential candidate for employment with the college. The second issue is how to fill the open position of information technology specialist at the college library.

Focusing on the next steps with Stephanie, Richard should set up a quick meeting with the college's legal counsel to seek advice on what is very quickly becoming a complex situation. Most professional organizations have a legal counsel, either an on-staff lawyer or contract lawyer who advises the organization on legal issues. Aliyah Andrews, the human resources director at Hartwell Technical College, is incorrect in her statement about there not being any relevant law to apply here. She may not yet be aware of a recent US Supreme Court decision giving federal protections to LGBTQ employees working in the private sector. Additionally, there are likely other legal issues pertaining to hiring employees that must be considered. Aliyah and Richard need to know that some counties and cities also have protections in place that will be relevant to how they proceed. Because Richard made the move of communicating to his superiors that Stephanie Smith was a "strong candidate," additional legal risk may be incurred by removing her as a candidate now. The organization's legal counsel can provide guidance on this.

Richard should also set up a meeting with the primary stakeholder, the library director, to discuss the situation. Stephanie's candidate status is quickly becoming a complex situation. In addition to being Richard's supervisor, the library director understands how this may impact the strategic implications of the outcome of this situation. The library director will likely have greater insight into how Stephanie's applicant status should be handled in light of all considerations at the college. Richard may want to include the library director in the meeting with legal counsel.

In short, Richard should not tackle this complex issue independently. He should seek out organizational support, internally within the library and beyond.

The second issue presented in this scenario is how the process of filling the information technology specialist position should have been handled differently. At the end of the scenario, the position has not been officially opened, yet candidates have been contacted on an ad hoc basis. Richard has handled this situation very unprofessionally by deviating from standard hiring policy. By leaving standard practice behind, Richard narrowed in on a single potential candidate, Stephanie Smith, before having the opportunity to neutrally evaluate a larger candidate pool. Stephanie may very well be a competitive candidate, but we have no idea if she is in the top tier of candidates since no other applications have been accepted. Even worse, Richard is calling an informal reference on a candidate before the position is even officially open, leading to even greater confusion and risk.

Discarding standard hiring practice creates significant legal risk for the organization. When a standard process is set aside, it is difficult to legally defend the rogue actions as fair to candidates. For example, imagine that, instead of this scenario, Richard had told Stephanie about the upcoming opening, taken her information, and informed her when the position officially opened. Then Stephanie could have applied and been evaluated against the other candidates via the normal channels. If selected for an on-site interview, she would have had the opportunity to assess the campus climate for herself to see if it was a good fit for her. Regardless of the information Richard found out regarding Stephanie's gender transition, the process is already compromised because he is zeroing in on a candidate before even opening the position. It's not specified in this scenario, but it wouldn't be surprising if Richard faced some sort of disciplinary action due to his actions in this case.

In the end, reaching out to the library director and legal counsel should be the first priority. Feedback from the library director and legal counsel will likely include guidance on how to proceed with Stephanie as well as how to get this hiring process back into normal procedure. Most importantly, Richard needs to take away from this scenario the importance of following that procedure from the beginning and not acting as a rogue recruiting agent.

The library community is small, as this scenario clearly demonstrates. It is common for there to be formal and informal connections between job applicants and hiring committee members. Keep in mind what your organization's policies are regarding hiring processes and references in these situations.

Rarely are human resource issues devoid of emotion. In a situation like this, there are likely strong emotions about the fairness of the situation to Stephanie. Issues like this can also involve very strong personal feelings and beliefs related to morals and religion. When this happens, take a step back, and see what resources are there to support you. In this scenario there is no rush to make a decision. Richard Berman and the Hartwell Technical College Library have plenty of time to sort out the situation and identify the best path forward, especially when following standard operating procedures.

Part Five

Staffing

Chapter Fifteen

Experience or Skills

A Staffing Scenario Using Problem Solving

SCENARIO

After a long and exhausting day on the interview panel charged with selecting the new librarian for Exhibition branch library, lead librarians Carrie Jones, Robert Klein, and Chris Haze watched the last candidate walk out of the room and close the door. Nora Rodriguez, staff analyst for the city's human resources department, addressed the group.

"Finally! That was our last candidate. Let's take a break for fifteen minutes and reconvene to make a selection. There's coffee on the table and restrooms just on the left as you go out the door. If you leave the room, please remember all your notes and interview material must remain in this room. Also, please don't discuss the interviews with anyone. Sound good?" Everyone agreed and ambled away in different directions to stretch their legs.

Jane Goodell was glad she had finished her interview. She hated scheduling interviews at the end of the afternoon because it usually meant that those on her interview panel would be tired and would likely zone out during her answers. The only thing that had lightened her mood a bit was seeing her old friend and fellow librarian Carrie Jones sitting on the interview panel when she walked in the room. Jane had worked at the Exposition branch library for eight years but had left her career to become a mother. While she was at Exposition branch, Jane's favorite colleague was Carrie—the familiar face she'd seen today on the other side of the interview table. She fondly remembered the many hours she and Carrie would spend sitting at the reference desk, helping library users, and forging a close working bond. Sure, she and Carrie had lost touch recently, but she knew her friend had respected her work ethic, and she was confident her friend would put in a good word of support for her with the others she'd seen on the panel just now. Jane was also happy to see Carrie had been promoted to lead librarian at Exposition branch, and she liked the idea of working with her again. She was just a bit nervous as she walked through the library on her way back to her car. There were so many computers now. Jane saw a computer just about every place she looked—even in the children's room! But it was the long line of patrons waiting to use the public internet stations that really alarmed her. Not only was each of the library's thirty public computers being used right then, but it looked as if there were at least ten people waiting to hop on as soon as a computer became available. *Where are the card catalogs?* Jane wondered. *This might be a good time to take a computer class. And look at all these kids on their phones in the library*, she thought as she walked out into the sunlight. *Things have sure changed. And I'm not sure they've changed for the better. Have libraries completely lost all human contact?*

During the break from their interviews, Carrie and Robert sequestered themselves away in the corner of the room and sipped coffee.

"That was exhausting!" Robert said. "Man, after the first six candidates, they all start to look the same, huh? Anyway, there are certainly lots of good candidates for you to choose from, Carrie. It's going to be tough for you to select someone."

"I don't know. It might be easier than I thought. I was glad to see Jane Goodell—that last candidate. We worked together at this very library a long time ago. I know her work ethic, and it's incredible. She's high on my list," Carrie remarked.

"Really?" Robert squinted his eyes. "I do remember her telling us about working at this library for a while. But she left, what, to raise her kids or something like that, right?" Robert took a bite of his bagel and gulped some coffee.

"Yes, that's right. I was a part-time librarian at the time she was here, and I remember her being one of the branch's best employees back then. She was well loved by the staff and the community, and she knew her reference books, that's for sure! She had a good human touch. I think we need more of that here," Carrie said. "Jane and I were pretty good friends too, but it was her work that impressed me back then. Now that her kids are old enough to take care of themselves, I totally understand her desire to come back to our library." Carrie stood up to put a little bit more cream in her coffee cup and started back to the table.

Robert called Carrie back, looking a little confused. "Carrie, didn't that candidate just tell us that she doesn't like computers and that she doesn't use the internet? And didn't she also confess to not even knowing how to use email? That seems pretty odd in this day and age—especially for an information professional—don't you think? Carrie, don't let your previous friendship with the candidate cloud your judgment."

Just then, Nora Rodriguez reentered the meeting room. "Sorry I'm late, everyone. One of your patrons trapped me on my way back to the room. They needed some computer help, and I was glad to assist. I just didn't think it would take as long as it did," she said. "Anyway, it looks like we're all here now, and you all look refreshed. So, let's discuss the candidates and make a selection."

Robert and Carrie dumped the rest of their coffee in the sink and rejoined the others at the conference table. The lead librarian for the main library, Chris Haze, was the first to speak.

"I really liked Desiree Embry. She's only a few months out of library school, but wow, what computer skills! And I'm sure the branch could take advantage of her experience teaching computer literacy at the senior center. The fact that she has such a large social media presence also shows that she knows the power of new technology platforms and how to take advantage of a whole new marketing arena for the Exposition library. Shoot, if I had a position open at the main library, Embry would definitely be my selection." Chris looked to Nora Rodriguez, who was nodding in agreement.

Then Carrie went to bat for her preferred candidate. "I have to consider how someone will work with my community and my team. Since I have personal knowledge of Jane Goodell's personal qualities and experience, I think she'd be the right fit."

"But you can't use that same criteria with the other candidates we saw today," Nora remarked. "None of the interview questions your panel created today would be useful to you in evaluating those qualities in the other candidates. Some of them may also fit into your team just as well."

Coming to Carrie's defense, Chris interjected, "Well, that's true, but can we use 'computer skills' or 'technology training' as our evaluation criteria then? I mean, neither of those qualities are in the job specifications."

"That's true, Chris," Nora conceded. "The current job specifications haven't been updated in over twenty years. They were probably developed long before the internet was even a household name. Our new human resources director has made it her priority to update every job specification in our city departments. Until then, we have to use the job specifications we currently have."

Carrie felt the tide was turning toward Jane, so she decided to pounce. "Look, technology skills, like email and web searching, can be taught. I can work with Jane to get her to a comfort level where that won't be an issue. But it's hard for me to train another person to have personal qualities they may or may not possess. I know Jane's qualities, and I know they are the right fit."

"I hate to point out the obvious," Robert said, "but obviously there is a huge need for technology-savvy staff at this branch. I mean, even Nora was waylaid by someone needing computer help just now. Sure, maybe Jane could learn tech skills, but it's not *your* job to teach her, Carrie, is it? And while Jane may have fit in with the staff here a long time ago, how will the current staff react to her lack of technology skills? I think you might be setting her up for resentment and failure if you place her in this position."

That was certainly a shot of realism that Carrie hadn't considered. How would the staff react to a technological luddite on the staff? Desiree Embry wasn't a bad candidate. She seemed nice enough. Carrie wished more than ever she'd asked some questions that would have told her a little more about Embry's personal qualities. Still, actual experience at the precise job site *had* to count for something, didn't it? Or was librarianship just about computers now?

Nora had to bring this process to a conclusion. She spoke up and said, "It's late, everyone. I know we all would like to call it a day. We need to make a decision. It looks like the panel has brought forth two good candidates from which to choose. So who will it be?" Carrie closed her eyes and, after a last moment of careful consideration, made her choice. "I'm going with my gut here. I'm choosing Jane Goodell."

EXPERIENCE OR SKILLS RESPONSES

Response 1
By Brian Sontag, operations manager, Stanislaus County Library System, Modesto, California

The "Experience or Skill" scenario presents an interesting dilemma. The previous working—and perhaps personal—relationship Jane and Carrie had established is a variable that makes it difficult for Carrie to be objective. We know her organization is looking for tech-savvy candidates. Yet, Jane does not meet this qualification. However, according to Carrie, Jane is great to work with otherwise. Jane sounds like a great example of a candidate who would be good for the organization in another capacity, but not in the position for which they are currently recruiting. In this situation it is easy to default to what one is most familiar with. For Carrie, that is her familiarity with Jane's work ethic. Carrie should have done her due diligence in assessing the qualifications of Desiree and Jane within the scope of the organization's goals.

In my experience, the recruitment process is an important and somewhat misunderstood part of the work environment. The Jane Goodell scenario is all too familiar. I have participated in recruitments for positions from library pages to library managers, and along the way I learned how to mitigate the uncertainty of the recruitment process. Libraries need dependable staff on all levels who carry with them a range of abilities and knowledge that make them effective in their communities. While it is tempting to look past some needs of the organization in favor of a few things we know to be true, we cannot ignore those needs altogether. In doing so, we shortchange our organization, and we likely set individuals up for failure.

I would recommend an improved approach to recruitments that could have helped Carrie avoid some of the conflict we see in this scenario. Whether a recruitment is internal (hiring from only within the organization) or external (opening up the recruitment to both internal candidates and qualified outside candidates), the process begins in the organization's human resources (HR) office. Get to know your library's HR representative. Having a good working relationship with HR will make you a more effective library manager. If your organization's HR representative is unfamiliar with library practices or works in another department, spend time to help them understand the library world you work in. Conversely, you should understand some of the HR world. Understanding your organization's approach to recruitments and the policies that guide them is a good place to start. There are often negotiations between library management and HR to figure out details of specific recruitments. For example, HR and library management might need to negotiate who will serve on the interview panel, the appropriate number of candidates to consider, how to screen qualifications, whether to accept experience in lieu of education, and whether job specifications are still up to date. Knowing about these sorts of issues would certainly have benefited Carrie in this case, as HR and Carrie could have talked about the importance of technology skills in the hiring process.

In this scenario, the recruitment panel discussed the outdated job specifications. Unfortunately, by this time it was already too late to do anything about it. Job specification reviews need to occur before any future recruitments. It is understood in this scenario that the new HR director has begun this process. However, Carrie should not have started this recruitment until that process had been completed. This would have helped her organization get a pool of qualified candidates from which to select, and likely would have pulled Jane out of the recruitment early on.

With the prerecruitment work of reviewing job specifications completed, Carrie must also ensure that interview questions the panel asks will be effective in getting the responses desired. An interview panel usually has fewer than a dozen questions to ask that allow them to interact with candidates and to ascertain their potential effectiveness on the job. Carrie needs to ensure that interview panels in the future design questions that make the most out of that short interaction with candidates. Carrie and her staff need to take time to discuss—with the assistance of the HR representative—how to design effective new interview questions and update antiquated questions they may be tempted to frequently use. This should be an integral part of any future recruitment panel and should take place well before the interviews begin.

Students reading this case scenario should note the role of the recruitment panel overall. Obviously, the individuals participating in the interview process will vary depending on the position and department where a vacancy exists. However, in most cases, the individual who will be supervising the position will participate in the interview and recruitment process. That was the case with Carrie in this scenario. Carrie has an understandable vested interest in the success of the recruitment. But she doesn't seem to have a good idea of the kind of employee she really needs in this position. If she did, she would have been looking more at technology qualifications. Carrie's remark that she could train Jane in the technology skills she lacks is also unrealistic and shows Carrie didn't prepare going in to the recruitment process.

Carrie's desire to have someone like Jane Goodell on her team, with her incredible track record of productivity and community service, is commendable. However, she has let her personal opinions outweigh her organization's actual needs in this case. Perhaps she could work on her own with Jane to get Jane's skills to a point where she would be more effective in this library. At some point, then, another recruitment will arise, and Jane can be encouraged to apply—if she meets those job requirements. Until then, Carrie needs to right her library's recruitment process immediately by working with the HR department and her library staff to update job specifications before initiating any further hiring.

Response 2
By Barbara Kerr, director, Medford Public Library, Medford, Massachusetts

The interviewing panel convened to select a new librarian for Exhibition branch library is about to make a mistake by hiring Jane Goodell. Although she has experience in the library and already has a good reputation there, you just can't hire someone who does not use a computer. It is impossible for a twenty-first-century library to operate without computer-savvy staff. A librarian must have at least basic technology skills, and Jane Goodell—by her own admission—does not even use email or the internet. She is completely unqualified. Libraries are not only "all about computers now," but you certainly must know how to use one!

The Exhibition branch library needs someone who can jump right in and handle the obvious technology need the users require—and that's not Jane. If Jane is hired, other staff are going to spend unreasonable amounts of time teaching her computer basics just to be able to function at a level necessary to complete basic tasks like answering emails and ordering material. Lead librarian Robert Klein is right—other library staff are going to resent Jane if she is hired, and the public will not get good technology service from her for a long time. If Jane had even basic tech skills, the decision to hire her would be a more reasonable one. But she has none, and that is just not acceptable. Experience is a good thing, but in this circumstance, it is the wrong *type* of experience, and it is not enough.

The fact that Exhibition branch library's lead librarian, Carrie Jones, wants to hire Jane highlights some problems with her management style. She would rather hire someone unqualified who is a friend than someone who has the precise skills that the library needs. Jane seems to be about to make a personal choice rather than a professional one. The human resources staff analyst, Nora Rodriguez, made a completely valid point that Carrie's friendship with Jane should not be a factor in hiring since it could not be a factor for the other candidates. However, Carrie is more concerned about her team getting along than she is about public service, and her choice is a poor one. It is obvious from the computer use described that this library needs tech-savvy staff. There is no comparison between the younger candidate, who teaches computer literacy, and Jane, who is nervous because she saw computers in the library.

Technology is not optional for a librarian, and it should have been a qualification for this position. This scenario points out the importance of having accurate, thorough, and updated job specifications that reflect the actual jobs an organization is trying to fill. The fact that the job specifications for this position have not been updated in over twenty years is extremely problematic. It's certainly good news to see that the new human resources director in this scenario has made it a priority for departments to update job classifications and specifications, but that won't help this current interviewing dilemma. The process has already begun, and interviews based on the current specifications have already taken place. Is the interview panel, then, forced to make a selection? Not necessarily.

Perhaps the best path forward in resolving this situation to the satisfaction of Carrie Jones, and to the benefit of the Exhibition branch library's user community, is to put the brakes on the current process and decide not to fill the position. This will allow the department to work with the human resources department to update the library's job specifications to include actual job requirements, like computer skills. Once this process is complete, the library can then start over and recruit more appropriate candidates with proper, usable skills that match the current needs of the department and its community.

To be honest, this process will not be quick and easy. Human resources reclassifications and specification updates are notoriously long and drawn-out projects. Still, this may give Carrie time to encourage Jane to get the skills she needs to join her team. It will also give the library an opportunity to seriously explore and analyze their classifications and positions to see if they need to be changed further. Perhaps there is an opportunity to reorganize and reshape this library to take advantage of whatever information they find in their exploration. Perhaps the library will recognize that they need lower-level technical assistants and trainers rather than another librarian. Or maybe they'll discover that they need a young adult librarian rather than an adult services librarian. Forcing the library to reevaluate their services and their needs in this way will take time and leave the current vacancy unfilled. This may be a stress on the existing staff, who will now need to take up the slack. Ultimately, however, it will result in a far more qualified employee that meets the department's expressed needs.

Turning back to the scenario, the scene ends with Carrie sticking with her gut and saying she wants to hire Jane. It is my hope that the other lead librarians and human resources staff analyst on the interview panel have better judgment and have come to this interview with expectations of an appropriate level of computer competency. Hopefully, they each have a vote and can overrule Carrie's decision and recommend a different course of action.

Response 3
By Elise Malkowski, director, Murrieta Public Library, Murrieta, California

Experience versus personality has been an ongoing hiring dilemma for many library managers over the years when considering the selection of new staff. Early in my career, I often landed on the side of experience when selecting staff; however, after many years working with challenging personalities that often made daily library operations difficult, I have shifted more toward the side of personality in making selections of otherwise equally qualified candidates, knowing that any required experience may be easily learned in training and mentoring.

If time permitted in this scenario, I would hold a second round of interviews, adding more personality-based questions. In these interviews, I might also recommend a branch coworker—one who is superior in the organizational chart—be invited to join the selection panel. There is value in those staff members who will be working alongside the new hire being part of the selection process. Customer service, friendliness, and a passion to help others are very important aspects of working in libraries and aspects that aren't easily taught or absorbed by everyone. Is it better to have a technology expert who doesn't really like people on your staff, or someone who loves helping people but isn't technology driven? I tend to side with the latter. In my experience, libraries are more about people than they are about the services they provide. By holding a second interview, the branch manager, Carrie, and her staff can determine the skill set and desire Jane has to work in a library that has changed and evolved since she last worked there.

Additionally, it will be important for the human resources person to conduct thorough reference checks on both Jane and Desiree. This, too, will help with the decision-making process. Checking two or more professional references from each candidate will certainly help focus the selection process on finding the perfect candidate. If the reference provided can be obtained from a previous supervisor—particularly in Desiree's case—the selection panel can get a better idea of the potential employee's work habits and interpersonal skills and work relationships. While we are to assume that Jane has been out of the workforce since she left the library, surely she has other individuals who'd be able to confirm certain aspects of her skill potential. It can be very telling when little is said about a potential hire.

When interview panels are established, each panelist will have different aspects they are looking for in the candidate. Perhaps Carrie should have recused herself from this panel once she saw Jane's name on the list of interviewees. Having prior knowledge of what a candidate is like to work with can cloud a decision, especially if they were or are friends outside of work. Has Carrie really thought about what type of employee she wants to fill her vacancy? She hasn't articulated what qualities will constitute a perfect fit for her library. She only knows that Jane has qualities she once liked. Carrie needs to consider how the current position differs from the position Jane worked in prior. Jane may not be as easy to work with this time if she is unhappy, overwhelmed, unprepared, and frustrated in the new position. I can sympathize with Carrie's desire to work with team players and personalities she is familiar with. Working with difficult personalities throughout one's career can certainly cause a manager to be more comfortable selecting someone familiar to work with. However, Carrie needs to be clearer in the second round of interviews about what the main job duties entail and to get a better sense of how these two candidates truly feel about the job duties and how they match her expectations about the type of person she wants.

Ultimately, managers want to hire the person with the best personality traits and skills. They want candidates who show a desire to learn and grow. In this situation, and barring anything unforeseen from a second round of interviews, I believe Carrie should hire Jane. Carrie knows Jane is a team player, Jane has a good work ethic, and Jane was well liked by the staff in her former position. Assuming Jane is on board with taking on additional training and acquiring her missing skills, which she will ascertain from questions asked in the second interview, Carrie should be comfortable with selecting Jane. In the experience I have had in managerial positions over the years, I have found that it is easier to train and mentor employees who possess excellent personality traits like Jane has than it is to develop interpersonal skills in an employee who doesn't have any.

Chapter Sixteen

Jack of All Trades

A Staffing Scenario Using Problem Solving

SCENARIO

Sharon Bond set the stack of new books needing Mystery labels on her desk and readied all the supplies she'd need to complete the task. Just as she sat down to begin, she glanced up and looked out the staff room window to see Jack Farrow, library director of Timberline Falls Public Library, gesturing at the city's landscape maintenance contractors.

"Are you kidding me?" Sharon exclaimed. "I just can't believe this!" Jim Scarsdale, the library's other library clerk, glanced up, concerned.

"What's wrong?" Jim followed Sharon's gaze out the window and saw what Sharon was seeing. "Oh my gosh. There he goes again. He's a Jack of all trades! He thinks he can do everything, but he's not very competent at anything!" The two sat and watched as Jack took the leaf blower from one of the landscapers and seemingly demonstrated the "proper" method of blowing grass and leaves across the sidewalk.

"Is he actually telling the gardeners how to do their job?" Sharon asked in disbelief. "That's got to be a first. Does his job description go that far?"

Reference librarian Carlos Rodriguez came up from behind, curious about what the two library clerks were so fascinated with. "What's going on? What are you guys looking at?"

"Jack Farrow. Seems he really *does* know everything. He's telling the landscapers how to do their job. Can you believe it?"

"Yes, he does like to put his fingers in everyone's pie, doesn't he?" Carlos watched through the window a few more moments and then added, "Just the other day he was telling me where to put certain books on our ready reference shelves. Oh, and he was actually telling the library pages how to sort material onto their book trucks to make it quicker for them. The funny thing was, the way Jack was telling them to do it actually took longer. When Jeanne found out, she told the library pages that she was their direct supervisor, and she wanted them to just keep doing it the way they'd always done it."

Leaving Jack to further instruct the landscapers, Sharon sat back down and started her labeling task. "He knows everything except how annoying he is," she remarked. Sharon and Jim shook their heads and got to work. Before the hour was over, however, the staff room door flew open, and the circulation supervisor came in. She looked to be nearly in tears.

"Jeanne? What's the matter? Are you all right? Here, sit down." Sharon got up to offer Jeanne her seat.

Jeanne sat down, grabbing a tissue from the box on Sharon's desk to wipe her eyes. "I've never been so humiliated. I'm the library's circulation supervisor. I'm supposed to be in charge of the activities that take place at the checkout desk. Apparently, our library director thinks he can do it better. I've had offers to work at other libraries that would appreciate my advice and input more than this place. I'm handing in my resignation. I can't take this disrespect anymore. This isn't the first time Jack has shot down my ideas, and I'm sure it won't be the last." Jeanne recounted the episode that had brought her to this point. She had spent several months researching new radio frequency identification (RFID) systems, and she had talked to several neighboring libraries that had had great success implementing their own systems. Jeanne had reached the point where she was ready to make a formal recommendation to the library director and library board to submit requests for proposals in order to get Timberline Falls their own RFID system and start experiencing some work efficiencies. Today, Jeanne recounted, Jack came into the check-in and sorting room and, after looking around the room a moment, started rearranging sorting shelves. When she asked him if she could help him with something, he—very condescendingly—started telling the staff how they could be more efficient if they'd set things up a little differently. Jeanne figured that this was the perfect time to spring her new proposal for RFID. She had been excited to share what she knew about the RFID systems, but Jack wasn't impressed. Jeanne told them how Jack had simply said the library didn't need to spend thousands of dollars on technology when they could achieve similar results with just a little "ingenuity." Becoming distraught once again, Jeanne told her library clerks that she was going home sick. She grabbed some of her personal belongings, put them in a box, and told everyone goodbye.

The next day, staff saw that Jeanne's name was crossed off the schedule. Figuring the library's circulation supervisor was still upset over her exchange with their library director, they set off to reassign duties and adjust lunch hours to cover the absence. At two o'clock, Jack sent out a memo to all staff announcing that Jeanne, Timberline Falls Library circulation supervisor, had resigned effective immediately. He thanked Jeanne for her years of service at the library and wished her well. The library would be recruiting for another person to fill Jeanne's position as quickly as possible.

"Did you see Jack's memo?" Carlos asked as he and Jim were having their afternoon break in the staff room.

"Yes. We're all pretty stunned in circulation. Jeanne was a great team leader. And to see this happen to her has really hurt morale in our unit," Jim said.

"Well, I'm not surprised really. This has been Jack's modus operandi for years, apparently. When I started at the library a couple of months ago, everyone warned me to watch out for Jack . . . and that Jack was a 'hands-on' type of guy." Carlos told Jim of several episodes where the director seemed to be micromanaging him and his colleagues. "Every time Jack came over to one of the librarians, they'd roll their eyes. I thought they were being overly dramatic. That was until Jack came over to *my* desk and saw my book purchasing request form stuck in one of the selection journals. He looked it over and questioned me on each and every book I wanted to select." Carlos had tried to explain the reasoning behind his selections, but the director had differing opinions for every book. And, as Carlos said, "Jack wasn't shy about sharing those opinions either." He chuckled. "But, you know, initially I was willing to give Jack the benefit of the doubt. I did some homework and looked over our circulation statistics. Numbers are up since Jack came on board. The library is doing more with less, and that certainly has to be a result of some of Jack's input."

"True," said Jim, "but what good are great numbers if your staff isn't happy? Jeanne certainly isn't the first person to quit. I think she's like the third one in as many years! At this rate, others could follow."

Carlos had to agree. There was a morale issue. "Having a boss who thinks they know better than you, or who doesn't trust you to do your job, well, it's really demeaning. We've all done our best to understand where Jack is coming from and to take what he says in a positive way, but I think I'm getting to the point where I just can't let go of the resentment and frustration I feel every time he comes around and tells me he knows better, or he can do it faster. I figured that, since I was 'the new guy' here at the library, maybe Jack was trying to coach me." Carlos shook his head. "Then I saw how other staff members were being treated the same way."

Jim agreed and shrugged his shoulders. "Not much we can do, right? He's the boss. You learn to choose battles you can win. Arguing with a know-it-all simply based on principle just isn't worth the effort. So, we've just got to accept it and find a way to do our job and interact with him amicably when he shows up. Oh, wow, break's over. Back to work."

Jim and Carlos left the break room just as Karen, the teen librarian, was coming in. "I need a break! Jack's been telling me how to run my teen programs. He was telling *me* the best way to handle kids. Him, telling me!" Karen lowered her voice a bit to say, "I've been a teen librarian for ten years. I've chaired the American Library Association's Young Adult Library Services Association group, *and*"—she raised her voice on that word—"*and*, I'm a parent of a two-year-old, and I have two other children who will soon be attending middle school. I think I know a little bit about child behavior. My husband is a principal at a high school, for Pete's sake!" Karen walked back to the ladies' room, shaking her head the whole way.

Carlos looked at Jim as they proceeded to their respective desks. "I hope she's not the next one to leave," Carlos said, raising his eyebrows in alarm.

Several months had passed at the Timberline Falls Public Library without additional incidents—at least none that the staff could see. In fact, things seemed rather status quo around the library—that was until Sharon Bond had arranged to have lunch with her former boss, Jeanne Lofranco, one weekend. Sharon had been holding on to some personal items that Jeanne had left behind after her sudden exit. Having lunch would give her the opportunity to deliver those items as well as to catch up on things with one another. The two sat down at a local restaurant and exchanged pleasantries. Sharon learned that Jeanne had accepted a job as a circulation supervisor at a local college library. She was very happy with the new working environment.

"The library's managers make us all feel valued—like equals. A real team," said Jeanne. Jeanne told Sharon how she had even convinced the college to purchase an RFID system and how much the system had improved efficiency at the college library. So much so, in fact, that Jeanne had received a commendation from the college president and advisory board.

"I really appreciated that recognition. I wasn't aware how detrimental Jack was being to my mental health at Timberline. He just made us all feel, like, so unimportant. At least at my new job, my opinion and my expertise count for something. At Timberline, I felt no better than, well, no better than those landscapers!"

Sharon had to admit that Jeanne looked happier and that the weight of the world had been lifted off her shoulders. "Wow, Jeanne, that's great. Do you need a library clerk?" Sharon was only half kidding. "Jack certainly doesn't seem to trust anyone on his staff. It's not right."

The two finished their lunch and wished each other well, promising to do lunch again soon. "Look, Sharon, if a clerical position opens at the college, I'll give you a ring," Jeanne said as she got into her car.

Sharon actually found herself hoping that Jeanne would call, and soon! When she arrived home, Sharon's husband asked her how her lunch had gone. "Well," she said, "I realized I want out of my current job."

"What? Why?" he asked, surprised.

Sharon went over the whole business. Recounting the years of Jack's know-it-all supervisory style and the way it was affecting staff. She was sure that some of the incidents were familiar to her husband from days she'd come home to sulk about them, but she felt she just needed to let everything out. A purge of the soul, she felt. "I just think a new, more positive work environment would be good for me. You wouldn't believe how much happier my old supervisor looks now that she's no longer at our library."

"Wow," Sharon's husband responded. "Have you, or anyone, ever said anything to him directly? Or maybe speak to the person Jack reports to—everyone has someone they report to. Whoever it is, they need to know how badly he is alienating the entire staff."

"I haven't said anything. It's not my place. I'm just a low woman on the totem pole. People who aren't happy, like Jeanne, just get to a point where they become so frustrated or angry that they resign. And Jack reports directly to the library board; they're the ones who interviewed and hired him. From what I've heard, the library board has been pleased with the library's numbers. They like that library usage is up, and they like that costs are down. They had a library satisfaction survey conducted two years ago, and the results showed that the community was happy with the library. I don't think they'd be likely to listen to staff members who don't like their boss. A lot of people don't like their bosses."

"But the board members are not seeing what you see, Sharon," her husband said. "Employee morale is an indicator of leadership. If the morale is bad, leadership is likely bad too. The signs may not be there now, but they'll show up soon enough! I think you should talk to them."

"I thought about that," said Sharon. "But I just don't feel comfortable going over his head. I think most of the board members would think negatively of an employee who came to them to complain about a mean boss. Remember, the library board appointed Jack. The members aren't going to do anything as long as the library isn't crumbling to the ground, which it clearly isn't. In their eyes, the library is actually functioning quite well. I'm not in a hostile work environment. I'm just in an environment where staff are not valued, and our creativity is stifled at every turn. Maybe the best way for me to handle this is just to stay low, do my job, and interact with Jack as little as possible."

"Keep in contact with Jeanne. Maybe you can get out of Timberline Falls soon. I just wish there was a better way for you to handle the situation now." Jeanne's husband gave her a hug and sat down to read. "I know you'll feel better if you find a way to resolve this without relying on leaving the library as your only option."

JACK OF ALL TRADES RESPONSES

Response 1
By Mary George, director of library services, Placer County Library System, Auburn, California

No one likes to be second-guessed while performing their job. Overmanaging, directing the details, and criticizing processes not in your lane, even with the best of intentions, will always fall short of productive management. When a library director like Jack Farrow speaks condescendingly to his teams and puts little trust in their discretion, professionalism, or expertise, staff morale will greatly suffer. When staff morale suffers, customer service will eventually suffer. Furthermore, when the public starts complaining, the library board will look for someone to blame, and all roads will lead to Jack.

Why would Jack, a man who has risen to the position of library director, take a leaf blower out of the hands of a trained maintenance professional and try to do the job himself? I would venture to say that it stems from a lack of trust in his own judgment and professionalism. It is far easier to make comments regarding the work of others than to enter the arena yourself. Grappling with library analytics, solving human resources issues, resolving conflicts with friends of the library, and tackling budget woes are challenging, and, unlike shelving or sorting, there is often no feeling of satisfaction or completion no matter how much work you put in. The work of a library director doesn't have a finish line, and decisions are rarely clear and precise like the Dewey Decimal System. Speaking from experience, being a library director is far tougher and sometimes lonelier than can be quickly explained. Sometimes I would love to disappear into the stacks and shelve for a few hours just to actually complete something. Alas, that is not what I get paid to do.

Compounding the situation, no one on staff seems willing to confront Jack. Additionally, the library board appears to currently support his leadership, even though their experience of Jack's performance appears limited to library statistics. The board seems to have no idea about deteriorating staff morale. So, while the emperor may have no clothes, staff would rather leave their positions with the Timberline Falls Public Library than speak truth to power. It is a mutiny, Mr. Farrow, plain and simple.

After thirty years as a librarian, I can tell you that the only way around conflict is through it. When seeking resolution, someone must attempt to explain to Jack that his behaviors are having a detrimental effect on staff morale. Specific examples and instances should be given. The key is to find someone Jack respects to deliver the message. Jack should be confronted with kindness, understanding, grace, and while assuming good intentions. Delivering the message requires bravery and finesse. Ultimately, the assumption that both parties want what is best for the library system must be at the forefront of the discussion, and the criticism should not be personal. An assistant director is a good candidate for delivering this message, especially since the assistant director is often the conduit between frontline operational staff and the library director. Look for the second in command to be a soft place to land with concerns related to the library director. If there is no assistant to turn to, a discussion with a trusted library board member may be warranted.

No matter who confronts him, Jack will not change overnight. He will inevitably fall back into the same behaviors. But, if Jack listens to understand and is willing to change, there is hope that staff morale will improve. If Jack is willing to improve his leadership and make some real changes, there are a few things he can do to be kinder and more approachable. It is clear he likes to "manage by walking around." Jack could take an hour out of his day to check in with staff and listen to what they are working on rather than give his typical unsolicited incorrect directives couched as advice. Listening for understanding is the key to Jack's success here. He should seek to understand the issues and not rush to solve them. A director's job is to move obstacles out of the way so that staff can shine and succeed, not to do every job or to resolve every issue. It's the "teach a man to fish" proverb that works best here. Instead of managing process, Jack should seek to coach the best performance from his teams.

Staff could benefit from changing a few behaviors themselves. Not rolling their eyes at the director or speaking ill of his intentions would be a good start. Jeanne, the circulation supervisor, could have made a formal appointment with Jack to sit down and discuss her important RFID research and proposal. Approaching Jack while he was on the floor of the library engaged in criticizing process did not put Jeanne at an advantage. Jeanne's professional assessment of the RFID systems and her analysis of the successes of neighboring libraries was lost on Jack, as he had no time to prepare for or adjust to what he was hearing and learning. Without preparation and context, Jack reached for his standard answer to innovation—no.

It's clear that the trust is broken between staff and leadership. Repairing trust takes time and sustained effort on the part of library leaders. The morale will improve if Jack's behaviors change. In the interim, some staff may leave the library, seeking more support and opportunity. Some say, "Employees leave managers, not jobs." That is certainly the case at Timberline Falls Public Library. Jack himself may leave (or be forced to leave) when the library board begins to see the effects of poor morale on its customers. In the end it will behoove the library board to evaluate the library director's performance not only on statistics but also on firsthand experiences from the staff.

Leadership is much more than insisting that your way is the right way. In fact, the best leadership happens when leaders move out of the way of their talented teams and embrace the ideas of others. Taking pride in selecting and coaching the best and brightest is more rewarding than criticizing process to no effect. Trust, coaching, positive feedback, and honest criticism can help repair morale and change a library culture for the better. In the end the customers win.

Response 2
By Kate Hall, executive director, Northbrook Public Library, Northbrook, Illinois

As someone who has been a director for a decade, I look at this situation and feel bad for the staff. One of the hardest things a director must learn is that their job is largely about managing people, not performing tasks. What we are seeing in this scenario is either a director who feels like he is the only person who can effectively do the job or someone so insecure in his abilities that he focuses on everyone's job but his own. Library director Jack Farrow might also be thinking that by "pitching in," he is showing staff that he doesn't think he is above the work that they do. However, good directors recognize that their library's most important attribute is their staff, and they will look for ways to empower and engage those staff. Unfortunately, that is not what is happening here at Timberline Falls Public Library. There are two angles from which to approach this situation: from the director's perspective and from the employees'.

In exploring how Library Director Farrow was behaving in this scenario, there are a few questions we can ask ourselves to better understand his actions. How long has he been a library director? Has he had any formal training on being a director? What support is he receiving from the library board? What changes has the library board asked that he make in the library? And, how long has he been exhibiting these behaviors? Exploring these questions might give us a clue as to why the director has decided he needs to place himself in the middle of his staff's roles and responsibilities. Jack may have been reprimanded in the past for not taking action on a personnel issue fast enough; he may have trusted staff to use good judgment and been burned for offering too much trust; or his library board may have given Jack specific instructions to change a policy or service. Still, if Jack had had proper training along the way to becoming a library director, he'd surely know that the principles of leadership stress delegating operational tasks to staff and allowing them to make decisions and learn from their mistakes. While directors should never be hesitant about asking questions, a well-trained leader knows when to step back and when it is appropriate to step in.

Even if Jack hasn't had any formal leadership training, or doesn't receive support from the board, it doesn't excuse how he is behaving. Because of his position within the organizational hierarchy, Jack can't look to others for feedback. Instead, he must learn to be self-reflective to improve. What he can do is create a culture that allows for honest feedback, both from him to his employees and vice versa. Right now, Jack is not giving feedback but is instead changing how everything is done to a way with which he is familiar. He should be concerned by the employees who are quitting—like circulation supervisor Jeanne. Apparently, Jeanne is the third person to quit in as many years. Jack should be questioning why his staff are abandoning ship. If Jack feels that his circulation supervisor is not running her department efficiently, he should be proactive in guiding and coaching Jeanne to higher performance. Instead, he is placing himself in the midst of operations, making staff feel uncomfortable, and making scattershot changes that confuse and demoralize his staff.

Jack needs to take a look at his management style and determine whether the short-term gains he is receiving in terms of increased patron engagement will be able to offset the ill will he is creating among staff. The library board may currently be happy that Jack is improving the library's performance measurements, but with staff at the boiling point, the library board will soon be forcing Jack to answer for his leadership style if he doesn't start looking at it himself right now. In my twenty-plus years of management experience, the gains in performance are not sustainable in an organizational culture that doesn't value staff.

To the employees, the director comes off as not caring what they think and not considering their expertise. An interesting question comes from the husband of one of Timberline Falls's library clerks, Sharon, when he asks her whether anyone has spoken to the director about these issues. Sharon tells him that she has not. While it can be scary to give feedback to someone in a position of authority, doing so can be one of the most effective ways to enact change. If Sharon is concerned about doing it alone, she could band together with a group of colleagues and speak to Jack together—an intervention of sorts.

When presenting their concerns to Jack, the employees should keep it factual and make sure not to place value judgments on Jack. For instance, Karen, the teen librarian, might tell Jack that she felt he did not respect her expertise with teens when he told her how to run her young adult programs instead of saying that Jack was a bad director because he told her how to run her programs.

If Jack doesn't respond to this method of feedback, the employees can then write to the library board—offering to meet in person with them if they would prefer. The letter should be addressed to the full library board, and it should provide information but not dictate any action (such as asking the board to terminate or reprimand Jack). Instead, the letter should lay out specific issues and ask the library board to investigate staff morale and engagement. Individual staff members should not go and speak to individual board members. This will only provoke a defensive response from Jack and won't lead to positive changes.

It may be that Jack doesn't realize how badly he is coming across, and having this brought to his attention by the staff or by the board will be a wake-up call for him. If Jack doesn't begin to question why his employees are quitting, and doesn't begin to check his leadership style, his library board will eventually be coming to him to explain himself. But I'd recommend the employees take it on themselves to meet with their library director to make him aware of their issues. If the employees never say anything to Jack or the library board, the problems will persist. More people will quit. Service standards will suffer. Innovation will die. And the Timberline Falls Public Library will be on the road to irrelevance. Every director can get better, but they need to be ready to engage in some serious self-reflection and always be open to hearing what staff really think. Jack needs to take a lesson from the Spider-Man stories, specifically the oft-cited Peter Parker principle: "With great power comes great responsibility." Jack obviously knows he holds a lot of power within the library organization.

What he has forgotten, however, is that he should be using that power for the greater good of his entire staff.

Response 3
By Faith Mason, reference librarian (retired), San Jose Public Library, San Jose, California

An underlying challenge built into this scenario is the fact that a workplace is not a democracy made up of equals. The power to make decisions and to influence the course of events is spread throughout an organization chart's chain of command. Those at the top of the chart have a lot of influence; those at the bottom, very little. Those at the top of the chart, such as Jack Farrow, are presumably hired in part for their experience in making sound, independent decisions; shaping the organization's structure; controlling who does what; and delegating work tasks effectively. In this light, the person at the top of an organization is something of a dictator, though the hope is that this person will fairly consider all sorts of information and will not be cold or cruel in carrying out their actions. It may be that the person at the top, or at least the person responsible for the employee who is complaining, is the person who will resolve a problem. In this scenario, however, the person at the top is, in fact, the person whom employees are complaining about. And in many workplaces, the higher-up does not take kindly to criticism from below.

There are a number of "fires" that seemingly need to be put out in this vignette. Before jumping to the main, core problem, it is useful to take a little time to look at various pointers presented in the scene.

- The director is blowing leaves off the library lawn, and on work time. This task is surely not included in his job description. Employees are irritated to observe this action, which they see as indicative of a bigger pattern of their director being in the wrong place at the wrong time and of meddling in the work of others.
- A long-term, dedicated, dependable employee, Jeanne, has left the system, having reached her limit of tolerance of Library Director Farrow's interference and humiliation. There are references to other employees being so dissatisfied with the library director that they have also left the library.
- While we do not know the nature and extent of Jack's education and training, it is common knowledge in management that a department director attends to the big-picture items—such as strategic planning—and they should appropriately delegate operational tasks to subordinates and then leave them to do the jobs they've been assigned to do.
- There is the question of how visible and participatory Jack is on a day-to-day basis. Is he seen doing his own work? Does he show up among the rank and file as an encouraging, appreciative presence, or does he only come to criticize or to meddle?

When considered together, these items seem to point to two key underlying issues that lead to one main problem. First, there is terrible workplace morale at Timberline Falls Public Library. Second, the chain of command at this library is not a useful tool in structuring organizational activities. Therefore, workplace activities have become more complex and confusing and less productive. These underlying issues are compounded by one main problem: library director Jack Farrow has lost faith in his staff, and he does not trust that they are capable of doing the jobs for which they are being held accountable.

What can be done to make this workplace more equitable, more a place with pride of ownership and mutual respect among staff, where people count themselves fortunate to work there? It has to start with Jack. A key employee should take it on themselves to talk confidentially with Jack's superior—whether this is a library board president or a city manager. This key employee should arm themselves with examples of the pointers listed above and must be frank in their discussion, outlining the potential for growing dissent and dissatisfaction. They should also recognize all the good work that Jack has done for the library (pointing to the positive library performance measures). Whatever approach is taken, the focus needs to be on getting Jack to stick to appropriate library director responsibilities and let his staff members shine.

Jack needs to be coached on when to take a role in the day-to-day operations his staff members are performing. Jack may not even be aware his actions are out of the ordinary. He may perceive his actions as a way to show he is engaged and concerned about staff. He needs to be made aware of the fact that, on the contrary, his current actions have caused problems. Before choosing to put himself into a subordinate's tasks, he should first consider how that task touches the library's core values. If he cannot find a direct connection to core values, he should have the subordinate's supervisor handle the issue. Before stepping into an employee's daily duties, Jack needs to ask himself whether something is going on there that seems counter to the library's strategic direction—provided he has crafted such a strategic direction. Doing so would prevent him from finding it necessary to show the landscapers how to hold a leaf blower. Jack should set himself a personal boundary to only involve himself, or intervene in, a subordinate's activities when those activities hinder or undercut library strategy. Otherwise, he should pass any concerns on to the subordinate's supervisor.

An effective library director needs to understand that the ultimate task of leadership is to motivate employees and create a vision and atmosphere for their department that not only respects the chain of command but also demonstrates a willingness to create success together. Jack needs to begin to create an organizational culture and vision for Timberline Falls Public Library that engages both the imagination and the energies of the library staff. He is currently failing at this core responsibility and needs coaching on how to change. Once he does, all the other issues this library is dealing with will likely disappear.

Chapter Seventeen

Weeding Out Bad News

A Staffing Scenario Using Skills

SCENARIO

Spencer Follet had to shake his head. Here he was, the new circulation supervisor at Santa Jacinta Public Library, a large, multibranch urban library system, and all he could think at this very moment was, *It's certainly a long ride down to the basement.* Spencer was working on the third day of his orientation. It had been a grueling three days introducing himself to his new staff, visiting new units in the library, and trying to remember the policies and procedures. It was a struggle not to drop the two large orientation binders in his arms as he tried to locate the library's materials deselection policy. Spencer's escort on today's tour, supervising librarian Zahara Cooper, was taking him to the library's basement to point out the discard shelves—or, as Zahara called them, "the place where old books go to die." She helped Spencer locate the deselection policy in his binder and tried to paraphrase the policy as briefly as possible. But Spencer kept thinking the elevator ride to the basement was taking a long time. Finally, the elevator doors opened, and Zahara escorted Spencer over to a back wall in a dimly lit area of the basement. The wall was lined with dozens of sections of shelves of old books. Zahara explained that the library's deselection policy was written about twenty years ago, and the staff were pretty familiar with the process of getting rid of the library's unwanted materials.

"Once an item is identified as needing to be discarded," Zahara said, "we check the material out to a temporary status called 'under review.' The item is then put on these shelves for review. Our system librarians have four weeks to come and review these shelves to see if they want to salvage the item or purchase another copy. After four weeks, you'll need to have one of your staff members process the materials for discard and remove them from the system. The items are then tossed."

"How often do the librarians come down here to evaluate these items? It looks pretty deserted down here," Spencer remarked with a chuckle.

"I rarely see anyone down here," Zahara said as she removed a book, gave it a glance, and then replaced it on the shelf. She wiped her hands together and wiggled her fingers in the air to remove some invisible dust, then said, "In fact, it's probably safe to say that a majority of the librarians forget this is down here, or they just don't have time to come down. 'Out of sight, out of mind,' you know? But that's our policy. The moment we don't give our librarian staff an opportunity to review these items, someone will certainly complain."

Spencer made a mental note to meet the library's head of collection development, Lily Moss, and discuss this discard process. Perhaps this was an area he could improve. But first, he needed to get through this orientation week. He barely knew the names of his own subordinates. He shouldn't be considering changing things about which he had little knowledge.

"Let's go back upstairs, Spencer. It's just about lunchtime, and we can continue when we get back." Zahara led Spencer back through the maze of books and shelves in the subterranean basement to the elevator for the long ride back to the surface.

Spencer's orientation week had concluded without much trouble over a month ago. He was settling in to somewhat of a daily routine, but he still had quite a lot to learn. At the front and center of Spencer's desk was a volume of policies and procedures he still needed to go through, along with several pages of questions he needed to find answers to. On that list was the question, "What happens to the discarded books on the basement shelves once they are pulled from review?" This was only one of the questions Spencer needed to ask about that whole discard process. Several days earlier, he had received his first list of overdue books checked out to "under review." This was the list that Zahara had told him about on his orientation visit to the library's basement. There were about thirty books on the list he received today. Wanting to see for himself what sort of material was being identified for possible deselection, Spencer journeyed down to the basement with the list in hand. After a quick spot check of several items, he couldn't understand why the library was going through these laborious steps. It was inconceivable to him that any of the books he found would be wanted by the library. They certainly could have been discarded without adding these "review" steps. Clearly there was a need for professional review of potential discards, but his staff was apparently going through a great deal of work for no apparent reason. He needed to meet with Lily, the head of collection development, in order to gain a better understanding of what the library was trying to accomplish here. In the meantime, he asked Frank, one of his library pages, to pull the overdue books from the basement's "under review" shelves and process them as discards.

When Spencer arrived at his desk the very next day, he saw a note attached to his chair from his supervisor, Zahara Cooper. It said, "Spencer, we need to talk as soon as you get in. Thanks, Zahara." Spencer went immediately to Zahara's office and knocked. She motioned for him to come in. Spencer entered and sat down in the chair in front of Zahara's desk while she spoke on the phone. "Yes, Spencer just got here. Can you come down now?" she said. She hung up the phone and asked, "Did you see this morning's *Santa Jacinta News*?" When Spencer indicated that he had not had an opportunity to read it, she thrust the paper over to him, folded to highlight a particular article. "Here. Read this over while I go see if the director can come down." Spencer picked up the article and read:

Library Tosses Hundreds of Books in Dumpster
The Santa Jacinta Library apparently doesn't need as many books as they claim. While the library has complained at recent city council meetings about the detrimental effect recent budget cuts have had on the library collection, hundreds—if not thousands—of books have been tossed in a big dumpster at the library's loading dock. A group of concerned citizens pulled many of these books from the dumpster and showed them off. Certainly, many of the items show their wear, but dozens and dozens of others appear to be brand new—unopened and unused. City councilman Rick Snyder told the *Santa Jacinta News* that he suspected "a drastic mistake or misunderstanding" had occurred and that he would "get to the bottom of this." The concerned citizens' group said they had been alerted to the practice of throwing books in the dumpster by an anonymous group of library employees. The group of librarians had said that as many as one hundred thousand books were

being tossed from the city's libraries annually. Our paper contacted library administrators for comment but had not received a reply by press time. We interviewed Susan Tupperman, one of the citizens who brought the library's practice to our attention. "I just could not see why we have some perfectly reusable books put in a recycling bin," she said. "Surely these books could be useful to schools or sent to other libraries that might need them." Tupperman declined to identify who had contacted her originally and said only that it was "library staff." Tupperman said that these library staff members had provided her with a copy of the library's policy, which states that Santa Jacinta Library tosses those materials deemed to be in poor condition or containing outdated information. "That's understandable," said Tupperman. "But many of these books look brand new and could certainly be used somewhere. The library should stop tossing out more books for now, and the city council should work to figure out a new policy on discarding its books." City Councilman Snyder promised the issue would be a focus of an upcoming council meeting. The *Santa Jacinta News* will be there when it is.

Spencer put the article down. "So, that answers *that* question," he muttered, referring to one of the questions he had written on his list of things for which he needed to find answers. "They just toss these books in the dumpster." It was a fairly common practice at libraries, Spencer knew. He was sympathetic with the library's need to get rid of outdated or unused materials in order to make room for new titles or technology. But there were good ways and bad ways to do this. He'd also heard that most nonprofit organizations and schools didn't want donated books. Spencer knew that book disposal needed to be handled sensitively and carefully to avoid a situation like the one his library was now facing. As he was thinking about the issue, Zahara and Lily Moss walked into Zahara's office.

"The director's got Councilman Snyder in her office. We'll have to meet with her later," Zahara was saying as she motioned for Lily to take a seat. "Lily, I'm not sure you two have met. Spencer, this is Lily. She's head of collection development at our library. Lily, this is Spencer. He's our new circulation supervisor. He supervises the library pages and shelvers."

"I've been meaning to set up a meeting with you, Lily," Spencer said. "It's just been a crazy few weeks."

"Lily says she's read the article, Spencer," Zahara remarked. "She also remembers the lady quoted in the article. Tupperman, I think her name was. Lily remembers her as a friend of Frank, one of your library pages."

"Yes. A few years ago Tupperman and Frank were dating, I believe. Frank would bring her to library staff functions like Christmas parties and staff picnics. At the time, I remember Frank asking me about the books in the basement and why we handled them the way we do. I think it was after he had been assigned the duty of tossing the unwanted items in the dumpster one day. I don't remember much of what I said to him, but I'm sure I explained the policy and the review process," Lily said. "I just bet Frank is the one who alerted the *Santa Jacinta News*."

"Frank was always quite vocal about library policies he didn't like," said Zahara. "After that incident, Spencer, your predecessor took him off that duty and never assigned it to him again." Looking back over the last several weeks, Spencer remembered that it was Frank who he had recently asked to process those books. Spencer was about to acknowledge that he had assigned Frank the task recently, but Zahara spoke up before he said anything. "We're going to need to talk to him. If he's sharing information secretly with the press, that's misconduct, and he might need some disciplinary action. Our library policy is quite clear that only the library director speaks for the library. If Frank has taken it on himself to go to the news in order to change a policy he doesn't like, well, I think that might be grounds for dismissal."

Spencer couldn't believe it. He hadn't even been at the library for an entire month, and already his department was embroiled in a press relations nightmare, it was sitting in the middle of a policy crisis, and he was facing having to handle disciplinary action with one of his staff members who was *perhaps* the source of information being inappropriately shared with the media. He tried to focus on the matter at hand. "Do we have any real idea of the numbers or the volume of materials that are being tossed in the dumpster?" he asked. "I mean, maybe several months' worth of books were being tossed all at once? That could explain a seemingly large load of discards ending up in the trash. Tossing twenty-five books in a dumpster once a week looks better than tossing a hundred books once a month. But the economics are the same. One way just looks better than the other."

Lily responded that she had discard statistics generated by the computer, but she couldn't say how many books Spencer's department actually tossed into the dumpster at the same time. "Just because your library pages are discarding twenty-five books from the system one week doesn't mean they are actually disposing of them at that moment," she said.

"Fair enough," Spencer agreed. "And I haven't been here long enough to understand how the staff are approaching this disposal process. It could very well be that they are hoarding material somewhere and creating a backlog to take to the dumpster together, all at once. Just to make it more convenient. I'll need to follow up on that."

Just then, library director Davina Darling entered Zahara's office. "Good. You're all here. I assume you've all read today's news article and realize we have a big problem? I've had Councilmember Snyder chewing my ear off for the last hour and promised I'd get to the bottom of the situation. So, tell me—what's going on?"

"From what we gather," Zahara answered, "one of our library pages, Frank Miller, has complained to the newspaper about the number of materials that end up in the dumpster after they are discarded from our system. Frank has also enlisted the help of a community group led by his girlfriend, Susan Tupperman. They believe the library is throwing out perfectly good material. We're not sure how many books were in the dumpster at the time the reporter saw them, but we guess that it was more than several hundred."

Lily interjected that, indeed, the library had perhaps been deleting more books than normal. "We started an aggressive book-weeding program early this year. Our senior librarians had not been proactive in their collection maintenance duties, and our collection has suffered. A regular weeding program is an important process that keeps the collection current and relevant for our users. I did some spot-checking of certain areas and found a good deal of the collection to be dated, unused, and in need of repair. So, I announced that librarians would be held accountable for weeding material." Lily picked up a folder of statistics from her lap and pulled out the recent discard statistics sheet. "According to our system, only twenty-two hundred books have been processed for discard this year," Lily added. "I also checked usage statistics on those before they were deleted, and nearly eighty percent of that material hadn't been checked out in more than three years. Spencer, Zahara, and I were just discussing that, while we know the number of items deleted from the system, we can't be certain how many items were actually thrown into the dumpsters."

"That's correct," added Spencer. "As the new circulation supervisor, I'm not aware of how your previous manager handled this material. It's possible that several months' worth of discards were hoarded and tossed all at once. I'll have to clarify with my staff."

"Well, let's get on this immediately," Director Darling warned. "I've been asked to address this issue at the next council meeting, which is a week from tomorrow." She left the office, and the others followed behind.

Spencer went immediately to the daily schedule, which showed the hourly assignments of each staff member in the library. Frank wasn't scheduled to be at work until five o'clock that evening. Spencer adjusted the schedule to ensure that Frank's desk assignment at five o'clock was covered so that he could meet with Frank regarding the discards.

That afternoon, Frank knocked on Spencer's office door and popped his head in. "Hey, Mr. Follet. You wanted to see me?"

"Yes. Come in, Frank." Spencer got up and shut his office door. "Frank, I don't know if you're familiar with an article that appeared in the *Santa Jacinta News* today, but I wanted to ask you some questions as a result of some of the information that was presented in that article." Frank listened as Spencer went on. "Last week I asked you to process some discards off the 'under review' shelves in the basement. I've since learned that part of that process involves my staff taking discarded material to the dumpster for disposal. Do you remember how many items you put in the dumpster last week?"

Frank was immediate in his reply. "I'd say it was close to a thousand books."

"A thousand!" Spencer exclaimed. "Are you sure?"

"Yep. It may have even been more than that. It took me a couple of hours of going back and forth between the 'under review' shelves and the dumpster to get rid of all the books," Frank said.

"Did you actually process that many discards at that time? I seem to remember only a couple dozen on the overdue list I gave you when I sent you down to the basement last week. Were some of the books you took to the dumpster that day some that had perhaps been kept aside from previous discarding processes?" Spencer asked. He was sure this was the key to the inordinate number of materials noted in the dumpster by the newspaper reporter.

"I only processed about thirty discards. Whoever has been deleting materials from the system hasn't been taking them to the dumpster. They've just been putting them in boxes and waiting for someone else to take them. I think a lot of staff do that," Frank said, shrugging his shoulders.

Spencer was still trying to get his head around the numbers. "The library's deletion statistics show that, over the last six months, about twenty-two hundred items have been deleted." Spencer did some quick math in his head. "That's fewer than a hundred items a month, which certainly does seem large but not abnormal for a library of our size. Lily tells me she has had staff completing an aggressive weeding program, which could also account for elevated numbers."

"Lily doesn't know what she's talking about, or the computer statistics are wrong. I'll bet there have been ten or fifteen thousand items thrown in the dumpster," Frank said. "When I tossed those books last week, the dumpster was already half full of items. I've even heard several librarians complaining about the numbers of items that are being jettisoned."

"But they can go down to the basement and 'save' items if they want. Why are they complaining?" Spencer asked.

"That's a joke." Frank gave a harsh laugh. "None of the librarians, especially the senior librarians, have time to go down to the basement. Who knows who's identifying items for deletion? They aren't being pulled with any expertise or criteria that we're aware of. At any rate, those materials show up on the review shelves, where they sit for weeks and then get thrown out. It's crazy!"

"Frank," Spencer said seriously, "you seem to know quite a lot about what's going on. Were you the person the newspaper cited as their resource? Because, if so, that's a breach of library protocol that I'm sure won't go unpunished."

All Frank said in response was, "I'm not saying that I am, but I understand there are protections for whistleblowers." He stood up and asked if the meeting was over. Spencer excused him. Tomorrow he intended to meet with Zahara and Davina about what he had learned.

The next morning, Spencer found he didn't have to convene the intended meeting. There was a note pinned to his office door when he came in. He grabbed it, opened it, and read it as he placed his jacket and backpack at his desk. "Spencer, please come immediately to my office when you get in. I have Zahara and Lily here awaiting your arrival." The note was signed by Davina.

Spencer walked to Davina's office and pulled up a chair to sit aside Lily and Zahara. They adjusted their own chairs to allow him room to join them.

"Spencer, I noticed that you had Frank in your office yesterday afternoon. What did you learn?" Zahara asked. Spencer updated them on what Frank had told him. From that information, the group put together the puzzle as best they could: thousands of books were being tossed in the dumpsters at one time rather than being disposed of in smaller increments; rather than twenty-two hundred books being disposed of, the number may have been closer to fifteen thousand; Frank was most likely the anonymous source of the information finding its way to the news; and, Lily's staff was in the process of an aggressive weeding program that was likely compounding the large numbers of unused materials being tossed.

Davina pounced on Lily's announcement about the weeding program she was implementing. "Why aren't the librarians more involved in this process on a daily basis . . . and don't tell me they don't have time!" Davina was clearly frustrated by these past several days of the library being in the limelight. She continued, "Who's pulling this material? Why aren't the senior librarians—our collection experts—more involved? I'm just so upset over this, Lily!"

Feeling a bit defensive, if not picked on, Lily quickly replied, "Our librarians are no different than any other librarian. You know, Davina, this is a professional mindset. In my twenty-five years of library service, I have never witnessed any librarian approach weeding with the regularity and rational mind necessary to keep a collection fresh, vital, and—most importantly—useful to the community it's intended to serve." Lily was clearly getting steamed. "On the contrary," she said, her voice rising slowly, "the overriding professional culture—including here at Santa Jacinta—has been to hold on to books at any cost. Like every other public librarian, our staff see us performing the role of an archive or research library, or—worse yet—a book warehouse! I am trying my best to instill in this staff that it is not only reasonable to weed our collection based on usage; it is also responsible! When I implemented this aggressive weeding program, I told my collection developers to leave their *personal* sense of nostalgia and sense of *personal* value out of the weeding process. Our users are telling us in no uncertain terms what *they* value and what *they* want to see in their public library—simply by the items they are checking out. As I told every librarian, we are not the Library of Congress; we can't keep everything. We have a limited amount of space. For that reason, the books sitting on our shelves, unused for many years, are not earning their keep. Our users don't want them and neither should we." Lily finally sat back in her chair, exhaling a deep breath.

The room fell silent for a moment. The Santa Jacinta library managers looked at one another. Davina finally broke the silence. "I'm not arguing with the validity of your program, Lily. I'm just shocked I didn't know about it. But let's return to the immediate problem. I have to present to council this coming week. The way I see it, there are two areas I need to publicly address. Zahara and Spencer, I want you to develop a clearer, if not better, way of handling library discards. I want you to particularly address how the library will dispose of unneeded material. Lily, I want you to work on how we identify unneeded material. Work quickly with your staff to develop a regular process of collection maintenance. I want to have complete confidence that the material being selected for discard has been thoroughly vetted by expert staff. We'll meet the morning before the upcoming council meeting. I'll expect each of you to bring your recommendations to me at that time. On my part, I will need to address the public relations aspect and talking with the news. Let's get to it."

Spencer, Zahara, and Lily each rose from their chairs and looked at each other momentarily. They put their chairs back in place, and each went their separate way to work out a plan.

WEEDING OUT THE BAD NEWS RESPONSES

Response 1
By Barbara Kerr, director, Medford Public Library, Medford, Massachusetts

At first glance, the Santa Jacinta Public Library seems to have it all worked out, with two huge binders full of policies and procedures. But as Spencer works his way through the weeding question, it quickly becomes apparent that there are some serious communication and supervision issues going on.

It is all very well to make sure you have written policies and procedures, but they aren't worth anything without supervision. Librarians are human, and like all the humans who don't read the directions for how to use the copy machine, librarians don't always read or follow the procedures correctly. A supervisor has to follow up to make sure the procedures are being carried out and make sense. All procedures and policies should be revisited regularly; libraries are not static places, and a policy that made sense when written may become outdated. This case study is a great example of what happens if you don't follow up and the public becomes involved. What should be a straightforward procedure turns into a public relations issue.

There are a lot of layers of supervision in this library, but no one seems to be paying attention to the entire weeding process. During Spencer's orientation, Zahara does take the time to show him the weeding shelves, but she is unconcerned about the fact that no one comes down to review the books. She says as much to Spencer and then follows up with the terrible phrase, "But that's our policy." That's a red flag; here is a senior supervisor who knows a policy is not being followed and has no intention of doing anything about it. Having a policy is not enough; you must follow up, and if staff are not doing what they are supposed to, you must communicate that and make sure things are done properly.

Lily seems to be a good communicator, but she is also at fault in this situation. She and her staff follow professional policies and procedures, and keep good track of numbers, but she did not follow up to the point of discard. As head of collection development, she should have followed the books from deselection to dumpster. Like Zahara, she didn't know what happened once the books left her hands, and she didn't care. And the "we don't have time" excuse is not acceptable; a supervisor finds the time. If no one can be bothered to follow up, you end up with a mess, and this is a mess. She should have been aware that there was a stockpile.

It would be easy to blame this all on bad behavior by "whistleblower" Frank, but he is actually the ugly end result of failed communication. Even though professional policies were followed, Frank ended up with an unreasonable number of books. Faced with the stockpile of items, he jumped to negative conclusions. And who can blame him? When he asked Spencer's predecessor about weeding, he was taken off discard duty. Frank's supervisor failed to communicate with him, and as a result Frank felt unheard by management. It is obvious from the records kept by Lily and Spencer that fifteen thousand items were not discarded, but to someone discontented, who has been punished for asking questions, this is an excuse to blow things out of proportion. If the procedure had been supervised and small batches had gone into the dumpster, this would probably not have blown up.

So, what does Spencer's future hold? Hopefully a better approach to communication. Weeding is a touchy subject; librarians understand the necessity, but to the public it can seem like waste. It is important to handle discards carefully, and this library didn't. Spencer and Lily must come up with a plan that provides supervision for the entire weeding process. More importantly, they must communicate this procedure to the rest of the staff at all levels. Even the most annoying Frank-like staff person should understand what they are doing. This library's policy may say that only the director can communicate with the public, but we all know that everyone who works at a library is a voice for the library. Everyone involved with weeding should understand how and why it is done. Add that to a little tidying up of the procedure, and things should go much better!

Response 2
By Alice Kuo, adult services manager, Beverly Hills Public Library, Beverly Hills, California

When looking at this scenario, it's important to separate the problems it presents into various categories. For example, the library director, Davina Darling, needs to decide what her most immediate problem is and which subproblems might also be necessary to tackle in order to prevent this or any other related problem from recurring in the future. In doing that, it should be clear that the most immediate issue here will be for library director Davina Darling to meet with her city manager and the city council in order to offer an explanation of what went wrong at the library with this weeding process, along with a plan of options for how it will be resolved. The last thing Davina needs right now is for those in her city who provide oversight and resources to lose faith in her ability to confront and resolve a public relations crisis like this. Director Darling's explanation to her city officials needs to admit fault in the library's weeding process. She needs to explain the "mistake" of tossing out thousands of books at once. Rather than faulting the necessary task of weeding library materials, the director needs to explain that the library was caught with a backlog of many months' worth of unused and useless books that were improperly tossed out all at once. Director Darling needs to acknowledge that she understands how and why this process made the library look bad. The practice of a systematic, regular weeding program is typical and necessary in libraries. However, the optics created here by the library's massive discarding of the backlog were that of an institution that did not value books purchased with taxpayer money and did not give careful thought to what is included in the community's library collection. The director needs to use this crisis as an opportunity to explain deselection and weeding in the simplest terms to city officials and the city council. Many officials and citizens who are not a part of the library profession do not understand that it is necessary to remove items due to age, content, condition, or relevance. This opportunity will help normalize the weeding process in the eyes of the library's funders and users. It will also help them understand that a policy is needed to back the process up. Helping the city council and public officials to understand the deselection and weeding process at this time will also be useful in other situations—such as when the director approaches them to seek additional funding for alternative disposal options for discarded books instead of just tossing them in the closest dumpster. For example, Director Darling will eventually need to consider offsite disposal services, additional secured dumpsters, or donation deliveries. These will come with a price tag, and the director can lay the groundwork now for the time when she'll need funds in her budget for her discarding mitigation efforts.

With the immediate issue addressed, Director Darling will now need to turn her focus toward resolving some of the subproblems the scenario crisis presents. For example, it should be quite clear that this library's deselection/weeding policy needs updating as soon as possible. Director Davina needs to empower her head of collection development, Lily Moss, to complete this update using the input (where appropriate) from the librarians as well as any supervisor of the staff involved in the discarding process—such as the circulation supervisor, Spencer Follett. The director will need to review the updated policy, provide input if necessary, and seek approval from the library board in a public forum. Once the new policy is approved, internal procedures must be adopted and appropriate staff fully trained. Responsibilities for following proper procedures (along with the consequences of not following the procedures) need to be understood by all staff.

There are additional subproblems presented by this scenario that need to be addressed. Poor communication is certainly one of them. Why wasn't the library director aware of the "aggressive" weeding put into process by the head of collection development? As a senior manager, Lily shouldn't have allowed the director to be caught off guard. Such an important process should have at least been brought up at a managerial meeting, if not in a simple email. Lily's rationale for implementing the large-scale weeding process is sound, but it was never shared with her library director or other necessary staff who'd surely be impacted by the activity. At one point in the scenario, circulation supervisor Spencer Follett recognizes that he needs to meet with Lily to "understand why the library was going through these laborious steps" in the discard process. He also ponders the need to gain a better understanding of just "what the library was trying to accomplish here" with the discards. Clearly, the purpose and goal of the library's discarding activities have not been effectively communicated. Library managers should be overly cautious about not forgetting to alert supervisors up and down the organization chart about important projects that impact the library and its community.

To specifically improve communication surrounding the issue presented in the scenario, staff will need to work on clarifying the goals of any weeding done at Santa Jacinta Public Library. The staff will need help in recognizing how weeding benefits the collection, how it improves circulation, and how important it is in keeping the collection relevant. Popular myths will need to be effectively debunked. Reminding the librarians that weeding is not harmful, that staff are not "throwing" away perfectly good books, and that "someone somewhere" will not necessarily want a book the library doesn't need, should be part of an aggressive retraining process. Whether this training is conducted by Lily Moss, or with the assistance of an outside consultant, it needs to be communicated with force and commitment.

There is certainly enough blame within the communication breakdown problem at Santa Jacinta Library to lay a bit at the feet of supervising librarian Zahara Cooper as well. While training her new circulation supervisor, Spencer, she seems fairly flippant and unconcerned about what she is training her subordinate on. As supervising librarian, Zahara needs to have a better understanding of the policies and procedures at the library. Her training seems to consist of dumping policy binders in Spencer's arms and dragging him through the library without much regard for the seriousness of the work ethic involved. Zahara is the intermediary between Lily and Spencer, and, as such, she needs to ensure they work effectively.

Finally, there are some interesting and inappropriate remarks made by Zahara and Lily regarding library page Frank's personal relationship with Susan Tupperman—the woman at the heart of the newspaper exposé. Gossip and innuendo have no part in library staff interactions, and it certainly shows poor judgment on the part of the library's leaders to include this in their discussions. Also, since it cannot be proven that Frank was the "source" of the information leaked to the newspaper, it should never have been brought up—especially as when

Spencer told Frank that if Frank spoke with the newspaper it would be "a breach of library protocol" that "won't go unpunished." Because Frank's involvement in leaking this news is an unproven piece of gossip, Spencer's remark could be viewed as a threat. Library page Frank's remark about "whistleblower protections" should be a clue that Spencer could be in for a future surprise if Frank takes this remark to his employee representative organization for further action.

In tackling this final subproblem, Davina Darling needs to reread (and revise if necessary) the current media relations policy. The scenario mentions there is a policy that addresses who "speaks for" the library, but the reader has no clear idea if such a policy is known to anyone other than the director. If Frank was, in fact, the one involved in starting this media crisis, it's likely that he would have thought twice about the potential consequences of secretly sharing data with the media. In the age of social media and instant communication channels, existing media relations policies are likely outdated and in need of a complete overhaul. Director Darling should take this opportunity to ensure that the media relations policy covers everything it should. If not, she needs to reopen it and begin the immediate process of updating it, having it approved, and—most importantly—communicating it to the entire Santa Jacinta Public Library staff.

Response 3
By Jolene Cole, associate professor of library and information science, Georgia College, Milledgeville, Georgia

This scenario represents a perfect storm of what can happen when several minor infractions and missteps in communication within a library—especially one the size of Santa Jacinta—occur. One may be quick to assume that the significant issue here is the negative publicity the library is receiving due to the vast number of discards. However, the more substantial problem is the number of missteps and the lack of follow-through from the library's staff. To begin, let's break down the errors committed by the Santa Jacinta staff.

The circulation supervisor, Spencer Follet, was initially overwhelmed by his new assignment, not an uncommon occurrence when starting a new position. Spencer had good intentions, but his first slip-up was not meeting with Lily, the head of collection development, before having his library page, Frank Miller, pull the items for discard. Spencer had some initial questions and concerns about the process, and it would have been wise for him to speak with Lily prior to taking any action. Approaching the discard process by asking additional questions, Spencer technically could have prevented the public relations issue altogether.

The library page, Frank, is the staff member who lights the figurative fire in this situation. However, Frank should not shoulder the entirety of the blame. We are led to assume that Frank is the individual who speaks to the press; if that is true and can be proven, then Frank should face disciplinary actions within the library's guidelines. Frank, out of frustration, also makes many assumptions about the discard process. It is paramount that Spencer investigate and address Frank's concerns. Honestly, the whole situation may have been avoided if the library administration would have addressed the issue when Frank was previously removed from the process by his last supervisor.

The head of collection development, Lily, was extremely passionate about implementing an aggressive weeding program. Unfortunately, it seems that Lily may not have gotten the buy-in from the librarians and library staff that she needed for them to successfully follow through on the project. If Lily struggled to get buy-in to the program, she should have reached out to her direct supervisor for assistance in implementing the new plan. At the very least, Lily should have officially updated the twenty-year-old weeding policy, clearly articulated any changes to staff at all levels, and implemented a method to assess the progress of the plan. Her supervisor should not only be informed of the proposed changes but should also have signed off on the whole effort and, at the very least, been informed of the expected increase in discards.

Supervising librarian Zahara Cooper plays a more ambiguous role in this scenario. It is hard to know precisely which areas Zahara officially oversees. However, it was evident in Spencer's tour of the library that Zahara was very disconnected from the process. She knew the weeding policy was over twenty years old, and she stated that she rarely saw anyone down in the basement evaluating the items and flippantly remarked "out of sight, out of mind" about the items. Zahara seemed to be content in the status quo and yet all but admitted that maybe the policy was not working. That is concerning for a supervising librarian—a position normally responsible for playing an integral part in planning, coordinating, and supervising specific library operations. Perhaps Zahara needs to reevaluate the twenty-year-old discard policy and check in with the library's collection development head along with all other departments that participate in the weeding process.

The library director, Davina Darling, has a full plate managing a large, multibranch urban library system. Without question, a director needs to be able to rely on their administrative staff to keep everything moving forward smoothly. However, the director also needs to find a balance between knowing all the gritty details and keeping everyone focused on the larger picture. Director Darling needs to reinforce staff expectations and policies and encourage yearly retraining sessions. There are probably too many unknowns in this situation to necessarily place blame solely on Director Darling. However, as the library director, the inevitable fallout is placed on her shoulders. At the very least, she will need to address the city council and may need to release a statement to the press.

The overarching issue of the public relations nightmare might be the trickiest to address. Libraries of all types face patron concerns over weeding policies. There will always be patrons who feel the library has not done enough to save items and others who are totally on board with a strict weeding policy. It is next to impossible to find a solution and strategy that works for every patron, every time. However, libraries should make a reasonable effort to fall somewhere in between those two extremes.

Cleaning up some of Santa Jacinta's communication issues and missteps above will help avoid problems like this in the future. However, in the meantime, they may want to issue a verbal apology, restate the library's current weeding policy, and inform patrons that the policy will be reviewed and updated as needed. Santa Jacinta should also explain the library's need to implement an aggressive weeding policy and emphasize that the current discards were in the best interest of the library's collection and patrons' needs. I'd also suggest the Santa Jacinta Library consider the option of having a used book sale once or twice a year to dispose of their unwanted titles instead of discarding them. It would be an opportunity for the library not only to assure patrons that items are going to good use, once discarded, but also an excellent opportunity to raise money for the library.

The staff at Santa Jacinta Library have some work ahead of them to avoid any future issues. Library representatives from each department should review and update the weeding policy. Library staff and administration should be trained on the new policy and procedures, and the administration should develop an annual or biannual check-in to assess that the policy is working and that there are no significant concerns from staff. At the very least, the staff need to learn to communicate more effectively with one another.

Part Six

Communicating

Chapter Eighteen

A Failure to Communicate

A Communicating Scenario Using Difficult Professional Topics

SCENARIO

Tanya Stewart arrived at work thinking about one thing: lunch! *There are so many good Mexican food places by our library now*, she thought, and it was making her hungry. *I think I'll go out for lunch today.* But first she needed to check the hourly desk assignment schedule to make sure she had enough time to really enjoy herself. She normally brought her lunch to work, but if she was going to go outside the library, she wanted to make sure she wasn't rushed.

As one of many librarians at the Williamson Park Public Library, Tanya was becoming aware of the increasing variety of users at the library, and she was finding it hard to balance her knowledge of library service with what the library's community needed these days. Almost on a daily basis, a library user would come in and ask for books in Spanish. When staff took them to the library's three meager shelves of books in that language, she almost felt embarrassed. Tanya had even looked for some Spanish-language selection resources and book reviews in hopes she could find and purchase some more recent and relevant materials. Unfortunately, she hadn't had much luck. And now the community demographic seemed to be changing further. Would Spanish material even be necessary in a year or so? She wasn't sure. To satisfy her curiosity, Tanya went to the US Census website to search for community information. She was surprised at how easy it was to find demographic information online. She even found she could enter the library's zip code to get specific neighborhood information. Tanya knew that most of this census information was only gathered every ten years and was therefore a bit dated, but she discovered the census also provided yearly population trends, estimates, and projections. She made a mental note to share this "discovery" with her colleagues.

Just as she was about ready to click on the table for her library community's population demographic on the census website, Tanya was interrupted at the reference desk. In front of her stood an Asian man who was noticeably uncomfortable asking a question in a language that was not native to him. Tanya smiled in an attempt to diffuse his discomfort, but she sensed she was not successful in that regard. For the next ten minutes, she tried to understand what the man needed. She became frustrated as she wondered to herself how one conducts a reference interview with someone who speaks almost no English. She heard the man say what she thought was the word "article," so she walked him over to the periodicals section. She glanced at the clock on the wall on her way. She was already late to her lunch break. Not really understanding why Tanya had walked him there, the man said "no" in his heavy accent and then, once again, turned to the language he was comfortable in. *What language is that?* she wondered. *Is that Vietnamese?* Tanya did her best to understand but was no closer to getting the man what she *thought* he needed than she had been twenty minutes ago. Seeing the library's circulation supervisor, Loretta Ramsey, walk up to the circulation desk, Tanya guided the man over there. Explaining the situation—a situation most in the library were already familiar with—Tanya handed the problem over to Loretta.

"I'm totally sorry to do this, Loretta, but I'm already working well into my lunch break," Tanya said as a means to disengage. As she walked away, Tanya noted several non-English-speaking moms gathered in the children's section. One of them was gesturing to a library card application she held in her hand. Tanya could only think to herself that these folks represented more communication problems in her future.

When Tanya returned after her lunch break, she found Loretta and inquired about the Asian man she had left in her hands.

"Oh, yeah. I got lucky," Loretta said. "After you left, the man's young daughter came over and started talking to her father in the same language. I think it was Japanese. Anyway, she was able to translate for us, and I found that all the man wanted was to apply for a library card. It was so cute. When I thanked the little girl for being such a big help, she said"—at this point Loretta put on a fake accent and repeated what the Asian man's daughter had said—"'Is no problem. No to worry about it.'" Loretta giggled. Tanya didn't look amused.

"It makes me feel like such an idiot when I can't help these people! I just can't understand them and vice versa. Ugh! And the problem seems to be getting worse," Tanya complained.

"Maybe they should start requiring library school students to learn a second language rather than worry about cataloging and metadata," Loretta said only half-jokingly.

"Yeah. The old neighborhood has certainly changed a lot from when I started here," Tanya said. "In fact, I was just noticing all the taquerias and ethnic food spots sprouting up as I drove in to work today. It used to be nothing but Japanese restaurants. But now there are just as many Mexican, Chinese, Somali, and Middle Eastern restaurants and shops around here. Sometimes I feel like I'm in a foreign country when I come to work." That jogged her memory about the census website she had looked over earlier, and she returned to her desk to see if she could make sense of any of that voluminous data she had noted.

Over the course of the next two hours off desk, Tanya had found—and tried to interpret—data from the last three census reports. Additionally, she charted some of the demographic projections and estimates, hoping she might be able to put her finger on where her community had been and where it would likely be going—at least according to the census data. Her initial thoughts were that the library's Japanese community had started to dwindle some ten years ago and year after year had declined. At the same time, the Spanish-speaking population around the library had risen. Although she wasn't exactly sure from her perfunctory research, Tanya had also noted a trend that seemed to show rising populations of Chinese and Middle Eastern families for the next few years. *Well, that's alarming*, Tanya thought. She obviously knew that the Williamson Park Public Library staff was predominantly made up of Caucasian women. In fact, Williamson Park was far from diverse. It could only claim one Japanese library clerk, named Cathleen Himoda, and one Spanish speaker, the assistant library director, Bob Lopez. The fact that Bob was also close to retirement age caused Tanya even more consternation.

At that moment, Loretta walked into the staff room and sighed. "Whew! That was a busy hour."

"How many of your patrons were non-English speaking?" Tanya asked.

"About half," Loretta replied.

Tanya called Loretta over to her desk and showed her the fruits of her research, pulling up her discoveries of the census tables and data.

"This didn't happen overnight, Loretta. It's been happening for a while. There is no reason administration could not—or *should* not—have been on top of this. We could have been better positioned."

"Tanya, I think we really need to talk about this at the next meeting, don't you?" said Loretta. "If more and more of our patrons don't speak English, and we don't speak their languages, it's going to be impossible to communicate with them, let alone serve their needs—at least in a timely manner."

"I agree. Let's bring it up with Joyce at the next staff meeting," Tanya said.

To her credit, Tanya was able to get a brief moment with library director Joyce Hogue before the meeting in order to ask her to put the topic on the agenda. "Just wanted to ask that the subject of communication be added to the agenda on Friday," she told Joyce, who was in her typical rush out of the building on her way to a meeting.

"Communication? What do you mean?" Joyce asked.

"Well, Joyce, several of us have been amazed by the tons of immigrants and non-English-speaking patrons coming into the library these days. It's getting really difficult to communicate with them."

"Oh, really? I guess I hadn't noticed," was Joyce's reply. "Maybe it's time to do another community assessment. Those are so expensive, though."

"I did a little research online, Joyce, and the library seems to have missed an opportunity to position itself better to react to the changing demographic," Tanya offered.

"Well," Joyce said, "community analysis is an expensive undertaking, and the community changes so quickly that, once a library has done the analysis, the findings are soon irrelevant. I think it's more important to focus on the actual users who come into the library. Make twenty percent of them happy, and you'll solve eighty percent of your issues. I remember that from my management class. It's called the Pareto rule. Twenty percent of your collection accounts for eighty percent of your circulation. Twenty percent of the users account for eighty percent of your problems. Stuff like that. I'll have to look that up again and refresh my memory. Anyway, yeah, okay, I'll put that issue on the agenda for the meeting, and we can talk more about it together," Joyce said. "Right now, I'm due over at a City Hall meeting, so I better run."

When Friday arrived, all the Williamson Park staff were assembled in the staff room awaiting the start of the regular staff meeting. They knew these meetings rarely ran longer than thirty minutes before Joyce was called away, so they were anxious to get going in order to talk about everything on their agenda. After taking care of regular agenda items regarding City Hall and library board issues, Joyce turned to Tanya's request. "So, Tanya tells me that several of the staff have concerns over our ability—or should I say *inability*—to serve our growing immigrant population. If any of the rest of you want to share your thoughts on this, please do so, but please keep your comments brief. We have to open the library soon."

"Well, since I am the one who asked to put this topic on the agenda," Tanya said, "I'll start. Many of us have talked about this while in the staff room, and as I told Joyce, we're just becoming really alarmed that, over the last few years, I think there have been so many new immigrants into our community that it's becoming really problematic to communicate." She relayed her recent experience with the Asian man who just needed a library card application and his daughter who rescued the staff from their failure to communicate. "I'm sure you've all had a similar experience. It's typical in here now."

"Well, it isn't only immigrants," Cathleen Himoda said. "There are a large number of African Americans and second-generation Hispanics living in our library's community now." As she looked around the staff room and the staff gathered there, she pointed out the obvious. "Just look. I'm the only Asian woman, Bob is the only Hispanic, and there are no black staff members at all," she said. "No wonder we're having issues. I'm thinking we could use an online translating software application or something to help."

"That might be a good idea, Cathleen, because guess who everyone comes looking for when a Hispanic person comes in asking for something," Bob Lopez said. "Yep! Me! And not all of those Hispanic patrons only speak Spanish—in fact, some do speak English and so don't even need my help. I think it's just because some of you are uncomfortable talking to non-white patrons. Or maybe we've lost our ability to conduct good reference interviews?"

"But isn't the ability to communicate their problem rather than yours?" asked Loretta.

"Not really. It's my problem too. It eats up my time away from the desk doing selecting or collection maintenance. It seems like whenever I sit down to weed books, someone needs my help to communicate with a Spanish speaker. I can't get anything done because you're all giving me problems you don't want to handle," said Bob. "It's not like I can only help brown-skinned patrons because my own skin is brown. I help white patrons too, so I should expect you to do the same with those with brown—or any other color—skin."

Loretta felt this meeting was beginning to slide down a slippery slope. "It's just human nature to be uncomfortable like that. You've been really helpful, Bob, and we all appreciate that," she said.

"Maybe a translation tool would be helpful," said Tanya. "But there are other things we can do too. We have a collection of mostly best sellers in English. I think we need to make changes there to meet the community demand. Our collection certainly doesn't reflect the needs of the current users in our community, right?"

Having been caught off guard a bit by the onslaught of anger and frustration, Joyce interjected something she immediately wished she could take back. "Okay, so what do you want me to do? I can't fire half the staff and replace them with blacks, Hispanics, and Asians! And I don't have the money to replace half the collection with foreign-language materials," she said. "And look, if we purchase more Spanish books tomorrow, who's to say that we will still need them next year? What if *that* community moves out and another one moves in? Wouldn't it be best to just focus on meeting the needs of the longtime users?"

"I'm not saying that either," Tanya demurred, sensing that she had set off a time bomb here.

Joyce's phone rang, and she immediately saw it was City Hall. "Look, it's opening time. We'll have to talk about this more later, everyone. I've got to run. In the meantime, if anyone has any more suggestions, give them to Tanya so she can relay them to me." Director Hogue grabbed her purse and left the room.

"Well, that didn't go well!" Tanya told Loretta.

"I know. Talk about a knee-jerk reaction," Loretta said.

"Where do we go from here?" Tanya asked. "Maybe the library board needs to be brought in on this?"

"Well, that's a thought. I've got to get to the reference desk. Looks like we're open now, and there's a new group of users pouring in the front door." With that, Loretta quickly zipped away. Tanya headed to her desk to gather more census data and devise a plan to take to the library board. But would that be going behind Joyce's back? Tanya suddenly had a lapse of courage. But where would the library go from here? If she didn't do it, though, who would? This was certainly a dilemma she hadn't anticipated putting herself in the middle of as she was driving to work days earlier. Tanya suddenly noted that the library's public phone line was ringing. *Loretta must be caught up in something*, she thought as she jumped to answer the reference help line.

"Williamson Park Public Library. May I help you?" Tanya asked.

"*Hola? Hablas español?*" came a soft voice on the other end of the line.

Tanya took a deep breath, let out a large sigh, and thought to herself, *We gotta do something about this. It's just getting worse.*

A FAILURE TO COMMUNICATE RESPONSES

Response 1
By Susan Hildreth, former director, Institute of Museum and Library Services, Washington, D.C.

There are failures to communicate on all levels in this library; it is rather stunning to see this happening in the twenty-first century! Successful libraries have in-depth knowledge about their communities and are constantly adjusting services to meet their unique needs. Sadly, that is not happening in this case. Dramatic change must occur here to improve library services for this community.

I have organized these issues and how they might be addressed by the key operational segments of library service: the library board, library director, library staff, and community.

Library Board

The library board has a duty to represent the interests of the community and ensure that all members of the community are being served. That responsibility is not being carried out for this community. Although some board members may think that the library director is responsible for making the board aware of community needs, that ultimately is the responsibility of the board. It is also the responsibility of the board to consistently evaluate the performance of the director. Even though director Joyce Hogue seems to be very involved in City Hall activities, it is not clear what those activities might be and if they are, in fact, moving the priorities of the library forward. The board must set the priorities for the library and make sure that the director carries out those priorities through regular communication and annual formal performance evaluations. If the director is not able to carry out these priorities, action should be taken to identify new leadership for this organization.

The library board should represent the diversity of the community. If the membership of the board reflects the lack of diversity that is represented in the staff, much work needs to be done. The board itself, the library director, and the political leadership of the community who may appoint board members must make diversity of board membership a priority. That diversity would bring more community knowledge and commitment to serving all populations to the board.

Library Director

Joyce Hogue, library director, is not prioritizing her staff or service to her community. Although it appears that she is involved in very important City Hall business, it is not clear that this involvement is moving forward the library's agenda in any way. Perhaps Joyce is promoting her own personal agenda. She does not respect open communication with her staff when she limits the staff meeting time and agenda and rushes off before discussion is complete.

Joyce is somewhat surprised when Tanya Stewart, reference librarian, informs her that immigrant and non-English-speaking patrons are using the library and are challenging for staff to serve. Joyce is definitely not spending enough time in the library. Her response that it may be time to do a community assessment, which could be very expensive, is appalling. Community assessments done on a regular basis are crucial investments to ensure that the library is knowledgeable of its changing community. Also, the library staff has tools and information available to them to facilitate annual updates of assessments that should be completed every ten years after new census data is available. The concern that Joyce has about assessments becoming irrelevant soon after they are completed is completely contradicted by the fact that population changes occur over time and can be readily anticipated and addressed by any agency with responsibilities for community service.

Joyce's philosophy of serving the users who come in the library is out of date and does not acknowledge or address the role of the public library in its community. The library's "power users" are going to avail themselves of the in-person or virtual services because they are knowledgeable and determined to do so. One of the key roles of the public library is to serve those who may not be aware of the services or are unable to access the services due to lack of public transportation, limited access to broadband, previous fine records, or a variety of other logistical and personal reasons. The library that overlooks or neglects the population of nonusers is not fulfilling its mission.

Although it is not surprising that Joyce may have been somewhat defensive in her response to the staff meeting discussion, her inability to anticipate the priority of increasing staff diversity and offering a more varied collection, including additional non-English materials, is very concerning. Joyce Hogue demonstrates a significant lack of engaged leadership that will hinder the ability of this library to meet the needs of its community.

Library Staff

The library staff is beginning to recognize that their community is changing and that effectively serving the diverse members of the community is challenging. It is rather astounding that the library staff, who acknowledge that the retail environment in their neighborhood has been changing, did not realize that these changes are also reflected in their patrons and service priorities. They may have noticed the changing environment but did not think it was their responsibility to modify their service strategy in any way. As Tanya Stewart noted, "There is no reason administration could not, or should not, have been on top of this. We could have been better positioned." This statement demonstrates the director's lack of leadership, yet, since these demographic changes have been taking place for at least several years, it is surprising that the staff has not brought these demographic and service changes to the attention of the director or the board sooner. It is particularly surprising that the assistant director, Bob Lopez, a Spanish speaker, did not address this situation, but that may speak to the lack of latitude or empowerment that is provided for staff in this organization.

The public service staff does not have a customer-friendly attitude. When Tanya was doing census research (which was long overdue!) at the reference desk, she was "interrupted" by an Asian patron with whom she could not communicate effectively. Her negative customer service attitude toward this patron could be affected by her desire to focus on research she was interested in or to avoid communication challenges with the patron. That inability to serve the patron effectively could trigger feelings of frustration and ineffectiveness. Basic customer service training for all staff would be a useful starting point.

It is extremely unfortunate that the library staff does not work as a team; they do not back each other up in various settings. Tanya handed off the Asian patron with whom she was unable to communicate to Loretta Ramsey, circulation supervisor, because Tanya was late to take her lunch break! When Tanya checked in with Loretta after lunch, Loretta informed her that the patron's daughter served as a translator for a successful resolution, then proceeded to make fun of the manner in which the patron's daughter spoke. Many staff refer persons of color, whether they are Spanish speakers or not, to Bob Lopez. This constant referral impacts Bob's ability to carry out other duties. It also demonstrates that the library staff generally are not comfortable serving persons of color or respectful of those who do not look or speak like them. This situation is exacerbated by the lack of diversity of the staff, with only one Japanese and one Spanish speaker on staff, all other staff being Caucasian, English-speaking women. The library needs to immediately provide cultural competency training for all staff and begin to identify opportunities to diversify the staff.

The lack of a diverse collection is another challenge for this library. Materials in languages that are prevalent in the community—Spanish, Japanese, and other world languages—must be included in a variety of formats for children, teens, and adults. Obtaining non-English materials can be challenging. This library needs to establish relationships with vendors providing those materials and/or work with neighboring libraries or cooperative systems to obtain these materials. Several staff suggested a translation service or online translation platform to facilitate communication with non-English-speaking patrons. This would provide immediate benefit until staff with fluency in various languages can be hired.

Community

Sadly, the lack of community engagement demonstrated by the library board, director, and staff does not suggest that this community is being well served by their public library. It is not clear whether there is a friends of the library group in place that might demonstrate some community connection. The non-English-speaking moms who were gathered in the children's section and gesturing about library card applications sadly represent communication problems for staff. These moms could be a potential group to advocate for family services in world languages to become a priority for the library. Hopefully, some members of the library staff and/or new library leadership will take serving all members of their community more seriously than is currently happening.

Response 2
By Lisa Richland, director, Floyd Memorial Library, Greenport, New York

The idea that a library staff of predominantly English-speaking white women is culturally or linguistically prepared to serve a multiethnic, multiracial community is untenable. The library director, Joyce Hogue, is right that she can't fire half the staff and remove half the collection, but that isn't the solution this issue needs. There are many other things that Joyce needs to consider that are equally untenable at this library. Joyce has chosen to tackle the easiest problem first—how to communicate with the Williamson Park Public Library's user community.

The scenario presents a fairly black-and-white portrayal of the library staff's lack of language skills necessary to communicate effectively with patrons. There is seemingly only one staff member—the assistant director, Bob Lopez—who speaks a language other than English, and he is close to leaving the library due to his pending retirement. So, in resolving the language communication problem, Joyce has at least five clear options on this front:

1. Joyce could look to reallocate resources in her organization chart by replacing retiring staff with multilingual professional staff. Since Assistant Director Lopez is retiring, his salary would support two new librarians with the language skills necessary for the community. While this reallocation process could be laborious and involve the organization's human resources department, it could be done.
2. Under Joyce's request, the city could strive to encourage more multilingual community members to apply for clerical positions. The circulation supervisor, Loretta Ramsey, should be keeping her eyes and ears open for likely multilingual library users who could become library clerks and work to recruit them.
3. Joyce could have her staff prepare information sheets in several languages that translate common requests and their answers ("Where are the restrooms?" "How can I get a library card?" and others). These translations could show visual cues as well. These immediately useful information sheets seem like a far more appropriate area for the library to place resources instead of the survey that Tanya Stewart is well on her way to compiling in house.
4. Joyce could work with her staff to encourage community members to suggest titles in their native languages. This would address Tanya's concern about the library collection's lack of usefulness and relevance to the community.
5. Joyce needs to address the staff's disassociation from its user community by bringing in a little sensitivity and diversity training for clueless employees. Loretta Ramsey could certainly benefit from this as well as Library Director Hogue herself, but obviously the whole staff needs some sort of help and training in this regard.

With attention focused on how the Williamson Park Public Library can better communicate with its users, there seems to be an equally critical issue Hogue needs to address—and that is her own lack of awareness. Why didn't she see the community changing? Joyce's comment that she "hadn't noticed" the staff's problems in communicating with patrons seems to indicate she has also failed to see the community change around her. Until her staff has pointed it out to her, Joyce has apparently pretty much ignored her library community's demographics. I'd bet that Joyce is one of those staff members who drives to the library, parks in the staff lot, enters the library by a backdoor staff entrance, stays in her office or at City Hall most of the day, eats lunch in the staff room, and—at the end of the day—exits the library at the staff door and drives home. The library's users could pretty much be space aliens for all she knows. Joyce's comment that performing a community assessment is "expensive" is also alarming. Joyce has failed in some of the most basic, critical library management skills: having a desire to meet and serve the library's user community, and having an ability to motivate, establish, and maintain effective working relationships with the public and with community agencies. Resolving the language communication problem may be a good short-term solution. But I would bet that—unless Joyce starts to pull the veil from her eyes and becomes more effective in interacting with her staff and the public—the Williamson Park Public Library will face equally onerous community-based problems down the road.

The "problem" here is an opportunity. The community is enthusiastic about the library. This is a wonderful problem to have. With just a little shift in focus from "can't" to "can" or from "no" to "yes," the Williamson Park Public Library can be a positive force for its new neighbors. Library Director Hogue needs to spend a little time in the building instead of in meetings at City Hall. If the community is changing so drastically, it will likely continue to do so. Director Hogue can position the library as a valuable resource for the new residents as well as for City Hall. However, she'll have to come out of her office and meet the people she and her staff are being paid to serve.

Response 3
By Donna Catron, branch manager, Muncie Public Library, Muncie, Indiana

What we have in this scenario is more of a failure of leadership than a failure of communication. There are a myriad of issues that this scenario brings forward, but let's start with Tanya's dilemma presented at the end of the scenario—should she circumvent her library manager and discuss her problem with the library board? Tanya is right to have second thoughts about going directly to the library board. At this point, it would be going over her supervisor's head, and right now she has nothing to offer the library board beyond the director's off-the-cuff remarks in a rushed half-hour meeting and some anecdotal evidence. Going to the library board now would risk losing her director's confidence and could have serious consequences for her career. Tanya also doesn't have any guarantee that the library board would listen to her or respond in a meaningful way, so even if she did approach the library board, there is a strong possibility that the community she wishes to help would remain underserved.

The better strategy would be for Tanya to do as her library director has suggested and do some solid research to gather concrete community information, demographic trends, and projections, and with that data in hand, she could then schedule a private meeting with library director Joyce Hogue to go over her findings and offer suggestions. Researching census statistics is a good start, and Tanya can also institute a grassroots survey to ask her coworkers to record all the questions they get in a certain week. Also, keeping a list of items customers are asking for that the library doesn't own can be a good indication of whether the collection is supporting library user needs. Armed with that information, Tanya should be able to vividly demonstrate that further action is required.

Whether or not Library Director Hogue will listen and take that action is another issue. As a library director, Joyce's attitude seems very short-sighted. Librarians cannot afford to ignore segments of the populations they service. A library that's supported by public taxes should reflect the entire population, not just the majority or the "longtime users." Ignoring a changing population is a missed opportunity and a good way to drive the library into obsolescence. Eventually, the longtime user base dries up, and—if the library does nothing to cultivate new customers and offer new services—then it will fail. Successful libraries change and adapt to meet their communities' needs. The library I started at thirty years ago is a very different organization today, even though it is the same library system. Adapting to changing technology, user needs, and population trends are all vital to the health of a library. Library Director Hogue has some explaining to do in her absence of judgment here.

Right now, Williamson Park Public Library is not a healthy institution. The culture is indifferent at best and downright toxic at worst. Shuffling a customer off to another employee in favor of going to lunch is very poor customer service. More troubling is circulation supervisor Loretta mocking a customer's accent. This shows a marked lack of cultural sensitivity and, even worse, bigotry that has no place in the workplace. The most serious issue is that of the allegations of Assistant Library Director Lopez—that staff are automatically referring Hispanic customers to him, even if they speak English. That kind of prejudice is simply unacceptable and shows laziness and a lack of concern on the staff's part. But the fault here lies less with the library employees than the library director. Joyce has put her employees in a situation that they are ill prepared for. It seems like most of them want to provide good customer service but haven't been given the resources to do so. This is extremely stressful, so it's no wonder the employees are looking at their patrons as problems rather than as customers to serve.

If Tanya is able to convince Library Director Hogue of the need for change, the good news is that there are things that can be done to transform this library into a responsive and healthy organization, both for the community and for the library employees. The first step is to start looking at the changing population as an opportunity for growth. A growing population, especially a diverse one, is a great boon to a community as a whole and gives the library a new opportunity for growth.

Ideally, as the library director suggested, a community needs assessment would be conducted. Yes, that can be expensive, but it doesn't have to be cost-prohibitive. Most cities have some type of community development office or chamber of commerce that may have already done a lot of the legwork as far as demographic and population trends. If the community is home to a university, there may be an opportunity to work with students on an immersive learning project to study community needs. It can also be enlightening to dig deeper into why the population is changing—are people coming for greater economic opportunity, social reasons, education, or other factors? Understanding why the population is changing will help in assessing their information needs.

Reaching out to schools, businesses, and other community groups that serve these populations will help in determining how best to serve these customers. Also, creating partnerships with these groups will help in developing programs and services to truly meet the needs of this growing population.

The language barrier is the most pressing obstacle to overcome in order to begin truly serving the new customer base. Hiring multilingual staff would be an ideal solution, but if that is impossible, there may be ways to develop a core of volunteers to assist in translating and facilitating interactions between library staff and customers.

The next step is developing a collection that meets the needs of all the library's customers. Spending a certain percentage of the collection budget on multilingual materials is a reasonable response if it meets community demand. Needs and tastes change over the years, and the materials will change over time. As is the case in any library, information needs change. When this happens, the library will need to acquire new materials. Most library book vendors can be quite helpful in pointing the library's material selectors in the right direction for acquiring books in other languages.

Changing staff attitudes is the greatest managerial challenge I see in this scenario. Cultural sensitivity training is a must for the group, as is basic customer service training. The American Library Association has resources that can help foster a greater understanding of diverse populations. Partnering with other community groups to create programs celebrating the different cultures would benefit employees and customers alike. Despite all efforts, though, there may be staff who simply don't want to change, and that reluctance may need to be handled through a disciplinary process.

Another must is instituting a diverse hiring policy, which includes actively recruiting minorities and providing opportunities for growth. This isn't just a good idea; it's the law. And, with the library's assistant director poised to retire, this would be the time to look at ways to create a new position or at least develop a new job description that would include reaching out to and working with diverse populations.

Turning this library's failure to communicate into an opportunity to grow and thrive won't be easy, but it will reap rich rewards for the community and for the library employees. If Tanya is able to persuade Joyce of the need to change, and Joyce makes the commitment to that change, things can turn around. If not, Tanya and her coworkers may very well need to go to the library's board or maybe even start updating their résumés.

Chapter Nineteen

Professor Privileges

A Communicating Scenario Using Difficult Professional Topics

SCENARIO

Kingston University's dean of libraries, Shiloh Chance, hated to worry, but the continual problems the university was seeing with their operational budget had put her in a general state of concern. She noticed the head of collection development, Jill Bayer, walking past her office and called her inside. "Jill? Do you have a moment? I need to talk to you about the university's collection budget." Jill stopped and did a quick about-face to walk back and into the dean's office.

"I hope it's not more bad news," Jill said. "The budget has been hacked to pieces the last few years, and I don't know where else we can find savings."

"Well, it's not good news, that's for sure. The university library has been told to reduce their entire operational budget by five percent. That's not as bad as last year's twelve percent . . . but, like you said, I'm not sure what's left to cut." Shiloh opened the folder marked "Budget" sitting on her desk and said, "Our book budget is pretty well decimated, and I'm not willing to cut there again. Do you agree?" Shiloh handed Jill a copy of last year's collection budget.

Jill took the sheet and quickly looked it over. "Yes, I agree. This book budget line item from last year had already been reduced from the year before that. And, if you'll remember, the faculty just about had a revolt when we informed them that their purchase requests would be limited, and most requests would go through an additional level of scrutiny."

"Right," said Shiloh. "I remember. They were so used to just submitting a request for the library to purchase a book, and we'd bend over backward to buy it. Then we told them that *library* faculty would be the final decision maker regarding purchases and that the library would apply strict criteria to future material purchase requests. When we told them the criteria included the cost of the title, the demonstrated need, and the availability of funds—well, we barely got out alive. I think that caused a lot of red flags to go up throughout our teaching faculty. They saw a power shift in purchasing decisions."

"Well, if we don't want any changes with the book budget allocation, where can we find any savings?" Jill had an idea of where Shiloh was taking this discussion. During their midyear budget review several months prior, Shiloh had brought up the university's skyrocketing annual subscriptions budget—particularly as it related to journals and databases. Prices for scholarly journals had been steadily rising, and—at that time—were about 5 percent higher than anticipated. Shiloh was concerned about how this increase was straining an already stressed budget. Together, they developed a few management strategies to maximize the value of their limited subscriptions budget. They canceled journals that the library also subscribed to online. They also sought to offset the cost of any new journal subscriptions by canceling others of equivalent value that were deemed less needed. Although the university had continued to utilize these strategies, the benefits they yielded seemed to diminish. Over just the last few months, Jill had received seven notices from publishers of rising annual subscription costs. Jill knew the subscriptions budget was in trouble and that it was becoming increasingly unsustainable. There would be no way the university could keep up with the demands of the scholarly journal information marketplace. Jill figured this was where Shiloh was taking their discussion, but she waited for her dean to finish before mentioning that she knew something that would throw a monkey wrench in the budget planning process.

As suspected, Shiloh spent the next twenty minutes in their impromptu meeting reviewing the university's journal costs. "We have over ten journal titles that cost more than four thousand dollars annually," Shiloh said as she pointed to the annual subscription costs. "That's a hit of more than forty thousand dollars each year to our subscriptions budget allocation! We just can't keep doing that, Jill. We should be meeting the needs of our students, not giving away our precious resources to greedy journal publishers!"

Jill decided the time had come to make this sticky situation even stickier. "Well, hold on to your hat, Shiloh. Wait until you hear this. I got a purchase request yesterday for a subscription to *The International Journal for Chemical Engineers*, and the price is eleven thousand dollars annually."

"What? You can't be serious. Eleven thousand dollars!" Shiloh's mouth fell open.

"Oh, it gets better," Jill said sarcastically. "On the same form was a request to subscribe to *ChemFinderBasicsDelux*. It's an online database with a limited licensing subscription rate of over ten grand!" Jill pulled the request form out of the folder she was carrying and showed Shiloh.

Shiloh took the request and looked it over with a smirk. "Of course! Lingford! Just who does he think he is? There's no way we can add these titles. Jill, is there even a need for these?"

"Well, not that I'm aware of," Jill said. "There's more, Shiloh. Looking over your list of subscription prices, four of the ten titles you identified as costing more than four thousand dollars annually were ordered by—you guessed it—Professor Lingford."

Chemistry professor Dr. Robert Lingford had been teaching at Kingston University for nearly fifteen years. During that time, he had earned a reputation from his peers as a respected instructor and expert in the field. Lingford was currently chair of the university's chemistry department, which came with certain privileges. However, Lingford was also villainized by many of his students due to his toughness and high academic expectations. His reputation among library staff tended to side with that given to him by the students. Lingford was demanding, impatient, and often rude. When he requested something, he wanted it right now! He didn't appreciate waiting, nor did he appreciate being told to do so.

"Why in God's name would Lingford need all these expensive resources? Does anyone use them—other than Lingford himself?" Shiloh asked.

"I'm not even sure that Lingford uses them!" exclaimed Jill. "The periodicals staff tells me that those journals are some of the least requested items on their shelves. Lingford doesn't require students to read articles from any of the journals, and they are not checked out. Our statistics show that not one of the journals we purchased for Lingford has ever even left the shelves." Jill leaned in closer to Shiloh and whispered, "From what I can tell, Lingford is on a power trip. He has had several articles printed in several of the journals over the years, and he just wants people to know that he's some sort of published bigwig!"

"What you're telling me, Jill, is that we're spending over forty thousand dollars each year to stoke the vanity of one of our professors? Is that right?" Shiloh could barely contain her anger. "And now he wants us to spend, what, another twenty thousand for more stuff that will sit unused?" Shiloh didn't give Jill time to answer her rhetorical question before she emphatically claimed, "Well, *that* will not happen. Lingford knows about the purchasing policy we implemented last year. These two requests certainly fail the 'cost' and the 'available funds' criteria . . . and I'm pretty sure they will fail the 'demonstrated need' criteria as well! Not even department chairs get unrestricted purchasing powers. Someone has to say no! I guess that someone is me."

"I'll warn you, Shiloh: Lingford can be a real"—Jill looked for a polite word—"well, he can be a bear."

"Return his purchasing request form with the 'under review' box checked. If he contacts you, refer him to me. And, Jill, cancel the subscriptions to the four journals we already ordered for Lingford. There's no need to keep paying for something we don't need." Shiloh had a look of satisfaction on her face.

"You do know, Shiloh, that standard operating procedure is to notify faculty members when we cancel any material orders or subscription they've submitted, right? Do you want me to notify Lingford? He's going to throw a fit."

"We have adopted university policy supporting us. If he complains, send him to me."

Three days later, Robert Lingford arrived at his office to a campus mailbox nearly overflowing with junk mail. But campus announcements, newsletters, publisher catalogs, and the like couldn't hide the one envelope that immediately caught his attention. The envelope was marked "purchase request," and it came from the desk of Jill Bayer, from the university library collection development office. Lingford quickly opened the envelope and unfolded the form inside. His eyes immediately focused on the words "under review." "What does that mean?" he mumbled to himself. Attached to the form was a cancelation notice. Listed on that form were four journals the library had acquired at his request years ago that they now intended to drop. The reason given on the form for dropping the journals were "non-use," "cost," and "limited funds." "What the hell!" Lingford stormed into his office, dropped the form on his desk, and dialed Jill Bayer's number.

Jill answered the phone on the first ring. "Hello. This is Jill."

"Ms. Bayer, this is Dr. Robert Lingford. I just received your notices about some journals I need that the library intends to cancel. I also had requested some important resources for our department that the library will not acquire. This is unacceptable, Ms. Bayer. Do I need to remind you that the library's mission is to serve the instructional and research efforts of the university's faculty? As chairman of the chemistry department, I'm notifying you that our department needs this material. All of it!"

Jill had anticipated this call for several days. She knew immediately what to say. "I've been instructed by our dean of libraries, Shiloh Chance, to hold off on new orders due to funding challenges. This will give our library selectors time to review educational needs and priorities before proceeding with purchasing. As far as the cancelation notices you received, as you know, the library has implemented policies to cancel materials that are not used."

"Well, that is simply not acceptable. Is Ms. Chance there? I need you to transfer me to her immediately. Never mind; I am coming over to the library now. This needs to be addressed, face-to-face, right now." Lingford hung up the phone, grabbed the notices he'd been sent, and walked across the campus to the library.

Lingford arrived at the university library only five minutes later. He stopped at the front desk and demanded to speak to Shiloh Chance. Taken aback by the professor's tone, the student assistant at the front desk stepped in the back room and told his circulation manager that there was "someone here to see the dean." Lingford, impatient as always, tapped his foot expectantly. The student assistant returned to the front and told Lingford that it would be a moment. The professor responded, "I don't have a moment. Where is her office?" The assistant told the professor that administrative offices were on the fourth floor, and—if he'd be patient—someone would escort him there. Lingford swung around and headed to the elevators.

When he arrived at the fourth floor, Lingford was met by the administrative secretary. She greeted Lingford politely, but he was in no mood for pleasantries. "I need to speak to Ms. Chance immediately."

"Certainly, sir. Who may I tell her is waiting?" she said.

"Tell her that the chairman of the chemistry department, Dr. Lingford, is here to speak to her about a library order," Lingford barked.

"If you'll have a seat, I'll let Dean Chance know you're here. I believe she has someone with her in her office at the moment." The administrative secretary rose from her desk and headed to Shiloh's office. Lingford remained standing. Just as she got to Shiloh's office door, it opened, and out came Jill Bayer.

"Oh, excuse me, Jill," the administrative secretary said. "I hate to interrupt, but there's a Dr. Lingford here from the chemistry department." Jill and Shiloh exchanged glances.

"I warned you he'd be here. I just didn't think it would be this quickly," Jill said.

"Bring him in, please. We've been expecting him." The administrative secretary left to bring Lingford back. "Jill, you are welcome to stay. In fact, I think it'd be a good idea."

"All right. Strength in numbers," Jill said.

Lingford walked directly into Shiloh's office and said, "Ms. Chance?" The administrative secretary was all too happy to close the door behind him and get out of harm's way.

"Yes. And you must be Professor Lingford?" Shiloh reached out her hand. The gesture was not reciprocated.

"It's Department Chairman Lingford, but I prefer Dr. Lingford." He slapped the paper he had received in his campus mailbox down on Shiloh's desk.

Shiloh ignored the paper and introduced Jill. "This is Ms. Bayer. She is head of our library's collection development."

"Oh, it looks like I've struck gold!" Lingford smirked, sarcasm dripping from his voice. "I want to talk to you about this order submission. It says that it is 'under review.' I find that offensive. As chairman of the department, I find it insulting to have my credibility and expertise questioned like this, Ms. Chance."

"I prefer Dean Chance," Shiloh replied. She thought she detected Jill stifling a cheer. "It is not our intention, Pro . . . I mean Dr. . . . Lingford, to offend or insult you—or anyone else on our faculty. As you are aware, the library's budget is not limitless. Just last year we were forced to implement a strict ordering policy that has been approved by the provost's office. It is a policy we have had in place for the last year. Part of that policy is to apply specific criteria to any acquisition request. We do this with all requests. Your requests for a new journal subscription and a specialized database totaled nearly twenty thousand dollars. Before we spend our dwindling resources on such costly acquisitions, we need to make sure that there is a demonstrated need. You have not provided that with your request."

"The fact that the chairman of the department is requesting it should be enough of a 'demonstrated need,'" Lingford scoffed. "Do you think there is someone on your staff who knows more about what my department needs than I do?"

Shiloh assured Lingford that he and his staff would be included in the decision-making process. "But since we are talking about need, let me address the journal cancelations we notified you about." Shiloh pointed to the notice Lingford had slammed on her desk when he entered. "Due to limited resources," she explained, "it is now library policy to review usage statistics of all journals before they are processed for renewal. Not one of these journals has been checked out in the six years we've subscribed to them."

"I find that incredibly hard to believe," Lingford said. "These are some of the most respected journals in the chemistry field. It would be an embarrassment to this university if we didn't have these in the library."

Jill Bayer decided to jump into the conversation at this point. "Dr. Lingford, my staff is not arguing about the quality of these journals. But if these journals are not useful to our students, it doesn't seem wise to spend thousands of dollars making them available. Think of the other journals or resources the library could acquire with the money saved in this case."

Lingford never looked at Jill. His eyes were focused like lasers on Shiloh's face. "As chairman of the chemistry department, I am its chief representative." Lingford stood up. "I facilitate the deployment of materials and other resources for our department, and I develop teaching curriculum with my staff. You have no idea what my department's needs and plans are and how these materials complement those plans. By canceling these subscriptions, and by questioning my purchase requests, you and your staff are severely jeopardizing our department's reputation and advancement, not to mention endangering our ability to recruit and retain faculty. I will take this to the university provost; you can bet on that."

"That's your choice, Dr. Lingford, but I believe your requests for these resources do not meet the university's established selection criteria. In fact, I will be checking just how much of the library's limited funds are being expended on the chemistry department and compare it with other departments in our university. I'll look forward to discussing this with the provost should he ask." Shiloh also rose to her feet. She walked to her office door and opened it. "Have a good day, doctor."

Lingford nearly ran out the door, never looking back. Jill noticed Lingford's purchasing request letter still sitting on Shiloh's desk. She swiftly picked it up. "Should I run after him?" Jill asked, showing Shiloh the letter.

"No," Shiloh said, calmly returning to her desk. "If he wants it, he can come back for it. I'm through coddling the egos of these prima donnas."

"So . . . " Jill mused. "Do you want me to cancel these four journal subscriptions? And what do we do with these two purchase requests 'under review'?"

Shiloh sat down in her office chair. She thought for a moment, taking Lingford's purchase request back from Jill's hands. "What do you think?" was all she said.

PROFESSOR PRIVILEGES RESPONSES

Response 1
By Jolene Cole, associate professor of library and information science, Georgia College, Milledgeville, Georgia

Unfortunately, this scenario is all too familiar for academic librarians struggling to keep budgets on track while balancing the needs of their patrons. It can be daunting for library management to keep everyone abreast of changing budgets and policies while managing various personalities. In this specific scenario, there are several issues to address. There is the overarching issue of shrinking budgets and skyrocketing journal costs, which is a major concern. However, the treatment of the Kingston faculty member and the head of collection development is the more immediate concern.

Dealing with faculty can be a tricky situation, especially when you add shrinking budgets and unreasonable demands to the equation. Dr. Lingford, the chair of the chemistry department, is an excellent example of a difficult and likely uninformed faculty member. Nevertheless, the way in which Shiloh, the dean of libraries, addressed the issue with Dr. Lingford is cause for concern. It is easy to sympathize with Shiloh and understand where her frustrations stem from; however, her quick-to-anger response style is detrimental not only to the library's relationships outside the building but also with Shiloh's immediate staff. Dr. Lingford may be on a so-called power trip, but he may also truly believe his requests are vital for his department's success. Remaining calm and thoughtful in this situation will get the library more goodwill and cause less overall frustration for the library staff. Shiloh needs to remain composed and professional and avoid jumping to assumptions when talking to—or about—her faculty members.

In addition, Shiloh needs to monitor her initial reactions with Jill, the head of collection development. It is easy for managers to get wrapped up in the moment, but Shiloh's response to the issue and her response to Jill are concerning. She didn't allow Jill any say in the initial response to Dr. Lingford, nor did Shiloh take time to consider her options with Jill in responding to the initial request. It would have been better for them to discuss alternative plans and next steps together as a team. It would also be helpful for Shiloh to forgo any disparaging remarks about another department head on campus in front of Jill.

The Kingston library also has a relatively new purchasing policy. This policy, although necessary, needs to be clear, widely circulated, and frequently explained in detail to the faculty. I assume that there are faculty, including Dr. Lingford, who may not be as familiar with the new policy. Faculty tend not to keep up to date with library policies or may not fully understand the larger picture. It should be our responsibility to remind them and assist them with these types of requests, when possible.

As for the purchasing policy, does the policy indicate how much money it allocates per department? Does the policy offer guidance on what are reasonable requests and what are not? Otherwise, faculty may not fully understand how to demonstrate their needs adequately or understand what a reasonable request should contain. Does the policy state when the library will review usage statistics of current journal subscriptions? Annually? Biannually? This should be done across the board for every department on a set schedule. In this scenario, Shiloh makes this determination as a retaliation to Dr. Lingford's behavior and uses the policy to cancel the subscriptions out of spite. Shiloh also escalated the situation needlessly when she threatened the chemistry department's entire allocation by comparing it with other departments at the university. Library collection allocation allotments didn't seem to be an issue until the heated exchange with Dr. Lingford. To be clear, I'm not advocating for library managers to be run over by overzealous faculty or that they should take emotional abuse from anyone in the workplace. Shiloh should make every effort to engage with Dr. Lingford and discuss how his interactions with library staff could be improved. Shiloh will have to carefully choose how she responds moving forward, in a manner that won't escalate rising tensions.

Suggestions for the future could include working with the chemistry department to make sure all faculty and their students are aware of current subscriptions. The library should also consider changing its policy from purchasing physical copies to purchasing only digital subscriptions. Getting students and faculty to use physical journals has honestly become obsolete. Eliminating physical journals could address the low usage numbers among the current chemistry subscriptions and widen their appeal to students and faculty. I would also add an option on the purchasing request form where library faculty can clarify an "under review" response and explain the next steps in the process. The policy, if possible, should be updated to assist faculty in the form resubmission process and answer any questions a faculty member may need addressed. This would allow the process to be more transparent and inclusive. In addition, I wouldn't cancel Dr. Lingford's current subscriptions unless the library was doing a campuswide evaluation of resources so that cancelations don't look like retaliation because of personal conflict. Finally, if all else fails, Shiloh may consider having a sit-down with the provost and Dr. Lingford to discuss the situation further.

Response 2
By Christine Schultz, library director and associate professor, College of Idaho, Caldwell, Idaho

Dean Shiloh Chance and the Kingston University Library are facing an all-too-familiar combination of circumstances. Budgets are shrinking, and subscription costs are rising. In today's higher education climate, the need to pay careful attention to budgets and expenses is not the exception but the rule in academic libraries.

Faculty, many say, are the lifeblood of the college or university. Unlike many staff members and administrators, who may come and go, faculty often stay at their institutions for the long term, earning tenure and even retiring from the same institution where they began their careers right out of graduate school. Though this may be changing as new, more mobile generations of faculty are hired and more institutions come to rely more heavily on part-time and adjunct faculty, it is important to remember that a faculty member such as Dr. Lingford may feel a strong sense of ownership at the university. Faculty members often enjoy a system of shared governance and will, in addition to control over curriculum and academic policy, and often have a strong voice in matters—including budgets—related to university operations. Any change, such as the recent power shift at Kingston regarding library purchasing decisions, that seems to discount or ignore the central role of the faculty in the life of the institution will likely be unwelcome and may be met with resistance. The common-sense spending controls that Kingston University and the library have put in place, however, have nonetheless received the appropriate approvals in the institution's governance structure and are now a matter of university policy, even if an unpopular one.

From what we see in this scenario, Dean Chance has two choices. She can either choose to cancel the four expensive and unused chemistry journal subscriptions immediately or she can establish a system for their evaluation for future cancelation.

Two elements may be important to consider. The first is fairness. While it is unlikely that any decision resulting in the immediate or even possible cancelation of these journals will be acceptable to Dr. Lingford (that is, it will not be possible to make him happy), such a decision would be far more palatable to many individuals in Dr. Lingford's position if they knew that decisions of this kind were being made according to a common standard across all departments and disciplines—that is, if Dr. Lingford was aware that the physics and business departments were also facing the possible cancelation of a handful of their more expensive journals.

I would suggest that staff at the library—perhaps the head of collection development, Jill Bayer—establish a benchmark maximum cost-per-use for all subscription titles in order to determine the "cost-to-benefit" of each journal subscription, thereby taking the subjectivity out of the decision making. This is a simple calculation that is determined by dividing the annual subscription cost of a title by the number of times it is used in that year. For a print title, this usage figure could be identified as the number of times the title is reshelved during the subscription period. For an online subscription, it may be the number of article downloads. For a bibliographic database, it may be the number of searches performed. The library can determine which methodology makes the most sense. Basically, the question is "How much does it cost every time a library patron uses this title?" And, "How much is too much?" Some libraries might determine that they should not be paying more per usage than the cost of obtaining an article from this title through a document delivery service, or more than it would cost for the end user to purchase an individual article online.

Once this maximum cost-per-use is established, the library should analyze the cost of all of its subscription renewals against this standard and flag any titles that exceed the maximum for possible cancelation. It may be necessary to adjust the standard somewhat based on patterns of need and use that are quite specific to the institution and its curriculum. For example, if a journal is used to support a course that is only taught on a two-year rotation, it may see heavy use, but only every other year. In this instance, it might make sense to use a two-year average cost-per-use. In addition, the cost-per-use will likely be higher for STEM-related titles (science, technology, engineering, and mathematics) and some titles in the professional studies, so a single benchmark maximum across all disciplines may not be sufficient.

In addition to fairness, it will be important to maintain transparency. That is, none of these decisions should be made under the cover of darkness. The methods used for calculating cost-per-use should be shared with the faculty, as should the usage statistics that are being used. Titles should be flagged for possible cancelation and this information brought to the faculty before any final decisions are made. If faculty are in the process of developing courses or assignments that will make greater use of these materials, these circumstances can then be taken into account and subscriptions can be placed on probation of a sort instead of immediately canceled. If faculty can see and understand the calculations (and they may question them, in my experience, but this questioning will likely result in tweaks to the process that will improve it), they will feel much more part of the process—as in the shared governance structures they are accustomed to—and much more likely to accept the results.

While, as Lingford has said, the library may have no idea what the chemistry department's needs or plans are (though this is unlikely if there is library representation on the university committee charged with overseeing the curriculum, as is common) and have no idea how the library materials complement those plans, the library *does* know what items are being used—and the titles identified in the scenario are not. No library in this situation (and what academic library isn't, in some way, in this position?) can afford to have materials sit on shelves unused. Developing, communicating, and fairly applying common-sense guidelines for such decisions seems like the appropriate path forward to resolve Dean Chance's problem. It seems likely that the cost of Dr. Lingford's subscriptions will exceed any maximum cost-per-use standard. Dean Chance will need to determine if the journals that Dr. Lingford has requested should be placed on probation or immediately canceled. In the spirit of fairness and transparency, if the budget allows, it might make the most sense to give Dr. Lingford notice that the journals will be canceled the following year if they do not see sufficient use.

Response 3
By Keri Moczygemba, head librarian, Austin Community College District, Austin, Texas

Much of a manager's responsibility, particularly when dealing with necessary relationships among departments, is managing expectations and interpersonal relations. The new collection development policy, which is quite a change from the previous status quo, coupled with additional budget cuts, makes managing expectations in relation to materials purchases especially important for Shiloh and Jill. The interpersonal issue in this scenario may seem extreme, but it is actually quite common. Now, how do you manage expectations of someone with a history of demanding and rude behavior? There are multiple parts to this predicament. While the activities necessary to handle this situation are listed in order below, they will actually occur simultaneously or at least with some overlap: managing bullying behavior, making difficult budget decisions, and, finally, communicating with the chemistry department chair.

Responding to a professor's bullying behavior is, unfortunately, part of the job of any academic librarian. A hardline decision and tough communication might seem like the way to go, but collaboration and diplomacy are important as tensions are high in all departments when budget cuts are mandated. Also, it is common for an individual's rude behavior or negative reputation to mask their legitimate concerns and requests. In this scenario, are the requests made by Dr. Lingford truly demanding and extraordinary or has Shiloh and Jill's judgment been clouded by his reputation for mistreating library staff? Shiloh and Jill must remain objective and professional as they interact with Dr. Lingford and make decisions about his requests. Venting about the exasperating and unreasonable requests behind closed doors is one thing, but those frustrations need to be put aside when making decisions, when communicating with library staff about the issue, and when communicating with Dr. Lingford. Responding to bullying behavior with bullying behavior is not the answer; it only leads to interpersonal conflicts, persistent aggression, and damaged reputations. So how do you respond to bullying behavior in a professional setting?

1.
   a. First, and possibly most importantly, resist the urge to respond immediately and instinctively. Remember to separate yourself personally from this professional situation. Recognize your instinctive mental response, and recognize that you have full control over how you respond to this negative situation. Verbalize this to the individual, if it suits you: "My instinct is to respond negatively to your request because (your tone is quite harsh/wagging your finger in my face is threatening/etc.)."
   b. Call out and separate the behavior from the matter at hand. Even in a professional setting, bullying behavior may include forceful tones, name calling, accusations and insinuations, threatening phrases, and threatening body language. Calmly respond with the behavior called out: "We are both professionals, and I'm sure you realize [insert bullying behavior] has no place here. If you want me to take this conversation/request seriously, please refrain from repeating that bullying behavior." You can try a less direct call-out if the individual has been reasonable in the past and this is a one-time or first-time negative situation: "Forceful behavior will not increase the library budget, so let's work together to find a solution that works for both of our departments."

2. Assert your authority. In this scenario, Dr. Lingford may be the respected head of his department, but Shiloh and Jill are both in authority positions when it comes to the library and its expenditures. Remember, a balance must be struck between maintaining positive and collaborative relationships between the library and academic departments while establishing the authority and expertise of the library dean and head of collection development.
3. Finally, redirect the conversation back to the matter at hand with assurances that you are vested in developing a solution that works for both departments.

Budget woes abound in academia, and libraries of all kinds routinely see their budgets tested. In this case, a substantial cut the year before resulted in a drastic new policy, and yet another cut is now in the works. The library must stretch the budget as far as possible to meet the academic needs of the students, and it is also necessary to adhere to priorities and deselection criteria. Maintaining subscriptions that are not used by students—or even faculty from the requesting department!—is not a sustainable budgetary decision.

In this scenario, the chemistry department chair's new requests have already been formally challenged and met with a negative response, and it is vital that the dean honors her promise of evaluating all department requests. This shows integrity on the part of the dean and the library, and it also establishes a data-based framework for making collection decisions. Shiloh and Jill, in coordination with their experienced team, need to pull all available data and examine it objectively. Which departments are truly requesting extraordinary expenditures compared to the use of the materials? What other factors should be used, objectively and across the board, when deciding which subscriptions need to be canceled? Use this time to develop lists of all unused materials by department and cost.

Once the data is pulled and examined, Shiloh and Jill should develop and justify their draft recommendations for purchases across all departments. Perhaps the requests by the chemistry department are in line with those of other departments, which could mean reductions in expenditures for all or several departments. A decision cannot be made based on the reputation of a department chair, and it is important to realize that the biology department, for example, might have just as many unused materials on the subscription list.

Knowing the library has the purchasing policy backing their ultimate decision, Shiloh and Jill should collaborate with requesting departments and faculty before final decisions are made. This gesture of goodwill allows all parties to contribute vital information and justifications for maintaining and discarding subscriptions while allowing transparency in the decision-making process. It also demonstrates the expertise and experience of library staff in responsibly expending university funds. Offer one-on-one or departmental consultations where collection development staff walk a faculty member through the data driving purchasing decisions. In this case, it could go something like this: "These budget cuts have been difficult for all of us, and we'd like to use your departmental requests as an example and learning opportunity for library staff and classroom faculty. For most cases, the addition of new subscriptions means cutting something existing. Are you or representatives from your department willing to have a meeting to review the new materials requested, existing subscriptions costs, and use?" Following and communicating established, administration-supported policies is always best practice, but in this case the policy is new and was controversial when announced. Pushback and confusion is completely normal from all involved parties as the institution adapts to follow and respect the new policy.

Establishing rapport is the first step to effective communication. In this situation, Shiloh needs to act quickly to communicate with the provost about the situation and her plan of action as well as communicating with Dr. Lingford about the process that will be followed before final decisions are made. The communication needs to be professional and objective at all times. Library staff should recognize the knee-jerk responses that bullying behavior may bring out and avoid them as much as possible. Due to the volatile nature of this situation, communication should primarily be in writing (email or letter) to preserve the information for reference.

Shiloh needs to recognize and convey to her staff the importance of maintaining a positive relationship with all departments, including the chemistry department. Any actions of library staff reflect on that of the library as a whole, whether positive or negative. The reputation of the library then impacts future communication and requests from all departments, including departments having confidence in the ability of library staff to purchase adequate materials for academic success.

In any communication with Dr. Lingford, Shiloh and Jill need to establish and emphasize their expertise in library science and collection development. Our vocation is reputable and requires advanced degrees, and positions are highly competitive. Librarians are devoted to providing the most accurate and timely information and assistance. Shiloh and Jill also need to be completely transparent about materials use, deselecting, and major budget decisions in all conversations with departments. This is achieved partly through collaboration, as described above. They should demonstrate that decisions are not made in a vacuum. Rather, a well-defined process is followed, which has been approved by the provost.

Chapter Twenty

She Seems Creepy

A Communicating Scenario Using Difficult Professional Topics

SCENARIO

Gerry hadn't been at his new library job a full week, but he could tell that this was a tight-knit unit he had joined. From the first group lunch at the Thai restaurant across from the Carlton branch library, the team had made him feel incredibly welcome. Everyone was friendly, laughter was frequent, and the joking was occasional. There was even a friendly bit of pranking. Not much, and not mean, but it made him feel there was a good sense of comradery with this team.

Gerry was used to being on a team like this. He had come from a previous position at Arbuckle University where most of the team were college students from fraternities. So, yes, he could get used to this job culture. Except for one thing. He was finding it hard to figure out Carlton branch library manager, and his new library manager, Dahlia Jao-Seng. She was certainly very nice, beloved by her entire staff, and a pillar of the community. But Gerry had felt that Dahlia had singled him out for extra attention—and not negative attention either.

It was his sixth day on the job. Gerry seemed to have completed most of his orientation period at the branch, since today he was working without direct supervision instead of shadowing one of the other staff members. It was relatively mindless work they had given him to do—preparing the new arrivals for circulation in the branch's media room—but Gerry didn't mind. He had rolled his book cart full of new materials next to the table and started in on the pile.

"Howdy," Dahlia called in to Gerry.

"Good morning, ma'am," he answered.

"How's the first week been treating you?" Dahlia asked, walking in and leaning against the book cart enough to bump it a bit into Gerry's foot.

"Fantastic so far," Gerry said, readjusting the book cart in order to move his foot.

"Glad to hear it. I remember when I started here, all the walking around and hand shaking, smiling, lunches with a dozen other folks, trying to remember all their names."

"I still haven't gotten that one nailed down yet!" Gerry said.

"Me neither, Terry," Dahlia joked.

Gerry laughed and picked up a few more DVDs to process. There was awkward silence as Dahlia seemed to linger a bit longer than normal as she watched him turn to the computer and back. *Is she evaluating me?* he wondered. Dahlia picked up the DVD on top of the pile nearest to her, *Into the Woods*.

"I love Sondheim," she said, setting it back on top of the pile. Gerry looked puzzled. "Sondheim's *Into the Woods*," she said, gesturing toward the DVD and singing, "No one is alone."

Again, Gerry looked puzzled. "From the musical . . . 'no one is alone,'" Dahlia sang again.

"I prefer Jerry Herman," Gerry answered. "*Hello Dolly, La Cage aux Folles*."

"Oh! Are you a Broadway nerd too?"

"Since birth," Gerry answered.

Dahlia looked wistfully off in the distance and said, "I used to work for the Nederlander Theatre, Broadway's biggest theater. I would watch Broadway shows sometimes seven days a week—five while working at the theater, standing in the back, and two as a spectator in the audience on the weekends."

"That would be my dream job," Gerry said.

"Hey, now, I'd hate to lose you. I mean if you left us," she replied.

"Don't worry. I'm loving the people here, and I'm not going anywhere," he said. Dahlia reached over and patted Gerry's shoulder then stood up.

"Well, that's good to hear, Gerry," she said, "and if you've ever got any questions, or just want to sing a little musical theater with me, head over to my office."

"Will do," Gerry said.

Dahlia dallied a minute, then finally headed out of the media room, leaving Gerry to his work.

As Gerry's third week on the staff of Carlton branch library came to a close, he was already a well-liked and firmly established member of the staff. He even had a nickname—Dice—given to him by staff members who noticed the dice logo on his favorite polo shirt. In fact, he had been wearing that shirt the day he had another awkward encounter with Dahlia.

Gerry was eating an early lunch in the break room. He always managed to get his lunch break at odd times, so he had the break room all to himself. It was a calm place, no windows, small fridge, a couple of ugly paintings, and a massive table that had obviously once been in the old study room. Gerry had just taken a big first bite of his typical Italian sub sandwich. He looked across the table, and there was the Arts section of yesterday's newspaper. He was pulling it over to read the reviews when Dahlia walked in.

"Gerry! It's nice to see you. Oh, I was just looking for that section of the paper."

Gerry looked up. "Hi, Dahlia. I wasn't reading it. Take it away." He pushed the newspaper toward her.

"Thanks," she said and tucked it under her arm. "It looks like you're well on your way to becoming one of our most popular staff members, Gerry," she said, taking a seat directly across from him and then, oddly, putting the Arts section back on the table.

"It's been a very nice couple of weeks," he said. "Everyone's been great."

Dahlia smiled a moment.

"Glad you like it here," she said, ending a somewhat pregnant pause. "You've been a very nice addition to my team, for sure."

Gerry, feeling slightly embarrassed, simply smiled and took a bite of his sandwich, fully aware that Dahlia was watching him. A few moments later, she asked a question that seemed appropriate—if out of context.

"Have you read any good books?" she asked. "It looks like the latest Franzen novel is getting good press. Have you read it?"

"No" was his only reply as he took another bite of his sandwich. He hadn't meant to be, but—in retrospect—he may have been a bit too dismissive.

"I'll let you get back to your lunch," she said, standing up from her seat. "You should swing by my office later. I'm interested in seeing your iPhone playlists. I bet we have a lot of overlap."

Dahlia opened the door and looked over her shoulder.

"By the way, you look good in that shirt, Dice." She laughed and left the room.

Gerry finished his lunch, running the entire exchange through his head over and over again.

The next day, Gerry and one of the branch's library assistants, Lena Carlisle, were prepping the children's room for story time before the library opened to the public. The two of them had developed a friendly working relationship, and they were often teamed since they had nearly identical schedules.

"Do the board books in the wicker basket need to be alphabetized?" Gerry joked.

"No, they're arranged by ISBN," she responded, her humor as dry as she could muster.

The pair continued prepping the room. Gerry felt he and Lena could open up about things, so he finally unloaded the topic that had bothered him since the first encounter with Dahlia.

"Lena, it's great here at Carlton," Gerry said. "I've never found a group as accepting as Carlton. You've been amazingly helpful to me in particular, Lena."

"And you got a nickname, Dice," Lena added, slyly.

"And I got a nickname."

As the pair finished up organizing and prepping the program room, Gerry cracked. "There's one thing though," he began.

"Yeah?" asked Lena.

"Well"—Gerry was tentative—"it's kind of been . . . well, Dahlia . . . I can't put my finger on it. Dahlia . . . "

"Yeah," Lena interrupted. "She can be tough!"

"No, it's not that. She's been"—Gerry stalled—"the times when we've been alone, she's been kind of . . . creepy?"

"Kind of creepy?"

"Yeah," Gerry said. "Like she'll linger around, making small talk that feels . . . "

"Flirty?" Lena asked.

"Maybe," Gerry said, hesitantly. "Or maybe just too personal, but not like, sexual, but not . . . "

Lena could tell that Gerry was conflicted about it.

"It just makes you uncomfortable?" she asked.

"She keeps bringing up how I should swing by her office," Gerry answered. "But not like, 'come by my office and we can get it on,' but it's things like 'we can talk about musicals' or whatever. I mean, maybe it's just Dahlia being friendly, or maybe it's something more, but I have no clue what's up."

"She's never been that friendly to me," Lena noted.

"She's nice enough," he said, "but it's when we're alone that things feel almost, sort of, expectant. In this age of the MeToo movement, I just think it's odd is all."

"Well," Lena said, "it might just be that she likes you, but I can say for sure that she's never been like that with me. In fact, Dahlia and I are rarely in the same room alone together."

Gerry mulled that over. Dahlia hadn't made any sort of overt move on him, nor said anything inappropriate, but he still felt awkward and uncomfortable with the way she interacted with him.

"Gerry," Lena said, "you might want to say something. You could bring it up with her, or if you feel strongly enough, maybe go higher up."

"I don't know if I'd do that," Gerry said. "That's just . . . Maybe I'm misreading the entire situation. How does the library define harassment these days? Is there a policy? I don't remember it coming up during my orientation."

"I don't know," Lena remarked. "I don't know of any policy. The last department staff training we had was years ago, on customer service. But, policy or not, Gerry, if you feel awkward, then maybe she's being highly inappropriate, and she'd appreciate knowing how you feel."

The pair finished their preparation and left the children's room, and Lena left to open the library doors. She noticed that Dahlia was sitting behind the circulation desk, going over something with a library clerk. Lena watched Dahlia as Gerry walked by her, and—sure enough—she seemed to be staring at him as he made his way to the reference desk. Or was she looking past him at the crowds flowing into the library?

Gerry managed to avoid Dahlia for the next two weeks, save for a couple of large-group meetings. She hadn't sought him out either, which made Gerry even more certain that he had simply misconstrued every interaction between the two of them, that he had imagined she was hitting on him, and that the strange feeling of discomfort he felt was simply a side effect of his overactive imagination. *She's just a supervisor taking an active interest in one of her employees*, he kept telling himself. He decided to let the whole matter rest.

Several days later, the Carlton branch library hosted the annual Young Poets Festival. It was the hottest day of the year so far, made hotter by the number of people crammed into the branch's community room. The Central Middle School Poetry Club members sat in chairs at the front while one speaker was standing, reading at the small podium. An audience of parents, Rotary Club members, local writers, and other school kids sat between the speakers and Gerry, who had done much of the setup for the event and, as a result, was sweating profusely.

"Thank you, Elizabeth," Mayor Ton Lyau said, reading from his notes as the third speaker left the podium, "and now it's Mike Galso's turn to read his poem 'Oranges on a Plate.'"

Gentle applause filled the room as the mayor, who was hosting the event, came to the podium and announced the next reader. At that moment, Dahlia walked into the room through the door roughly halfway between the speakers and the back wall. She did a quick scan of the room and then caught that Gerry was standing at the back. She made her way back, eventually leaning against the wall next to Gerry.

"Goodness, Gerry, have you been working out?" Gerry gave her an odd glance, and she pointed to his sweaty shirt. "Don't you think our young poets are as exciting as the work you did during your slam phase?" Dahlia asked Gerry, never taking her eyes off of the young child reading his poem at the podium.

"How did you know I did poetry slams?" Gerry asked, taken aback.

"I follow you," she said, "on Twitter and Instagram. You took a lot of amazing photos back then, especially of the one in Boulder. You were wearing that shirt that looks so good on you."

"Thanks," Gerry mumbled, getting that feeling again, but again, she hadn't said anything sexual or even slightly suggestive.

"I wrote my share, back in my early post–New York days. A lot of stories of local girl done wrong, gone wrong. I wanted to be T. C. Boyle meets Ursula K. Le Guin meets Anaïs Nin, but it never quite came together."

Gerry tried to wrap his head around that combination. He came up short at every careening turn. "That's an interesting trio," Gerry said, flatly as he could manage.

"I'll let you read some of it," Dahlia said, finally looking over at him, "if you like." And at that, she walked forward, taking the final free aisle chair, leaving Gerry leaning against the back wall, wondering exactly what had been going on.

The next day, Lena and Gerry were walking back inside the library with armloads of books after emptying the drive-up book drop. The rain was heading in this afternoon, and emptying the book drop was even less enjoyable with the water pounding down.

"How's things with Dahlia?" Lena asked.

Gerry had to reposition the books he carried as he walked back to the library. "I don't know," he said. "It's not . . . "

"Sounds like you're even more confused now than the last time we talked about it," Lena said.

"We were standing in the back of the poetry thing, and she came and stood next to me." Gerry told Lena the story of yesterday's poetry program as they scanned the barcodes to check in the books. Lena listened to his recounting of the event and the way Dahlia had spoken with him.

"So," Lena said, "have you talked to her since?"

Gerry shook his head as he slid another book under the scanner, listening to the highly satisfying gentle beep.

"She hasn't come by to see you since then?" Lena asked.

"Nope," Gerry answered, sliding several more books. "In fact, I haven't seen her at all today."

"I hear there's some sort of brouhaha back in City Hall that has a bunch of the department heads pulling long meetings," Lena said.

Gerry finished his set of books and started arranging them on the cart. "Oh," he said. "I was sort of hoping that she had realized that she was being inappropriate and decided to back off."

"Was she being inappropriate?" Lena asked.

"That's what I have not figured out," Gerry said. "Because it's never clear."

"Well, look at how she's been making you feel, Gerry. Isn't she making you feel awkward?" Lena asked, starting to scan her stack of books.

"Honestly"—Gerry paused—"not really."

Lena kept scanning.

"Are you at all interested in seeing her?" Lena asked.

"No," Gerry said. "I'm pretty set for the moment. Plus, she's my manager."

"And are you uncomfortable when she approaches you?" Lena asked, more probingly.

"I don't know if I'd say uncomfortable," he stated. "I mean, it's odd, and a bit confusing, and I think I'd enjoy chatting with her in other circumstances, but it's also a bit too, I don't know, raw. It's like she has something in mind, and I don't."

"That's pretty much what I'd think of as being uncomfortable," Lena said, sliding more books under the scanner, "but this isn't happening to me. Maybe you should talk to the human resources department anonymously?"

"I'm new, and I have no idea what to expect from Dahlia as a manager. If she's the hands-on, get-to-know-ya type or what, you know what I mean? I have no way of knowing how she is as a supervisor and if this is at all abnormal," Gerry said.

Lena paused her scanning.

"Over my first year, after she hired me, I think she spoke to me twice, and both times were to confirm schedule changes. I can't say I've seen her get personal with any other employee. She's pretty by the book. If she's lavishing attention on you, you might be the only one."

Gerry took that in.

"She doesn't interact with other folks like that?" he asked.

"Not that I've seen."

"That's . . . that makes it weirder," Gerry said. "I mean, there are about a dozen guys on our entire staff, and I'm the only one she's talking with regularly?"

"Maybe," Lena said. "I mean, I had no idea she was talking with you so often."

Lena resumed her scanning.

"Is she single?" Gerry asked.

Lena guffawed. "Why, you interested now?"

"No, but it would make things . . . " Gerry trailed off.

"I have less than zero idea," Lena said, "but I'm pretty sure she's never brought anyone to any of the staff events, so maybe?"

Gerry started to pile Lena's books on the cart.

"If she's not single, then I'm probably making it all up in my head."

"Or," Lena said, "she's super sketchy, or polyamorous, or this that or the other thing."

"I have no idea how to deal with this," Gerry said.

"I can think of one thing," Lena said.

"I could ask if she's single?"

"You could ask what her intentions are, or at least try to let her know that you're having issues with the way she's been interacting with you."

"So, you're saying I—a new employee—should approach our manager, say 'Hey, have you been hitting on me the last few weeks?' and hope that it doesn't backfire?" Gerry asked, a touch sarcastically.

"Probably not," Lena said, "but you need to clarify the situation. She's a manager, and I'm pretty sure the city frowns on managers flirting with their employees. I think they must put managers through training for this stuff. If she's being inappropriate, she knows it. If she's just not approaching things the right way, then she can explain that too."

Gerry seemed unconvinced.

"You could go up the ladder? Talk to Manuel over at human resources," Lena offered once again.

"I don't think I can do that," Gerry said. "What if I'm totally off base?"

"You're obviously all tied up about it," Lena said, "and if it's just her being awkward, then it's cool, but if it's something more, then maybe there's a pattern the rest of us aren't seeing, and maybe administration knows about it and can deal with it."

Gerry thought she might just be right. They finished filling the carts in silence, then Gerry spent the rest of the afternoon reshelving, running over the possibilities of every potential action he could take. There didn't seem to be a good answer, but the worst seemed to be waiting. He had to take a step, but in what direction, he wasn't sure.

SHE SEEMS CREEPY RESPONSES

Response 1
By Julia McKenna, circulation services manager, Jacksonville University, Jacksonville, Florida

In this scenario, the major issue is the level of attention that Dahlia, library manager at Carlton branch library, is giving to Gerry, a new library employee. Whether or not Dahlia means to make Gerry feel uncomfortable, singling him out for long, non-work-related conversations—

without engaging with other staff—is inappropriate. Because of her position of authority, she needs to be careful about how she treats her staff and not selecting favorites or potential romantic partners among those she supervises. Managers have to keep a level of authority and equality that Dahlia is not presenting in this scenario. Her following him on social media is especially inappropriate and is a red flag that she is not treating their relationship professionally.

It's understandable that Gerry isn't sure how to react to Dahlia's conversations. Many times, harassment in the workplace starts off subtly. Employees internalize that the aggressor is "just being nice" or that they may be reading too much into things. In addition, Gerry wants to create and maintain a good working relationship with his manager, which is essential for career success. However, it's also not okay that Gerry feels constantly uncomfortable at work. His library manager should be the person he turns to for career and problem-solving advice, and his discomfort is infringing on that. Gerry feeling uncomfortable around Dahlia has the potential to set back operational efficiency. Dahlia may well be damaging Gerry's professional development, thereby preventing Gerry from achieving professional growth and taking part in promotional opportunities he might be able to otherwise.

Gerry has four primary options when it comes to addressing the issues with Dahlia. The first is to simply ignore the issue and remain professional at work. This option leads to the lowest amount of conflict and avoids the risk of his manager taking retaliatory actions. However, it also does not solve the problem and leaves Gerry feeling uncomfortable in his workplace, where he spends the majority of his time.

The second option would be to approach Dahlia directly about the issue. This has a high potential to be an extremely uncomfortable situation. Because of the power imbalance between Gerry and his boss, he may not feel comfortable speaking as candidly as he needs to. However, it has the benefit of him addressing the problem directly without bringing in any outside parties. Depending on Dahlia's management style, she may value his willingness to address issues directly with her and could be horrified that she is making him feel uncomfortable. However, it also has the potential for her to either take retaliatory measures (either directly or indirectly) or make inappropriate advances while alone with Gerry.

The third option would be for Gerry to go to the organization's human resources (HR) department and ask for assistance. This option has the benefit of accountability, as many HR professionals would be concerned to find out that a manager in their organization is singling out a staff member and making them feel uncomfortable, and they'd want to ensure that if something inappropriate was happening that they would take immediate action to stop it. If there are prior complaints of inappropriate behavior with Dahlia, HR would know this and be able to follow up and take action. HR could offer Gerry advice and suggestions on how to approach a conversation with Dahlia in the workplace and how to go about documenting his interactions to provide HR with more information. HR may even facilitate an internal meeting between an HR representative as a neutral party, Gerry, and Dahlia. However, there are risks with this third option. It has the potential to create an awkward work environment with Dahlia, damaging any possibility for the two of them to have a good working relationship in the future.

The final option would be for Gerry to approach Dahlia's immediate supervisor with his concerns. Every employee—including Dahlia—reports to someone. Library branch managers often report to a district manager or directly to the library director. Gerry can schedule a meeting with this person and lay out his issue. This option has the potential for the most impactful action. Since Dahlia reports to her superior, she knows she will be held accountable by them or face disciplinary action—and may even face termination. However, she may be angered by Gerry "going over her head" and attempt to take retaliatory action. In addition, Gerry may feel uncomfortable with this option due to the power dynamic of approaching a high-level superior.

If I were Gerry, I would first voice my concerns with human resources. This sort of scenario is exactly why HR exists. They can offer Gerry advice, offer a neutral outside perspective, and document his concerns in case they become a pattern (or take action if this has been a documented pattern of Dahlia's). In addition, human resources departments can ensure that Gerry does not face retaliation. No one should feel uncomfortable at work because of a supervisor's behavior. While addressing the issue may feel uncomfortable, taking no action at all leaves Gerry in the same place—dreading coming to work and avoiding his manager. By taking action, Gerry can ensure that Dahlia's behavior does not affect his career growth and can find a more comfortable workplace in the future.

Response 2
By Tammy Garrison, executive director, Ross Library, Mill Hill, Pennsylvania

It should be noted that Gerry, the new employee at the Carlton branch library, has done nothing wrong in this situation and that Dahlia, the library's branch manager, is indeed behaving inappropriately. Many people are awkward or have issues in social situations where they cannot read social cues correctly. This may even be the situation with Dahlia. While it may be an explanation, it does not excuse her intrusive and inappropriate behavior, nor should Gerry have to put up with it. Talking about shared interests is one thing, but commenting on appearance, even in a positive manner, is another thing altogether. While following an employee on social media may not violate policy directly, it is still not appropriate for a manager to do so. Employees are entitled to a life outside of the office, one in which a supervisor is not constantly checking up on them.

Dahlia also seems to be singling out Gerry for attention she would not bestow on other employees. In fact, Dahlia doesn't seem to speak much to her other library employees at all—at least not from the information we've been given in the scenario. Yet, here she is offering to compare playlists with Gerry. Comparatively, Dahlia is overstepping a boundary that she, herself, made in how she deals with subordinates. Again, all of this may or may not be in direct violation of a specific code of conduct, but it *is* inappropriate behavior for a supervisor.

Gerry's first step should be to obtain and review the entirety of the library's policy manual. He may not find a section on harassment that covers his situation, but it may be covered in another section. It may, in fact, be a part of the larger city organization policy manual. As city employees, library staff would be covered by those policies as well. Reviewing the policies and codes of conduct that effect the library will arm Gerry with valuable information that he will need in order to make a decision on how to proceed.

After arming himself with the relevant policies, Gerry has two options. First, he can talk directly to Dahlia about how uncomfortable she is making him feel. His second option is to bypass Dahlia, his supervisor, and go directly to human resources, anonymously or not. Both options are complicated, and Gerry needs to think about how he would like to handle the situation, what he feels most comfortable with, and what option would produce the most desired results. Either way, there is the potential for blowback with Dahlia, who may not take kindly to being confronted in the first option, or may not like that Gerry went behind her back to human resources in the second option.

In the first option, Gerry needs to have a clear and candid private informal meeting with Dahlia. He should use recent examples in his discussion and explain that those subjects are not welcome and he does not want to share private, personal details at work. It may feel blunt, but he needs to be so there is no misunderstanding. In fact, if Gerry comes to Dahlia directly, she may appreciate that he is coming to her personally without involving the human resources department, giving her an opportunity to clarify herself and adjust her interactions with Gerry. However, going this route could also be both professionally detrimental and personally embarrassing. Approaching Dahlia directly could backfire, and Gerry should be prepared for a negative reaction. It may affect the way Gerry's branch manager treats him from that point on, which can have a direct impact on his career.

In preparing for a one-on-one meeting with Dahlia (or for any other option as well), Gerry needs to make a detailed account of all the situations between them that have made him uncomfortable—logging their dates and approximate times. He should write down what he wants to say and practice it. Repeating his message over and over will also help to dull the emotional effects of the situation and help him keep his composure in what could be a nerve-wracking situation. Difficult conversations often go better with rehearsal so that no points are missed, under- or overplayed, or added to in a way that distracts from the seriousness of the conversation. Gerry should focus on how *he* feels and why he is uncomfortable rather than criticizing Dahlia. He should also be prepared to make direct statements that when behavior X occurs, he feels Y. He should not minimize his feelings for anyone's sake. Gerry should make it clear that he is uncomfortable talking about personal matters with someone who is taking an unwanted special interest in his personal life. He needs Dahlia to understand that there is a difference between a boss asking, "Did you have a nice weekend?" and a boss saying, "I saw on your Facebook page that you went to the movies this weekend. Who did you go with, and what did you do afterward?"

If Gerry is uncomfortable with direct confrontations, or—after careful analysis—he believes that the situation merits it, he may wish to choose another option: taking the problem directly to human resources. Most managers tend to believe that it is appropriate to bypass going directly to your boss, and instead to go over your boss's head, when the situation involves something unethical, illegal, immoral, or harassing. Getting human resources involved would take the responsibility of handing the situation away from Gerry and put it in the hands of the human resources department. Their staff will handle things according to their policies and their own analysis of the situation. In some cases, however, bringing an interpersonal relationship concern between you and your boss to human resources will not work out in your favor. It may produce ill feelings among the rest of the staff or result in unanticipated actions—such as Dahlia being terminated or Gerry being transferred. These results will be out of Gerry's control, so he needs to be comfortable with giving control of the situation over to someone else.

Whether or not the situation described in this scenario is actually harassment should drive Gerry's decision here. The organization's policy will help Gerry decide if he is really being harassed or if Dahlia is just being unwittingly inappropriate. Actual harassment presents a legal risk to the organization, and they will take it seriously. But if Gerry comes to the decision that he really doesn't think he *is* being harassed by Dahlia, then the best he could hope for by going to human resources would be professional and helpful advice from them about how he needs to talk to Dahlia directly. For this reason, the best option seems to be the first one—talking to Dahlia one-on-one. This is going to be difficult for someone who is a new employee and who does not like confrontation. However, the problem will persist or grow worse if it is not addressed. Gerry does not deserve to work in an environment where a supervisor is behaving inappropriately toward him, and the best person to articulate this to Dahlia is Gerry himself.

Response 3
By Joshua Kunkle, adult services librarian, Beaumont Library District, Beaumont, California

When it comes to professional relationships in the workplace, there are times that interactions can be seen as uncomfortable or awkward. These interactions become more pronounced when conducted between staff and managers. In the case of Gerry and the Carlton library's branch manager, Dahlia, the focus of Gerry's confusion surrounding Dahlia's behavior becomes a blurred line between her being inappropriate and her taking a benign, personable approach toward a new employee. Stress from these situations can cause people like Gerry to become confused about their feelings or to develop a fear of addressing the issue lest they become the target of negative reactionary behavior.

In seeking to ascertain Gerry's next steps with regard to what he has experienced, it helps to build an idea of what the problem actually is. In this case, Gerry has been the recipient of unwanted behavior by his manager, Dahlia. The important point here is that Dahlia's behavior is *unwanted*. Gerry is uncomfortable addressing the issues out of fear they are probably unfounded, and he doesn't want to "create waves" so early in his career at the Carlton branch library. Gerry's feelings stem from Dahlia asking him a number of personal questions as well as approaching him with what he perceives as overly personal and flirtatious behavior. It should be noted when listing these facts that perception is in the eye of the beholder and should be taken into account so as to avoid personal bias against either side in this situation.

As Dahlia has not overtly conducted herself inappropriately in Gerry's eyes, he needs to take account of—and research—a number of facts before deciding what to do. The first step would be to look at the law and what constitutes harassment. Gerry can do this on his own, but he likely should enlist the assistance of the organization's human resources department. While Gerry isn't quite sure what to call what is happening to him, he is lucky that there is written legal doctrine he can research that does define what constitutes harassment when a person is receiving unwanted attention. Gerry can use this knowledge as a benchmark to compare his perception of the situation with stated legal doctrine. Though all organizations have their own policies surrounding harassment, they are based on legal doctrine that exists at both the state and federal level, and it would behoove Gerry to seek that information so that he can have a better understanding of how he is protected in the eyes of the law. Perhaps more importantly, he can use this knowledge to validate whether what he is feeling falls in line with harassing behavior.

It follows that if Gerry is to have more facts at his disposal before moving forward with a decision, he should also seek out other employees in the library to ascertain their own interactions with Dahlia. By so doing, he will not be relying so much on a single coworker's perceptive evidence. This can, and should, be done without drawing attention to his personal dilemma and with regard to his privacy. Since we are only seeing incidents in this scenario from Gerry's perspective, we need to be sensitive to the possibility that Dahlia's side of the story might be somewhat different and change the recommended focus and direction Gerry should take. As was suggested above, Gerry should not rely so heavily on one coworker's testimony of how Dahlia treats the other staff in the library and that other personnel may have had similar interactions to Gerry's.

Gerry is the focus of this story, and his ultimate decision on how to deal with Dahlia's behavior toward him is what will resolve the issue at hand. Though Gerry has been presented with a number of options to resolve his issue, he feels confused about what direction to take. Once he has researched the existing documentation that pertains to harassment—with or without the help of human resources personnel—and once he ascertains whether Dahlia's behavior is unique to him, he will have armed himself with the important information and legal guidance necessary to make a well-founded decision on what direction to take. At the very least, he will have given himself the confidence to have the much-needed uncomfortable conversation with Dahlia regarding *unwanted* behavior. Ultimately, Gerry will need to approach Dahlia and have a difficult conversation about her intentions. Gerry can perhaps ask Dahlia why she has been focusing her attention on him more so than the other staff (without mentioning the awkward conversations that had occurred previously). This approach allows Gerry to broach the unwanted behavior issue without touching on the harassment issue. It can also help Dahlia tactfully modify her behavior before it becomes an even bigger issue.

It should be noted that the way a manager or superior interacts with individuals—subordinates or otherwise—can change from one person to another. Human behavior is often not black and white, and we often misinterpret one another. Dahlia may just be trying, perhaps clumsily, to make Gerry feel accepted on the library's team. If, however, the case arises where Dahlia's intentions are indeed considered inappropriate, Gerry's prior fact finding would have the backing of the human resources department and the knowledge from his own research to move forward with protecting himself, if not other personnel in the library. Communication, ultimately, is key in situations like this. Gerry hasn't communicated his discomfort with anyone—including human resources. He hasn't defined what is, and what is not, proper in this situation. Until he does this, he will be stuck in the same confused fog he is in now. His first step is to begin the process of defining what constitutes unwanted behavior. Once he has done that, the rest of the steps—including what he should do next—will fall into place.

Index

ALA. *See* American Library Association
American Library Association, 93, 130, 133, 134, 218
American Library Association Bill of Rights, 42, 43, 44, 127, 128, 130, 131, 132, 133
American Library Association Code of Ethics, 43
American Library Association Freedom to Read, 44
American Library Association Office for Intellectual Freedom, 43, 44, 131
American Society of Association Executives, 21
Americans with Disabilities Act, 91, 93–94, 97

Barclay, Donald, 18–20
Begraft, Lyn, 28–30
Block, Peter, 120
Bohannan, Kelly, 96–97, 158–159
Broyles, Amanda, 44–46
budgets, 33, 56, 61–72, 99–108, 143–145
bullying, 229–230

Carson, Jenn, 118–120
case histories vs. scenarios, xv
Catron, Donna, 217–218
change management, 29–33, 119
Civil Rights Act of 1964, 169
Cole, Jolene, 204–205, 225–227
collection development policies, 43–44, 45, 48, 152, 229
Comito, Lauren, 146–149
communicating, xxi, 209–243
communication, 9–10, 55–56, 58, 68, 104–105, 117, 201–202, 203–204, 215–216, 230–231
community assessment, 214, 218
consensus, 28, 102, 107
controlling, xx, 125–174
cost-to-benefit analysis, 227–228

data-driven decisions, 70, 118, 146

delegation, 30, 190, 192
deselection. *See* weeding
difficult professional topics scenarios, xxii
Disher, Wayne, 32–34, 105–107, 171–173
Dragon, AnnaLee, 144–146

Equal Employment Opportunity Commission, 169
Estes, Beth Wren, 20–21

Fayol, Henri, xix
Flaharty, Mary Grace, 67–69
floating collections, 108
format, ix
Fuller, Rachel, 81–82
fundraising, 17, 68, 145

Garcia, Carol, 30–32, 92–94
Garrison, Tammy, 57–58, 240–241
George, Mary, 188–190
groups, working in, xviii
Grubb, Jason, 103–105

Hall, Kate, 190–192
Hicks, Deborah, 58–59
Hildreth, Susan, 213–215
homeless, 94
Hovanec, Jennifer, 71–72
HR. *See* human resources
Huddle, Katherine, 43–44, 142–144
human resources, 169–171, 174, 180–182, 216, 239–240, 241

in loco parentis, 46
intended audience, viii

Kerr, Barbara, 120–121, 181–182, 201–202
Kreimer vs. City or Morristown Library, 93
Kuni, Kayla, 7–9

Kunkle, Joshua, 242–243
Kuo, Alice, 202–204

labor unions, 70
LaRue, James, 44
leading, xx, 77–121
lesbian, gay, bisexual, transgender, queer, plus, 145–146, 173
LGBTQ+. *See* lesbian, gay, bisexual, transgender, queer, plus
library board agendas, 19
library board management, 17–18, 18–19, 20–21, 213
library commission management. *See* library board management
library mission, 106, 117, 121
limited public forum, 94

Mai, Theresa, 83–84
Malkowski, Elise, 182–183
management style, 118
managerial functions, ix, xix–xxi
managerial insecurity, 33–34
Mason, Faith, 192–193
McCafferty, Bridget, 159–161
McKenna, Julia, 11–12, 238–240
Moczygemba, Keri, 229–231

National Council for Behavioral Health, 92

organizational culture, 59, 72, 82–83, 104, 191, 193, 217
organizing, xx, 37–72

Palascak, Helen, 17–18, 46–48, 157–158
Parker, Kathy, 116–118
Patriot Act, 128, 133, 133–134
performance evaluations, 9, 10, 11, 213
performance improvement plan, 12
personality conflicts, 119
Pilate, Terri, 107–108
planning, xx, 3–34
policies, 157, 226

Price Waterhouse v. Hopkins, 170
privacy, 132–133, 133, 134
problem-solving, xxii, 57, 59, 85
programming, 142–145
Public Library Association, 21

radio frequency identification, 186, 189–190
recruitments, 180–181
Request for Reconsideration of Library Material Form, 47
Rerat, Cari, 85–86
RFID. *See* radio frequency identification
Richland, Lisa, 55–56, 215–217
Robert's Rules of Order, 21
Rosenblum, Lisa, 132–133

scenario: analysis, ix–xii; benefits, xvii–xix; classification, ix, xix–xxi; context, x, xi; labels. *See* scenario classifiation; triggers, ix, xxi–xxii
scenarios: supposition, xxii; using in the learning process, xvi
Schuldner, Dina, 9–11
Schultz, Christine, 227–228
scope, viii–ix
Sednek, Samantha, 94–96
sensitivity training, 96
service models, 29–30
skills scenarios, xxi
Society for Human Resource Management, 170
Sontag, Brian, 179–181
Spencer, Brenda Robertson, 169–171
staffing, xx, 177–205
strategic plans, 19–20, 21, 30–32
Sunshine Act, 21

team building, 57, 83
Todaro, Julie, 69–71
Tompkins County Public Library, 68
triggers. *See* scenario triggers

weeding, 108, 202–203, 204–205
Whitehair, Kristin, 173–174
Williams, Philip, 133–134

About the Editor

Wayne T. Disher is a retired public library director for the City of Hemet Public Library. He obtained his master's degree in information and library science from San Jose State University in 1994. He is an associate lecturer for the San Jose State University School of Information, teaching library management and collection management classes. He was recognized as instructor of the year for San Jose State University's School of Information and was president of the California Library Association in 2012. Mr. Disher is the author of several library science textbooks and is both a popular library trainer and a professional development speaker for library leaders and staff around the United States.

www.ingramcontent.com/pod-product-compliance
Lightning Source LLC
Chambersburg PA
CBHW082033300426
44117CB00015B/2462